Zora Hurston
And the Strange Case of
Ruby McCollum

Zora Hurston
And The Strange Case Of
Ruby McCollum

C. Arthur Ellis, Jr., Ph.D.

Gadfly Publishing, LLC ▪ Lutz, Florida ▪ www.gadflypublishing.com

"Changing the world, one book at a time."™

Zora Hurston And The Strange Case Of Ruby McCollum

Gadfly Publishing, LLC ▪ Lutz, Florida

Oil painting illustrations executed by Chinese artist collective under artistic direction of Min Zhang, based upon original sketches and photographs by C. Arthur Ellis, Jr., Ph.D.

Edited by Michael Carr

Publisher's Cataloging-in-Publication data

Ellis, C. Arthur

Zora Hurston and the strange case of Ruby McCollum / by C. Arthur Ellis, Jr., Ph.D.

p. cm.

ISBN 978-0-9820940-0-6

1. McCollum, Ruby, ca. 1915- --Trials, litigation, etc. 2. Trials (Murder) --Florida --Live Oak. 3. Race discrimination --Law and legislation --United States. 4. Segregation --United States. 5. Hurston, Zora Neale. I. Title.

KF224.M356 E45 2009

305.896--dc22

2008909001

Printed and bound in the U.S.A.

Downtown Live Oak, Florida
1952

P*reface*

In the 1930s, Zora Neale Hurston, the famous African American anthropologist and celebrated writer of the Harlem Renaissance, studied the practice of "paramour rights" in the timber camps of North Florida. This unwritten law of the antebellum South allowed a white man to take a "colored" woman as his concubine and force her to have his children. Twenty years later, Hurston accepted an assignment from the *Pittsburgh Courier* to cover a murder trial in the small North Florida town of Live Oak, where Ruby McCollum, a wealthy African-American woman, had shot Dr. C. Leroy Adams, her white lover who had recently been elected to the state senate. At the time, the *Courier* was the country's most widely circulated black newspaper, and Hurston expected the upcoming trial to be an unprecedented forum for a "Negress" to testify in her own defense after being forced, through paramour rights, to bear a powerful white man's children.

Eager to begin her writing assignment, Hurston traveled to Live Oak, only to find that presiding judge Hal W. Adams had issued a gag order banning all but defense attorneys and close relatives from visiting the defendant. When Hurston sought interviews with locals during the course of this Kafkaesque trial, the entire town—white and black alike—seemed complicit in what she called a "conspiracy of silence, operating behind a curtain of secrecy."

After the trial, Hurston appealed to renowned author William Bradford Huie to take up the case where she had left off. But when Huie visited Live Oak, he encountered the same conspiracy of silence. For over half a century since then, the case has haunted countless curiosity seekers, who continue to visit Live Oak hoping to hear "the real story," only to find that the conspiracy of silence continues to this day.

Reading *Dust Tracks on a Road*, I realized that what made Ruby's case so compelling was right there in Hurston's stated motivation for writing her own life story: "There is no agony like bearing an untold story inside you." Hurston's insight gives Ruby's plight a universality that appeals to our deepest fears of being wronged without legal recourse and left without a voice.

In creating Hurston's "voice" for this book, I have tried to be true to the voice in her newspaper coverage of the trial, and to her world-view as expressed through the totality of her surviving works.

Ruby McCollum's story is supplemented from my memories of the event and its aftermath, interviews with my family members and others who were willing to share information, and hundreds of hours spent searching through newspapers and public documents of the time.

Undoubtedly, Hurston unearthed much of this same information during her stay in Live Oak, but many of her letters were totally or partially burned during the housecleaning after her death, including a 1953 letter to the *Courier*, blasting the paper for misquoting her. That half-burned letter is preserved in the Florida Archives at the University of Florida.

It is equally intriguing that none of Hurston's surviving letters mention reading Huie's *Ruby McCollum: Woman in the Suwannee Jail.* This was uncharacteristic of Hurston, who had earlier corresponded with Huie to praise his *Execution of Private Slovik.*

We will never know whether there ever was such a letter or, if so, what Hurston might have thought of Huie's take on Ruby McCollum's story.

PART I

Zora Hurston Arriving In Live Oak, Florida

Chapter One

Hissing hydraulic brakes, humming tires on wet asphalt, and hard, cold glass against my face roused me to the uncomfortable awareness that I was not at home in the warmth of my bed. Feeling my possessions safely beside me, I breathed a relieved sigh and cleared a spot on the fogged-up window to see damp gray sidewalks glistening in the dim amber light of a streetlamp.

"Li-i-ive Oak." The Greyhound driver's laconic drawl, along with the light in my eyes, forced me to accept that my sleep, however fitful, had come to an end. Seeing an aisle crowded with zombies staggering in the dingy cabin light, I decided to grab a little shuteye until the path cleared. That's when I told myself I was getting too old for this sort of thing.

It's not the first time I've had this conversation with myself. The end result is always the same—something in this nappy old noggin reminds me that I still have to work for a living. Spot has a puppy now, so there's the extra mouth to feed. That brings the total to three if I include Jean McArthur. Not that I have to worry much about her, since there are always enough squirrels in the oak trees around the house to keep a cat with her hunting skills fat and sassy.

Then there's the matter of the roof over our heads. Taking on a new assignment meant that I would be able to buy the house I'm renting now, with its own backyard where I can grow vegetables, and a fenced front yard where I can cultivate my favorite flowers. Who cares if I have to slice bacon so thin I can read the morning paper through it? At least I'll finally have a place to call my own.

Besides, I've not made much progress on *Herod the Great* lately—seems as if all of my efforts to make great strides have resulted in nothing but jumpin' up and down in the same set of footprints. I suppose it doesn't help that everybody thinks I'm crazy for conjuring up a biblical epic in the first place.

That's why I thanked my lucky stars when I got the telegram from Sam Nunn, editor in chief of the *Pittsburgh Courier*, about a Negro woman named Ruby McCollum. Seems she shot this mucky-muck white physician and newly elected state senator in the little farming town of Live Oak, Florida, almost three hundred miles north of where I made my home in Eau Gallie.

Nunn told me he had learned of the murder in this otherwise quiet little town after being contacted by Releford McGriff, the McCollum's family attorney. McGriff had sent him a copy of the August 8, 1952, *Suwannee Democrat*, its front page emblazoned with Adams's campaign photo and the headline DR. ADAMS SLAIN BY NEGRESS.

Not "Ruby McCollum," you understand, but "Negress," following the time-honored Southern tradition of reporting the trespasses of "Negroes" without names, villains without voices—a special breed of faceless creatures who were, by the very color of their skin, the usual suspects in any crime.

Nunn also informed me that he had already sent two senior staff reporters, Revella Clay and John Diaz, to cover the trial, supported by Alex Rivera, the paper's lead photographer. Sometime toward the end of September, however, Nunn decided that the story had the potential to rise from journalistic slug lines to great Southern literature. He had even considered the possibility of serializing Ruby McCollum's life story in the *Courier*.

That, he told me, was the reason he had called me into the case and pulled Revella Clay back to the office to edit my work. Needless to say, I crammed my typewriter into my suitcase and hit the road, anxious to cover a story that had all the drama and varied play of human emotions that fill the pages of great literature from Plutarch to Shakespeare.

From what I understood, it also offered a rare opportunity to cut to the heart of a murder mystery involving a sordid interracial love affair between two people who were equally prominent within their respective communities.

Nunn was right: there might be a book in it.

"Don't your ticket say Live Oak?" a voice boomed overhead.

"Yes, sir," I replied, grabbing my purse and briefcase with one hand and my tired old coat and hat with the other. Stepping off the bus and pulling my overcoat tight around me against the cold damp mist, I caught the smell that rain leaves after falling on dirt baked too long by the sun.

"Need a ride?" a cheerful voice greeted me as I was retrieving my luggage. I bent down to see an elderly colored man flashing a toothless grin. Gasping after lugging my belongings to the curb, I managed a "Yes, please," making a mental note to cut down a pack a day on my cigarettes.

The driver jumped out of the cab like a twenty-year-old, circling it to grab my suitcase.

"Be careful," I warned, thinking of my typewriter packed inside. "It's heavy."

"I'm use' to it," the driver replied, securing my suitcase in the trunk. "It do be a bit heavy, though."

As soon as he had me settled in the backseat, the driver ran to his side of the car and started the meter. "Where you headed, miss?"

"I need to go to the corner of Woods Avenue and Southwest Sixth Street," I replied.

"That be Matt Jackson's place...you kin?"

"I'm a friend of the family."

"You looks like one of them reporter fellas been snoopin' 'round here lately...only you's a woman."

"How'd you guess?"

The driver chuckled, stealing a glance at me through his rearview mirror. "You lucky you come when you did—rain's started to cool things down a mite. Before today, we ain't had none in months. Had some hail, but that just made things worse—ripped up folks' 'bacca sump'm awful!"

"I'm glad the weather has improved," I commented, too tired to participate in the pleasantries expected of folks in this part of the country.

The driver stared at my reflection again. "Before you goes nosin' 'round 'bout Ruby McCollum, I might oughta tell you she gots a date with Old Sparky."

I knew that the driver was referring to Florida's electric chair at Raiford, the very prison that Ruby had first been rushed to after the murder.

"You know her?"

"Ever'body know Ruby McCollum...ever'body."

"You want to tell me about her?" I asked, intrigued by what the man might know.

"Like I done told you, miss, she a dead woman," the driver insisted, bearing left to follow the bend in Highway 90.

"Do you think she shot Dr. Adams?"

"Everbody know she shot the doc. Rich niggah got upset about her doctah bill and done gone and shot the only doctah in Suwannee County visits colored folks. Gottah be a special place in hell for the likes of that woman."

"Sounds like you already have her tried, convicted, and sentenced."

"Miss…"

"Hurston—Zora Hurston."

"Lijah Johnson."

"Good to meet you, Lijah."

"I don't know where you from, lady, but 'round these parts Ruby be lucky she made it to the jailhouse. 'Round these parts, most niggahs that shoots a white man done be swingin' from some big oak tree befo' sunset."

"So why's this McCollum woman so different?"

"Humph!" Lijah muttered. "'Cause she be rich, that why. If it'd be any other niggah, things be a whole lot different, I can guar-awn-tee you that this instant minute."

"A rich colored woman in Live Oak?" I challenged, hoping to draw more out of the driver now that the rhythm of his voice, falling into the cadence of his native dialect, told me he was becoming more comfortable with me.

Lijah turned left onto a dirt road and stopped in front of a well-maintained two-story Spanish-style home with a tall Mexican palm planted in the middle of its circular drive. A thick twelve-foot bamboo hedge surrounded the house on three sides, almost touching the stucco walls, embracing it like a mother protecting her child. The driveway had a low brick fence guarded by two concrete lions. It was difficult to tell by the dim light of the streetlamp, but the house appeared to be some shade of light tan or yellow stucco.

"You see that place?" Lijah asked, pointing to the house.

I leaned over to take another look. This time, in the glow of the streetlamp, I saw a large detached building to one side, apparently a garage.

"That be the McCollum's." He paused for my reaction.

"My house would probably fit quite nicely inside the living room."

"So would mine—'long with the outhouse." Lijah turned and pointed across the street to one of the tin-roofed bungalows surrounding the McCollum house. "And that be Matt Jackson's place."

"In that case, I suppose I've arrived."

Although it was hard to make out in the dark, Matt Jackson's house, sporting a fresh coat of white paint, appeared to be better maintained than the other shanties in the neighborhood. Even so, it was eclipsed by his sister's mansion.

Lijah got out of the cab to unload my suitcase and ferry it up the front porch steps. "That be fifty cents, ma'am."

"Thank you," I said, fishing four quarters out of the bottom of my purse. "I appreciate your handling that heavy suitcase."

The old man flashed a broad grin. "Thank you kindly, ma'am. You give me a call if you needs to get 'round town while you's here. Matt got a phone and he know my number."

"I will," I assured him, and he got into his cab and drove off.

While I walked up the porch steps enjoying the cool evening breeze scented with wood smoke from the neighborhood fireplaces, I felt a little uncomfortable about entering a relative stranger's house when he was not at home. Matt had insisted that I stay as his guest while I was covering the trial, assuring me that I could help by keeping an eye on the house while he had to be out of town on family business. And I had already prepared myself to accept the inevitable gossip that was bound to circulate about a strange woman staying with him while his wife was out of town. So, I concluded that my uneasiness had more to do with the sense of responsibility I felt being charged with looking after someone else's property.

Opening the front door with the key Matt had left under the doormat, I dragged my suitcase inside and flipped the wall switch to see a simply furnished, neatly kept living room: small overstuffed sofa and matching armchair with white crocheted lace doilies pinned neatly on the backs and arms. I stepped to a potbellied stove between the living and dining rooms and found it still warm enough to comfort my cold, arthritic fingers.

Having warmed my hands, I found a 1952 wall calendar from Mizelle's Feed Store, hanging beside a door that Matt had told me led to my bedroom. Inside, I found the bed carefully made with a plush white chenille bedspread. The covers were invitingly turned down, and a small lamp on the bedside table cast a warm glow on the yellowing flowered wallpaper. On the wall in front of the bed was a mirrored dresser with a vase filled with bright bronze and gold chrysanthemums.

Throwing off my shoes, I fell back onto the bed. This is heaven, I thought, sinking slowly into the delightful feather-stuffed mattress that reminded me of home.

McCollum Home

Saturday morning I was awakened by an impatient rooster, urging the sun up. Enjoying a luxurious stretch, I savored the sound—a comforting reminder of a bucolic childhood that I much preferred to the blaring horns and screeching brakes in New York City, where I had made my home for a few years.

Feeling the fresh fall breeze blowing gently through the sheer white lace curtains of the open window, I pulled the covers up around my neck, recalling the time I left my patroness's gilded cage in the Big Apple after what I still regard as my gifted telling of Hans Christian Andersen's "The Red Shoes."

Like the little girl in the fairy tale, I decided that I had become seduced by lavish surroundings and fancy tailored outfits, enslaved by the glitter of material things. Whereas the girl in the story cut off her feet to free herself from the magical red shoes that possessed her, I had only to cut off my financial footing to regain my creative freedom.

It had been a painful but liberating experience. "Perhaps it is true," I told the woman I still call Godmother, "that all great art is born of suffering."

Now, looking across the bedroom, I smiled at my tailored outfits hanging in the open closet, tired old reminders of how I had left Godmother with the gift of being able to experience poverty vicariously, all scrubbed up and idealized for its virtues, rather than up close, raw, and unrelenting, as I have lived it.

"You up yet?" a voice called through the bedroom door.

I yawned. "That you, Matt?"

"Yes'm, it me."

"I'll be right out," I called, throwing off the covers. Freeing myself from the thick feather mattress was another matter—a bit like trying to climb out of a giant marshmallow.

Tapping gently on the shared bathroom door, I stepped inside to rush through my morning ritual. When I got to the lipstick, I winced to see it feather along the fine age lines around my lips. "Wake up, old gal," I chided myself in the mirror. "Time to go to work."

After throwing on a dress, I entered the dining room to find breakfast on the table, and Matt, a short, pleasant-looking gentleman in his late thirties, so thin that I could see his Adam's apple bob up and down when he swallowed.

"Mornin', Zora. Thought you'd like some bacon, eggs, and grits and some of my cane surp to go with these biscuits I made."

"What a treat, Matt!" I exclaimed, pulling up a chair to a table laden with enough food for a good-size family. Sopping my biscuit in the syrup, I took a bite, careful to avoid dripping it on my chin. "My goodness! This is absolutely the best cane syrup I ever tasted."

He smiled. "Glad you like it."

I could see that this was a person who took pleasure in watching the people he liked enjoy their food. To me, the only thing sweeter than the cane syrup was the smile on his face.

"How was your trip?" he asked.

"Just fine. How is your family?"

Matt's face fell. "They be doin' as good as they can with how things is, I reckon. Sometimes I wonder how sweet Jesus can let such misery out on this old world of ours."

"I know what you mean, Matt," I conceded, thinking of the hard circumstances I had had to brave in my own life. But unlike Matt, my consolation did not come from a Sunday school Jesus. To me, organized creeds had always seemed to be mere collections of words around a wish, selfish attempts to place a wedding ring around the vast expanse of the universe and claim it for themselves.

It hurt to see Matt so depressed, so I tried to think of something to lighten the mood in an attempt to raise his spirits. "I see some dried-out corn stalks there in the side yard," I said, "and a seed catalogue on the lamp table. You do much gardening?"

"I loves to grow things," Matt acknowledged, making the closest attempt at a smile I had yet seen from him.

"What kinds of things do you like to grow?

"Oh, just 'bout ever'thing: cane, melons, corn, string beans, taters, and radishes, mostly. Ain't had much luck this year with the drought, though, 'cept for the melons. Little bit of rain that started when you got in town be the first real rain we got this year."

"You really are a serious gardener," I said, thinking how most of my gardening was dedicated to cultivating rare ornamentals, rather than growing the more pragmatic plants that end up on the supper table.

"Cane's my favorite. I runs it through the press and bile down the juice for that surp you're eatin' there. Then my wife, Bessie, takes some and cooks it down to make pull candy for the kids."

I was pleased to see Matt's mood picking up. "You have a mule?" I asked, knowing that the screw-driven press for squeezing the juice out of the sugar cane stalks required one to power it.

"No'm, but my neighbor, Jake, down the lane do. I gives him a couple of gallons of surp to borrow his mule ever' year come the end of summertime." He got up from the table to go into the kitchen and returned with a Mason jar full of his treasured cane syrup. "Put this in your room and take it back home with you when you go."

As I was thanking him, there came a knock at the door, and Matt got up to answer it.

"Come on in, Releford—Zora Hurston's here," said Matt, stepping aside for the visitor, a dark-skinned, handsome figure of a man dressed in a smartly tailored brown wool suit. "Zora, this is Releford McGriff."

McGriff came to my side of the table to take my hand. "I'm delighted to meet you, Miss Hurston. How was your trip?" he asked in a rich baritone.

"My trip went well," I said, feeling a little giddy when I looked into a pair of deep-set eyes that sparkled with the kind of superior intelligence and sophistication that I have always found irresistible in a male. His briar pipe gave the room a delicate scent of burley tobacco and cinnamon-baked apples that blended deliciously with the aroma of bacon and coffee. "Won't you please call me Zora?"

"I'm glad your trip went well—and please, call me Releford."

"Unless I'm mistaken, you're the gentleman who called Sam Nunn about the story."

"That's right, Zora," he replied, taking a seat at the table. "I thought old Judge Adams might need the press nipping at his heels to keep him honest."

"No doubt that was smart thinking," I agreed.

"As you know, Diaz, Revella, and Rivera have been covering the trial so far."

"Yes, I've followed their articles in the *Courier*. Any idea where they're staying?"

"We arranged housing for them with friends of the family. Matt can give you their addresses."

"So, Releford," I ventured, "what's your specialty? All I've been told is that you're the McCollum family's attorney."

"I'm with a Jacksonville firm that represents civil rights issues statewide, but my personal interest is probate. I also practice a good bit of business and contract law for the McCollum family. Do you want me to brief you on Ruby's case?"

"Please."

"When Ruby reached Raiford, a Jacksonville attorney named P. Guy Crews showed up unsolicited to represent her. Buck, Sam's brother, paid him the five-thousand-dollar cash retainer he requested, whereupon he recommended that his associate, John Cogdill, be retained because his cousin works at the prison. For another three thousand, he guaranteed preferential treatment for Ruby."

"The good-ol'-boy system."

McGriff nodded. "Crews and Cogdill then made an appearance before Judge Adams to file two motions, the first of which was for a change of venue."

"What was the ruling on that?"

"When Crews pointed out that the head of the Florida Highway Patrol in Tallahassee directed local officers to transport Ruby to the state prison at Raiford for her protection, the judge ordered that she be transported back to the county jail here in town. He then cited that action as proof that she was safe here—oh, thanks, Matt," he added, sipping the cup of coffee that had appeared at his elbow.

"Clever."

"The second motion was a suggestion of insanity, which was met with the appointment of two local physicians to examine Ruby in her jail cell when she was returned to Live Oak."

"When is the hearing scheduled?"

"It's already been held."

"What was the outcome?"

"Since both the court-appointed physicians admitted they were not qualified to practice psychiatry, Crews convinced Judge Adams to call Dr. McCullagh, a well-known psychiatrist from Jacksonville."

"So when is Dr. McCullagh due to testify?"

"Monday morning."

"Looks like I arrived in the nick of time," I concluded.

"I'd say so."

"By the way, who's Pigeye?"

"Oh, I should have mentioned that P. Guy Crews prefers to be called 'Pigeye,' a nickname he picked up in college. From then on, I'm guessing he preferred Pigeye to Pearl, his legal given name."

"Understandable," I acknowledged, thinking that some parents should be horsewhipped for the names they saddled their children with. "Is Judge Adams related to Dr. Adams's family?"

"No," Releford assured me. "Judge Adams is a transplant from Missouri, and all of Dr. Adams's family came from Jasper, just a few miles north of Live Oak." Releford paused to take a draw on his pipe. "There is one more thing I should tell you, though."

"What's that?"

"Cogdill was just temporarily disbarred for mail fraud."

"No!"

"That leaves Ruby with Pigeye as her only attorney."

"Will this compromise the case?"

Releford relit his pipe. "No. Pigeye is a great strategist. He's handling all the pretrial motions just fine."

"I must have a million other questions," I said, trying to work in a spoonful of grits to assuage my growling stomach. Although my yard hens provided plenty of fresh eggs, it had been a long time since I could afford real butter for my grits — even buying a dime stick of margarine was stretching it.

"I have a lot of questions myself," McGriff admitted. "I want to know all about this Adams character."

"Would it be possible to take a look around inside Ruby's house?" I asked.

"I don't have a problem with that as long as Matt comes along — he and Sam Junior are trustees for the estate."

I turned to Matt, who had been sitting quietly during the conversation. He nodded.

"When can we go?"

McGriff stretched, collecting his pipe. "No time like the present."

When I started to get up, he came around to my side of the table and pulled my chair out for me. "Thank you," I said, unable to recall the last time any man had performed this simple act of courtesy for me.

On the front porch, I thought how out of place McGriff's shiny new black Chrysler looked in this neighborhood, though of course, it would have looked quite at home in the driveway of the McCollum house across the street.

While we crossed the road to the McCollum house, I wondered what I could tell about Ruby just by walking through her home. How neat was the house? How was it furnished? What kinds of personal articles would I find? The first thing I noticed was that the detached building I had seen last night was a three-car garage—clearly a rarity in Live Oak.

Matt unlocked the front door and stepped back for me to enter.

Inside, there was no foyer and no separation of living and dining rooms. Instead, each area achieved its own sense of intimacy through the felicitous use of Persian rugs and heavy furniture with distinct personalities.

I admired Ruby's placement of an inviting camel-colored velvet sofa in the living room to focus her guests' attention on the stone fireplace, and her use of a large gilt mirror over the massive buffet in the dining room, strategically positioned to catch the light of the crystal chandelier.

Lavish surroundings in a colored home did not surprise me since I had visited the homes of the newly emerging American Negro aristocracy in New York and Chicago, spearheaded by the likes of Madame C. J. Walker's rise from poverty through her cosmetics empire for women of color.

What did surprise me was that such wealth could be acquired here, by a Negro family living in the segregationist South, not to mention that they dared live in finer surroundings than most of the white folks in town.

"What's in here?" I asked, indicating a swinging door beside the dining room buffet.

"That's the kitchen," Matt volunteered. "Go on in. We'll wait out here."

When I pushed the door open, I let out an audible gasp. Never had I seen such an elegant kitchen, even in the homes of the wealthy. "Two stoves," I whispered, running my hand along the top of first the gas range and then the electric. "Now, that's a woman who likes to cook." I also marveled that the refrigerator, unlike mine, did not have its coil on top.

Opening the dishwasher, I tried to determine how it worked. What happened to the food left on the plates? I wondered. That, I decided, would forever have to remain a mystery.

As I admired the checkerboard floor, reflected in the finish of the cabinet doors, the kitchen reminded me of an ad for Crosley appliances that frequently ran in the *Courier*: "A carefree kitchen is the heart of your home, so set your heart on Crosley!"

"Like the kitchen?" Releford asked when I returned to the dining room.

"What woman wouldn't? It's a fitting backstage for a feast."

Matt nodded sadly. "Ruby managed to put out a nice hot supper ever' night for Sam and the kids."

At the end of the living room, against the wall by the staircase, I saw an upright grand piano, a Baptist hymnal on the music stand. "Who played the piano, Matt?"

"Ruby played a little. But she bought it so the kids could take piano lessons. Kay got pretty good at church music. My favorite was 'In the Garden'..." Matt's voice caught, and he turned away.

"Would you like to see upstairs, Zora?" Releford asked, graciously affording Matt some private time.

"Yes, thank you," I replied, knowing how difficult just being here in the house must be for Matt.

On my way up the stairway I turned to look at the family photographs on the wall. A large hand-tinted photograph of Ruby and Sam, embossed in the lower right corner with "Mims Studio," was mounted in a gilt frame. Ruby was dressed in a smartly tailored outfit with a mink stole, and Sam was wearing a pin-striped suit. I noted that Ruby was wearing several diamond rings, with a large canary yellow diamond solitaire on her ring finger.

Smaller black-and-white pictures of Sam Jr., Loretta, Kay, and Sonja surrounded the central portrait of their parents. From what I could determine, it looked as though each of the children's photographs was taken when they were around seven or eight years old, except for Loretta, Ruby's child by Dr. Adams, who was much younger and lighter-skinned than her siblings.

Continuing up the stairway, I found a long corridor with doors along either side. I said, "These must be the bedrooms."

McGriff nodded. "All except the door down this short hallway to your immediate left—that's a bathroom—and the first door to your right—that's Ruby's office."

"Is it all right if I take a look around?"

"Make yourself at home," said Matt.

"Thanks," I said, unaware that he had followed us upstairs. I opened the door to the office, illuminated by the sunlight coming through a window at the far end of the room. To my left, I saw a huge safe with a gaping hole in the side. "Why on earth would Ruby and Sam have a safe with a hole in it?" I asked McGriff.

He chuckled. "Keith Black, the prosecuting attorney who's making it his mission to get his hands on the McCollum money, got a court order—he was standing right where you are when the welders cut that hole."

I must have looked confused by Releford's chuckle.

"Zora, you should have seen the look on Black's face when they finally got that thing open. It was as bare as old Mother Hubbard's cupboard."

Releford's laughter was so engaging that I found myself laughing—really laughing—for the first time in years. "I'd love to have been there," I managed, wiping the tears from my eyes.

Continuing the tour, I walked into Ruby's bedroom. Aside from the beautiful four-poster bed and dresser, what caught my attention were the mirrored double closet doors. I said, "If there's anything that makes more of a statement about a woman than her kitchen, Releford, it's her closet."

"Go right ahead," he invited, amused by my feminine curiosity.

I opened the closet to find tailored dresses, furs, extravagant feathered hats, and dozens of pairs of coordinating shoes. "Now, there's a woman after my own heart," I observed, pulling a hat off the shelf to try it on.

"It looks lovely on you," Releford was sweet enough to say.

"Thank you," I beamed, flattered by the compliment; then I felt a sudden sadness. "It's a shame Ruby won't have a chance to wear it...at least for a while," I said, almost reverently placing the hat back where I had found it.

In the bathroom I found the usual collection of creams and cosmetics of a woman who is comfortable spending what she pleases on her looks. Alongside several rows of lipstick, I found a jar whose label read, "Dr. Palmer's new double-strength skin whitener—be lighter, be lovelier, be loved!" Putting the jar down in disgust, I marveled at how colored women hate their dark complexion. And yet, as an anthropologist, I understood why. Throughout the "civilized" world, the shameful truth was that light-skinned women were considered more desirable.

For all my distaste, I had to admit that the skin lightener had no doubt made Dr. Palmer a very rich man.

Entering the hallway to look into another bedroom, I saw that it was furnished with a crib and a bassinet with a porcelain-white Shirley Temple doll lying inside beneath a baby blanket. I picked up the doll to see its glassy bright blue eyes pop open. When I placed it back in the bassinet, the eyes closed again and a mechanical voice ground out, "Now I lay me down to sleep, I pray the Lord my soul to keep. If I should die before I wake, I pray the Lord my soul to take. Amen."

When I looked at the doll in the bassinet, I laughed and said, "I didn't know dolls came with souls these days."

Releford laughed, too. It was then I realized that Matt was standing at the doorway.

"That's the new prayin' doll that come out just last Christmas. Ruby bought all the girls one."

I could feel the blood rush to my face, embarrassed that my comment might have offended Matt. "It's lovely, Matt," was all I could think to say.

Around the room were several other dolls, all of them white. I stood silently a moment, considering what the choice of all-white dolls and skin-lightening cream revealed about Ruby.

The colored Saralee doll, manufactured by the Ideal Toy Company and marketed through Sears Roebuck, had come out in time for Christmas. I was quite familiar with the doll, since its designer, Sara Lee Creech, a white woman from Bell Glade, Florida, had consulted me out of concern for creating an "anthropologically correct" doll. After Creech conceived and designed her doll, Eleanor Roosevelt hosted a tea where many famous Negroes chose the precise skin color before it went into production.

"This was Loretta's room," Matt continued. "Doctah Adams bought her the basinet."

I was not surprised at the gift. It seemed to be a hallmark of Southern "gentlemen" who sired children by their colored mistresses to look with a certain degree of affection on their bastard children. While never acknowledging them, these men often kept their mistresses and their children with enough food and clothing to scrape by—reason enough for some colored women to seek out such an arrangement when men of their own race could not afford to support them. I quickly concluded that this was not the case with Ruby.

"That's the only good thing I can say 'bout him," Matt said. "He come by to see Loretta all the time and bought her lots of toys and things."

I nodded, thinking better of pressing with any more questions about Adams right now, since I could see by the look on his face that being in the house was too personal, too humid with memories of what used to be.

Leaving Loretta's room, I continued my tour in the next bedroom. There I saw two twin beds, several white dolls sitting around the room, and two or three children's books that had fallen to the floor. "Sonja and Kay's room?"

Matt nodded. At the end of the hallway, past a closet, was another bedroom.

"Whose bedroom was this, Matt?"

"That be Sam Junior's old room."

Entering the room, I noticed that it was cleared of anything that might say something of who had once lived there.

"That be all the rooms," Matt informed me, "'cept for one bedroom downstairs that Ruby used to th'ow things in."

"Thanks for the tour, Matt," I said, leaving the room to head downstairs. "I always like to get a feel for the stories I cover."

"I 'preciates you writin' 'bout this. Maybe if they know they bein' watched, Ruby get a fair trial."

Moved by Matt's words, I put my hand on his shoulder. "I'll do my best."

Matt and I left the house that was no longer a home, and waited in the circular driveway while Releford locked up.

Releford McGriff glanced at his gold Rolex. "It's about time I headed on back to Jacksonville. If there's anything you need, Matt, just give me a call."

After thanking him, Matt added, "Buck say he be up soon's he can make it. You comin' back then?"

"Give me a call when he gets here and I'll drive over."

Releford gave me a concerned look. "Zora," he said, "I want you to be careful while you're in town."

"Any particular reason?"

"This case opens up a can of worms. Lots of people had their hands in Sam's business, and he operated under the full protection of the law up until Ruby shot Dr. Adams. I'd recommend that you keep a low profile so folks don't get nervous."

"I'll do my best," I assured him, knowing full well that I usually managed to find myself in the limelight during the times I tried hardest to avoid it.

Releford shot me a grin that told me my reputation got off the bus before I did. "In any event, when I get back in town, I'll stop by to update you and Matt on what's happening in the legal filings and to answer any questions you might have about the trial."

"I'll look forward to that," I replied, crossing the road to his car with him.

After he left, I returned to the front porch to take a seat in the rocker beside Matt. I have always been amazed at how rocking away on the front porch calms the nerves. No matter how stressed a body may be, a good rocking chair has a way of pumping the worries right out the soles of your feet.

"Would tomorrow be a good time to ask you about Ruby and your family, Matt?" I ventured.

"I don't mind talkin' right now if you want to."

"I'll run inside and fetch my notepad."

Suwannee County Courthouse

Chapter Three

When I entered the Suwannee County Courthouse around 1:45 on Monday afternoon and found my way to the balcony reserved for coloreds, I was surprised to find only a dozen or so people seated on the church-style wooden pews.

Looking down onto the main floor, I saw that the white citizens of Live Oak were much better represented, with perhaps seventy-five people sitting in padded seats. I had to wag my head at Suwannee County's interpretation of the "separate but equal" ruling by the nation's Supreme Court.

Against the quiet murmurings of an expectant audience, I reflected that there are two reasons why people in Suwannee County meet in the courtroom. The first is to "yaw" over property lines and things like that so that neither party gets too personal in a small town where getting too personal doesn't sit well. The second is when matters get totally out of hand and the living heirs of the losing party take it to court after the funeral is over. In the first instance, the courtroom attendance consists of the sparring parties and their attorneys, with the judge officiating. In the second, most of the county shows up for the drama, and all that is missing is the popcorn.

Today the courtroom was brightly lit by the sunshine flooding through the tall open windows, and ceiling fans whirred softly, circulating the cool fall breeze.

Brass spittoons were stationed in the jury box, by the judge's bench, and in the areas provided for spectators on the main floor as well as the balcony. Several red-rimmed enameled buckets with blue-handled dippers provided communal drinking water.

While everyone was waiting for court to begin, the janitor, an elderly man whom Matt had identified as the McCollum's former groundskeeper, lugged in a bucket of ice water and dipped it into pitchers for Judge Adams and the attorneys. Matt also told me that the man had ingratiated himself with the judge by carrying his briefcase each morning, becoming what I call a "pet Negro."

When Ruby McCollum entered the courtroom with Crews, I noted that her hair was neatly pressed and lay to one side on her shoulder. She was dressed simply in a short-sleeved blue and white checkered frock. From my tour of her closet, it was apparent that Crews had dressed her down for the trial.

Aside from her attire, I noted that she was a diminutive woman, dwarfed by Pigeye Crews, a portly man in his mid-forties with squinty little eyes set in a puffy, pink face. It was obvious that more than phonetics had figured in his nickname of "Pigeye."

Ruby's expression was stoic as Crews seated her at the table provided for the defense.

While spectators passed the bucket of drinking water to quench their thirst, their curiosity would not be so readily slaked: How could a Negro woman have the audacity to murder the county's most prominent white man?

Murmurs spread through the gallery, but I resisted the urge to pull out my notepad just now for fear of quelling the flow of information that I might overhear.

"Why she shoot him over that doctor bill?" the woman next to me asked the man seated on her other side. "The McCollums always paid they bills."

Curious whether the local dogma regarding the dispute over the doctor bill might be called into question, I turned to the woman. "Do you think there was something else going on?"

"Hush up!" a woman behind me warned with a note of urgency. "Folks don't need to be askin' so many questions."

Shortly after Ruby and Crews had taken their places, Arthur Keith Black, the state's attorney—a short, stout, balding man in his forties, wearing a rumpled blue suit and rimless spectacles—entered the courtroom with his inconspicuous assistant, O. O. Edwards, and sat at the table provided for the prosecution.

The murmuring continued in the balcony, blending with the soft ticking of the pendulum clock mounted above the whites' entrance to the courtroom. I heard an old man beside me whisper to his friend that Black was "a gettin' fool." Recalling my cab driver's conviction that Ruby was headed for "Old Sparky," I decided that Black had earned himself quite a reputation with the locals.

At about 1:50, ten minutes before court was scheduled to be in session, a frail silver-haired woman carrying a knitting bag entered the courtroom to sit in the front row by a younger woman with a small child in her lap. Removing her needles and yarn from her bag, the old woman settled in to begin her work.

While I thought the woman's diversion a perfectly reasonable way to pass the time, I also recalled reading that women during the French Revolution would often bring their knitting, missing a stitch here or there as they enthusiastically cheered the fall of the shining guillotine blade, followed by the thud of the condemned's head tumbling into the basket below.

At 1:59 by the clock on the wall, the court clerk gave a stentorian "All rise," heralding the entrance of Judge Hal W. Adams, a tall, thin man with receding gray hair and bushy eyebrows, who appeared to be in his late sixties or early seventies. Given a beard, he could have passed for Abraham Lincoln. From where I sat, the door through which he entered was so carefully concealed by the wood paneling that it was as if the elderly jurist had been magically spirited onto the stage—a fitting entrance for a man who, in many ways, held the power of life and death in his hands.

When Judge Adams took his place on the bench and the audience settled into their seats, the proceedings began with a devotional. After the prayer, two resounding clangs in the courthouse dome coincided with the pounding of Judge Adams's gavel, declaring court in session.

Black and Crews immediately approached the bench to engage the judge in a whispered conference, and while they conferred, John Diaz took a seat beside me. "I tried to catch you outside," he whispered. "If you're interested, I have a meeting scheduled with the old man in his chambers after the hearing."

I nodded, glad to see that Diaz was including me in his conference. "Where's Rivera?" I asked.

"Taking the day off—nothing for him to shoot today since the judge banned cameras." Diaz motioned toward the front of the court-room. "You see that microphone sitting beside the court reporter?"

"Yes…that's strange."

"I found out the old man's having the trial electronically recorded. I'm told it's a first."

After Crews and Black returned to their respective positions, Judge Adams asked if Crews was ready to call his expert witness on his motion of suggestion of insanity.

When Crews called Dr. McCullagh to the stand, he asked the usual preliminary questions: Could he please state his name for the record? What was his training? Where was his residency? Was he board certified in psychiatry? Where did he practice? McCullagh's qualifications as a psychiatrist were impressive, including certification by the

American Board of Psychiatry as well as the American Board of Neurology.

"I believe, Your Honor, that the witness is qualified," Crews concluded.

The judge leaned forward. "I already knew that, Mr. Crews. This gentleman has been in my court upon many occasions."

Then Crews came to the point. "Did you receive authorization from this court to examine the defendant, Ruby McCollum, here in the Suwannee County jail?"

"Yes, I did."

"Would you state when and where and under what circumstances that examination and observation was made?"

"I understood from the order that some sort of written report was required, and so I have a written report that I have addressed to the judge."

"Will you read it?" Crews asked.

Dr. McCullagh pulled a sheet of paper from a file folder. "As authorized in the court order dated September 29, 1952, I have made a neuropsychiatric examination of Ruby McCollum, and report as follows: History of the examination indicates that Ruby McCollum is not psychotic (not insane) at the present time. It is my opinion that she was not psychotic (not insane) at the time of the alleged offense. I have been treating this patient for a nervous disorder classified as a psychoneurosis, depressive and hypochondriacal being the predominating symptoms."

"What do you mean by that?" Crews asked.

Judge Adams added, "Will you please tell us in plain, everyday language what that means, if possible?"

McCullagh returned his report to the folder and settled back in his chair. "Yes, sir. I said that I have treated this patient for a nervous disorder, and the name of the nervous disorder, I said, was a psychoneurosis, depression and hypochondria being the predominant symptoms. I treated her and put her in the hospital."

"What hospital was that?" Crews asked.

"Brewster Hospital."

"In Jacksonville?"

"Yes, sir."

"When was that?"

"She was there first in January, where she was a patient for about twelve days, I think, and again in February, where she was there about nine days, and I think she was there on a third occasion in May, when she was there about a week. That was all in 1952."

"That was January, February, and May of this year?" Crews asked.

"Yes, sir."

"And what did you find to be wrong with her?"

"I can tell you what I meant by 'depression' and 'hypochondria.' By 'depression' I meant she was emotionally despondent, or blue and worrying, and by 'hypochondria' I mean that she was preoccupied with feelings that she was having. For example, she was complaining of discomfort of her chest, but X-rays of her chest and examination of her heart and lungs and blood pressure were made and nothing was found. She was also complaining of pain in her back and lower abdomen, and we made studies of that area and many X-rays of that area, which were interpreted to be normal."

"And that is what you meant by 'psychoneurosis' and 'hypochondria'?"

"Yes, sir," the physician affirmed.

Having established the state of Ruby's mental condition in the months before the murder, Crews continued, "And from your recent examination of the patient, you found nothing at this time that would change your opinion about her present condition?"

"No, sir."

"Your opinion at the present time, and your previous opinion, is that she is able to determine right from wrong?"

"Yes, sir."

"And able to present a rational defense?"

"Yes, sir."

Black's response was a matter-of-fact: "I have no questions."

Judge Adams immediately ruled that Ruby was sane and capable of presenting a rational defense.

Following the judge's order, Crews stated that he had a "bill of particulars," which would establish his client's temporary insanity at the time of the murder, but that he needed two weeks to prepare.

Judge Adams interrupted Black's immediate objection by stating that he had been in conversations with a colleague about the problem of his current term nearing an end and that the earliest date he could set for the trial would be November 18, which would be sufficiently into the next term to cover the eventuality of a new judge needing time to prepare.

After consultation with attorneys, Judge Adams set November 15 as the date for drawing the venire of one hundred names for selection of the jury, and November 18 for the veniremen to appear in court for questioning.

When the session was adjourned, I whispered to Diaz, "Did you hear Crews get Dr. McCullagh to testify that Ruby had three psychiatric commitments just before the murder?"

"That pork chop politico might be smarter than he looks," Diaz responded.

I nodded, thinking of how many brilliant Southern senators had bushwhacked their unsuspecting Northern colleagues who mistook drawling quotes from Scripture as proof positive of a limited education.

Downstairs, Diaz and I were intercepted by Sheriff Sim Howell, a slim figure of a man with an expression so dour he may well have just bitten into a green persimmon.

"Y'all from that colored newspaper?"

"Yes, sir," Diaz acknowledged.

"The judge sent me out to bring you to his office. Before I do, though, I need to tell y'all we don't need no outside interference in this trial. I hope y'all don't plan on goin' 'round town stirrin' things up."

"We're reporters, Sheriff, not troublemakers," I blurted out before I had a chance to think.

Howell frowned. "We'll see. Follow me."

Judge Hal W. Adams

Chapter Four

On the wall we faced when entering Judge Adams's chambers were ceiling-high dark wood bookshelves housing hundreds of legal tomes, the tools of the jurist's profession. The only natural light came through a single window behind the massive oak desk, but floor and wall lamps provided sufficient light for reading.

On either side of the window were photographs of the judge, including several with past Florida governors and other state dignitaries. Then there were various awards and honors he had received. Of the seven counties of North Florida making up the Third Judicial Circuit, covered by Judge Adams, I knew that Suwannee County, with approximately fourteen thousand souls, was the most populous, so it was the most likely of the seven courthouses he frequented to display these status symbols.

"Y'all come on in and have a seat," the judge called over his shoulder from the small closet where he kept his robes.

"Thank you, Your Honor," I returned, taking a seat beside Diaz in front of the judge's desk. Since he had removed his robes, I could see that he was wearing a dark blue serge suit and high-top black boots of a style that had gone out in the previous century.

"Hope you folks don't mind if I make a couple of notes on my calendar before we begin," he said, closing the closet door. "I have to admit that my memory isn't as good as it used to be."

"Not at all, Your Honor," Diaz assured him.

While the judge sat at his desk to open the ledger-style calendar, I noticed a picture frame on the wall behind his desk, with two oval-matted photographs. The one on the left showed the judge as a much younger man, riding a mule, while the one on the right side, taken fairly recently, showed him standing in a convertible beside Governor Caldwell, against the background of a bridge. Below the two men, a very determined-looking young girl held scissors above her head to cut a ceremonial ribbon.

"I hear y'all are from the *Pittsburgh Courier*," the judge announced suddenly, closing his calendar.

"That's correct," Diaz affirmed. "I'm John Diaz, senior Florida reporter for the *Courier*."

"Pleased to make your acquaintance," the judge greeted without extending his hand.

"And I'm Zora Neale Hurston. While you were attending to your calendar, I was enjoying the photograph with the young lady about to cut a ribbon."

"That's my granddaughter. That was quite an honor, having a bridge in my circuit named after me. They ran that photograph on the front page of the *Democrat* back in 'forty-seven."

"The young lady looks quite determined."

"Stubborn as a mule, I always say. Her mother claims she's the spitting image of her grandfather."

I smiled, thinking how well the mother knew her daughter and her own father. "And the picture of you riding the mule?"

"That's Jeb. Back when I first started riding the circuit, Jeb and I crossed over the old wooden bridge that stood on the same spot as the newer bridge you see there."

"You certainly have roots here," I acknowledged.

"Actually, I'm a transplant from Missouri, but most folks around here don't remember that far back." The judge spit a stream of tobacco juice into the ceramic spittoon beside his desk. "But enough about me. I'd like to talk about your book that came out a few years back. I believe the title was *Seraph on the Suwannee*."

"That's right," I replied, pleasantly surprised at the judge's familiarity with my work.

"My wife asked me to prevail upon you to autograph her copy."

"I'd be delighted." Regardless of his intent, the judge had a disarming charm about him.

As I was autographing the book, there was a tap on the door.

"Come in," the judge called.

The door opened to reveal a young, tall, broad-shouldered man with a ruddy complexion and dark hair, carrying what appeared to be a small suitcase. Closing the door behind him, the man placed the suitcase on a table beside Judge Adams's desk, opened it, and pulled out a cord to plug into an outlet.

"I don't know that y'all have had the chance to meet the newly elected district attorney. Mr. Slaughter, this is Zora Hurston and Alex Diaz from the *Pittsburgh Courier*."

Slaughter nodded nonchalantly, continuing to set up the recorder.

I had a passing thought that the judge was giving Slaughter an opportunity to become acquainted with a trial that he would ultimately inherit from Black, since he had defeated Black in the recent election.

"I hear that you folks have requested a press table on the main floor of the courtroom," Adams said.

"We have, Your Honor," Diaz responded.

The judge leaned forward, signaling Slaughter to turn on the recording device. "Let me tell you how I feel about allowing reporters to have a press table. First, I expect that the good folks of Suwannee County will attend this trial to the full capacity of the room. From my best recollection, the courtroom accommodates up to a hundred and fifty souls on the main floor and about fifty in the balcony."

"That is what I calculated," Diaz agreed.

"I'm glad we're in agreement on the numbers." The judge smiled narrowly, revealing a set of tobacco-stained false teeth.

"Do you mind if I change the subject for a moment to ask Your Honor why you've chosen to record our conversation?" Diaz interjected.

"Not at all," the judge assured Diaz. "As I explained to your paper's staff photographer a while back, with all the reporters covering this case, I have no idea what might come out of it."

"How is that, Your Honor?"

After expertly firing another brown stream into his spittoon, he replied, "What a lot of folks don't understand is that this is just another murder, like any other murder that I see several times a year in this circuit—it's not a bit different. And I'm going to give this woman a fair and square trial, just like I would any of the other cases that come before me in my courtroom."

"I can appreciate that, Your Honor," Diaz conceded.

"A lot of folks outside the area have their minds set on what they plan to hear, and their imaginations take off, regardless of what actually transpires in the courtroom." The judge paused. "You would agree that the mind is a powerful thing?"

"Yes, Your Honor, it is," Diaz agreed.

"I believe it was Shakespeare who wrote something to the effect that the poet's pen gives airy nothing a local habitation and a name."

"That's from *A Midsummer Night's Dream*," I volunteered.

"Very good, Miz Hurston. I see that you know your Shakespeare. And I'm certain that you can understand my desire to protect what is said in the courtroom, as well as what is said in my chambers, from any sort of flights of fancy."

Heinz could have wrung enough vinegar out of the sour look Diaz shot me to run his whole pickle works for a year.

"Your Honor, do you mind if we return to the topic of the press table?" Diaz persisted.

"Not at all—I've decided to deny the request. As I said, the citizens of this county deserve a chance to attend this trial."

Diaz was stunned. "But, Your Honor, I can't believe that you are denying us a press table simply because it might take up the space of a couple more seats."

"That is my determination."

"But that means we'll have to sit in the balcony while the white reporters get a ringside seat."

At that point I could see the fire kindling in the judge's eyes.

"I'm sorry to hear you refer to my courtroom as a circus. That's exactly why I have remained firm in taking any measures necessary to ward off the intrusions and misrepresentations of outsiders who would try to sensationalize this case to their own ends."

Diaz had walked straight into the judge's trap, and I could see by the look on his face that he knew it.

"It's not about sensationalizing, Your Honor," Diaz protested.

"Be that as it may," the judge persisted, "it is my considered decision that there will be no table set aside for use by the press."

Diaz gripped his knees. "I suppose that's that."

In the silence that ensued, I wondered whether the judge embraced the local dogma about Ruby shooting Dr. Adams over a doctor bill and, if he did, whether his acceptance was native to his spirit or sprang from his roots in the geographical emotions and traditions of his ancestors.

Sitting there, I realized that Judge Adams's closest spiritual ancestor was General Robert E. Lee, a military genius with more nobility of soul than the common soldier, who hated the institution of slavery and had freed his own slaves. In his heart he devoutly believed in the Union and regarded secession as the ultimate death of the nation, and yet, when the fighting began, he sided with Virginia and its sister rebel states.

With this revelation, Judge Adams became the foremost figure of interest to me in the trial. Ruby McCollum had already admitted to murdering Dr. Adams, so only the degree of her guilt was to be decided. The real drama lay in the evidence to establish mitigating circumstances and in whether Judge Adams would allow or bar its presentation to the jury. Not until after the trial would I have a full measure of this man's character. It was still too soon to know whether he could rise above his Jim Crow heritage or whether his soft and courteous manner was simply a mask to hide his true nature.

"There is one other matter, Your Honor," I ventured. "I would like to set up a time, agreeable to you and Sheriff Howell, to speak with Ruby McCollum."

Judge Adams settled back in his chair.

"Well, Ms. Hurston," he said, his lower lip tight against his teeth to hold the chew in place, "I can appreciate your desire, as a member of the press, to speak with the defendant. It is, after all, in the nature of reporters like yourself to gather information and to report what you find to your readers. Needless to say, I understand and respect that."

"Yes, sir," I responded, thinking that this was the kind of man who had to drive his buggy around the courthouse several times before eventually hitching his horse.

"But I have to respond to your request in the same manner that I have responded to all the others. My position all along has been that I don't want to subject Ruby to any further stress or embarrassment. I also don't want the community to be subjected to the outrageous claims of outsiders about matters that are certain to arise out of reporters' needs to sensationalize the trial."

"I can assure you, Your Honor," Diaz protested, "that I am a legitimate journalist, and my intent is to report the facts."

"I have no doubt that you are honorable," the judge continued, "but I have to use the same rule for everyone. I can't make an exception for the two of you, no matter how much I believe in your keen sense of journalistic ethics. As to your interest in the facts, that is what this court is in the business of establishing."

Diaz was incredulous. "Doesn't it bother you at all, Judge Adams, that you are denying Ruby McCollum her First Amendment rights?"

"I've had to address that question with a couple of reporters who drove up from Miami, and I'll tell you the same thing I told them." The judge paused, ran his tongue inside his lower lip to dislodge the wad of tobacco, and spat it into the porcelain cuspidor. "There is considerable confusion among reporters about First Amendment rights. In unusual circumstances, when the course of a trial might be diverted from the fair and equitable treatment of the defendant by unreasonable attention to details irrelevant to the case, it is within the discretion of the court to bar the press from speaking with the defendant. And these are just what I have determined to be the circumstances in this trial."

"What could we possibly do to derail your trial?" Diaz asked.

"I'm not implying that you would try to," Adams persisted. "I'm just saying that this defendant is going to get a fair and square trial, and I'm not going to let anything get in the way of that."

Seeing Diaz's rigid posture, with both arms of his chair in a stranglehold, I decided to bring the conversation to a close. "Well, Your Honor," I said, "it appears that you've made up your mind on the matters we came to discuss. We appreciate your taking the time to speak with us."

Judge Adams stood up. "Y'all come by anytime. I'm always available to the press."

"Thank you," I replied cordially, standing to leave.

Diaz managed to get out a restrained thank-you. After that, he remained silent until we were outside on the courthouse steps. "I can't believe we spent a half hour in there just to leave empty-handed," he said. "I need a drink."

"Know a good place?"

"Yeah...and I'll bet Rivera's already beat us to it."

Sam McCollum's Three Spot

Chapter Five

Diaz parked in front of the Three Spot, a small, whitewashed concrete-block structure nestled beneath ancient live oaks richly draped in Spanish moss. Though the building had apparently once been someone's home, in its current incarnation it had brightly painted tin Coke and Camel cigarette signs covering the windows for its customers' privacy.

That one of Sam McCollum's jooks, or "jukes" as they are called in the South, was located in a colored neighborhood directly across from the fenced white school grounds and less than twenty yards from the African Baptist church was a testament to folks' uncanny ability to hide their heads in the sand and pretend that such places didn't exist in their town.

In front of the juke, two elderly colored men in overalls and broad-brimmed straw hats sat playing a game of bottle-cap checkers. Nehi held the board for one player, and Coke for the other. A steel barrel with flames licking its rim sat nearby, furnishing warmth for the players. Innocent though they appeared, I knew that the men were lookouts, much as in the old speakeasy days, and that a doorbell button wired under the table would sound the alarm inside should anyone approach who didn't look quite right.

"Afternoon," I greeted them, getting out of the car.

"Afternoon," the men responded with simultaneous tips of their hats.

"How are you two gentlemen this fine afternoon?"

"Reckon we be two steps 'head of the devil," the Coke player quipped, jumping his Nehi opponent to add a cap to his collection.

"You gentlemen see Alex Rivera today?" Diaz asked.

The Nehi player smiled while making his move. "Crown me, brother." He glanced toward the juke. "He be inside with Thelma right this instant minute."

"Thank you, sir," said Diaz, pulling the screen door open for me to enter.

Inside, Count Basie blared from the Wurlitzer at the back of the room while several men sat around little tin-topped tables with female companions who hung on their every word in exchange for a steady supply of liquor and cigarettes.

In the back corner I spotted a conspicuously well dressed man in his thirties, smoking a cigar and nursing a drink. I guessed from his bronzed skin and fine facial features that he was of mixed African and Latin ancestry, the same as Diaz. At the man's side, a very dark, stout woman in her thirties was thoroughly enjoying his attempts to undress her with his eyes.

"Mind if we join you, Alex?" Diaz asked, interrupting the couple's tête-à-tête.

"Pull up a chair." Eyeing me from head to toe, he added, "You must be Zora Hurston."

"Yes," I replied, shaking his hand. "And you must be Alex Rivera."

"Zora, I'd like you to meet Thelma," Rivera said, gesturing toward his companion. "Thelma Curry, this is Zora Hurston. Zora's the boss's latest darling."

I ignored the barb, knowing that it stemmed from Rivera's resenting my assignment to the story. "Good to meet you, Thelma."

Thelma giggled, playing with the wedding band embedded in her stubby finger. "Likewise."

I felt an instant distaste for Thelma's girlish demeanor. It was obvious that she had outgrown her marriage as well as her wedding ring. It was equally apparent that she and Diaz had been drinking for some time before we arrived.

"Thelma was Dr. Adams's nurse," Diaz interjected.

"Dr. Adams's death must have come as quite a shock to you," I said.

The smile disappeared from Thelma's face. "I was sorry to lose my job—I suppose that's what upset me the most."

I sensed that Thelma's seemingly callous response was probably disingenuous—perhaps she was closer to Adams than she would like to admit. Apart for her personal feelings for the dotor, I could understand her concern about her job. The term "nurse" in a small Southern town is not necessarily associated with a formal education, quite often referring to a clerical worker who has been around long enough to learn what the doctor needs to support him in his practice. "What was he like?"

"He had his good side...and his bad," Thelma reflected. "I guess I just usually managed to stay on his good side."

"Did Ruby really shoot him over her bill?" I persisted, pulling out a cigarette.

Thelma laughed. "That woman might be crazy, but she's got more money than most rich white folks got." Cupping her hand, she lowered her voice to a stage whisper. "One thing's for sure, she didn't shoot him over no doctor bill...leastways not over the money part."

"Then why did she shoot him?" I persisted. This was like pulling teeth.

"She started goin' crazy when he shoved her out 'bout the time he run for senator. But what pushed her over the deep end was that last bill when the doc wrote..."

Diaz glanced nervously around the room to see several men looking over to our table. "Thelma, I think you'd better slow down on the booze."

Rivera had obviously blazed this trail before I arrived. "So," he said, "how long are you two staying in Live Oak, Alex?"

"Didn't Nunn tell you?" Rivera shot back. "I've been summoned back to Pittsburgh for another assignment. First Revella, now me. It seems they've called in the 'famous writer and novelist Zora Neale Hurston.'"

"I thought we'd work as a team," I ventured.

Rivera's nostrils flared. "You thought wrong. Like Nunn told me, the *Courier* can't afford to keep half its staff down here."

"Sorry to hear that," I said, meaning it. "Maybe you'll get a chance to come back before it's over."

"Maybe," Rivera sulked. "By the way, Diaz, how was your luck with the old man?"

"Owe you twenty," Diaz lamented, pulling out his wallet.

Rivera laughed. "I don't know how you thought you'd pull off what the guys from the *Miami Herald* couldn't."

"So what shots have you managed to get so far?" I asked Rivera as Diaz folded a twenty and grudgingly tossed it across the table.

"One of Ruby leaving the courthouse. Several of her family, including that bright kid of hers, Loretta, when they brought her back into town for a day. I also got one of the McCollum house, along with one of Adams's house and the colored entrance to his office."

I reflected on Rivera's use of "bright," referring to the light-skinned Loretta. It was one of the many words in the colored lexicon that conveyed ambivalent undertones about our people's sense of racial inferiority.

"I've seen some of your work. You're the first photographer I've ever known who's taken pictures of Jim Crow signs."

Rivera gave a grim smile. "Somebody has to put a face on Jim Crow in the South."

"I wonder why no one else has?" I pondered, more as an aside to myself than a question for Rivera.

Rivera glanced at Thelma. "I suppose it's not the kind of photograph a colored man can feel proud about showing to his lady friends."

Thelma giggled and held her hand over her mouth like a school girl.

Seeing beyond Rivera's attempt at a joke, I looked into his eyes to recognize the all-too-familiar hurt that comes with documenting hate.

Chapter Six

On the morning of October 10, I sat rocking on Matt's front porch, collecting my thoughts. Both Rivera and Diaz had been called back to Pittsburgh, confirming Rivera's assertion that Nunn was depending on me to cover the trial. I had until November 18, over a month, until the next court date—plenty of lead time to research the case.

I had already drafted an article on the sanity hearing, suggesting as a title "Ruby Sane." Not very literary, but then, sanity hearings are the venue of psychiatrists, not poets.

Matt had left me to mind the house while he visited his family in Zuber, and, since I had finished all of the leftovers in the refrigerator, I was trying to decide where to go downtown to get a hot meal. I had to be tight with my finances, since I had precious little money remaining from the paltry hundred-seventy-five-dollar advance that Nunn had sent for expenses.

Then I remembered that Matt had told me about the Saturday special of boiled peanuts and ham hock at Sam's Café. "You gets all you wants if you orders a pitcher of beer," he confided. Aside from sounding like something I'd enjoy, I just might casually glean snippets of gossip from the café's patrons.

Walking the mile to the center of town rather than taking a cab would save another seventy-five cents. Besides, the weather was good, and I would have an opportunity to see what had changed in Live Oak since my last visit, back in the thirties.

Leaving the front porch to stroll down Woods Avenue to Fifth Street, I took in a deep breath of fresh fall air, laden with the scent of burning leaves. That smell always transported me back to my childhood, when I would jump into the neatly raked piles of leaves, reveling in the crunching sound they made when they swallowed me up in their cushiony softness. It was a wonderful diversion from raking the yard, until my mother would run out of the house and chide me. "Zora Neale Hurston," she'd say, "you better not let your daddy catch you scatterin' those leaves all over the place, or he'll take it out of yore hide." I smiled, recalling her voice protecting me from my less forgiving father.

Turning right on Fifth Street, which at this point was also Highway 90, I counted myself lucky that my work usually put me in the Southeast, where the mild climate allowed me to move about freely most of the year.

Immediately past the sharp bend in Highway 90 known locally as "Dead Man's Curve" was McKeithen's Grocery. Matt had confided that Sam met in an outbuilding behind the store with his colored schoolteachers who sold bolita tickets. From what I understood, it was one of the many secret meeting places where Sam's bolita business extended into the white community. From these collection points, Sam's "lieutenants" reported to the back room of Mott's auto dealership, the final destination where the numbers wheel was spun to choose the lucky winner, and the week's gambling take was driven to the McCollum residence two blocks away.

Crossing Walker Avenue, I saw Dr. Adams's house, situated at the edge of the Suwannee County Hospital grounds. In comparison with Ruby's home, Adams's ranch-style brick home was modest.

Reaching the hospital in its lovely setting of moss-draped live oaks, I sat on one of the concrete benches by the fountain in front. Lighting a cigarette, I watched the goldfish swim through the thick, fernlike elodea, surfacing occasionally to grab a wayward bug. At times, I could swear they stared back at me.

When I had last visited Live Oak, the old colored normal school stood here. The school had started out as a half-built courthouse, abandoned by a bankrupt developer who fled town in the middle of the night. Its reincarnation as a colored liberal arts school was funded by a group of African Baptists in 1868, just three years after the area's slaves were freed and allowed to learn to read. The school lasted until around 1941, when it closed down, reopening in St. Augustine.

Putting out my cigarette, I continued along Highway 90, passing Cannon's Lumberyard, and made a left past McMullen's pea-shelling plant. At the corner where Highway 90 became Howard Street, I looked across the road to see Childress's fruit stand, with the Seaboard Coastline Railroad tracks running directly behind it.

The scene took me back to the 1930s, when I had researched the history of Live Oak and documented the Negro folktales told around evening campfires in the surrounding turpentine camps. Lawd! These old bones had certainly seen their days.

In the midst of the Depression, long before the fruit stand, the Sea Island Ginning Company stood here, an institution that served as the most reliable barometer of Suwannee County's economic and industrial progress over the years. Spanning a century, the cotton gin's groaning wheels had sounded the death rattles of the old South, while its newly installed steam whistle had heralded the New Deal.

The wooden structure once housed the most modern ginning machinery of its time, and farmers for many miles around had reaped handsome profits through its enterprise. Long-staple cotton was the platinum crop for many years, furnishing the raw material for giant weaving looms in the industrial North, where Yankee ingenuity transformed the ginned cotton into yard goods for New York's burgeoning garment industry.

But the cotton boom faded by World War I, and the gin operated at reduced capacity, serving the needs of an industry devastated by the boll weevil. By the mid-1920s, the plant had shut down, and the rhythmic chug-chug heartbeat of the cotton gin was heard no more.

Since it was constructed of the best timber, the plant was far too valuable to demolish, so it was gutted of its equipment and reborn for a brief time as a mule barn. By the early 1940s, when tractors replaced mules, the structure was again resurrected — this time as Ottis Brown's Tractor Dealership. I have often reflected that one of the greatest ironies of modern history lies in how the Industrial Revolution, in one giant wave of irreversible change, made the slaves as well as their mules obsolete, replacing both with machines.

Aside from the transformed cotton gin, Live Oak showed other signs of a slowly evolving economy. Favored by two main transportation arteries, Highway 90 and the Seaboard Coastline Railroad that paralleled it, the town was connected to the seaport of Jacksonville and points west. With these favorable means of shipping goods, Live Oak could grow its new cash crops of tobacco and corn and also get the turpentine and lumber from its vast surrounding timberlands to market.

And yet, even with these rich resources, it had remained a poor country town during the 1930s. But few people during the Great Depression suspected that entrepreneurs in this little community would prosper by meeting the postwar demand for cigarettes and timber as hordes of soldiers returned home, built their houses to start their families, and enjoyed an unlimited supply of the cigarettes they had longed for in the foxholes of Europe and the Pacific.

Knowing the place's history as I did, I could see why the McCollum's business had taken root and flourished in Live Oak. With thousands of poor workers eager to gamble their dimes and quarters for the chance to play it rich for a weekend, Ruby and Sam had struck pay dirt.

From personal experience, I knew the emotional high that comes when a long spell of poverty is broken, however fleetingly, by a sudden influx of cash—just buying an exotic plant for my garden was a whim I could indulge only when an eagerly anticipated royalty check showed up at the post office. While prudence dictated that the quarter squandered on a butterfly plant would be better invested in a few loaves of day-old bread from the corner bakery, my ability to forgo the simple pleasures in life had its limits.

To my right, the morning sun illuminated the brilliantly colored stained-glass windows in the First Baptist Church, a stately brick edifice with Romanesque arches, which marked the beginning of downtown Live Oak. The church, along with a nearby school for whites, had been built by the pioneering Parshley family, who had contributed just as generously to the Baptist-sponsored colored normal school. The Parshleys had also built the office building where Dr. Adams had his practice, and had played a role in designing and constructing the Suwannee County Courthouse.

Crossing the street, up ahead I could see the hill that was Live Oak's colored shopping district. Locally it was known in the colored community simply as "the Hill," and in some segments of the white community as "Nigger Hill." Occupying a single block, the Hill backed up against the railroad tracks.

I entered Sam's Café to see an obviously tipsy woman perched on a bar stool, alongside several men who had also had their share. I walked to the back of the café, hoping to find a secluded booth where I might overhear their conversations and take some discrete notes. Playing the role of shameless voyeur was, after all, second nature to a cultural anthropologist.

"I don't care what nobody say," one man at the bar protested, "Ruby got what she deserved. That uppity niggah thought she was too good to wipe off the soles of her feet on my back."

"Yeah," his buddy agreed. "If she needed a outside man, she shoulda stuck with her own kind, 'stead o' runnin' after no white man."

"How you know she don't want a white man 'cause he better 'twixt the sheets?" the drunken woman challenged.

"Shut yo' mouth, niggah!" the first man snarled. "Ain't no white man know how to plow the field like a colored man do."

Seeing that the man was not backing down, the woman relented and took another swig of her beer.

"Lawd knows if my woman ever got knocked up by a white man, I'd be the one to put a bullet in her head," the first man said. "I sho' 'nuff wouldn't wait fo' *her* to kill *him* soon as she find out what it all about."

"Well," his friend retorted with a raised eyebrow, "with that sweet young schoolteacher he had on the side, who you think you rather have in bed, Ruby or her?"

"Ain't that the Lawd's truth!" his friend guffawed, slapping his knee. "That Ruby sure ain't no looker, no matter how gussied up she get with them furs and them big diamond rings."

Seeing me sitting in the back of the café, the stout barmaid ambled over to my booth, chomping her gum, and tossed out an indifferent "Take your order?"

"I'll have your special," I replied, unable to rid my mind of the image of a cow chewing its cud.

"We gots two specials," the bovine waitress announced, slinging her hips to one side. "The boiled peanuts —"

"I'll take that," I interrupted, glad to hear that the special was still available.

"Anything else?"

"No, thanks," I said, reaching in my purse for a cigarette and stealthily pulling out my pad and pencil.

As soon as the waitress turned and disappeared behind the bar into the kitchen, I began my note taking, but the first man at the bar caught sight of me, elbowed his buddy, and rolled his eyes toward me.

I smiled at the men, knowing that my watering hole had just gone sour, and pushed my notes aside. Sitting back to light a cigarette, I considered that I should come back during the week, when I could catch a new crowd and be a little less obvious with my chronicling.

A few moments later, the waitress returned with a pitcher of beer and a quart-size bowl of boiled peanuts topped with a large piece of ham hock.

"Here you go, honey," she said. "You want anything else?"

"This is fine, thank you."

"Let me know if you change your mind."

"There is one other thing," I ventured.

"Mm-m?"

"I'm new in town and wondered if I might ask you a few questions. Do you have a minute?"

The waitress stole a covetous glance at my pack of Lucky Strikes and squeezed into the booth opposite me. "I guess I can take a smoke break."

"What's your name?"

"I'm Annie Mae."

I handed her a cigarette and my lighter. "It's a pleasure to meet you, Annie Mae. My name's Zora."

"Glad to meet you, Zora—and thanks for the cigarette. How can I help you?"

As Anne Mae flicked open the Zippo, I leaned forward to whisper, "I'm a reporter for the *Pittsburgh Courier*. I'm here in town to cover the Ruby McCollum trial."

Annie Mae's eyes widened.

"Would you happen to know anyone who might talk with me?"

Annie Mae looked over her shoulder and pulled my notepad over to her to scribble a name and telephone number.

I was delighted. "Thanks."

"Don't you tell her I give you her name. She's my boy's teacher out at Douglas High."

I secured the note in my purse and took out an unopened pack of cigarettes to pass to my newfound friend, knowing that it was a gesture I could ill afford.

Annie Mae slipped the gift into her apron pocket. "Since you been nice to me, I'll tell you somethin' else. You might want to stay off the streets downtown tonight."

"Hey, Annie," a male voice called from the kitchen. "You through with that smoke yet? I could use some help back here."

"Comin'," Annie Mae returned, extricating herself from the booth with the cigarette dangling from her mouth.

I touched Annie Mae's hand. "Thanks."

She smiled and gave a quick wink. "Hope you enjoy them peanuts. And don't forget what I told you 'bout tonight."

Enjoying my meal, I gave a passing thought to Annie's warning, but knew that it would not deter me from my evening stroll. Somewhere in my soul, I had always believed in Churchill's admonition that there was nothing to fear but fear itself, and I was certainly too old to change now.

When I finished my boiled peanuts, I left the café to continue my exploration of Live Oak's downtown, to see what else had changed in the past fifteen years.

Turning left outside the café, by the cabstand and the little shoe box of a police station, I passed an appliance store, the *Suwannee Democrat* offices, a clothing shop, a jewelry store, a shoe store, and a barber shop.

I looked across the street to see Seward Fleet's, Gilmore's and Sharple's department stores sitting between the Commercial Bank and the Blue Front Grocery, which anchored the block. I had always been fascinated with these pioneering Jewish families who had started out peddling rags on the streets of New York and Baltimore to build the capital they needed to become clothing merchants along the Eastern Seaboard from New York to Miami.

Crossing the street to Gilmore's Department Store, a lovely brown tailored outfit caught my attention. Unfortunately, I could not afford such an extravagance until the *Courier* paid the first real installment on my story.

A few shops later, I looked into the window of McCrory's five-and-ten and made a mental note to shop for toiletries.

Continuing past McCrory's to the courthouse, I sat on a bench a few yards away from the jail and had a needed smoke. From my vantage point, I could see the Cities service station, where the *Suwannee Democrat* had reported that the three witnesses ran screaming for help when Adams was shot. I could also see the painted white brick front of the Parshley Building, where Adams spent his last days practicing medicine. Now Ruby sat in her cell in the shadow of the courthouse, where she would soon be tried for killing the most important man in Suwannee County. The story, as well as its setting, had all the makings of high drama, and I felt lucky to be sitting center stage.

As the sun disappeared behind the jail, the streets grew strangely quiet and a fog rolled in out of nowhere. In the distance, coming from the general direction of the First Baptist Church, I heard drumbeats drawing closer. Although I had never seen a Klan march that had a drummer, I recalled Annie Mae's warning to stay off the streets after sundown tonight and concluded that perhaps here in Live Oak things were different.

Retreating to the safety of the shadows beside the jail, I heard the sound of the drumbeats moving closer. Moments later I saw a dozen hooded figures draped in white, falling into step behind their leader, who set the pace with his drumbeats. Directly behind the leader, another Klansman held a Confederate flag, and several of the men carried bright, smoking torches that cast flickering shadows at their feet.

Boom...boom...boom... The deep bass rhythm of the drum echoed the pounding of my heart. Boom...boom...boom... The sound evoked images of the fiery massacre at Rosewood some thirty years ago. Boom...boom...boom... The footsteps of hatred incarnate clothed in white, the color of innocence, marching along the streets of Live Oak.

Chapter Seven

On Tuesday afternoon I rushed to Matt's mailbox to see if the October 10 edition of the *Courier* had arrived, and was thrilled to find it safely packed in a brown wrapper and mailed first class to "Zora Neale Hurston, c/o Mr. Matt Jackson."

Rushing up the front porch steps, I eagerly unwrapped the paper to read the headline: "Zora's Revealing Story of Ruby's 1st Day in Court!" My working title had been "Ruby's Day in Court." Technically, Ruby had already appeared in court on a number of occasions, but I didn't mind the journalistic liberty that Nunn had taken, since his title was more dramatic than mine.

Farther down the page was the photograph of Ruby that Matt had given me, with the heading "Drama on the Suwannee." I eagerly skimmed through my credits. "One of America's most illustrious women novelists, Mrs. Hurston is a recognized authority on the manners and mores of the people about whom she is writing. She knows the people who live on the banks of the Suwannee River. She knows places like Live Oak, Florida." Nunn was obviously referring to my work in the turpentine camps of northwest Florida, and my last novel, *Seraph on the Suwannee.*

Aside from noting that the *Courier* addressed me as "Mrs." even though my last divorce was many years ago, I was impressed with the layout of the story and the citation of my professional credits. As to the "woman novelist," I reflected that the gender reference would take at least another generation to become irrelevant.

All in all, it was a good first article, but what I really wanted to report was the underlying drama of the story, not just the legalistic maneuverings of attorneys in the courtroom.

Then I noticed that the *Courier* had added a copyright line, and my heart sank. It was apparent that I should have had a written agreement retaining the right to use my research for anything I might pen in the future. Unfortunately, it was too late now.

Pulled from my reading, I saw Matt driving onto the front yard, followed by a black Cadillac limousine.

"Mornin', Zora," Matt called as he got out of his car.

"Mornin', Matt," I returned, leaving the porch to meet him.

Matt opened the passenger door of the limousine. "I'd like you to meet Sam's brother, Buck."

I leaned over to reach for Buck's outstretched hand.

"Mornin', Zora," Buck said, gripping my hand warmly. "It's goin' to take a minute for me to get out with this bum leg of mine."

Although Matt had told me that Buck was younger than Sam, making him less than forty years old, his face was etched with the kind of lines that pain sketches on the faces of those it afflicts, aging them beyond their years.

I was admiring the carved ivory handle of his walking cane when he grabbed it with his left hand, revealing a canary diamond on his ring finger that was the size of my index fingernail. "I'm so sorry to hear about your brother."

"Thank you, Zora. Sam's passing was a shock to all of us."

"Did you have a chance to see Ruby yet?"

"Zora don't know what happened, Buck," Matt intervened.

Recalling the Klan march, I looked questioningly at Matt, fearing the worst.

"Ruby had a miscarriage, Zora," Buck confided. "We've been down at the jailhouse since yesterday."

I was stunned—I had not known that Ruby was pregnant. "When did this happen?"

"Friday night sometime, from what we can tell. Pigeye Crews drove over here Saturday mornin' to meet with Ruby in the jailhouse. When he got inside, he found her layin' in a puddle of blood and hardly breathin'."

"Oh, my God!" I gasped.

"When he found her, Crews used her bed sheet to stop the bleedin', then ran down to the hospital and got some penicillin and some stuff to clean her up with. After that, he stayed with her till the doctor came."

"When did you find out about this?"

"Pigeye didn't call us until Sunday night. We drove straight up, but Sheriff Howell wouldn't let us see her until they had Dr. Workman check her out early this mornin'. We sat up in the car all night, waitin' until they'd let us in."

"How is she now?"

"She's not out of the woods yet," Buck lamented. "Good thing Crews was a medic in the Army. If he hadn't helped her, she'd have died for sure."

"Do you know how it happened?" I asked, wondering if it had anything to do with the Klan march.

"We don't rightly know," he admitted.

Buck's chauffeur, a powerfully built middle-aged, dark-skinned man, got out of the car to assist his boss.

Buck winced. "Thanks, Willie."

When we entered the house, I felt a deep sickness in the pit of my stomach. Though I had never had a child, I could empathize with a woman who had just had her insides ripped out only to deliver a stillborn baby.

Buck fell into Matt's easy chair. "We sure appreciate you comin' here to put this story in your paper, Zora, but I'm goin' to ask you if you'd keep this part to yourself. If things get stirred up much more here, Sheriff Howell might not be able to keep the Klan from breakin' her outta there. Hell, from what I've heard, he's one of 'em."

I took a seat, lighting the cigarette I so desperately needed. "Does Releford know about this?"

"Pigeye called Releford from the Suwannee Hotel, and his secretary told him he's out of the office but he'll call in for his messages today."

I felt relieved to hear that a call had gone out to Releford.

Buck motioned to Willie to help him out of the chair. "I'm goin' to get cleaned up, Zora. I'll see you later on."

"I'll be sitting on the porch," I replied, feeling that a breath of fresh air would be good for me right now.

Taking a seat in the rocker, I watched Willie unload the luggage from the trunk of the limousine while a dozen questions swirled in my mind. First of all, who knew that Ruby was pregnant? Did the Klan play a part in the abortion? Was somebody trying to murder Ruby as well as her unborn child?

Seeing Willie stagger to the front porch with several suitcases, I stood to open the screen door.

"Thank you, ma'am," Willie groaned, struggling to squeeze through the narrow doorway.

While the men were cleaning up, I decided to go back inside and try my hand at preparing a meal. Opening the refrigerator, I found a smoked ham and a bowl of eggs, so I decided to cook what would usually be considered breakfast. A pot of coffee also seemed like a good idea.

Just as I had finished setting the table and bringing out my rather basic attempt at a meal, the men came into the dining room.

"Somethin' sure smell good in here,'" said Matt.

"Hope you don't mind, Matt."

"No, ma'am," he said, taking a seat with Buck and Willie. "I sure be glad you fixed somethin' fo' us, 'cause I knows I ain't up to it."

Buck stabbed a couple of slices of ham. "This is the first time we've ate since we drove up here."

The mood around the table was predictably somber, so I tried to divert the conversation from their gruesome ordeal. "Buck, I've heard about bolita in my travels, but I'd really like to hear it from a professional."

"Well, it's a game of chance that started down in Cuba and worked its way up through Miami. I use the numbers broadcast over the radio out of Miami, and pay out based on our ticket sales after holding back a percentage for ourselves. Sam's setup was the same, but he used a numbers wheel in the back room of Mott's auto dealership since Live Oak's a small town and he found out folks bet more if they can watch the numbers bein' rolled."

"I've heard that you and Sam had other business ventures."

"I also own the Central Life Insurance Company down in Tampa. Sam was a stockholder and drove down every month for our board meetings. We sell mostly burial policies, and we have several funeral homes the folks sign their policies over to so they don't have to depend on their families to get a decent burial. When I taught Sam the business, he did the same thing up here in Live Oak."

"So how did Sam manage to steer clear of the law?"

"First off, the law don't give a damn what happens in the quarters. If somebody can keep the liquor clean and the colored folks happy with jookin' and gamblin', it just makes their jobs easier. Throw in a little bit of cash money and a few floozies for the white boys, and you got yourself a business."

So why did the *Democrat* print so many articles about bolita and liquor ruining the community?" I asked, thinking of the series of articles Louie Wadsworth ran to condemn the gambling and liquor running that went on in Suwannee County.

Buck raised an eyebrow. "Zora, you remember Prohibition. All those churchgoin' folks thought they could stop everybody from drinkin' by makin' it illegal. I don't have to tell you how that started the biggest jump in liquor sales in history. Men like Louie Wadsworth just don't understand that there ain't no way to stop folks enjoyin' their booze and gamblin'."

"Good point," I conceded. Here was a man who knew human nature. "Aside from the obvious, why do you think Judge Adams wants to keep the press away from Ruby?"

Buck, who appeared to have an answer ready for anything, fell silent, his face solemn.

"Do you think it has anything to do with the affair between Ruby and Dr. Adams?" I suggested.

"That's only part of it. Sam made lots of friends in the white community by making loans to help folks start up their businesses. He never expected the white folks to pay him back...just goodwill stuff. All of it's cash money, and the only record of it is in Ruby's little black book."

In a flash of insight, I realized the implications of what Buck was telling me. Since the whites who received Sam's loans never planned to pay him back, all these "loans" were considered undeclared income by the IRS and thus subject to interest, severe fines, and even jail time.

"The tax boys invaded Live Oak like a plague of locusts after Sam passed," Buck continued. "They gave Sheriff Howell a run for his money lookin' for Sam's cash. First thing they tried to do was to get their hands on Ruby's book."

"So, you think Ruby's affair with Adams is the least of the community's worries?"

"It matters 'cause of their pride," Buck acknowledged. "But keepin' out of the jailhouse and protectin' their butts from the IRS is what's most on their minds."

"Did the sheriff seize any of the McCollum's money?"

"He didn't, but the Doc's errand boy, Jeff Elliott, got his hands on the safety-deposit box down in Tampa where I put Sam's money. From what Releford tells me, though, he ain't bein' honest with the court about how much he took."

"How much do you think is missing?"

"At least ten thousand, from what I can tell."

"So how do you think this will all play out in the trial?"

"All I know is, Pigeye Crews used to be a state representative, and he's still got buddies over in Tallahassee. If he can't keep Ruby out of the chair, I don't know who can. Besides, my gut's tellin' me he's got somethin' up his sleeve."

"How's that?"

"When I saw him today, he bet me five thousand dollars that Ruby will walk out of the courthouse a free woman before they can pick a jury. Told me to have the money and a getaway car ready when we come to the courthouse."

Chapter Eight

On the evening of November 4, almost a month after I met Buck McCollum, I stood on the courthouse lawn with a few hundred people who had gathered to watch the results of the presidential election on the largest television set that I had ever seen.

It was quite an elaborate setup: scaffolding covered with curtains and fan-shaped flag bunting to form a proscenium arch for the TV. Behind the television, a neatly lettered banner announced, "1952 Presidential Election Results Courtesy of Kirby Appliance Store, Your Friendly GE Dealer."

The project had taken a crew of men the better part of a day, with workmen using the city's fire truck ladder to install the TV antenna atop the flagpole beside the courthouse to pick up the signal from the nearest station in Jacksonville.

In front of the stage area, about two hundred folding chairs had been set up by the Brodie Harris Funeral Home. The courthouse clock struck the half hour, and I looked up to see that it was now 8:30. The whites who had arrived early staked their claim to the precious seating to watch Walter Cronkite present the CBS coverage of election night. Coloreds crowded to both sides of the seated white audience to find a place to stand or sit on the ground.

I stood watching, curious about Cronkite's statement that although the opinion polls overwhelmingly favored Stevenson, Univac, the huge computer that took up an entire floor of a specially cooled building, was predicting hundred-to-one odds that Eisenhower would win by a landslide.

"What the tarnation is a computer?" one of the old men in the crowd asked the man sitting next to him.

"I read all about it in *Popular Mechanics*. It's just a bunch of radio tubes," his friend responded. It don't know nothin'."

I wasn't surprised that most of the talk centered on the election. Suwannee County voters had overwhelming supported Stevenson, the Democratic candidate endorsed by President Truman, even though Eisenhower promised to bring the troops home from Korea and clean up the bribery scandals uncovered among Truman appointees.

But feelings ran high in Suwannee County when it came to the need for welfare, health care for the poor, and farm subsidies—issues that were Democratic carryovers from the golden age of Roosevelt's New Deal. Roosevelt's Civilian Conservation Corps was all that had stood between many farmers and starvation during the Depression only a little over a decade ago, and it was still engraved in the public memory, underscored by this year's drought and farm foreclosures.

Nationally, the campaign had been one of the strangest that I could remember. Both candidates used radio and television to their advantage, and both campaigned hard, but neither could directly attack the other in the duke-it-out scenario that had dominated so many previous elections. Eisenhower was a war hero, so Stevenson was reluctant to attack him directly. Stevenson, on the other hand, had not been part of the Truman administration, so the Republicans could not hold him accountable for the administration's mistakes. Thus, both parties had rightly determined that a traditional frontal assault was not the road to victory.

It was clear to me, though, that the Republicans had crafted the winning strategy. On the one hand, they sent out "hatchet men"— Dewey, McCarthy, and Nixon—to campaign against the Democrats with their antiwar, anti-bribery, and anti-Communist message. Nixon took the lead in personal attacks, labeling Stevenson an "egghead" for his intellectual and seemingly arrogant manner. On the other hand, they sent out Eisenhower, whom the public generally considered friendly and accessible, distributing the ubiquitous "I Like Ike" buttons ahead of him.

Another brilliant move by the Republicans was to recruit women voters—a first in campaign history—with appearances by Mamie Eisenhower wearing an Ike button at rallies in support of her husband. Republicans took further advantage of what women could do for their campaign by staging all-women phone-calling parties and local political get-togethers where women could talk about traditional values in the home. The American public was still looking for stability after the war, and the Eisenhower family represented just that, holding to the traditional values of home and family. Stevenson, on the other hand, had a divorce tucked away in his closet. I suspected that Univac's vacuum tubes weren't far off course in predicting an Eisenhower victory.

With all the excitement of election night, I knew that my chances of hearing anything about Ruby were slim, but I had come prepared. By now I had learned my lesson about sticking out like a sore thumb with my tailored outfits and briefcase. Tonight I was wearing a simple house frock and a sweater, hoping to blend in with the crowd.

"Hello," I called to an elderly colored woman standing with her husband.

"Hey," the woman replied, still staring at the TV.

"Lots of folks out tonight."

"Yes'm."

"I'm just passing though town, and I heard about some sort of trial you're having here...something about a colored woman who shot a white doctor."

"Yes'm," the woman acknowledged. "That Ruby McCollum was a mean woman. She shot the best doctah we ever had."

"That's a shame," I said, knowing I would get little more from the woman than the standard litany I could now recite by heart.

"Hey, Zora...Zora Hurston," came a voice over my shoulder. I turned to see Thelma Curry.

"Hello, Thelma. This is quite a do."

"I'll say. I thought I'd come down to see what's going on."

"Do you mind taking a minute to talk with me?"

"Oh, I better not. Sheriff Howell told me not to talk to anybody before the trial's over. You know they subpoenaed me to testify."

"No, I didn't," I replied, although I suspected that Pigeye would want to have Thelma on the stand to testify to any interchanges she had seen between Ruby and the doctor. Then there was the doctor bill that she had started to tell me about that afternoon at the Three Spot.

"You might try to speak with Mr. Charles Hall over there," Thelma suggested, pointing to a man standing at one of the benches near the street. "He owns the colored funeral home in town, and he worked with Sam."

"Thank you, Thelma," I said, happy for even one lead today.

"See you later," Thelma called, working her way through the crowd of spectators.

Charles Hall was still talking with a man by the bench, so I approached him. "Mr. Hall, I'm sorry to interrupt. I'm Zora Hurston. I wondered if you would talk with me for a few minutes."

"I know who you are, Miz Hurston. You have to know by now that I run a business here in town. So I'll ask you this: if you was me, would you talk to a reporter?"

"I suppose not."

"Nice meetin' you, Miz Hurston. You have yourself a good night, now."

Hall left me standing by the bench while he sought out more desirable company.

I could see a few inmates of the jail looking through the barred windows of their cells, though their view of the television was blocked by the draped scaffolding. Looking up at the faces staring through the iron bars, I could only imagine how tormented Ruby must be, lying in a bed under guard, terrified of what might happen to her in the days that lay ahead.

Chapter Nine

Open court was scheduled for today, Tuesday, November 18, exactly two weeks after an overwhelming Eisenhower victory stunned the voters of Suwannee County. Now, along with losing their favorite U.S. senator, Claude Pepper, in the 1950 election, and their recently elected state senator, Dr. Adams, at the hands of a Negress, they had to suffer the indignity of their home state's unprecedented swing to a Republican presidential candidate. Things were not going well for the citizens of Suwannee County.

I suppose most people in north Florida felt that they were being invaded by outsiders, people whose values and traditions differed from their own—and the presence of reporters from the *Courier*, including myself, didn't help matters.

Thinking back to the meeting with Judge Adams, I could understand why he was adamant about cutting Ruby off from the world. Despite his protestations to the contrary, he knew instinctively that what had happened in Live Oak was more than a murder—it was a rip in the very social fabric of the segregationist South, a break in the great chain of being that stretched, uninterrupted, from the throne of the Almighty to the very lowest creature on the face of the earth. Thus, it promised to be the most sensational trial held in the South since the Scopes "Monkey Trial."

My schedule was tight today because the jury was slated to be empanelled and I had a meeting after following up on Annie Mae's lead. When I called the number she gave me, I discovered that it belonged to Lucy Brown, Sam's girlfriend and a teacher at Douglas High, the colored high school.

After changing into my tailored gray suit and matching hat, I glanced at the clock on the living room wall. I was running late, so I had no choice but to call for a cab. Five minutes later, a familiar voice called, "Howdy, Miss Hurston."

"Well, hello, Lijah," I returned, climbing into the backseat. "I didn't expect to see you again."

He grinned. "Only three of us drivin' the cabs, so it ain't like waitin' for a blue moon."

I smiled. "No, I suppose not."

Rounding the corner onto Highway 90, Lijah ventured, "You hear 'bout that Klan march last month?"

"Yes, I did. How often does that happen around here?"

"Last time I 'members was when they drownded Willie James up at Suwannee Springs."

"Do you have any idea when that was?"

"Reckon'bout 'fo'ty-fo'."

"What did Willie do?"

"He sent a Christmas card to a white woman."

"That's as good a reason as any," I quipped, knowing that we were living in an era when "eyelash rapes" — the conviction of Negro men for looking white women in the eye — were only now being overturned by the higher courts on the grounds that rape had to involve some form of physical contact.

"Folks say they be after you next," Lijah shared, looking in his rearview mirror.

"What!" I gasped.

"Folks say they don't want no niggah reporters in town."

"You know, Lijah," I said, "when I was a little girl my papa used to warn me that the stiff neck I carried my head around on would eventually upset a lot of white people. He told me that one day a rope-carrying posse would hunt me down and string me up from a big oak tree."

Lijah chuckled. "Your papa was a smart man."

"The way I figure it, I've managed to live out my three score. After another ten, Mother Nature might just beat 'em to it."

"You sho' is somethin', Miss Hurston. We at the Hill now — where you want me to pull over?"

"In front of Sam's Café will be fine," I answered, my hand trembling as I rummaged through my purse to find a few quarters. Experience had taught me that it takes a while for my courage to catch up with my tongue.

"Thank you, ma'am! I sho' 'preciates it. You jest call me whenever you needs me. You stay safe now, you hear?"

"Thank you," I called back, closing the cab door.

As I stepped up on the curb, two women passed by, staring in my direction and whispering to each other.

"Good afternoon," I greeted.

They hurried their steps to avoid speaking with me.

"Nothing like being the town pariah," I chuckled, strolling into the café.

Inside, I settled into a back booth, lit a cigarette, and enjoyed the music of Duke Ellington while I waited for Lucy. When the next record loaded in the juke box, a lovely mulatto woman in her early thirties entered the café, dressed in a stylish tailored red dress and broad-brimmed hat and carrying a red leather purse and a big shopping bag. She could easily have been a model were she taller than five feet three.

One of the men at the bar turned around to flash a snaggletoothed grin. "Howdy, Miss Brown. Teachin' anybody anything new?"

Ignoring the comment and the laughter that followed, Miss Brown made her way to my booth. "Mrs. Hurston?"

"Lucy Brown, I presume."

She smiled. "I'm honored to meet you," she greeted, graciously extending her hand.

"Please call me, Zora," I said, grasping her hand. "Looks like you didn't have any trouble spotting me."

Lucy laughed. "How many colored women in Live Oak have you seen wearing tailored suits, Zora?"

Without thinking, I glanced down at my suit, embarrassed by the frequent mending it had endured over the years since I had left New York. "You've had a heavy shopping day, I see."

"Actually, I took the day off just to meet with you," she said as the waitress approached the table.

"What can I get for you two ladies?" Annie Mae asked.

"Good morning, Annie Mae," Lucy greeted.

"Mornin', Miss Lucy, Miss Zora."

Lucy glanced at me. "I see you two have met."

I felt the blood rush to my face. "I've been in a time or two. The specials are great, and the conversation at the bar made for good material until my cover was blown."

Lucy glanced at the men at the bar. "No doubt."

"I don't know about you, Lucy," I said, anxious to engage her in conversation, "but all I really want is a mixed drink."

Annie Mae rolled her eyes.

"Have you forgotten where you are, Zora?" Lucy asked. Suwannee County went dry back in 'forty-six. All you can get now is low-alcohol beer…if you're an outsider." Lucy winked at the waitress. "Set us up with two of Sam's special iced teas, Annie Mae."

Annie Mae grinned. "Sure thing, Miss Lucy. That be all for you ladies?"

"Yes, thank you," I replied. When the waitress had gone, I whispered, "I can't wait to taste Sam's iced tea."

Lucy leaned across the table. "It's the best high-octane iced tea you can get anywhere! Sam's place brings in the good stuff through his cabstand."

"So Sam owned that, too?" I asked.

"That and all but one of the businesses on the Hill," Lucy murmured, suddenly preoccupied with something in her shopping bag.

On my first visit to Live Oak, it had struck me as odd that the colored shopping district was downtown, in the middle of the white shopping area, rather than next to the colored neighborhoods on the outskirts of town. Now, knowing that Sam McCollum owned most of the businesses on the Hill, it made perfect sense that downtown, right in the middle of commerce, was the perfect location to front his gambling and liquor operations, with police protection right next door.

Lucy lifted two books from her bag to place them gently on the table.

"Well, I'm certainly flattered!" I said. "*Seraph on the Suwannee*, my most recent." I was beginning to wonder if everyone in Suwannee County who could read had a copy.

"I loved it. But this is my favorite," Lucy said, handing me her copy of *Their Eyes Were Watching God*.

"More time has passed since I wrote that than I care to remember!" I said fondly.

"I really related to Janie," Lucy confessed. "Shame she had to go through two husbands to find Tea Cake."

"You liked my young primitive, did you?"

Lucy thought for a moment. "I liked the way he let Janie have her freedom."

"Your kind of romance, I see."

"Zora, you, of all people, know that Negro women with our education have a hard time finding suitable men of color. It's the law of supply and demand—there are too few quality Negro men to go around."

I nodded, thinking of my own personal experience. "Was Sam a 'quality Negro man'?"

Lucy smiled, fondling a locket around her neck. "Sam was...Sam was special."

"Want to tell me about him?" I asked, watching her discretely brush a tear from her eye.

"I'll cut a deal," Brown offered, managing a playful grin. "You autograph both of your books, and I'll tell all."

"You have yourself a deal," I agreed, uncapping my pen. I could see that she had the kind of spunk and sense of humor men find attractive in a woman.

"And the other one? My favorite?" she asked, sitting on the edge of her seat.

"Why don't we talk awhile?" I suggested. "That way I'll be able to learn more about you and give you a personal autograph…something meaningful."

Lucy leaned back and grinned. "Oh, you are the clever one. I extort your autograph with the subtlety of a sailor on shore leave, and you wangle my interview with the finesse of a diplomat!"

I crossed my arms in mock defiance.

"That's fine," Lucy conceded. "Before I forget, though, I need to tell you that Mr. Blue called me the other day and told me he would really like to speak with you."

"Who's Mr. Blue?"

"He owns Blue's Lodge. If you go out to Highway Ninety, it's about half a mile west of where you're staying at Matt's place."

"What on earth could this gentleman want to talk with me about?"

"Believe me, Zora, you really need to speak to him. He made me promise not to say anything else."

"Did he know Dr. Adams?"

"He considered Adams his best friend until after the funeral, when he found out some things that made him change his mind."

Now she had my curiosity peaked. "Can you share what he said to you?"

"He really wants to tell you himself," Lucy insisted.

"I'm dying to hear what he has to say," I said, sensing that she was being sincere rather than coy.

"You won't be disappointed, I assure you."

"So, what can you tell me about Ruby?" I asked, anxious to move on to better mining ground.

She looked down at her lap. "Do you know the difference between a mistress and a girlfriend, Zora?"

"I have my own theories — you go first."

"A girlfriend is a dreamer—she lives in a fantasy, always expecting her man to divorce his wife and marry her. A mistress, on the other hand, is a pragmatist—she wants her lover to stay married so she can enjoy the best he has to give while still maintaining her freedom."

"That's certainly true," I agreed, beginning to understand why Lucy related to Janie's character in my book—and why Sam would feel safe with her as his mistress.

"Sam was special enough to have two women," Lucy mused, her eyes softening. "Both of us working hard to make him feel powerful, proud, and self-assured. I always believed that a generous and capable man like him was valuable…worth taking care of."

"So you helped take care of him?"

"I did my part."

"Get you ladies anything else?" Annie asked as she served two glasses of Sam's special tea with several paper napkins.

Lucy shook her head. "No, thanks."

Annie gave me a wink as she left the table.

I took a sip of the drink and smiled. "Has a nice kick to it!"

"I told you it was good."

"Please, go on with your story."

"First, I'm curious about your opinion of how Ruby's trial is coming along."

"Well, as you know, Judge Adams ruled Ruby sane, so now they're selecting a jury."

"All white males, no doubt."

"I think the white male power structure has it so ingrained in their subconscious that they are uniquely qualified to mete out justice, it wouldn't even occur to them that anyone else could possibly be on the jury."

"When will the trial reconvene?"

I glanced at the neon clock over the juke box. "In a few minutes."

"Good," she said, picking up the tall glass and revealing elegantly manicured nails perfectly coordinated with her outfit. "We still have some time. Now it's my turn to find out about Zora Hurston."

"What on earth could you possibly want to know about me?"

"I always wondered what you meant when you wrote the line 'slave ships in shoes.'"

"Oh, yes. It's been some time…let me see," I considered, assuming my best stage persona. "It went something like, 'There is something about poverty that smells like death. Dead dreams dropping off the heart like leaves in a dry season and rotting around the feet; impulses smothered too long in the fetid air of underground caves. The soul lives in a sickly air. People can be slave ships in shoes.'"

I could see by her expression that Lucy was awestruck. "God...that's powerful."

"Many people read it wrong, though. The key words are 'can be.' We needn't be enslaved if we start thinking of ourselves as free."

"Then you don't turn a jaundiced eye toward the world because you're colored?"

"Honey, I'm too busy keepin' my oyster knife sharp!"

Lucy let out a hearty laugh. "May I have that autograph now?"

"Of course," I said, picking up my pen and reading aloud as I autographed the second book. "To Lucy, my friend and an honest woman. May she always walk in the shoes of freedom and keep her oyster knife sharp as a razor!"

Lucy took the book to look at my inscription. "Would you like to join me at my house for a drink later this week?"

"I certainly would," I replied, jumping at the opportunity to speak with her privately.

Carefully, almost reverently, it seemed, Lucy placed the two books back in her bag, then jotted her address on a napkin. "How about this Friday night? I always like to unwind at the end of the week. God only knows I could use some company."

"I'll be there." I looked at the clock again and put a dollar on the table.

"It was a pleasure meeting you, Zora," Lucy said, standing and reaching out her hand.

The instant I took her hand and looked her in the eye, I knew that Lucy would turn out to be my best source.

Suwannee County Courtroom

Chapter Ten

After meeting with Lucy, I entered the courtroom balcony to find Judge Adams nearing the completion of his *voir dire* examination of the prospective jurors, who stood lined up along the railing behind the attorneys. As I took my seat, I looked down toward the front of the courtroom audience and spotted the lady with the knitting, occupying her usual front-row seat.

Leaning forward over his bench, the judge seemed particularly concerned that this was a case of a Negro woman who had murdered a prominent white man. "We might as well get down to brass tacks now," he said. "You knew Dr. Adams, the deceased, one of the most prominent physicians in this section of Florida, and a white man who came from an old pioneer family in another nearby county. The defendant, Ruby McCollum, is a colored woman, and she is charged with killing Dr. Adams. Now, search out your consciences." The judge paused, adjusting his bifocals to stare down at the veniremen.

The men stood silently along the railing during the break in the judge's questioning. While I couldn't see their faces, several of them were nervously shifting their weight from one leg to another, and the man in the middle reached underneath the back of his jacket to manage a discrete scratch.

Judge Adams, seeming satisfied that there are no responses, resumed his questioning. "Are you in a position to give her, under those circumstances, a fair, square, unbiased, impartial trial upon the facts? And after you have heard all the testimony and the charge of the court and retire to your jury room to consider your verdict, can you consider it without any thought of the color or standing or the position of the deceased or of the defendant? And unless you are convinced from the evidence beyond reasonable doubt of her guilt under the evidence or the lack thereof, are you in a position to act in accordance with your judgment in that connection, whatever it may be?"

The men stood silently again, which led me to believe that their lack of response indicated that they could perform the duties the judge was asking of them.

As the judge completed his *voir dire* examination and prepared to empanel the jury, a stone-faced Sheriff Howell approached the bench to whisper in his ear. The judge looked concerned, whispered something back, and took a sip of water before addressing the courtroom audience.

"In the course of the activities of mankind," he began, "whatever they may be, and in the course of every individual's life, unexpected things will happen." The judge paused for his words to garner the attention of everyone in the courtroom. "So it has happened here and, in this particular case, has hampered and hindered fair progress therein and has brought to Suwannee County and the state of Florida considerable expense that could have been avoided."

The judge gestured toward two men standing by the sheriff at the courtroom entrance. "I desire at this juncture to make of record the thanks and commendation of the court to Mr. Malcolm John and his associate, Mr. Parks, both of whom are representatives of the Associated Press in Tallahassee. Had it not been for their alertness in passing on the matter to this court that took place in the Supreme Court of Florida today, this case would have tumbled into a pile of wreckage beyond repair."

The two AP reporters nodded their appreciation of the judge's acknowledgment.

Judge Adams turned back to the courtroom audience. "But you all recall that news of this trial and all of its proceedings have been broadcast not only over this state in the press, but also in publications of national circulation from Maine to California and from the Canadian border to the Gulf, attracting national attention. Beyond that, I have word that the news has spread across the Atlantic."

Lowering his bifocals to fix his gaze upon Crews, the jurist's face darkened. "Now, in the face of these widespread reports, I am astonished beyond explanation to have before me the absolute, official information that on this very day, when this trial is to begin, there has been entered a judgment against Mr. Crews, the attorney for the defendant, which precludes him from proceeding further in that capacity." The judge regarded a red-faced Crews over the top of his bifocals with palpable contempt. "I have other expressions I would like to make, and I am fairly gritting my teeth to keep from making them."

Judge Adams turned toward the jury. "Gentlemen, this case cannot proceed further at this time. It can proceed later, but in justice to this defendant, it would not be fair to her—in fact, it would be an outrageous denial of her rights—for us to attempt to proceed any further until she has had a fair time to make arrangements to be further represented. For this, I am truly sorry."

The men in the jury box nodded modestly.

Scowling, the judge paused to fire a stream of tobacco juice into his spittoon while dead silence prevailed in the courtroom. "What is your motion, Mr. Black?"

While Black made the necessary motion for a new trial, I reflected on the judge's soliloquy. It was apparent that the old man was the grand master of the circus of human emotions that played out daily in his courtroom. He had come to expect the unusual and the bizarre as part and parcel of his daily fare and had developed the ability to meet with calm control each stumbling block that fortune threw in his path.

Hurrying out of the balcony and into the common hallway of the courthouse, I cornered Pigeye Crews. "Mr. Crews," I called, "may I speak with you a moment?"

He halted to wait for me, moving into a side alcove along the hallway to avoid blocking the exit from the courtroom.

"Mr. Crews, I'm Zora Hurston from the *Pittsburgh Courier*. Can you please explain what all this means?"

Crews stared me straight in the eye. "Well, Ms. Hurston, it means that my client has to find another attorney."

"What would have happened if the jury had been empaneled before the court got the news that you were disbarred?"

He shrugged. "Guess they would'a had to let Ruby go."

"Didn't you know you were up for disbarment?" I asked incredulously.

"Well, Ms. Hurston," Pigeye drawled, "I guess that depends on what you mean by the word 'know.' Far as I'm concerned, those boys on the bench over in Tallahassee don't have the right to do what they're doin'. If you recollect, they disbarred Cogdill right after he took this case—now they got me. If you really believe all that's just a coincidence, then you must still believe in the tooth fairy."

Pigeye donned his hat, and with a knowing wink, he went on his way out of the courthouse.

In my confusion, I recalled Crew's wager with Buck McCollum. Did this mean that he owed Buck five thousand dollars for losing the bet? And what about his conspiracy theory? Was there some plot to deprive Ruby of her attorneys?

"Zora Hurston?" called a voice from behind me as I turned to leave the courthouse.

Catching the scent of snuff and Ben-Gay, I turned to see the woman who had been knitting in the front row.

"Yes?" I responded, surprised that she knew my name.

The lady dabbed the perspiration from her forehead with a lace handkerchief and set her knitting bag down to catch her breath. "I just had to find you, to tell you what really happened here in Live Oak."

I was stunned. After all the silence, was this the break I had been waiting for?

"Well," the lady began with the greatest of sincerity, "I want you to know that Dr. Adams would never have done anything mean to anybody. He was the finest Christian man I've ever met. That McCollum woman, on the other hand, was a mean colored woman who didn't want to pay her doctor bill." The lady caught herself. "What I mean is, we all love our colored people here and they love us. Why, when any of our family passes, they always come in to clean without charging a red cent."

Once again, the litany about the doctor bill and the "pet Negro" system, wherein Negroes can be good as individuals but scoundrels as a race of people. Over the years, I had come to believe that this sort of racism sprouts from the seeds of a special hybrid of delusional thinking best nourished by richly composted Southern soil. It is the only explanation I have for the persistence of false belief in harmonious racial relations in the South in the face of indisputable evidence to the contrary.

"May the Lord bless you," the lady concluded with a kindly smile, picking up her knitting bag to file out of the building with the other spectators.

Blue's Lodge

Chapter Eleven

The Thursday following my meeting with Lucy, I set out to visit Mr. Blue at his lodge, intrigued that he would send word asking to speak with me. He had certainly succeeded in whetting my curiosity.

Since Lucy had told me that Blue's Lodge was only a short distance west of Matt's house, I decided to walk rather than call my cabdriver friend, Lijah, even though there was a bit of a chill in the air.

Just after I left Matt's house and turned left at the end of the block onto Highway 90, the nature of the neighborhood changed from colored to a poor section of town occupied by whites and outcast mulattos, known as the Bivens' Quarters. Shortly after that, I passed Mott's auto dealership and crossed a railroad track, and there were the twin brick towers of Blue's Lodge, just ahead on my right where the railroad track took a turn to run in front of the lodge.

When I reached the section of railroad track in front of the lodge to cross it and walk between the twin brick towers, I saw that Blue's Lodge consisted of a large red brick central building, surrounded by some fifteen brick cabins, each of which contained four small dwellings. Immediately in front of the lodge was a concrete fountain inscribed with "1937." Although I was used to jotting down such information for later reference, I reflected that it was the same year that my novel *Their Eyes Were Watching God* was published, so it would be easy for me to remember.

When I opened the main door of the lodge and stepped inside out of the cold, I felt as if I were in a scaled-down version of one of the many federal park lodges built by CCC workers during the New Deal. The rough-hewn ceiling beams high above my head gave the impression of a much larger interior than I had guessed from the building's outside dimensions.

The room was filled with tables covered in white linen cloths and adorned with small but cheerful floral centerpieces. Toward one end of the room was a 1930s Wurlitzer juke box, and at the other end was a big limestone fireplace with a roaring fire. Seeing no one around, I stood in front of the crackling fire to warm my hands, admiring the fossils embedded in the limestone and recalling my days spent along the Suwannee studying its ancient legacy recorded in stone.

"Can I help you?" a voice came from my left. I turned to see a short white man, probably in his thirties, wearing a dirty apron.

"I'm here to see Mr. Blue," I responded.

The man frowned. "He ain't hirin'."

"I'm not here for employment," I assured him. "He's expecting me."

"He'll be back in a minute," the man returned curtly, eyeing me from head to toe.

Looking behind me at the sofa, I asked, "May I sit while I wait?"

"Suit yourself—I don't own the place."

I sat on the overstuffed sofa, expecting the man to disappear back behind the door he had entered, but he maintained his position, staring at me.

"You from outta town?" he asked, shooting me the kind of look I was now accustomed to getting in Live Oak.

"Yes."

"My name's Jimmy," he offered, not moving an inch.

"My name's Zora."

"You here to snoop around about Dr. Adams?"

"I'm with the *Pittsburgh Courier*."

"Well, I'm here to tell you that Dr. Adams was the finest Christian I ever knowed. He come out to my house in the dead of winter when my wife was sick as a dog, 'thout askin' for a dime. He even give me money to buy kerosene so's we could keep the house warm, and kept comin' back until she was up and around."

"Sounds like he was a fine man."

"You bet your keester he was," Jimmy assured me, his lower lip trembling. "And that Nig...colored woman...that Ruby McCollum, she was a mean woman."

"I suppose you miss the doctor."

"You got that straight," he shot back without hesitation. "Doc promised me a job over in Tallahassee when he won the 'lection. 'Cept for Ruby, I'd be in the high cotton by now."

"Jimmy!" came a stern voice to my left, "you need to get back in the kitchen and finish peelin' those potatoes. I'm not payin' you to flap your jaw with visitors."

"Yes, sir," Jimmy answered sheepishly, retreating through the door into the kitchen.

I turned to see a stooped elderly man with a round face and horned-rimmed glasses. "Nice to see you, Mr. Blue," I greeted, standing to shake his outstretched hand. "I was told that you might be willing to talk about the McCollum case."

"I'd be delighted, Mrs. Hurston." He pointed at the sofa and said, "Please, keep your seat."

"Thank you," I replied, returning to my place on the sofa. Blue sat in a chair just to the right of me and pulled out his pipe. From the look on his face, he seemed pleased that I had accepted his invitation. "I've been wanting to talk with you ever since I heard you were in town. You're somewhat famous here, you know."

"Me?" I asked, unable to comprehend why anyone in town would consider me a person of interest, other than to resent my being here to cover the trial for a Negro newspaper.

"That article you wrote in the *American Legion* magazine last year... Let me think, I believe you called it, 'Why the Negro Won't Buy Communism.' That article stayed up on the bulletin board at the Post for several months."

"My goodness, I had no idea."

"'Course, folks don't take kindly to your being here now for the trial."

"I'm painfully aware of that," I acknowledged.

"The only person I could think of to get in touch with you was Sam's girlfriend, Lucy Brown. I knew she had to hook up with you sooner or later, so I gave her a call."

"I'm glad you did."

"If I might ask, how long do you plan on stayin' in Live Oak?"

"Certainly for the duration of the trial—that is, if the Klan doesn't burn a cross in the front yard where I'm staying."

"Oh, the boys won't do you no harm. Judge Adams'll see to that."

"The judge is a member of the Klan?"

"I can't speak to that," Blue demurred, but I can tell you that I marched with 'em until Ruby saved my life."

"Saved your life?" I asked incredulously.

"Yes, ma'am, that's what I said."

"The fellow who just left the room—I believe he said his name was Jimmy—described the good doctor as something of a messiah."

Blue smirked. "More like the Antichrist, if you ask me. That Jimmy's a fool. He got caught up in the Doc's charade like every other yokel in this town. Shoulda heard the doc talk about him...called him a slobberin' idiot. No doubt Leroy took care of the man like he took care of every poor cracker in the county—all for his own ends, of course."

"Sounds as though you have a story to tell."

"I should say I do." Blue settled back in his chair to light his pipe. His face became sullen and distant, reminiscent of some ancient shaman preparing for a recitation of ancestors back to the Great Father. "I came to know Leroy Adams some years ago," he began. "Over time he came to be my personal physician, as well as my closest friend." He emphasized this last point with a shake of his pipe. "The murder came as a shock to me, although I knew Leroy was skatin' on thin ice. I knew that Ruby's last child was his and that she was pregnant again with another one just before she shot him." Blue paused, lifting an eyebrow. "And I knew that a situation was brewin' that could lead to one of those two gettin' shot."

I nodded when he stopped speaking, letting it soak in that Blue knew that Ruby was pregnant with Adams's second baby when she shot him. From the look on his face as he sat silently, the old man seemed to be having an internal monologue, considering what to say next. Listening to the gentle ticking of the mantel clock and the occasional crackle of the wood burning in the fireplace, I began to wonder if he was now even aware that I was sitting next to him.

"The last time I saw Leroy was the Saturday night before Ruby shot him the next mornin'," Blue continued without warning. "He came out here bellyachin' about her drivin' down to the hospital and tryin' to get him to come out of the operatin' room to talk with her. He said he told one of the nurses to go out and 'tell that goddam nigger woman to go to hell.' Then he stormed out of the hospital, deckin' Dr. Sims over some argument before he left. Knocked the poor man out cold, from what I hear."

"What happened with that?" I asked.

"Sims was okay, and Leroy died the next day, so I guess that took care of that."

"Yes," I said, "I suppose it did."

"I was an honorary pallbearer at the funeral, and I shed many a tear as I mourned my loss. Leroy was like another son to me, especially after I lost my own." Blue choked on these last words and paused to regain his composure. "Well, sir," Blue continued, "come two or three weeks after the funeral, Jeff Elliott, Keith Black's errand boy, came in the office and asked me if I had made out a will leaving all my property to Doc Adams. 'Why, of course not,' I said, more than a little shocked at the question. 'I intend for my property to go to my nephew in Illinois.'"

"'That's odd,' Elliott said, 'cause according to the will me and Mr. Black found in the doc's files, you left everything to the doc.'"

"Needless to say, I called my lawyer right after he left. He advised me to draft a new will. He then made a demand on Keith Black and Florrie Lee, Adams's widow, for the will they found in his files. Black then officially transmitted it to me through my lawyer."

Blue winced, pushing himself up out of his chair. Walking over to the corner beside the fireplace, he took down a framed copy of the forged will and handed it to me to inspect. "Here it is, plain as the nose on your face, neatly typed out, dated April third, 1951, and signed by 'LaVergne Blue.' I recognized the handwriting as Leroy's. As you can see, he even had it witnessed by two men who are still living."

"That's amazing," I said, feeling a cold chill run down my spine when I saw that the will gave Adams charge of Blue's remains. There was no doubt that I was looking at the prelude to a death certificate.

Blue's face fell as he nodded sadly. "When I first held that will, my hands trembled and I thought I'd faint. It was Leroy's work, all right, right down to the grammar. He never could tell the difference between 'their' and 'there' when I helped him write up his campaign speeches...and never could get 'receive' right, either—you get the general idea. I started askin' myself over and over again, What kind of friend was this man Clifford Leroy Adams? All the time he was alive, he had been plottin' my death—or at least to profit from it—and he had been plottin' to defraud my rightful heir."

"I understand why you feel that he was planning to profit from your death by inheriting your lodge, but do you have any evidence that he was actually planning to murder you?"

"I can't prove anything. All I know is that a week or so before he died, the medicine he gave me for my heart didn't seem to be workin' as good as it had been. I asked him to kick up the dose, and that didn't work, either. After Ruby shot him, I went to Dr. Workman right before the funeral and asked him for the same medicine. When I took it, I felt better again. I guess that started me to thinkin'."

"So that's why you say Ruby McCollum saved your life?"

"You're darn tootin'. I owe my life to Ruby McCollum. She was the first one to discover that he was a monster, and she shot him—an act of community service, if you ask me. I think the town ought to raise a monument to her."

"I wouldn't wait for the ceremony," I quipped, thinking how Blue had created his own private fortress within his lodge to protect Ruby's name, while the wheels of public retribution turned inexorably outside its walls to avenge the death of their beloved physician.

Chapter Twelve

"Zora! Please come in," said Lucy, stepping back for me to enter her small living room.

"Thank you," I said, trying to conceal my surprise at her gossamer evening attire.

She smiled. "Hope you don't mind that I'm so casual."

So much for hiding my reaction. "It's certainly a beautiful peignoir you're wearing."

Lucy looked down to stroke the black lace lovingly. "Thank you. It was a gift from Sam. Please take a seat," she offered, gesturing toward the sofa while she settled into the plush armchair in front of me. You know, I really should have told you to bring something to sleep in—this is likely to turn into a pajama party. I have a nice new pair if you'd like to borrow them."

"Oh, I'll be just fine," I assured her, taking a seat as I glanced around the room. Lucy's sense of style came through in her choice of antique furniture crafted of rich cherry wood and upholstered in white antique satin. Accented with deep-pile Persian rugs and table lamps with textured silk shades, the setting was warm and inviting—the kind of decor designed for romantic evenings.

On the coffee table in front of me was the latest edition of the *Courier*. "I see that you've been following the trial," I said.

"I have to say that the coverage has improved since you came on."

"Why, thank you."

"May I get you something to drink?"

"Not right now, thanks. Mind if I smoke?"

"Go right ahead," Lucy invited. "I think I'll have one myself. I've been trying to cut back, but so far I haven't had much luck."

"It's one of the few pleasures I allow myself these days," I admitted, leaning over to light her cigarette.

Lucy's face lit up with a mischievous grin. "If you really want to get downright sinful, I'll bring out some of Sam's panatelas and we can brew some Cuban coffee laced with cognac. Sam brought me back lots of gifts from his last trip to Cuba."

"Not right now, thank you," I said. "But later on I might take you up on that."

"How was your meeting with Mr. Blue?"

"How did you know I saw him already?" I asked, caught off guard.

"You have to know Mr. Blue, Zora. He's a lonely old man with nobody to listen to his story about his best friend betraying him, so the first thing he did after you left was to pick up the phone and thank me for sending you out to see him."

"He was a fount of information—what he didn't know about Dr. Adams probably isn't worth writing about."

"Blue was always there for Adams," Lucy acknowledged, throwing her feet up on the ottoman. "You'll have to forgive me, Zora. I know you came to talk about Ruby, but I haven't had an educated person to talk with since I graduated from college some years back.... My relationship with Sam hasn't exactly helped me win friends on the faculty." She took a long, luxurious drag on her cigarette. "So what did you think of the outcome of the presidential election?"

"Believe it or not, I predicted the results."

"Really? You might be surprised to know that I voted for Eisenhower."

"Actually, no, I wouldn't."

She smiled. "I won't be so selfish as to take up your time talking politics all night. I invited you here to give you information for your story—speaking of which, did you see today's *Democrat*?" she asked, pulling a copy from the magazine rack and handing it to me.

"'Suspension Blows Trial Sky High,'" I read. "Quite a headline."

"Keep reading—it gets better."

"Let's see... Oh, yes, here it is: 'Crews was accused by the Florida Bar of agreeing to file a divorce suit for Charles R. Abrams, accepting fees for the service but failing to file the suit and not returning the money."

"Yes. But did you see how long ago that happened? It was back in 1933, almost twenty years ago."

"That's odd."

"Very odd," Lucy agreed. "Don't you think twenty years is just a bit long for a client to wait before complaining about an attorney's representation?"

"This explains what Pigeye was trying to tell me when I caught up with him outside the courthouse. He implied that some unnamed higher-ups had conspired to torpedo Ruby's defense team."

"I think he might have something there. Both of Ruby's attorneys were from Jacksonville, since no local lawyer would take her case. Without representation, she'd be left with the public defender—that certainly would make things a lot easier for Keith Black."

"They underestimate the McCollums," I said. "Matt told me Crews has already spoken with a gentleman by the name of Henderson, who practices up in Jasper."

"Has he agreed to take the case?"

"Only in the capacity of cocounsel. He feels that it might hurt his practice to take it on by himself. I understand Releford is talking with some lawyers over in Jacksonville."

"I'm glad to hear that. You sure you don't want something to drink?"

"A glass of water with a few ice cubes would be good."

Lucy headed to the kitchen. "How much luck have you had talking with anyone else about Ruby and Dr. Adams?"

"Not much. Ordinarily, I don't have this kind of trouble ferreting out the facts of whatever I want to explore. I suppose it's because I was born curious about things, and research is nothing more than organized curiosity—poking and prying with a purpose. This one has me stumped, though. The only people who'll talk to me recite the usual: Dr. Adams was a fine Christian man, and Ruby was a mean colored woman. I swear, they have it down pat."

Lucy smiled, turning on the kitchen faucet to fill a glass. "I get the picture. People around here are suspicious of outsiders."

"Especially an outsider who asks too many questions. Just mention the name Ruby McCollum and they duck and cover as if an atom bomb had gone off."

Lucy laughed, stirring her martini. "It's different with me—I'm a schoolteacher with a town full of former students. They feel safe with me. Stepping out of the kitchen to stand by a small hallway, she said, "If you'd like, you can see some of them over here in the hallway."

Curious, I stood up and stepped over to where she was standing to see a row of classroom photographs neatly framed and mounted on the hallway wall. In each one of them, Lucy sat at her desk with a classroom full of students, and I gathered that each represented a different school year.

"Doretha, there cleans the courthouse," she said, looking fondly at one of the photographs on the wall. "She's capable of more, but she can't afford to go to college. In the picture next to her is Billy. He cleans Keith Black's office in Lake City. In a very real way, all of them give me eyes and ears just about everywhere—most white people don't think much about what they say around the colored help."

I nodded, taking the glass of water she handed me. From my work as a domestic through my college years, I knew that what she was saying was true.

On our way back to our seats in the living room, I said, "I suppose the first thing I'd like to ask is if you know anything about what Thelma Curry was trying to tell me concerning a doctor bill Ruby received shortly before she shot Dr. Adams. Unfortunately, she was cut off by an associate of mine, and I never heard the rest of what she was trying to tell me."

Lucy crossed her legs and rolled her eyes. "Oh, yes, the doctor bill. It's not something I'm proud to admit, but I might as well own up to it: Sam paid for my abortion."

"Was it..."

"Yes," she admitted, sipping her martini. "Thelma certainly knew since she sent out the bills. And no matter what she testifies, I know she looks at them before they go out. Thelma's such a gossip—can't keep her tongue after the second drink."

Even though I was beginning to understand the complexities of the dual triangles of Ruby, Sam, and Adams on the one hand and Sam, Ruby, and Lucy on the other, Lucy's abortion still came as a shock.

Lucy threw her legs up on the footstool. "So, Zora, where shall we begin?"

Trying to recover from Lucy's revelation while considering its implications for Ruby's motive in shooting Adams, the best I could manage was something from Lewis Carroll. "Well, I believe Alice in her Wonderland adventures was advised to start at the beginning, go through to the end, and then stop."

Lucy smiled, taking another sip of her martini. "How apropriate. I can see how you would feel like Alice in Live Oak."

I laughed, enjoying the comparison. "Sometimes, I suppose. I certainly get the feeling that things are not the way they appear—or at least the way people would have me believe."

It's such a pleasure to have someone like you to talk with, Zora. Around here people only quote the *Bible*—and even then they get it wrong more often than not."

"You mean Live Oak isn't filled with literati?"

Giggling, she said, "Ever try to look for a bookstore in this town? The most you'll find is the magazine stand at Howland's filling station, across the street from the courthouse. If you rule out what they sell from under the counter, you can elevate your reading to the most recent issues of *True Crime* and *True Story*. Our library opened two years ago, and they still haven't honored my interlibrary loan request for Darwin's *Origin of Species*." Pointing to a bookshelf in the corner, she said, "I had to drive to Jacksonville to buy that copy you see over there — and I don't dare take it to school with me. But again, I digress. You've come to hear my story."

"I'm ready," I said, feeling myself stiffen with anticipation. Watching Lucy tuck her legs up to her chest and hug them, I couldn't help thinking that although she was obviously a sophisticated woman, in that position she looked as vulnerable as a schoolgirl with ribbons in her hair.

"I'm the first to admit I'm far from perfect," she confessed, "but I try to live my life without harming others. Some people would say I harmed Ruby, but I never felt that I did. I always wished her the best. I didn't run out to get Sam; he ran to me."

I could see that this was going to take a while. I had come to gather information on Ruby and Adams, and now I realized I must sit through a confessional before I could get to the meat of the story. Patience, Zora!

"You might as well throw your shoes off and get comfy."

"Don't mind if I do," I admitted, glad to see that Lucy was willing to confide in me. "Will it bother you if I take notes?"

"Not at all. Telling you the whole story is my only outlet. It's the only way to let the world know what kind of man Adams really was — and it's the least I can do for Sam."

"I'm ready when you are," I said, pulling my pad and pencil out of my purse.

Lucy stroked her chin. "Well, let's see. 'Start at the beginning,' you said. I suppose the best place to start would be October sixth, 1945. I remember the date because that was the day Sonja was born. Adams was new in town that year, and he was the only doctor who would make house calls to coloreds. It wasn't an easy delivery, and Ruby was sick for some time. Then she got the flu and Adams drove out to see her every day. After she got better, he didn't come out to the house until he was called out again at Christmas... So I suppose the story really started around Christmas, 1946."

PART II

1946

Christmas Eve, 1946, found the McCollum household filled with the sounds of holiday music and sparkling laughter. Spicy fragrances of gingerbread cookies and percolating coffee mingled with the fresh scent of evergreen boughs to create the timeless essence of Christmas.

In front of the fireplace, a giant slice of fruitcake sat invitingly on the coffee table next to a glass of milk, awaiting Santa's visit. A sprig of mistletoe dangling from the chandelier completed the setting for romantic gazing into the lingering embers later in the evening, after the children had fallen asleep.

At the foot of the staircase, Sam, a tall, thin, dark-skinned man in his early forties, bent down to pick up Kay in her pink flannel pajamas so she could put a smiling celluloid angel atop the Christmas tree. "There!" she announced proudly, pleased to see the angel looking down on the boughs of haphazardly hung ornaments and strands of colorful lights.

Sam Jr., sporting a Santa Claus outfit and a white cotton beard, finished anchoring the chains of red and green construction paper to the corner of the ceiling and descended the stepladder.

Kay pursed her lips and pointed a demanding finger at her brother. "Santa, I want my presents!"

"Ho, ho, ho! Not until I get my fruitcake and milk," Santa bargained, gesturing toward the coffee table.

Kay crossed her arms to mount her best pout. "Daddy! Make Santa give me my presents!"

Sam grinned, his intense gray eyes sparkling as he gave her a peck on the cheek and lowered her to the floor. "Not until tomorrow mornin', baby doll, bright and early when Mr. Sunshine comes dancin' through your bedroom window — that's when you'll get your presents."

"Promise?" Kay asked, her big brown eyes twinkling with a six-year-old's sense of delight and wonder.

Sam crossed his heart and bent down to give her a hug. "You know that Daddy always keeps his promises."

Kay kissed her father on the cheek, happy with the compromise.

Across from the expansive living room, the dining room table was draped with a cream lace tablecloth and set with gold-plated flatware, gold-rimmed Lenox china, and crystal stemware. In the center of the table, a spray of red and white carnations with green candles furnished the crowning touch.

On the mahogany buffet, a pair of cut crystal vases filled with American Beauty roses flanked a bowl of fresh fruit, all of it set aglow by the dining room chandelier's reflection in the gilt mirror.

Ruby, wearing a bright poinsettia-print apron around her matronly waist, entered from the kitchen, the spring-hinged door swinging shut behind her. "Sammy," she called sternly, bringing her somehow imposing five feet two inches to bear, "I thought I told you to take Kay on over to your uncle Matt's house."

"Can't I roast some more chinquapins in the fireplace before we go?"

Ruby shot back a staccato "No!" that left little room for negotiation.

"Pl-e-e-ease, Mama?"

"I told you those were special and I wanted to save some for Christmas day. It's going to be cold tomorrow, and I'm looking forward to us all having some when we sit around the fireplace and open our presents."

"All right, Mama," Sammy acquiesced, knowing better than to cross his mother when she was in high gear for the holidays. Pulling his beard off by its rubber band, he took Kay by the hand.

Kay hugged her mother and blew a kiss to her father on the way out the front door.

"Now, you be a big girl for Uncle Matt and Aunt Bessie and don't cry to come back home tonight," Ruby called after her.

"Oh, Mama, I'm too old for that," Kay objected in her best grown-up voice, grabbing her teddy bear on her way out the front door.

"Whew!" Ruby exhaled, sinking onto the living room sofa. "What a day!"

Sam pulled out his monogrammed gold pocket watch to check the time. "The boys'll be here in a few minutes. You got everything ready, baby?"

"Yeah," Ruby murmured, removing her apron. "I need to go on upstairs and get dressed. Would you mind throwing another log on the fire?"

"Sure thing, baby."

He watched her climb the stairs. Even with the inevitable physical changes brought on by age, she was still a desirable partner in every way, and he loved her as much as ever.

Shooting a quick glace up the stairway to make certain that she was out of sight, Sam pulled a small black velvet box out of his trouser pocket and opened it to look once more at the glittering diamond solitaire inside.

While Sam stoked the fire downstairs, Ruby, upstairs in the master bedroom, was pleased to see that Beulah had laid out her new red-sequined dress for the evening.

Beulah straightened her apron and said, more by way of conversation than anything else, "You send Sammy and Kay on over to Matt's house?"

"They just left. I don't want them underfoot when Sam's men get all liquored up tonight—and I sure can't take care of the baby."

"Don't blame you, Miss Ruby, Beulah agreed, watching Ruby apply her lipstick and eye shadow in the dresser mirror. "'Specially the preacher. He ain't got no business gettin' liquored up, him bein' a Baptist an' all."

Ruby stepped out of her duster to lift her prized new dress off the bed. "From what I've seen, Beulah, Baptists do more than their share of drinking."

"I guess I ain't got no argument with that," the maid sighed, helping Ruby with her zipper.

Ruby winced, feeling the zipper squeeze its way slowly up her back. "Do you think it's too tight, Beulah?"

The older woman giggled. "No, ma'am. You gots on a good girdle."

"You're lucky you don't have to put up with these infernal contraptions."

"Yes'm," Beulah chuckled, securing the zipper. "Mama always told me I come out like a string bean and never did fill out."

"Did you get the table all set?"

"Just like you wanted, Miss Ruby," Beulah announced proudly, stepping back to admire the dress. "I put out those nice new napkins and that fancy new tablecloth you bought over in Jacksonville... They sho' do look fine with that good china of yours."

"Glad to hear it," Ruby replied distractedly, holding a plain ruby cabochon up to one ear, and a dazzling red crystal pendant up to the other. "Which do you think?"

"I like the one with those dangly things—it look better with your dress."

"I think so, too," Ruby agreed, returning the cabochon to her jewelry tray. With the pendant earrings in place, she stepped back to view the overall effect in the mirror. Sighing, she picked up a jar of skin cream from her dressing table. "Do you think my face is just a tiny bit lighter than it was last week, Beulah?"

"What that you be puttin' on your face, Miss Ruby?" Beulah asked, taking the jar from Ruby's hand to read the label. "Dr. Palmer's new double-stren'th skin whitener—'be lighter, be lovelier, be loved!'" Beulah clucked disapprovingly.

"I thought I'd give it a try," Ruby said a little defensively, seizing the jar from Beulah. "I saw it advertised in the *Courier* last week."

"Honey, you ain't never gonna be no white woman—I don't care what that stuff say!"

Ruby set the jar back on her dresser, ignoring the comment. After all, Sam seemed to be paying more attention to her lately, so the cream was worth every penny.

"I'm so happy tonight, Beulah," she sighed. "It's going to be a wonderful Christmas."

"It sure is," Beulah agreed. "Ain't never seen so much food in my born days. Think I needs to work on that tree, though."

"Oh, don't fret about the tree. At least it kept the kids busy. I'll finish it up in the morning when I have a little time.... That the doorbell?"

"You askin' the wrong woman, baby. The closer I get to the River Jordan, the harder it be to hear the voice of the Lawd!"

"Would you just get the door, Beulah?" Ruby asked impatiently.

"Fast as these old bones will carry me," the old woman groaned, scurrying out of the bedroom.

Ruby stepped to her mirrored closet doors to practice several seductive poses. "Wait until Sam gets an eyeful of this!" she thought out loud.

Pleased with what she saw in the mirror, she left the bedroom to find him in the office, dialing the combination to the safe. Leaning against the doorjamb in her slinkiest come-hither pose, she waited for him to notice.

"Nice dress," Sam complimented, turning to admire her outfit.

Ruby slithered toward him, running her hands slowly up her sides to her breasts. "I thought I'd give you a special Christmas present after the party, big boy," she whispered in a throaty voice. "Real special."

"You're sure hot tonight," he grinned, planting a wet kiss on her lips.

Ruby felt a warm rush flow through her body when Sam embraced her.

"What's that perfume you got on?" he whispered in her ear.

"Your favorite—gardenia. The same one I wore on our honeymoon."

Sam kissed her neck.

"Not until we're through with business!" Ruby teased, pushing him away to slink down the hallway. At the head of the stairs, she glanced in the mirror to see him still looking at her. "Keep the engine runnin', baby."

Downstairs, Ruby leaned against the wall to catch her breath, listening to Beulah greet Sheriff Hunter at the front door.

"Oh! Sheriff. I didn't know you were here," Ruby cooed at the middle-aged white man. "Beulah just warmed some nice, big pieces of fruitcake in the oven and brewed a fresh pot of coffee..."

"I don't mean to be impolite...," Hunter stammered, removing his hat to fidget with the large leather satchel at his side.

"Not at all, Sheriff," Ruby replied with a dismissing wave of her hand. "Beulah, take Mr. Hunter's hat for him."

"Sam upstairs?" Hunter asked, handing his hat to Beulah.

"He certainly is," Ruby returned. "I'll take you up to him."

Halfway up the stairs, Ruby called down, "Beulah, honey, would you please make up a plate with a nice big piece of that warm fruitcake for Sheriff Hunter to take with him when he leaves?"

"Yes'm," Beulah called, heading back to the kitchen as Ruby led Hunter into the office, where Sam was busily arranging stacks of bills in the safe. "Sam, honey, Sheriff Hunter's here."

"Sheriff Hunter, sir, it sure be good to see you!" Sam greeted him, switching smoothly to his best "good nigger" talk—a skill that had earned him the nickname "Dyna-glide" among his friends.

Hunter nodded but did not extend his hand. "Been a long time since I last seen you, Sam. You just get back up from Tampa?"

"I'se been back 'bout a week, Sheriff. How thangs be here in town?"

"Pretty good, Sam," Hunter replied, "so long as I can brag about bustin' up a still or two ever' now and then."

Sam laughed. "Yassuh, Sheriff. I keeps my men busy buildin' new ones ever' time your men busts 'em up."

Hunter grinned, slapping Sam on the back.

"Sam, honey," Ruby interjected, "the sheriff wondered if you could take care of business so he can get on home to be with his family."

"Sure, Ruby."

Hunter turned the satchel over to dump a mound of cash and paper slips onto the table.

Ruby bit her lip. She had asked Sam to let his white writers know to bundle up the bolita tickets—the small slips of paper now mixed with the cash on the table—so they would be easier to tally. Now she would have to spend extra time sorting them before she could compare the tickets sold against the cash collected, to calculate the profit after the payout.

"Looks like Christmas was good to the white folks this year," Sam laughed, pleased with the week's take.

"Yeah," Hunter agreed, flashing a broad grin.

Turning to the safe, Sam picked up a large box wrapped in green paper and secured with a red ribbon. "Ruby and me wanted to give you somethin' extra to show our appreciation for all you done for us this year."

"I wrapped it special," Ruby added, clasping her hands. "Green on the outside and green on the inside."

The sheriff and Sam laughed at Ruby's presentation of the protection money.

"Thank you, Sam, Ruby," Hunter said, taking the present and retrieving his empty satchel from the table.

"Let me walk you down to the front door, Sheriff," Sam offered. "I know you has to be gettin' on."

"Good night, Ruby," Hunter called on his way out of the office.

"Good night, Sheriff. Merry Christmas to you and the family."

"Merry Christmas, Ruby."

While Sam and Hunter headed downstairs making small talk, Ruby counted the mound of cash with the proficiency of a bank teller, quickly sorting denominations of ones, fives, tens, and twenties, recalling the time when she had to count mounds of dimes and quarters. After sorting the bills, she tallied each stack, flipped through the receipts, and punched the numbers into the adding machine, pulling the handle to hear the familiar crunch of gears calculating the running total.

After punching in the last figure, she held her breath and pulled the handle. *Thank you, sweet Jesus!* she said to herself when she saw the grand total. *This week they didn't cut us short.*

Placing the receipts with the cash in a metal box in the safe, she recorded the bolita income for the week, alongside the payment for protection money that would be distributed to the sheriff and the police. She then secured the safe and left the room, straining to close the heavy safe door behind her.

Downstairs, she found Sam wiping his hands on his trousers after finishing Santa's fruitcake.

Sam smiled. "You sure are fine tonight, baby…you look like you're on fire."

"Careful, baby, you might get burned!" Ruby cautioned with a seductive smile, ignoring the cake on his trousers. Now was not the time to point out his bad habits—not if she wanted to have a romantic evening.

"Burn me baby, burn me!" Sam crowed.

She planted a kiss on his lips. "Baby, I was right about you from the start—you're my big man…always was, always will be."

Sam returned a quick kiss. "Just you and me, brown sugar."

Ruby gave him a push. "Better be just me, baby…better be."

The radio began playing "White Christmas."

"Let's dance," Ruby cooed in his ear, holding him and swaying to the music.

The doorbell rang, interrupting the dance.

"Showtime," Ruby sighed.

Beulah swung the front door open to Sam's men, dressed in flashy pin-striped suits and broad-brimmed hats.

"Merry Christmas, Beulah!" the men chimed in chorus.

"Come on in, brothers!" called Sam, greeting each of his men with a handshake and a pat on the back.

Beulah stood to the side, dutifully collecting hats and overcoats while trying not to sneeze from the overwhelming scent of Old Spice.

On their way in, the men greeted Ruby circumspectly with "Nice to see you, Miss Ruby"; "Merry Christmas, Miss Ruby"; "You sure look nice, Miss Ruby."

Unlike Sam, Ruby looked at her husband's "lieutenants," the men who led teams of "soldiers" who wrote bolita tickets, as paid employees, not friends.

Charles Hall handed Ruby a Mason jar filled with bright red-orange jelly, topped with a red bow. "My woman sent this jar of mayhaw jelly to you and Sam. The mayhaws was real fat and juicy this summer."

"Please tell Louise thank you from me and Sam," Ruby said graciously, taking the jar to retreat into the kitchen.

As soon as the door swung shut, she put her ear against it to hear the men snickering in the living room. "Hmph!" she snorted, tying on her apron. "Passel of no-good vermin," she mumbled, stirring the soup and checking various pots on the gas and electric ranges. Opening a side cabinet, she took out a bottle of pills and swallowed two.

Beulah noted that long after delivering Sonja, Ruby continued to take her pain pills when she was upset. She had intended to talk to her about it, but there was no good way to bring up the subject. "Leave it be, Beulah," her sister had admonished. "Most rich folks drown their troubles in liquor and pills. Ain't nothin' you can do to stop Miss Ruby nohow—she'll just hate you for tryin'."

"I know you don't cotton to them fellas, Miss Ruby," said Beulah. But you gots to remember, honey, they's Sam's men, and without them runnin' the numbers, collectin' the juke box money, and sellin' the liquor, you wouldn't be livin' here in this great big house of yours."

"Yeah, but every time Sam gets together with 'em, he bosses me around like a field hand."

Beulah laid her hand gently on Ruby's shoulder. "Sam just bein' a man, Miss Ruby. Menfolks always got to be the boss of the house. He don't mean nothin' by it. 'Sides, he know you be the one keepin' the books and takin' care of his chillum."

Ruby sighed. "I've never been this upset around his men—what's this make, at least ten years of Christmas parties with those bums? I don't know what's changed lately."

"Somethin' else is botherin' you, Miss Ruby; that's what's changed."

"I guess I still haven't got over finding out about Sam's fling with that high-yellah whore out in the Bivens' Quarters," she admitted.

Beulah gave her a hug. "You gots to forgive and forget, honey child. Believe you me, Sam ain't 'bout to leave you for no young trash like that. Deep down in that man's heart he loves you—and God knows he loves his chillun."

"You're right about that," Ruby agreed. "Let's get some food stuffed into 'em before they get all liquored up."

"Now you're talkin', honey!" Beulah said, relieved to have cheered her up a little. "After we put the food on the table, can I get on back home?"

"I'll take care of the mess after they all leave, Beulah. You need to be with your family on Christmas Eve."

"I sho' do thank you, Miss Ruby. I'll stop by tomorrow to help with the cleanin' up."

Ruby gave Beulah a hug, then carried the tray of food into the dining room, where she found Sam pouring another round of liquor.

"When y'all finish your appetizers, bring your business on upstairs," Ruby instructed, passing the men on her way to the staircase. "And don't be gettin' drunk," she snipped.

Halfway up the stairs, she heard Hall say to Sam, "Your woman's in a tizzy tonight. You ain't been neglectin' her lately, has you?" She quickened her pace up the stairs to distance herself from the raucous laughter that followed.

In the office, Ruby sat at her desk, determined to set aside her ill humor. As she began leafing through the ledger, she let her thoughts drift into daydreams about taking a trip to Jacksonville and shopping with her friend Leona. But then Sam walked in, his troops behind him.

"You ready for us, baby?"

"I'm ready," Ruby answered wearily, her daydream evaporating.

After the men dumped their stacks of bills onto the worktable, she began her count while Sam removed several small gift-wrapped boxes from the safe.

"Ruby and me wants to give y'all some Christmas, brothers," Sam said, handing out the gifts.

"Why, thank you, Sam! And you, too, Ruby," the men said with their usual feigned surprise as they accepted the same Christmas presents they got every year.

"Ruby, we're gonna wait for you downstairs."

"I'll be down after I finish," she called back distractedly.

"Better hurry up—I can't hold 'em off the food for long."

She glared at Sam's back as he left the office, resenting the way he treated her around his men. Then, turning back to the task at hand, she finished counting the cash and reconciling the income with the bolita receipts—two thousand for the week, not counting liquor sales. Not bad, though they had certainly done better.

While Ruby completed her work upstairs, Sam poured another round of liquor for the men.

"You got the winning numbers for this week's, sermon, Sam?" asked the preacher.

"They be three, one, and six," Sam announced.

"Praise the Lord!" cried the preacher. "That be my favorite sermon—John 3:16." Holding a turkey leg to his mouth as if it were a microphone, he said, "I'll be sure to yell it out loud and strong. Half the folks in church come every Sunday just to hear me call out the numbers."

"Amen, Preacher!" agreed Hall, clapping his hands. "The only thing they prayin' for is to hit the jackpot."

Shouts of "Amen!" and clinking glasses filled the dining room.

"When you're through playing with your food, Preacher, we'll all sit down to supper," Ruby called icily over the banister.

The preacher put the drumstick down to pull out his chair. "Sorry, Miss Ruby. Guess we jus' got caught up in the spirit of fellowship."

Ruby shot the preacher a disapproving look and took her seat opposite Sam at the head of the table.

"That's what we're all here for, ain't it, fellas?" Sam said, raising his glass to propose a toast. "Well, boys, here's to a mighty fine endin' to a mighty fine year."

"I'll drink to that, brother," agreed the preacher, seizing the opportunity to get past the awkward interchange. "And I'd like to toast Suwannee County goin' dry last year."

"Oh, yeah!" Hall agreed. "Since then we've had the best liquor sales ever."

"Ain't that the truth," Little Sam slurred.

Ruby raised a censorious eyebrow. "Is anybody going to ask the blessing?"

Without missing a beat, the preacher bowed his head and folded his hands over his belly. "Dear Lord Jesus, make us thankful for this food, Amen."

Sam laughed. "Preacher, that's the shortest blessin' ever come out your mouth."

As the men fell to their dinner, there was little conversation beyond the obligatory compliments to Ruby for the "fine vittles." They were into second helpings when suddenly Little Sam leaned over and vomited onto the Persian rug.

"Little Sam!" Sam exclaimed. "You all right?"

Little Sam wiped his mouth with the lace tablecloth. "Yeah, Sam, I be fine. Jus' a little too much whiskey too fast—I just needs to go to the kitchen and get cleaned up."

"Ruby," Sam called impatiently, "get Beulah to come clean up this mess."

Ruby was disgusted. "Beulah's gone home for the evening."

"Well, get somethin' and clean up this mess so we can eat."

"I'm not cleanin' up that mess!" Ruby retorted, furious at Sam's demeaning conduct in front of his men.

"Ruby," he repeated sternly, "I told you to get that mess cleaned up."

Ruby stood up and headed for the stairs. "No!"

The preacher nudged Hall. "Guess she done tol' him!"

"You can sure tell who wears the pants 'round here!" Hall said under his breath, not intending his comment to reach Sam's ears.

"Ruby!" Sam called angrily. "You get your behind over here right now and clean this mess up like I told you!"

Ruby stood with her hands on her hips at the foot of the stairs. "You want that mess cleaned up? There's towels in the kitchen!"

In one swift motion, Sam lunged to the stairway, grabbed Ruby by the arm, and dragged her into the living room.

"You're hurting me!" Ruby cried.

"Not as much as I'm gonna if you don't get your big ass over there and clean up that mess!"

"No! I'm not going to—"

Sam's slap across her face sent her sprawling against the sofa. She looked up to find Sam standing menacingly over her. "Get up, woman, and do what I told you!"

"Sam, stop!" Ruby pleaded, holding her arm up to defend herself. "I'm pregnant! You're going to hurt the baby."

He froze. "You… you're pregnant?"

"Yes," she managed, guarding her injured side.

"We can play poker some other night, boys," Hall stammered, getting up and retrieving his hat and coat.

"Yeah," Little Sam agreed, staggering to his feet. "I needs to get on home and clean up."

"Sorry to eat and run," the preacher chimed in, grabbing a thick slice of fruitcake for the road before filing out the door behind the other men.

Ruby curled up in a fetal position on the sofa, sobbing bitterly.

Sam paced nervously, torn between his anger at being embarrassed in front of his men and his regret for hitting Ruby — and their unborn child.

"Where you going?" Ruby called to him as he headed out the door.

"I don't know!" he yelled, slamming the door behind him.

Watching the fire die down in the fireplace, Ruby sobbed herself to sleep under the shimmering Christmas tree lights.

Chapter Fourteen

As Christmas Day dawned clear and cold, Ruby lay in her bed, holding an ice bag to her forehead. By now her tears had given way to consuming anger. Yet it still did not mask the pain that lingered even after the second double dose of pain pills she had taken during the night.

How dare Sam demean her, the woman who had shared his dreams and worked beside him to make them all come true! With their wealth, along with their church work, she and Sam had earned the respect of the colored community. And, for many children in the neighborhood, Sam was the only Santa they knew.

What would happen when those poor kids woke up this morning expecting to see Santa Claus? What would happen with *her* children today? With Sam gone and her face swollen, what would she tell them?

Sonja was only a baby, so she would never know. Kay, at six, would accept the explanation that Mommy was sick and Daddy had to go out of town on business. On the other hand, Sam Jr. was another matter — old enough to sense that something was wrong.

Ruby knew she had to be strong. She had to get on with her life for the sake of her family, regardless of how she settled the matter with Sam. But just when she thought she could hold her own, a sudden wave of anger pulled her under, gripping her in its undertow. *Next time that nigger hits me, he's gonna find himself staring down the barrel of a gun!*

While Ruby lay bruised and scraped in her bed, somewhere in her heart, Sam fell off a shelf. At first the feeling was vaguely disturbing, as if a part of her were missing. Then it felt as though a burden had been lifted, leaving one less thing for her to dust off, one less thing to take care of amid life's daily chores.

"Ruby?" Beulah's voice called through the bedroom door.

Ruby stayed quiet, hoping she would go away.

"It's me, Beulah! You in there, Miss Ruby?"

"Come on in," Ruby called, knowing she wouldn't leave without talking to her.

"You all right, Miss Ruby?" Beulah asked tentatively, cracking the door to poke her head inside. "I dropped by to wish you a merry Christmas and clean up the kitchen. Then I seen all the food still sittin' out downstairs.... Is you sick?"

Ruby turned her face away to hide the puffiness around her eyes. "Merry Christmas, Beulah. I'm fine, thank you."

"What happened to you, baby?" Beulah asked, seeing the ice bag.

"Reckon you won't stop pesterin' me until I tell you," Ruby returned with a touch of irritation in her voice, returning the ice bag to her forehead.

"No, ma'am, I reckon I won't," Beulah acknowledged, nervously pressing her apron with her hands.

"Sam hit me."

Beulah's jaw dropped. "Sam...?"

Ruby nodded. "I got him to stop by telling him I was pregnant."

"Sweet Jesus!" Beulah moaned, sitting on the bed beside her. "You ain't said nothin' to me 'bout bein' pregnant." She leaned over to examine Ruby's face. "I don't like the looks of them bruises, baby." Beulah reached for the telephone on the bedside table. "Hello, operator? Get me Doctah Adams's house. I gots a 'mergency."

Ruby lunged toward her. "Beulah! Put that phone down!"

But Beulah stood her ground. "No, I ain't! You gonnah be seen by a doctah, Miss Ruby. Ain't nobody got to know 'bout this if you don't want 'em to, but you carryin' a baby now, so you ain't the only one needs lookin' at."

Ruby resigned herself to her caretaker's advice, feeling strangely comforted. After all, it couldn't hurt to have Dr. Adams come out to the house. Besides, he had delivered Sonja last year, and he had helped her get through a case of the flu that she thought would kill her, so he might be able to do something about the pain.

"Doctah Adams? I gots a 'mergency out at the McCollum house," Beulah announced. "That's right. Miss Ruby got some cuts and bruises need lookin' after. Five minutes? Thank you, Doctah!"

Ruby took Beulah's hand and closed her eyes. "Thank you, honey."

"You gonna be just fine, Miss Ruby." Beulah straightened the bedclothes and tucked her in as if putting a child to bed, then took a seat in the rocking chair by the window while her charge dozed. Looking outside to watch for the doctor, she thought about what to tell him when he arrived.

Beulah was no stranger to domestic violence. She had seen so much of it in her own family that before she married, she issued an ultimatum to her fiancé. "Thomas," she had said, "if you so much as raise a hand to me, I swear to Jesus I'll leave you 'fore the sun come up next mornin'. And if we got kids, they goin' with me."

And Thomas had scrupulously heeded her words for nearly fifty years now. Dealing with the problem in her employer's home was another matter, of course, but the end result would be the same—she would not stay in a home torn apart by violence.

Seeing Dr. Adams's car pull into the driveway, Beulah ran downstairs to let him in.

The tall and paunchy physician, wearing a rumpled long-sleeved white shirt and black trousers with matching loafers, stood holding his trademark black satchel. "Mama, you know I always come out when you call me," he bantered, greeting her with a broad grin and a gentle pat on the back. "Now, what's this about an emergency?"

She looked down and pressed her apron nervously with her hand. "I better let Miss Ruby say."

"That's all right, Beulah," Adams replied warmly, turning to look at the dining room table. "What's that that smells so good?"

She giggled. "You ain't changed a bit since I seen you last, Doctah. After I run 'crost the street to ask Matt to keep the kids the rest of the day, I'll scoot on into the kitchen and fix you a mess of fresh collards and cracklin' cornbread to take with you.... You'll find Miss Ruby upstairs in her bedroom."

As Beulah disappeared into the kitchen, Adams walked upstairs. Passing the office, he saw the McCollum's huge black safe. "Damn!" he mumbled, continuing to Ruby's bedroom, where he tapped lightly on the door. "You in there, Miss Ruby?"

She sat up to straighten her covers. "Come on in, Dr. Adams."

"Merry Christmas, Ruby," Adams greeted cheerfully, closing the door behind him.

She turned her face to hide her bruises. "Merry Christmas, Doctor Adams."

Watching him roll up his sleeves to place his satchel on the bed, Ruby felt something strangely warm and soothing in his presence. He still had the same graying hair, deep-set brown eyes, and massive build, but now she felt safe and protected when he came close to her.

The doctor stared at her face. "Some pretty bad bruises you got there, Ruby. How'd you come by those?"

Turning away again, she said, "I fell down the stairs."

"Let me take a good look," he replied, holding her face gently to examine either side. "Um-hm." Placing his big hand on her abdomen, he pressed inward.

"Oh, my God!" she screamed, guarding her side.

"You want to tell me what really happened?"

"I fell..."

"I can't treat you if you ain't straight with me, Ruby. Who did this to you?"

"Sam hit me."

"Sam did this?"

She nodded.

"Looks like you got yourself a couple of cuts, so I'm gonna have to clean 'em up," he announced, reaching into his bag.

Ruby moaned. "Can you give me something for the pain?"

"After I finish cleaning up these cuts, I'll give you a shot to help you rest, but tomorrow before Thelma leaves at five, you need to have somebody drive you down to my office so I can take another look at those cuts and get an X-ray. I'm pretty sure you got yourself a cracked rib."

Beulah opened the door, nervously kneading her apron.

Where'd you come from?" Ruby snapped, annoyed at the intrusion.

"I just come back from Matt's place," she explained, stepping inside the bedroom. "He say he'll take Sammy out to play Santa Claus while Bessie keep Sonja and Kay."

"What'd you tell Matt?" Ruby managed, flinching from the burn of the mercurochrome as the doctor cleaned the cuts on her face.

"Just that you be sick and Sam had to go outta town. I thought it be up to you what you tell your brother." Beulah backed out of the room, closing the door behind her.

"That woman's worth her weight in gold," he said, dabbing at the scrape on her chin.

Adams pulled a bottle of pills out of his satchel and placed it on the nightstand. "I'll give you a pain shot right now. Later on, you can take these pills if you start hurtin' again before mornin'."

"Can you write me a prescription for the pills you're leaving me?"

"That's got morphine in it, Ruby," Adams warned. "Don't you still have those pain pills I gave you after you delivered Sonja? Thelma tells me you keep callin' in for a refill, and I always okay it since it ain't nothin' too strong."

"Well, my rheumatism kicks in from time to time, and my back…"

"If you think you need something stronger, that's fine with me, but I have to tell you that it can get to be a habit."

"Thank you, Doctor…. There is one more thing."

"What's that, Ruby?"

"I told Sam I'm pregnant…. I don't know what he's gonna do when he finds out I lied."

Adams grinned, swabbing her hip with alcohol. "Oh, I think I can take care of that."

"Whatever you can do, I'd sure appreciate," she said, grimacing from the shot.

"Now, you just lay back and relax," he soothed. "In a minute or two, you'll be feelin' fine."

Suddenly, Ruby felt herself floating, drifting weightlessly over the bed, her body filled with a warm sense of inner peace. "Oh, doctor, you're an angel," she breathed.

Adams smiled, stroking her thigh as she nodded off. "That's right, Ruby. I'm your angel for today."

****

In her dream, Ruby was transported back in time to her parent's home, admiring her youthful body in the mirror on the closet door in her bedroom. Dusting her breasts with talcum powder, she decided that poverty did not become her. This was the smooth dark-chocolate skin of a Nubian princess, she mused, a sensuous body deserving of gold chains and elaborate silks, with bodyguards, their bulging muscles dripping sweat, standing ready to fulfill her every wish. The vision made her smile as she slipped her flannel nightgown over her head and coaxed it down over her hips, luxuriating in its soft warmth.

In 1927, her senior year of high school, Ruby realized that Zuber, Florida, was not big enough to contain her dreams. Zuber was just a two-street town in the middle of orange groves, peopled mostly by Negroes eking out a bare living by the sweat of their brows, much as their grandparents had done as slaves. The termite-riddled remains of slave shanties, standing in silent rows like so many crumbling tombstones in an ancient graveyard, still remained on the old plantations, decaying testaments to a not so distant past.

There were no rich families here. Instead, rich land barons employed white overseers to manage their orange groves while they lived in comfort a few miles south, in Ocala's elegant Southern mansions. From what Grandma Jackson had told her from working in the home of one of the grove owners, his family tree was framed on the sitting room wall, embroidered in colorful threads of silver and gold. Completing the iconography of good breeding and wealth were hand-colored photographs of parents, tintypes of grandparents, and oil paintings of great-grandparents comfortably seated in high-backed chairs while their Negro house slaves served afternoon tea. There was a certain likeness among the white faces on the wall, each being a reflection, as it were, of a common ancestor along a vast hall of genetic mirrors that stretched back through countless generations.

Here in Zuber, Ruby knew that she would always be a poor colored girl, the daughter of a man who had worked odd jobs to scrape together a meager subsistence for his wife and seven children until he was found facedown in the field beside his plow, dragged ceremoniously into the Negro church for a recitation of "Ashes to Ashes, Dust to Dust," and returned to the earth whence he came. Somewhere in her grief, at a point between the "ashes" and the "dust," Ruby decided that she was going to escape Zuber's smothering world of thou-shalt-nots and grinding poverty to breathe freely in the world of her dreams.

Although she would miss the bright explosions of phlox and daisies in the spring and the delicate perfume of the chinaberry and cape jasmine blossoms scenting the summer evenings, Ruby was willing to forego these simple pleasures for the wealth and prestige she so desperately desired.

Backing away from the mirror to sit on her bed, Ruby decided that her immediate problem was whether the prom dress she wanted was still waiting for her in the general store.

"I got it in just yesterday," the elderly white saleslady had told her when she asked about the dress. "You needn't get your heart set on it, though—it's priced at ten dollars, and I know Mr. Appleton won't budge a red cent."

But Ruby didn't want anyone walking away with that dress until she could earn the money to buy it herself. And so, even though the prom was months away, she was already planning for it, picking oranges at a nickel a crate and storing her wealth in a coffee can hidden in the back of her dresser drawer.

Ruby ran her fingers gently over her prized chenille bedspread, a festival of yellow roses with green leaves entwined over a white, tufted background. She had paid dearly for that treasure, parting with an entire year's savings to claim it for her own. But it was more than a bedspread—it was a talisman, her promise to herself that she would one day have the finer things in life.

Ruby rested her head on her pillow and imagined walking into the general store to hand the saleslady cash and watch her jaw drop in disbelief that a colored girl had bought the most expensive dress in the store. But would she make it to the store in time? Would someone else buy the dress before she had the chance?

Tired but still fretting over the dress, she filled her mind with images of clouds, trying to fall asleep.

Ever so slowly, the cool evening breeze wafting through the gossamer yellow curtains by her bed lifted her gently on her magic bedspread, transporting her to a land of wealth and plenty.

Chapter Fifteen

Doctor Adams entered Blue's Lodge to find LaVergne Blue serving breakfast to a family at a table by the fireplace. The father looked at the glowing coals and asked, "Mind if I throw another log on the fire, Mr. Blue?"

"Make yourself at home, friend," Blue invited, turning to pin the festive garland of holly back in place where it had detached from the mantel.

"Thanks, Mr. Blue."

"Hey, LaVergne," Adams called.

"Merry Christmas, Leroy," Blue replied, pouring coffee. "I'll be with you soon as I've helped these folks."

Blue finished waiting on the table and ambled over to Adams and Sheriff Hunter to pour a cup of coffee. "Start you out right this mornin', Leroy."

"Thanks, LaVergne."

"Want a little warm-up, Arch?"

"No, thanks, LaVergne. Had enough for one mornin' — too much makes my heart jump like a jackrabbit."

"Got to watch that coffee," Adams advised.

While Blue retreated to the kitchen, Adams turned to look across the room at the family opening their Christmas presents. The father was showing his son how to load film into his new Kodak Brownie Junior.

Adams scowled. "Must be rich Yankee tourists."

"Yeah," Hunter agreed. "I seen those little gizmos down at the drugstore when they first come out right after the war. My wife told me she wanted one, but I told her it cost too damn much. You know how that goes — hardheaded woman waltzed right down to Kennon's pharmacy and put one on my bill."

"Damn Yankees don't deserve to be makin' that kind of money."

"Here we go, Leroy," Blue announced, returning from the kitchen with a tray of eggs, grits, sausage, and buttermilk biscuits.

"Looks mighty good, LaVergne," Adams complimented, plowing into the grits before Blue had a chance to place the rest of the food on the table.

"How's the new hospital plans comin' along, Leroy?" Blue asked.

"They got a good deal on that place where the old nigger college used to be—already paid the architect to draw up the plans."

"Senator Pepper making any progress with that Hill Burton legislation?"

"Last I heard from him, he says we can plan on breakin' ground next year."

"Be a lot better for folks around here when it opens," said Blue.

"Yeah," Adams agreed, stirring the butter into his grits. "Instead of sendin' my patients up to Valdosta or over to the VA in Lake City, I can take care of 'em right here."

"Anything else goin' on?" Blue asked.

"Stopped by to see a nigger woman this mornin'."

Hunter chuckled. "Anythin' unusual 'bout that, Doc?"

"Yeah, I shoulda said, a rich nigger woman."

"Oh, you mean Ruby McCollum, Bolita Sam's wife," said Blue, taking a seat to join the men.

"You don't say! I delivered her baby some time back, but I had no idea what Sam did to build a nice house like that."

"He's the man who runs all the gamblin' in Suwannee County," Hunter volunteered.

Adams paused with a forkful of sausage suspended in the air. "Ain't gamblin' illegal here?"

"Why, hell, yes. But then, there ain't no way to track cash money, now, is there, Doc?"

Adams laughed. "You got that straight."

"They run shine, too," Blue added. "Now the county's dry, that's one hell of a business."

Hunter nodded. "Yep, they been doin' just fine."

"Goin' dry sure knocked me for a loop," Blue lamented. "Folks drive over to Lake City now if they want a glass of wine with their supper."

"So how does Sam run the liquor, Sheriff?" Adams asked while stabbing another piece of sausage.

"Well, Doc," Hunter said with a chuckle, "he set up his very own cabstand. Now anybody can take a taxi ride and get dropped off with a couple jars of white lightin' a lot cheaper'n they can drive over to the County Line Liquor Store for a fifth o' Early Times."

"Sounds like he's got a good thing goin', so long's he don't get caught."

"Hell, Doc, it don't pay for us boys to go chasin' after Sam when we got bigger fish to fry—you know, the outta-town bootleggers usin' old car radiators with lead in 'em to pump out jake-leg rotgut.... Least Sam keeps his liquor clean."

Adams cocked an eyebrow. "He show his appreciation from time to time?"

Hunter winked over his coffee cup. "Oh, you know how it is for us boys—we get paid chicken feed. Got bills to pay, an election to start savin' up for... It all adds up."

"Ain't that the truth," Adams agreed, piling more grits and butter onto his plate. "You know, Sheriff, I was thinkin'.... Way things are now, Sam has to deal with a lot of white folks holdin' their hands out, right?"

"So what's on your mind, Doc?"

"After I leave here, I need to drop by my office. What do you say about roundin' up Sam and bringin' him down there tonight so you and me can cut him a deal?"

"Fine with me, Doc. What time you want me to have him down at your place?"

"Oh, 'round eight'd be good."

Hunter glanced at the mantel clock across the room. "Guess I better be gettin' on to catch up with my paperwork." He pushed his chair back and put three quarters on the table. "I'll see you down at your office at eight sharp, Doc."

Dr. C. L. Adams's Office
Colored Entrance

Sam parked behind Sheriff Hunter's car in the alley behind Dr. Adams's office. Leaning back to pull a handkerchief out of his pocket, he wiped the sweat from his forehead, wondering why the doctor would have the sheriff escort him here on Christmas evening. Something didn't feel right.

Seeing Sheriff Hunter go inside the office, he sat for a moment to collect himself, then got out of his car and opened the screen door marked, "C. L. Adams, M.D.—Colored Entrance."

"Doctah Adams?" Sam called, seeing no light inside.

Adams loomed out of the shadows in the hallway by the colored waiting room. "Merry Christmas, Sam," he said affably. "Come on in; I've been expectin' you."

"Merry Christmas, Doc," Sam replied nervously, following Adams down the dark corridor, toward the light coming from his business office.

"Have a seat, Sam," Adams offered, maneuvering his way around his desk to fall into the padded leather chair.

"Thank you, Doctor Adams," Sam replied, sitting down in a barrel chair and only then seeing Sheriff Hunter, seated in the corner.

"You know Sheriff Hunter, don't you, Sam?"

"Yassuh, I sho' do," Sam responded, flawlessly executing his Dyna-glide shift into "good nigger" talk.

"Did you know I came out to your house this mornin' to see your wife?" Adams asked.

Fidgeting, Sam glanced up to meet the doctor's intense stare. "No, suh. Guess I was down at the Three Spot when Sheriff Hunter found me. She sick again or somethin'?"

"Ruby told me what happened, Sam."

Sam went suddenly rigid and the unctuous smile melted from his face. "I ain't never done nothin' like that befo', Doc," he protested.

"I don't give a goddamn about your personal life, Sam," Adams returned matter-of-factly. "I will tell you, though, Ruby had a miscarriage after you beat her up."

Sam was stunned. "Suh?"

"She lost her baby. It was real early on, so there wasn't much to clean up."

Sam buried his head in his hands.

"You can't go slappin' a pregnant woman around like that, Sam. Next time make sure she's not carryin' a baby."

"I never done nothin' like that before, Doc," Sam cried, the tears rolling down his face.

Adams opened his desk drawer to hand Sam a tissue. "Clean your face up and stop bawlin' like a baby. Ruby's gonna be fine. And you ain't got nothin' to worry 'bout from Sheriff Hunter here. Besides, you need to start lookin' at the two of us like friends."

Sam's hands trembled as he wiped his face and waited for Adams to continue.

"I called you here to talk business," Adams explained.

"Business...?" Sam managed, trying his best to follow the thread of conversation.

Adams leaned forward. "After comin' out to your house to see Ruby, I says to myself, 'A successful colored man like Sam must have to deal with a lot of white men holdin' their hands out—that's enough to make any man come home and kick his dog and beat on his wife.'"

"Well, suh, that be true," Sam agreed, fingering the crease in his trousers.

"Then I was talkin' to the sheriff here, and I says, 'Arch, what if Sam had only one big man to settle up with, and that man took care of all the little men for him?'"

"That's what you said, Doc," Hunter affirmed.

"Well, sir, then I figured, if that big man went on to become a state senator, then you'd have a friend over in Tallahassee."

"Ain't nobody like the doc here to come up with a good idea," Hunter added.

Adams cocked an eyebrow. "You reckon we can do business, Sam?"

"Oh, yes, suh!" Sam agreed, relieved to be off the hook for the incident with Ruby. "We can do business just fine, Doctah."

Adams stood up. "I'm glad to hear that, Sam."

Expecting to be dismissed, Sam was surprised when the doctor walked around the desk to put a comradely arm around his shoulder.

"Sam, Sheriff Hunter here tells me that Ruby keeps your books."

"That she do."

"Well, like I said, I don't give a damn about your personal affairs, but if I was you, I'd leave that woman alone so she can count our money."

Sam laughed. "Yes, suh. I'll do just that, Doctah. You say she gonna be all right?"

"I'll make sure she's just fine. But you know, Sam, I think it'd be a good idea if you left town for a month or two to give this thing some time to blow over."

"I was plannin' on drivin' down to Fort Myers to see my brother for New Year's."

"I wouldn't worry yourself none about things up here. I'll be out to your house to take care of Ruby. I'm sure the two of us can manage the business just fine until you get back."

"I sho' 'preciates that, Doctah...I sho' 'nuff do. You's a fine man for doin' that. Yassuh, a real fine man."

Chapter Seventeen

Just before noon, Sam gave up looking for a parking space and pulled onto the grass in front of Buck's Lucky Flamingo Club. Unlike Sam's unassuming neighborhood jooks in Live Oak, the Lucky Flamingo, a pink stucco art deco building with a flashing neon flamingo, was Ft. Myers's hottest night spot for coloreds and Latinos.

The place was packed with New Year's Eve survivors. At the bar, several men had swiveled around on their stools to cheer on a garishly dressed sport with striped baggy pants and a purple necktie, who was swinging his good-time girl, her ruffled red dress and long braided hair swirling about her in rhythm with the jitterbug music blaring from the Wurlitzer.

In the booths beyond the dance floor, several pretty young waitresses served the traditional New Year's fare of black-eyed peas and fatback with corn bread. Circulating among the diners was a young mulatto girl peddling Cuban cigars and cigarillos, bending over to display her ample cleavage, which served as a tip repository.

"Happy New Year, José," Sam called to the bouncer, a Puerto Rican bodybuilder who was gathering up a group of fallen friends who had rung in the year with a bottle of Smirnoff that now lay empty on the table.

"¡Feliz Año Nuevo, señor!" the friendly giant returned with a broad smile. "Happy New Jear, señor Sam."

Sam laughed. "Looks like you got your hands full."

"Sí. Your brother, señor Buck, he sent his hearse down to load up these borrachos—the cabs, they full."

"Bet their womenfolk are gonna throw a hissy fit when that thing drives up to their front doors."

"Oh, jes, señor. These zombies, I think they don't do this again for some time, no?"

"See you later, José," Sam laughed, seeing his brother at the pool table in the rear of the club, just past the Wurlitzer.

"Oh, man!" Buck's opponent lamented, watching the balls bank and roll into the pockets precisely as called. "Why you have to go and do a thing like that?"

Buck grinned while the man pulled out a fifty-dollar bill to make good on his bet.

Sam walked up behind his brother, thinking how much higher the stakes were in Ft. Myers. "That the best you can do, brother?"

"Hey, Sam!" Buck greeted, patting his brother on the back. "What took you so long to get down here?"

"Flat tire. Spent the night alongside the road until I could walk to a fillin' station early this mornin'."

"You ain't changed much. You remember when you and me was back in high school and I was always tellin' you to keep a good spare in your trunk?"

"Yeah, yeah, I remember."

"So, you want somethin' to eat?"

"I'd sure like to get somethin' to drink."

"Hey, Queta!" Buck yelled toward the bar. "Bring Sam here a pitcher of ice water, a glass of milk, some corn bread, black-eyed peas, and a big chunk o' that ham hock."

"Yessuh!" Queta called back, retreating to the kitchen.

Buck looked at Sam's face. "Want to settle in back in my office? Looks like you need to talk."

Sam returned a weary nod.

Buck called over to the bartender, "Jake, tell Queta to bring Sam's food to my office."

"Yessuh," the man called back.

"And tell her to send me a draft."

"Yessuh, I sure will."

Following Buck to his office, Sam wondered how much he should tell his brother about the fight with Ruby.

"How's Ruby doin'?" Buck asked, pushing a button on the top edge of the doorjamb.

Sam hung his head.

"Have a seat," Buck offered, closing the door behind him.

The office was lavishly furnished with a big carved-mahogany desk, a conference table, and window curtains covering the steel door of the back entrance to give the appearance of a window in a room that had none.

Sam settled into a leather-upholstered chair at the conference table. "Ruby's still takin' all those pain pills that Doc Adams give her when Sonja was born."

"Do you think she should see another doctor?"

Sam's eyes widened. "You think I'd try to tell her that? After the doc delivered Sonja, she worships the ground that white man walks on."

Buck grinned. "You ain't jealous, is you, brother?"

"Of a white man?"

Buck raised an eyebrow. "When's the last time she worshipped the ground *you* walked on?"

"I got a bad feelin' in my gut 'bout that man. He's already movin' in on my business—had Sheriff Hunter bring me down to his office and tell me he'd be the only white man I had to deal with from now on."

"You forget that's the same way I operate down here, little brother." Seeing the green light flash on his desk, Buck called, "Come in, José."

The door opened, and Queta carried in a tray of food and drinks while José stood guard. "Here you go, fellas. Let me know if y'all need anything else."

"Check back a little later, sweetheart," Buck told her. "José, if anybody asks, I'm out. Sam and me'll leave through the garage when we're through here."

"Sí, señor Buck," José acknowledged, following Queta out the door.

"And one more thing, José," Buck added, remembering that Sam's car was parked outside. "Keep an eye on Sam's car till I can send Willie and John back for it."

"Jes, señor Buck. Already my eye is on it," José replied, closing the door behind him.

"Like I said, Sam, havin' one white man to deal with ain't bad."

"Maybe," Sam sighed halfheartedly, taking a drink of water. "But I'm afraid it won't be long 'fore he looks at Ruby and me like a big pile of cash."

"He's a doctor, brother—he's already got his own money."

Sam rolled his eyes. "He treats mostly coloreds."

"Well, he makes money from whites; you can believe that."

"I don't like him up there with Ruby all by herself."

Buck lit a cigar. "So why'd you come down here?"

"Me and Ruby had a fight."

"You couldn't stay over at your gal friend's house?"

"If I parked over there, Ruby'd be sure to hear all about it."

"You wanna tell me 'bout it?" Buck asked tentatively, sipping the foam from his beer.

"Me and my men was havin' our Christmas party, and Little Sam threw up on the rug right at the supper table. Then he wiped his face with Ruby's new tablecloth."

"Little Sam never could hold his liquor."

Sam nodded. "Well, I told Ruby to get Beulah to clean it up, but Beulah had already gone home. Then I told *her* to clean it up, and she told me I could clean it up myself. Next thing I remember, I grabbed her and slapped her and she fell and hurt herself."

"Sorry to hear that, Sam. She all right?"

Sam teared up. "The doc told me she lost her baby."

Buck choked on his beer. "Jesus Christ, Sam! Didn't you know she was pregnant?"

"No, Buck, I swear I didn't," Sam cried. "Anyway, all I remember doin' is slappin' her 'cross the face. After that, she fell."

"Is the doc treatin' her?"

"Yeah, he said he'd take care of her while I was gone."

"Well, Sam, this sure ain't gonna be easy—guess you'll just have to give it some time. You know you can always stay down here with me."

"Will you call Beulah for me tomorrow to see how Ruby's doin'?"

Buck finished his beer. "You know I will, brother. Right now, though, you ain't touched that food sittin' in front of you and I need another beer."

Sam stared at the plate of black-eyed peas and cornbread. "I feel like hell, Buck. I don't know what to do."

"Well, I can tell you, first thing you do is send her a couple dozen roses every week while you're down here. Then you go out and buy her the biggest damn diamond you ever seen, brother."

"I just bought her a diamond for Christmas—still got it in my pocket."

"Take it out and let me take a look."

Buck opened the black velvet box that Sam handed him, and saw the half-carat solitaire. Cocking an eyebrow, he held up his hand and wiggled his ring finger, flashing his three-carat canary diamond. "Take it from me, brother, you better start lookin' for this one's twin."

Sam stared at Buck in disbelief. "But…what do I do with the one I already bought?"

"Buy another one just like it, so you can have the jeweler make her a pair of earrings to boot."

1947

Chapter Eighteen

Adams slammed the *Democrat* down on his desk. "Damn that Wadsworth!"

Sheriff Hunter fidgeted, leaning over to reach for the newspaper. "He's got to write about somethin', Doc."

"Yeah, well, who the hell's he think he is, anyway?"

Hunter pulled out a pair of bifocals from his shirt pocket to look at the front page. "Louie's a war hero, you know. Now that he bought the *Democrat*, looks like he's usin' his 'Thinking Out Loud' column to preach against liquor and gamblin'."

"Wonder how much he knows."

Hunter looked up over his bifocals. "Well, this week it looks like he's got his sights locked on Sam as the gamblin' kingpin."

Adams scowled. "That's fine, but we sure as hell don't want him fingerin' us."

"I don't think he'd have the balls to do that, Doc," he said, returning his bifocals to his shirt pocket and folding the newspaper to toss it back on the desk. "Besides, Louie knows better'n to dig up dirt between whites and niggers."

Adams licked his fingers to thumb through a stack of hundred-dollar bills. "Last year the same goddamn paper was runnin' ads for all the saloons in town. Now that the county's gone dry, I guess he figures he ain't got nothin' to lose by steppin' into a hoopskirt and turnin' into a goddamn Carry Nation."

"Before you get too riled up, Doc, don't forget, tobacco season's comin' up in a few months, so Louie's got to get busy sellin' ads. Once he gets out and around, folks'll start askin' him if he ain't got nothin' else to write about. Hell, you know how many boys in town depend on sellin' bolita tickets to help pay their rent."

Adams grinned.

"Besides, when WNER goes on the air next year, the boys out at the station are talkin' 'bout runnin' the tobacco auctions live, with ads in between sales. That's gonna give Wadsworth a run for his money."

Adams snickered. "Funny thing 'bout that is Sam's talkin' about how the new radio station's gonna help his business."

"How's that, Doc?"

"When he called me from Fort Myers last week, he told me the station's goin' to run the nigger church's sermon live on Sundays as a public service. Preacher always announces the weekly jackpot with his scripture of the week. Like Sam explained, John 3:16 tells the poor suckers that three-one-six is the winner."

Hunter chuckled. "Smart nigger—now everybody can hear the winnin' number at the same time."

Adams finished counting the bills and secured the stacks with rubber bands. "Looks like we done better'n last week."

"It's the same every year, Doc. Everybody's short of cash till their crops come in, so lots of folks are tossin' out their pocket change, hopin' to hit the jackpot."

Adams nodded and scowled. "Ain't right, people 'round these parts suckin' hind tit while those goddamn rich Yankee Jews down in Miami live in the lap of luxury."

"Least we get some of their racetrack money since our boys in Tallahassee made 'em cough up some of the gamblin' taxes they take in down there."

"Drop in the bucket, Arch."

"I know it is, Doc," Hunter agreed, still trying to placate Adams. "At least Senator Pepper's got us the first county hospital in the whole country, and a radio station's goin' in, and we got that brand new bridge they're puttin' up over the Suwannee. You gotta admit, comin' so soon after the war, that's a lot of progress for one dirt-ass-poor county."

Adams peeled off several bills to secure them in a desk drawer, slid a bill over toward Hunter, and then stuffed the remainder into a satchel. "You goin' down to the bridge dedication next month, Arch?"

"Bet your bottom dollar, Doc," he said, reaching over to pick up his payoff and the satchel for his evening run to the McCollum house. "Gonna be the biggest Fourth of July shindig we ever had 'round these parts."

"Got my own personal invite from Judge Adams," Adams announced proudly, sliding his center desk drawer open. "Here, take a look."

"Hmm, fancy," Hunter commented, taking the invitation to run his fingers over the raised printing.

"LaVergne told me it'd be a good chance to rub elbows with all those politicians who'll be drivin' down there to grab a piece of the old man's glory."

Hunter smiled, handing the invitation back to Adams. "Old man Blue's right, Doc—it sure can't hurt."

Hal W. Adams Bridge
Madison Road Over Suwannee River

On either side of the road leading up to a gleaming steel structure that looked for all the world like a gigantic Erector Set project, rows of black steel-drum grills billowed smoke as men in aprons toweled the sweat from their foreheads and served up platters of barbecued beef and pork ribs. A small army of women ferried the ribs to the red-white-and-blue–draped folding tables set up in the shade of the slash pines, while laughing children darted about spitting watermelon seeds at each other.

Along the banks of the river beneath the bridge, dozens of old men with cane poles sat in the shade eating their barbecued ribs and watching their corks, pulling in an occasional bream or catfish from the glistening tea-colored Suwannee to throw in their ice chests for supper. Beyond the reach of the fishing lines, some teenage boys had shed their shirts to cool off in the river.

On the banks up above, firecrackers went off, and the band played "God Bless America" to announce the arrival of the horse-drawn surrey carrying Judge Hal Adams and his wife and young granddaughter.

When the judge and his party got out of the surrey and took their places at the head table, one after another distinguished guest had to be introduced, including Governor Caldwell and his entire cabinet, three former governors, and just about every circuit judge, state representative, senator, and county commissioner in North Florida.

Following a string of long-winded speeches, Governor Caldwell accepted the certificate of completion from a representative of the firm that erected the bridge.

Next, F. Elgin Bayless, chairman of the State Highway Commission, dedicated the structure, followed by former governor John W. Martin, who pulled the cord to reveal a cast-bronze plaque reading "Hal W. Adams Bridge, 1947."

"Thank you, Governor Martin," Judge Adams said. "You and I go back a good ways."

After arcing a stream of tobacco juice onto the ground, he continued, "We stand here, on July 4, 1947, marking the dedication of our great state's first and only suspension bridge, an engineering marvel standing fifty feet high and spanning four hundred and twenty feet between its towers. I want to congratulate the folks from the state as well as the L. J. and W. J. Cobb Construction Company of Tampa, whose teamwork gave us this fine bridge."

Applause spread slowly through the crowd, rising to a thunderous din as the host of rib eaters finished wiping their hands to join in.

"It seems like just yesterday when I crossed the Suwannee here on my way down to Mayo back in 1907, over a wooden bridge that creaked under the weight of our surrey. On that trip I brought my new bride, who stands here beside me today, as beautiful as she was then."

Applause again rippled through the crowd.

"Through the years, I've been blessed with children and grand-children, and I'm honored to bring along my granddaughter, Miss Kay Airth, to help with the ceremony."

Scattered applause welcomed the judge's granddaughter.

"Aside from the fact that I'm being honored today, this bridge also marks a new era in the history of our country, ushered in by the end of a war we fought to bring about world peace."

Rebel yells erupted through the roaring crowd until the judge raised his hand. "That new era will also bring another first to our area, and one that I hope all of you good folks will have the chance to attend next year. I'm speaking, as you know, of the dedication of our new Suwannee County Hospital. Thanks to our own Senator Claude Pepper, this will be the first hospital in the nation to be constructed with the assistance of federal Hill-Burton funds. And with it comes yet another first—a brand-spankin'-new X-ray machine that will allow our fine doctors the opportunity to bring us the most advanced medical care available in the world today."

Cheers spread through the crowd.

"I think I'm safe to say that every last one of you know Dr. Leroy Adams."

"Yea, Doc!" someone yelled, triggering a round of whistles and clapping.

"Y'all know him because, more likely than not, he's come out to your place in the middle of the night to take care of a loved one....So now I'd like to as ask Dr. Adams to say a word about the plans for the new hospital."

The crowd roared when Adams stepped up to the podium to give a broad wave. "It's a great honor to stand here today, celebrating the dedication of this bridge to a man who has meant so much to all of us.

It's also an honor to look out and see not a crowd but people I know, people whose homes I've visited when they needed me."

More applause broke out, along with heartfelt smiles and cheers from the doctor's patients.

Adams raised his hands. "What I'm up here to tell y'all is that soon every last one of you will have a place to come, day or night, where I have everything I need to treat what ails you. Ain't nobody gonna worry about their baby. Ain't nobody gonna worry 'bout the old folks. What's more, you ain't gotta have a thin dime in your pocket for me to see you."

The masses fell silent as women wiped tears from their eyes, recalling the stillbirths and infections that were all too common in a county with no medical facilities.

"I want to ask Senator Pepper to stand up, to let him know how much we appreciate what he's done for the folks of Suwannee County in givin' us the first hospital funded with the Hill-Burton legislation he fought so hard for."

Pepper stood to another round of enthusiastic applause.

"Well, I don't plan on takin' up any more time, since today belongs to Judge Adams."

After Dr. Adams left the head table, the judge, along with the governor and the judge's granddaughter, got into the lead car, a white Cadillac convertible with its top down, and drove up to the ceremonial yellow ribbon to pose for photographers.

When little Kay, with a fierce determination beyond her years, managed to cut the ribbon, the convertible rolled slowly forward to cross the bridge, accompanied by a spirited trombone rendition of "Way Down upon the Suwannee River."

Chapter Twenty

Ruby sorted through a rack of dresses at May Cohen's in Jacksonville with her friend Leona, a tall, bronze-skinned woman with a cover-girl figure and an exotically attractive, almost feline face.

"You know, Leona," Ruby lamented, "it seems like I can measure my life by the dresses I've worn."

Leona laughed. "Honey, that's true of any woman who loves her clothes."

Removing a floral-print jersey dress from the rack, Ruby held it up in front of her. "Do you think this would be good for church?"

"That's an old lady's dress, honey," Leona advised, pulling a stylish tailored suit from another rack. "This is what all the young women are wearing these days."

"That costs as much as three of my dresses!" Ruby objected.

"Look again," Leona urged, pointing to the tag. "It's on sale—half off. At least try it on to see how it looks on you."

Ruby slipped into the dressing room and changed into the outfit, then admired her reflection in the mirror. Not as slender as Leona, but then, her friend had to stay thin for her modeling job.

"Well?" Leona called through the dressing room door.

Ruby stepped out to strike a pose in front of the three-way mirror.

"Sexy, huh? When we get back home, I can show you some new makeup that'll knock Sam's socks off."

Ruby sighed, stepping back into the dressing room. "I'm afraid it'll take more than that."

"Uh-oh. Sounds like you and Sam got a bad case of too-long-married-to boogie."

"During the last few years, I've had to work hard to get his attention. That's what I was trying to do last Christmas before..."

"Tell me, girl!" Leona interrupted. "We girls have to work harder the older we get, just so we can keep our men home between the sheets. And it ain't just us, you know—that thing they got don't kick-start like it used to. Nowadays it takes a lot higher octane to get it cranked and keep it pumpin'."

Giggling, Ruby emerged from the dressing room with her new outfit. "Honey, from what I can tell, it must take some kind of rocket fuel."

Leona grinned. "You gettin' hungry?"

"I'm beginning to," Ruby decided, rubbing her stomach. "We could eat at the lunch counter downstairs—they have a colored section."

"I thought we might treat ourselves to something special. What about the country club? We can get there in less than an hour."

"That would be wonderful."

"Good. Let's check out and drive on up there."

With their purchases in hand, the women crossed the parking lot to Leona's car, a red 1946 Cadillac convertible with a white canvas top.

"I still can't believe you had a suit carrier installed underneath the backseat," Ruby said, laying her new outfit neatly in the custom-built chest. "And lined with cedar, no less!"

"Designed it myself," Leona announced proudly, lowering the white leather seat cushion back into position. "Had to have some way to carry all my outfits for my photo shoots and still enjoy my convertible."

"You mean they don't have your clothes ready for you when you get there?" Ruby asked, getting into the front seat.

"It depends. Sometimes they want me to tailor them myself before I show up for work. I'm the only model who'll still do that, so I have some old regulars."

Leona cranked the engine and turned onto Bay Street, then made a left a short distance later to cross the Acosta Bridge, spanning the St. Johns River. "Mind if we stop to pick some sea oats when we get out to the beach?" she asked, catching a glimpse of the sailboats gliding along the river. "I thought I'd dry some out back on the patio and paint them gold for an arrangement on my foyer table. It's all the rage this year, you know."

"I'd love to walk barefoot on the beach. Can't remember the last time I did."

A few miles out of town, they turned onto Highway A1A, the beach route through the marshy savannah that stretched east to meld seamlessly into the Atlantic Ocean. A few seagulls, fishing in the high grass of the saltwater spawning ground, squawked their annoyance at the intruding car.

"You know that sexy black lace bra and panty set I bought the last time that we were over here?" Ruby asked.

"That was way back last summer," Leona recalled. "What made you think of that?"

"Well, I went home and starved myself for a month. When I finally looked decent in it, I planned a romantic evening. That night I put on my best perfume—his favorite, mind you—and sashayed into the bedroom decked out in it. Girl, I was even wearin' high heels and black nylons to boot."

Leona giggled. "Details?"

"He asked me if I was getting dressed to go out somewhere."

"No, he didn't!"

"Oh, yes, he did," Ruby assured her.

"I know what you mean, honey. My baby's done lost the scent, too. Ain't been bird-doggin' me for years now."

"Do you think that Jake and Sam have women on the side?"

"You know a man who *don't* once his woman's titties start headin' for her belly button?"

Ruby shrugged. "I've been so busy with the house and keepin' the books, Sam could have himself a harem and I wouldn't know."

"Honey, foolin' around is in a man's nature. As time moves on, he's bound to roam while the woman stays at home."

"And you think that's fair?"

"Girl, since when you got the notion that women can do the same thing their menfolk can?"

Ruby sat silent for a moment. "Leona...you ever look at another guy and wonder what he'd be like in bed?"

She cut her eyes toward her friend and smiled. "More than a few times, if you want to know the truth."

"What kind do you like?"

"That's easy," Leona mused, leaning back in her seat. "I like mine tall and muscular—but not too bulky—with smooth, chestnut brown skin." Leona hugged herself and giggled. "And they got to be real sweet on me."

"I don't care so much what my men look like. I like them to be successful—you know, make lots of money. And I don't really care what they do for a living."

"Lord, girl, you always did like your 'big men.' I can still remember picking oranges with you out in the groves and you saying, 'I always pick my oranges off the top—just like my men.'"

"That's me," Ruby admitted. "I don't care what size, shape, or color he comes in, just so long as he knows how to get what he wants."

Leona pulled over to the side of the road. "Looks like a good stand of sea oats over there on that dune. You mind reaching in the glove compartment and grabbing those scissors?"

Pulling off their shoes to walk barefoot along the sand dunes, they took several handfuls of golden sea oats, choosing the stalks with the fullest wheat-like heads. A curious gull approached but then veered away when he saw that no food was likely.

Standing mesmerized by the sound and gentle lap of the sparkling waves, Ruby felt the cool breeze waft over her, making little ripples in the endless expanse of sea oats crowning the dunes along the shore. Drinking in the moment, she felt a flow of energy surge through her body, and a sense of inner peace that had not been hers for years.

"Jake and I rented a beach house out at the colored beach last summer," Leona said, breaking the spell. "First thing I did was open all the windows and let the salt breeze blow through.... It was heaven."

"Sam and I have never done that," Ruby replied, thinking how odd it seemed that she could no longer visualize spending time with the man who had been her husband since she was eighteen.

"Well, maybe we should plan a weekend together sometime."

A short walk later, after stowing their sea oats collection in the trunk of the car, Leona lowered the roof and pulled back onto the road. "So, how do you like riding in a convertible?"

"I love it—but it's not for me."

"Why not?"

"Can you imagine me riding through downtown Live Oak in a red Cadillac convertible with the top down? Every farmer in the county would be out at my house that very night with torches and pitchforks."

The car swerved over the center line of the highway as Leona burst out laughing. "Ruby, you kill me!"

A long silence ensued while Ruby thought of how to tell Leona about her separation from Sam without getting derailed as she had been back at the department store. It was a difficult subject to broach, because the two couples had been friends since they first married—bringing it up might lower Sam in Leona's eyes. And yet, if she couldn't discuss it with her best friend, how could she ever get it off her chest?

"I don't know how to tell you this," she blurted, "but Sam and I have been separated since Christmas."

"No! That's eight months!"

Ruby nodded sadly.

Leona patted her shoulder. "What happened, baby?"

"We had an argument in front of his men...."

"And?"

"Then he hit me."

Leona's foot came off the gas pedal. "Sam hit you?"

Ruby nodded, avoiding her friend's eyes to discretely wipe the tears from her own.

"That son of a bitch!" Leona scowled, looking back at the road. "If Jake ever hit me, I'd put a bullet in his belly for sure."

"That thought did occur to me," Ruby admitted. "Then I thought about the kids."

"I wondered why you two drove all the way over here in separate cars.... So what now?"

"We're going to try to get back together. I'm going to give it my best shot, Leona. Deep down, I know Sam's a good man."

"Men certainly can be difficult. Sometimes I think they measure their virility in decibels when they're out to make a point.... By the way, I wonder if Jake and Sam worked out a deal on those two bird dogs Sam had his eye on."

Laughing, Ruby said, "Jake could name just about any price and Sam would agree. He's crazy about those dogs of his."

"Here's our turn," Leona announced, making a hard right at a landscaped sign announcing the Lincoln Golf and Country Club, a nationally famous resort founded by one of Florida's first colored millionaires, Abraham Lincoln Lewis. The crushed-limestone driveway leading up to the club, a two-story Spanish-style building of bright yellow stucco, was bounded by a golf course on one side, with a low lime rock fence and a neatly trimmed hedge of pink oleanders. On the other side, the rhythmic waves of the Atlantic pounded the sun-bleached coral jetties, spraying a rainbow of salt mist over the driveway.

Under the green canopy in front of the club, a valet helped Leona out of her car, and she joined Ruby at the massive carved oak doors of the club entrance.

The doorman bowed as he held the door and bade them a good afternoon.

"My!" Ruby whispered. "They've remodeled."

"Just wait until you get inside."

In the foyer, they were greeted by a rush of cool air and a tuxedoed maître d'. Leona identified herself with Jake's membership card, and when they were seated at a corner table with a view of the ocean, a liveried waiter filled their water goblets while simultaneously shaking the swan-folded napkins to place them on their laps.

"I hardly recognize the place," said Ruby after the wine steward had come and gone.

"The last time you were here, Releford McGriff and his wife joined us—they've done a lot of redecorating since then."

Looking at the wrought-iron balconies with gas lamps and cascading silk bougainvilleas, Ruby took a bottle of pills from her purse. "It reminds me of New Orleans."

Leona watched her take a pill, and said, "Are you still on medication?"

"Oh, it's just something my doctor gave me for my rheumatism. Bending down to cut those sea oats started it up again."

"Sorry to hear that. But if it's working for you, I'd sure like to know what it is."

The wine steward returned, and then they ordered the fried catfish dinner.

The two friends sat quietly for a few minutes, sipping their cabernet and looking out the window at a seagull hovering effortlessly on the ocean breeze, his wings motionless. Squawking, the bird climbed higher in the air and spiraled downward, gaining speed on his descent. Then he folded his wings and dove suddenly to hit the water and disappear below. Momentarily, he surfaced with a fish in his mouth. Several other seagulls, encouraged by their companion's stroke of good luck, slanted their wings to swoop low over the glittering ocean surface, catching the panicking fish as they skipped over the water.

"You know, Ruby," Leona began, breaking the silence, "the best way to get Sam's attention is to not criticize him. What I mean is, make him feel like he's the lord of the castle—especially when his men are around."

"I suppose I have been hard on him about inviting his men over for their poker parties."

"You still got Beulah?" Leona asked, running her finger around the rim of her wine glass.

"Of course."

"So what's the problem, girl? Just make sure she stays to clean up the mess next time."

"I don't know. I guess it has something to do with the fact that they're just a bunch of no-good drunks."

Leona shot back a wry smile. "They may be obnoxious, honey, but Sam's men keep you sittin' pretty—don't ever forget that."

"So I've been told," Ruby acknowledged, remembering her conversation with Beulah last Christmas. "But I wish Sam wouldn't lower himself to their level."

The waiter returned to the table carrying two platters heaped with fried catfish fillets and hush puppies. As they started eating, Leona said, "I know it's hard, Ruby. Your side of the business is a one-person operation—you do all the bookkeeping by yourself. But Sam has to depend on his men to run his end. That kind of job calls for the kind of men who hang out in the jooks and other places that people like you and me would never go."

Ruby sipped the last of her wine, considering her friend's advice. "You're right, Leona, but they still aren't the class of people I like to have in my house. Anyway, I think I'll try that catfish now."

"You sure you don't want to share a pitcher of beer? You know it's what really goes with catfish."

Ruby threw up her hands. "What the heck. I'll start back on my diet when I get home."

****

After lunch, the two friends stood beneath the porte chochere in front of the club while the valet went for the car. "Mind if we drive back through downtown?" Ruby asked.

"You got your mind set on anywhere in particular?"

"I saw a jewelry store I'd like to check out...thought I might find something for Sam to give me on our anniversary."

"Jacobson's?"

"How'd you know?"

"'Cause I know you only shop at the best, girl," Leona said, fishing two quarters out of her purse for a tip.

Ruby laughed as the valet drove up in the car and opened their doors for them.

"It has certainly been a lovely day," said Leona with a satisfied sigh, pulling out of the property to turn south toward Jacksonville.

Ruby took a deep breath and let it out slowly. "I love smelling the ocean. Someday I hope I can talk Sam into buying a beach place over here."

"Want me to keep an eye out? One of Jake's clients is an investment realtor."

"Not right now. Things are just too up in the air with Sam and me."

"I can understand," Leona sympathized, reaching over to squeeze her friend's hand.

Back in Jacksonville, they were greeted in the jewelry store by a clean shaven, short, balding white man in a suit and tie. "May I help you?" he asked with the arrogance of a bankrupt aristocrat forced to work for a living.

"Yes," Ruby returned cheerfully. "I'd like to look at your ruby and diamond rings."

"Very good, madam. My name is Mr. Jacobson—please follow me."

"Madam?" Ruby whispered to Leona.

Leona shrugged, stifling a giggle.

Following the proprietor along a long row of glass display cases, Ruby marveled at the broad selection of jewelry, noting that the diamonds were toward the back of the store.

"Ah, here we are," he announced, circling behind a jewelry case to remove a small ruby-and-diamond cocktail ring from a tray of much larger rings. "This is a lovely little piece."

Ruby waved the ring away. "I want something with about six rubies the size of this one," she explained, removing her engagement ring to drop it on the counter.

Pleased, he put the smaller ring back and pulled out the largest in the tray. "This cascade cocktail ring has six pigeon-blood rubies and twenty-four diamonds, for a total of seven carats' gem weight. It's our finest ruby-and-diamond ring, set in eighteen-karat rose gold and crafted in the art deco style after an original Tiffany."

"Oh…! It's beautiful!" Ruby breathed.

"Would you like to try it on?"

"Yes!" she exclaimed, holding out her hand.

The proprietor slipped the ring on her finger, watching her face. It was a perfect fit.

"Come home to Mama, baby!" Ruby laughed, showing the shimmering ring to Leona.

"It's gorgeous!" Leona enthused, holding her hand to admire the dazzling gems. "Don't you want Sam to see it first?"

"He don't know nothin' 'bout jewelry, honey, let me tell you! How much is it, Mr. Jacobson?"

"It's priced at fourteen hundred."

"I'll take it," Ruby declared without hesitation, looking behind the jeweler to see herself in the mirrored wall. *Get a load of this*, she thought, enjoying the way the ring looked on her finger. It would certainly be the envy of all the women at church.

He beamed. "Would you like to wear it?"

"Yes, I would," Ruby responded, unable to take her eyes off her new treasure.

"May I put your old ring in a box for you?" he asked, noting Ruby's engagement ring lying abandoned on the counter.

"Yes, please."

"I'll be glad to clean it first if you'd like," he offered.

"No, don't bother," Ruby replied, still mesmerized by her new purchase. "It's quite old. I'll save it for one of my girls."

The man walked to the front cash register while Leona and Ruby followed, browsing in the cases along the way.

"That will be fourteen hundred and forty-two dollars, including the tax."

Ruby opened her purse, took out her wallet, and began peeling off fifteen hundred-dollar bills.

After counting back her change, Jacobson said, "Anytime you ladies come in, I'll be glad to have your rings cleaned for you while you shop."

Outside, Leona glanced over her shoulder to see a vagrant sitting against a storefront, drinking from a bottle in a paper bag. "Ruby," she murmured, "I'd turn that ring around backwards if I were you—this isn't Live Oak, you know."

"You're right, girl—guess I just got excited." Getting into the car, she said, "That man sure knows how to make you want to come back."

"Doesn't he, though!" Leona laughed as they drove away. "He's like any good merchant who knows how to do business."

Ruby held out her hand to admire her new ring. "What impressed me was the way he treated me like I was a white woman. You get much of that around here?"

"Let's just say I stick to the places that treat me right."

"Don't blame you."

Reaching her two-story suburban house, Leona parked in the circular driveway, behind Jake's red pickup.

"I can't wait to show Sam my new ring!" Ruby gushed, getting out of the car.

"Do you think that's a good idea?" Leona blurted. Catching herself, she said, "I mean, maybe you should slip your engagement ring back on, put the new one in the box, and let him give it to you."

"Aw, Sam doesn't care, honey," Ruby assured her, dismissing the suggestion.

Leona unlocked the front door. "Anybody home?"

"We're in the kitchen, baby," Jake called.

The two women crossed the formal dining room to find Jake and Sam having a beer in the kitchen—much to Ruby's surprise, since Sam rarely drank.

"Come on in, girls," Sam invited. "I want to show you a picture of my new huntin' dog...."

"Sam," Ruby interrupted, waving her hand in his face, "look what I bought."

Seeing the ring, Jake leaned back in his chair and laughed. "Brother Sam, if you want to pay me on time for that dog you picked out, it's all right by me."

"I have my own money," Ruby snapped, her protest underscored by Leona's disapproving glare.

Sam's face fell. "Where's the ring I gave you when we got married?" he asked, seeing the elaborate piece that had taken the place of her modest ruby engagement ring.

"It's in my purse," Ruby explained. But she knew from the look on his face that she should have listened to Leona. "So...tell me about that new dog of yours."

Chapter Twenty-One

Sam lay in bed with his head nestled between the fulsome breasts of a lovely bronze-skinned young woman.

"I don't know, Lucy," he lamented. "From what I can tell, the doc's got Ruby hooked on those pills. When we was in Jacksonville with Jake and Leona, she had a purse full of 'em."

Lucy ran her fingers along his neck and gently stroked his cheek. "One thing I've learned, Sam, you can't stop somebody from drinking or taking drugs. They have to stop on their own terms."

He frowned. "No tellin' how long that's gonna take."

"She's been by herself for months—that's hard on a woman. Things'll settle down now that you're home, you'll see."

"You won't believe what she did in Jacksonville," Sam grumped.

"What's that, baby?" she asked, stroking his chest.

"She bought this huge ring with rubies and diamonds for me to give her for our anniversary."

"She didn't ask you to come with her to help pick it out?"

"No. And what's more, I already bought her a ring," Sam complained, reaching for his trousers on the bedpost. "Here, take a look."

Lucy's jaw dropped when she opened the box. "Sam! I've never seen anything like this—not even in a jewelry store. It must be almost three carats."

"Three and a half."

"Where on earth did you get a diamond like this?"

"Buck took me to a place that had it shipped down from New York."

"My heavens!" Lucy breathed, slipping the ring on her finger to admire the brilliance of the diamond.

"Looks good on you," said Sam as the diamond fell to one side on her petite finger.

Lucy pulled the ring off and put it back in the box. "Your wife's one lucky woman."

Sam returned the box to his pocket. "Problem is, I don't feel like givin' it to her now."

"Why's that?"

"When she showed me the new ring she bought, it was on the same finger she used to wear her engagement ring on."

Lucy took his hand. "That must have hurt."

"She's changed. Somehow she seems different than when I left at Christmas."

"You hit her, Sam. What do you expect from her? To welcome you home with open arms?"

Sam just glowered.

"Like I said, baby, it's gonna take time—women hold on to things. You can't expect her to pretend something like that never happened."

"I didn't mean to..."

"Doesn't matter, Sam. There's no excuse for a man hitting a woman, and you know it."

"Yes...I know," he admitted, looking like a little boy who had been scolded by his mother. "It's gonna be hard going back. Doc Adams has really moved in on the business since I left town. He has Sheriff Hunter droppin' in to check on the boys when they count up their tickets at the end of the week. And from what I can see, Ruby's turnin' over a lot more of the take to the doc than we used to pay out to all the white folks."

Lucy smiled, kissing his forehead. "You're the poorest rich man I know, baby. You told me last week you're takin' in more this year than you did last."

"I am," Sam admitted. "Since the war ended and the county went dry, business has more than doubled."

"So how much of a dent is the good doctor making?"

"I'd reckon about five percent more than before."

"So, by my math, you're still pretty far ahead of the game."

He laughed. "That's what I get for gettin' hooked up with a schoolteacher."

Lucy smiled. "I never heard you complain before."

"I ain't complainin', baby," he protested, planting a kiss on her cheek.

"All you have to do is play this white man's game. He's still skimmin' off a lot less than he could be."

"Buck says it's about the same as he pays out."

"There!" Lucy said, giving him a playful punch on the arm. "You see? I was right."

"I still don't like the man," he grumped.

"You don't have to like him, brown sugar. You just have to let him eat out of the trough enough to keep him happy. Besides, the last time I checked, you ran a cash business."

Sam grinned. "Yeah, I always hold some back to cover the hard times — only way I made it through the thirties."

"Well, then," she chirped, getting out of bed. "Care for a glass of orange juice? I'm goin' to mix myself a screwdriver."

"Sounds good, baby."

Lucy left the bedroom to return a few minutes later with the drinks.

"Thanks," Sam said, taking a gulp of orange juice. "You look worried, baby."

"Oh, it's nothing I can't handle," she assured him, setting her drink on the bedside table and sitting on the edge of the bed.

"Come on, baby, you can tell your daddy," he urged, pulling her down onto the bed to tickle her.

"Stop it!" Lucy demanded with a laugh. "Well...if you must know, I'll tell you — you know I can't hide anything from you. I have to take my car down to get a new set of tires this week. Thought I'd wait until payday, but I sure don't want to have a flat on my way in to school."

Sam laughed. "Is that all? Don't worry that pretty little head of yours," he assured her. "I'll stop by Mr. Andrews's station tomorrow mornin'. Drop your car by there after school and he'll fix you up. I'll tell him to put anything you get on my account from now on."

Lucy sat up to give him a peck on the cheek. "Thank you, Sam; that's sweet of you."

"Almost your birthday, anyway."

"You're all I need for my birthday, sugar," she cooed, reaching for her drink.

1948

Chapter Twenty-Two

Against an impressionistic background of multicolored phlox carpeting a sun-drenched field, dozens of small children ran searching beneath clumps of grass for their brightly colored Easter treasures. Ruby sat at a picnic table beneath the lacy shade of a pecan tree, counting the proceeds from the African Baptist Church bake sale. Finishing her work, she closed the metal cash box and sealed the ledger sheets in a manila envelope.

The Reverend White hobbled toward her with a piece of cracklin' cornbread in one hand and a quart jar of buttermilk in the other. "How'd we do, Ruby?" the rotund minister asked expectantly, washing a mouthful of cornbread down with the buttermilk.

"Fifty dollars and forty-five cents."

"Praise the Lord! Looks like 'forty-eight's turnin' out to be the best Easter yet."

"I don't know if we're quite there yet, Reverend. From what I'm told, the price of the organ just went up. Anyway, I put the ledger sheet in the envelope for you to return to the office."

"You're a blessin', Miss Ruby. I sure 'preciates you comin' down here on a Saturday to help with the bake sale."

"I do what I can," she responded graciously, handing the envelope to the minister. "I'll take the money on down to the bank first thing Monday morning."

"How's the baby doin', Ruby?"

"She's just fine, Reverend. Thanks for asking."

"What's her name again?"

"Sonja."

"I'm sorry, Ruby, it's just that this old noggin's like the old gray mare — ain't what it used to be."

"That's all right, Reverend," Ruby assured him with a patient smile.

"My, my!" he said, adjusting his bifocals to stare at her hand. "That sure is a fine ring you got there."

"Oh, this..." She fingered the canary diamond solitaire. "Sam just gave it to me."

"Mighty fine man, that Sam."

She managed a forced smile.

"You know, Ruby, since you and Sam come to town, this church has made a lot of progress, starting with those ceiling fans y'all donated." Turning toward the children on the playground, he added, "But I think the nicest thing y'all done was to donate that playground equipment. I can't tell you how much difference that's made—not just for the church but for the whole neighborhood. I just love to see our church members share the bounty the good Lord sees fit to bless 'em with."

"We're always there to help," Ruby assured him, trying to find a way out of the conversation before the minister could bring up the price increase on the organ. Spotting Kay picking up an Easter egg nearby, she seized the opportunity. "Kay, honey, you need to come on. We've got to get back home."

The Reverend White smiled, tipping his hat. "I know you've got plenty to keep you busy on over at your place. You have a nice afternoon, Miss Ruby."

"Thank you, Reverend," she replied, relieved to have broken free of the old man so easily.

"Can't I stay a little longer?" Kay whined, running to her mother with her Easter basket.

Ruby picked up the cash box. "No, baby, I'm tired and I need to take a nap before I start my bookkeeping. Did you have fun?"

"Yes, ma'am, I had lots of fun. See all the eggs I got?" she asked, holding up her Easter basket.

"Oh, how nice! You really did find a lot," Ruby said, walking hand-in-hand to the car. "You want me to make deviled eggs out of them for supper?"

"Would you?" Kay beamed.

"I sure will. You didn't eat too many cookies, did you?"

"No, Mama, just one...and a little piece of chocolate cake."

Ruby laughed. "Guess you won't be hungry for a while, then. Let's get on home."

A few blocks down the road, Ruby pulled over to look at the site of Dr. Adams's new house.

"Mommy, why are we stopping here?"

"I'm just looking at the new house they're building, baby."

"Whose house is it?"

"It belongs to Dr. Adams."

"Isn't he your doctor?"

"Yes, baby, he is."

"Is his house going to have rooms upstairs?"

"No, baby. It's just one story."

"Why doesn't he have a big house like ours?"

"Guess he likes the one he's building, baby."

"Must not have many kids," Kay concluded.

Signaling to pull back onto the road, Ruby noted that the gas gauge was hovering above empty. "Uh, oh," she said. "We've got to get some gas." She turned onto Highway 90 and drove two blocks past the site of the new hospital to Andrews's service station.

The young attendant grinned, hearing the engine sputter to a halt. "Looks like you coasted in on fumes! Second one today. Fill 'er up?"

"Yes, please," Ruby responded, noting that she did not recall seeing the boy before.

When he finished pumping the gas, checking the oil, and washing the windshield, he announced, "That will be three eighty, please."

"You're new here, aren't you?"

"Yes, ma'am—just started yesterday."

"My husband, Sam McCollum, has an account with Mr. Andrews. Would you be kind enough to add this to our bill and let me see how much we owe this month?"

"Sure thing," said the boy, and he retreated into the small cinder-block service station to look through the card file for the McCollum account. Finding the card along with a ticket clipped to it, he returned to the car. "We take cash or check."

Ruby saw the extra ticket when she took the card. "I'm sorry, this isn't mine," she said, handing it back to the boy. "It says 'Lucy Brown' at the bottom. She's a schoolteacher out at Douglas High School. It must have gotten attached to my bill by mistake."

"I know who she is. She's a real nice colored lady. She showed me how to fill out the ticket and told me to put her gas on the McCollum account along with the oil change—she said Mr. Andrews would explain."

"You're sure about that?"

"Yes, ma'am, real sure."

"I see." She paused a moment to consider what the boy had told her. "Well, I'll pay everything but that other woman's part until I can talk with my husband to see what that's all about."

"Fine with me. I just work here. The rest of the ticket comes to fourteen twenty-five."

Ruby peeled a twenty from a roll of bills and handed it to the attendant.

He handed her the receipt and said, "I'll be right back with your change."

"Thank you," she managed, feeling a silent rage growing deep inside her. Drumming with her fingers on the steering wheel, she considered her options: shoot Sam, or kick him out of the house. The first choice, though it would feel better, could not be reversed. That left the second.

When the attendant returned with her change, she thanked him, then slammed the car into gear and sped out of the filling station with the sound of squealing tires and the smell of burning rubber.

"Is something wrong with the car, Mama?" Kay asked.

"Nothing's wrong with the car, baby," Ruby assured her through clenched teeth.

"Are we going home now?"

"Yes, baby. When we get there, I want you to go on over to Uncle Matt's place and play on the swing in his backyard. Be sure to ask Aunt Bessie to help you change out of your Sunday clothes before you do."

"All right, Mama."

Ruby accelerated past the hospital grounds to round the hairpin Dead Man's Curve, made a screeching left turn onto Wood Street, and slammed on brakes in her driveway.

Kay jumped out of the car with her Easter basket, saying, "Gee, Mom, that was fun! Let's drive like that again!"

"See you soon, baby," Ruby called after her before hurrying into the house. Inside, she found Sam lying on the sofa and Beulah helping Sonja down the stairs. "How's Sonja?" she asked Beulah.

"She's just fine, Miss Ruby," Beulah reported, lowering her voice to a whisper on seeing Sam asleep on the sofa. "She's been a good girl all mornin'. Been babblin' up a storm."

"Would you mind taking her next door and asking Matt to keep her for a few hours? I don't feel so good, and I want to get some rest."

Beulah looked concerned. "You gonna be alright, baby?"

"I'll be just fine.... I just need some time to myself. You can go on home right after you take her over there."

"Thank you, Miss Ruby. You just take care of yourself."

"I will," Ruby assured her, managing a smile.

After Beulah left with Sonja, Ruby circled the sofa slowly, like a lioness closing on her prey.

"Ruby...you back already?" Sam asked, rubbing the sleep from his eyes.

"Yeah...I'm back," she replied icily.

He sat up to stretch. "How'd the bake sale go?"

"Oh, the bake sale went just fine, but I had the strangest thing happen down at Mr. Andrews's service station."

"Oh?"

"Yes. I went to pay our bill and found that somebody tried to charge a tank of gas and an oil change to our account." She paused to gauge Sam's reaction.

"Must've been a mistake," he suggested nervously.

"The attendant was a boy I'd never seen before. He explained that it was a schoolteacher from out at Douglas High. Matter of fact, he showed me the ticket—it was signed by Lucy Brown."

Sam's jaw dropped.

Seeing the face of guilt, Ruby put her hands on her hips and glared menacingly. "You know—one of Sam Junior's teachers?"

Sam was stunned. He had relied on Mr. Andrews's discretion.

Having confirmed her suspicions, Ruby grabbed a pillow from the sofa and had at him with all the strength she could manage.

Sam threw up his arm to guard his face. "What's wrong with you, woman!" he shrieked, jumping up from the sofa to avoid her assault.

Ruby's eyes blazed. "You're using our money to pay for your god-damn whore, that's what's wrong!"

"What the hell you talkin' 'bout, woman?" Sam yelled with feigned innocence.

"I'm talkin' about gas and an oil change for Lucy Brown, for Christ's sake!"

Sam froze, mortified that he had been caught.

"How dare you give that bitch our hard-earned money?" she raged, feeling violated by his infidelity.

Sam felt trapped. "Ruby, baby, I'm sorry," he said softly, hanging his head in an attempt at false contrition.

"'Sorry' don't cut it, Sam," she sobbed bitterly, sinking onto the sofa to hug the pillow. "You swore you gave up whorin' around years ago. And now...now I can never trust you again."

"It ain't like that, baby," he soothed, reaching over to hold her.

"Don't touch me!" Ruby screamed, pushing him away in disgust. "I want you out of my house!"

"Your house? Since when is it your house?"

Ruby threw the pillow at him. "Since you started spending money on your goddamn whore!" she screamed, jumping up from the sofa to head for the staircase. "I worked right alongside you all these years to get everything we have, and I never saw her high-yellow butt keeping your books!" Turning away, she ran upstairs, seething.

Feeling the room spin dizzily around him, Sam sank back on the sofa and buried his head in his hands. "Damn," he groaned, realizing that he was cornered.

Lucy had always been there, providing comfort and sanctuary when he needed it most. True, he loved Ruby, but things had changed over time—the thrill of young love had faded into the past.

Then there were the kids. What would he tell them? What would Ruby tell them?

"I want you out of the house!" Ruby demanded behind his back.

Sam turned to see her standing in the middle of the staircase with his revolver leveled point-blank at his head. "Ruby," he cautioned, "you need to put that gun down."

"I said out of the house, nigger!" she screamed, tears streaming down her cheeks.

"What about my things?"

"I'll get Beulah to send them down to Buck's place on the Greyhound."

Sam stood up and approached her cautiously. "You need to calm d—"

Just get out! Now!" she screamed, pulling the trigger. With an ear-splitting crack, the gun fired, blowing a hole in the floor by the sofa.

"You're crazy, woman!" Sam yelled, running out the front door.

Ruby sank to the stairs sobbing, dropping the pistol beside her.

Chapter Twenty-Three

Bolting out of bed, an eighteen-year-old Ruby Jackson threw on a pair of tattered blue jeans and a cotton blouse to enter the kitchen, where her mother, Gertrude, stood at the kerosene stove, pan-frying toast in butter. A blue-and-white-speckled enamel pot of grits bubbled gently on the back burner, while eggs swimming in bacon fat sizzled sunny-side up in the cast-iron skillet. The aroma of freshly brewed coffee filled the room.

"You up early for a Saturday, Ruby. You ain't doin' more pickin' in the groves today, is you?"

"No, ma'am," Ruby answered, rushing past her mother. "I'm headed downtown to buy that dress for the prom."

Her mother laughed, flipping the toast. "Well, I know better'n to git in the way of a hurricane. I'll keep a plate covered for when you git back."

"Thanks, Mama!" Ruby yelled behind her, bounding out the screen door and off the creaking front porch.

In the dirt road that ran in front of the house, she felt the warm sand squish through her open-toed sandals. Three blocks later, she stopped in front of the general store to assure herself that her treasure was still in the window. Rushing inside, she reached in the display to touch the coveted red satin dress.

"Will you be buying the dress today, Ruby?"

Vaguely realizing that someone had spoken to her, she turned around.

"Ma'am?"

"I said," the saleslady repeated sternly, "will you be buying the dress today?"

Ruby smiled. "Yes, ma'am."

"I'll get it for you, then," the saleslady said, sounding dubious of the colored girl's ability to pay for the fanciest dress in the store. "Here," she said, carefully handing the dress to Ruby. "You may try it on in the colored dressing room at the rear of the store."

Ruby took the dress from the saleslady like a new mother receiving her baby for the first time. She couldn't believe how soft and silky it felt.

The saleslady-turned–store detective followed Ruby to the dressing room. "I really need to be certain you're going to buy this dress. Like I told you when you asked to try it on, it's priced at ten dollars. I have other customers who have looked at it, and I can't afford to have it soiled."

"Yes, ma'am. I have cash money."

"Good," the saleslady replied, relieved to know that this was not just a dress rehearsal for an event quite beyond a poor colored girl's means. "In that case, you'll need a crinoline. I'll pick one out for you."

Ruby rushed to the back of the store, to a door labeled "COLORED DRESSING ROOM." The saleslady, scurrying to catch up with her with the crinoline, opened the dressing room door to point a bony finger at a hook on the wall. "Hang the dress up there and I'll hand you the crinoline."

"Thank you, ma'am," said Ruby, hanging the dress as instructed.

The saleslady handed her the crinoline. "Please be careful with the dress."

Ruby closed the dressing room door and shucked off her jeans and blouse, feeling like a butterfly anxious to break free of its cocoon. Wearing only her underpants and tattered brassiere, she slipped into the crinoline, then carefully pulled the dress over her head, instantly transforming in her mind's eye into a beautiful princess.

Stepping out of the dressing room, she caught sight of herself in the full-length mirror mounted on the wall. "Not bad for a colored girl going on eighteen," she whispered, admiring the hue of her chestnut brown skin against the ruby red satin.

Although the prom was months away, she had been meticulously planning for the event, acquiring treasured objects one at a time to complete her ensemble. The dress was the crown jewel of her acquisitions. She stood admiring her reflection in the mirror, imagining her mother's strand of cream-colored freshwater pearls draped around her neck.

Ruby pressed her hands to the bodice, feeling the coolness of the silky cloth with her palms, then slowly slid her hands down her sides, all the way to her hips. Savoring her image in the mirror, she felt a power well up within her that she knew would not be denied.

As she stood daydreaming about dancing with Sam and being the best-dressed girl at the prom, the saleslady's reflection appeared over her shoulder in the mirror. "May I ring up the dress, Ruby?"

Ruby stifled a giggle, thinking how much the scowl on the sales-lady's face reminded her of the evil queen's picture as she stood in front of her magic mirror in Snow White. "Do you have a bag to keep it just the way it is…nice and new?"

"I believe I still have the one it came in from Jacksonville."

"Did you say it came from Jacksonville?" she asked, curious about the lineage of the dress.

The saleslady, assured of the sale, warmed somewhat in the heat of Ruby's enthusiasm. "Gilmore's Department Store, over in Jacksonville, sent it to us on approval, trying to get us to carry their merchandise. They said they had sold several in this line as far away as Live Oak, so they thought our customers might be pleased with this one."

"Gilmore's?" Ruby confirmed.

"Yes, they're Jewish clothing merchants, but I understand that they have a reputation of selling only quality goods."

"Oh, that's good," Ruby said, wondering what the merchant's religion had to do with the quality of their merchandise.

"I'll check on a bag while you're in the dressing room."

"Yes, ma'am."

While the saleslady retreated to the stock room, Ruby paused to take another look at herself in the mirror. Reaching to open the door to the dressing room, she caught a glimpse of the door with the sign "LADIES' DRESSING ROOM." Without thinking, she turned and opened the door to find a spacious room with a sofa on a Persian rug in front of a raised three-sided mirror designed for fitting dresses.

Ruby's spine tingled at the strange thoughts rushing through her mind. *Why did I come in here? Why shouldn't I come in here? I just bought the most expensive dress in the store, didn't I? What'll happen if a white woman finds me in here?* With this last thought, she slipped out of the dressing room to find herself face-to-face with the saleslady, holding the bag for the dress.

"Did you lose your way, Ruby?"

She thought fast to cover her transgression. "I…I guess I just got turned around."

"I see. Well, now that you've found your place, let me know when you're ready to hand the dress out to me."

With the saleslady standing guard outside, Ruby reentered the colored dressing room. Moments later she cracked the door to hand the dress out.

"Is this a graduation gift from your parents, or perhaps a boy-friend?"

"No, ma'am," Ruby said proudly. "I earned the money myself, picking oranges in the grove."

"Well, you certainly are a hardworking girl. I just might have some housework for you when you're a little older."

Ruby closed the door to the dressing room to remove the crinoline. *Boyfriend! Housework!* she mused. *I don't need a boyfriend to get what I want. And I'll hire my own housework, thank you, ma'am!* Continuing to dress, she sighed. *But then again, I wouldn't mind having a husband to buy me lots of nice things.*

Looking into the little mirror on the wall with its aged silver backing, she retreated into her favorite daydream. *I want a big man who treats me nice, buys me diamond rings and nice cars, and builds a fine house for me to live in.* She twirled and curtsied to the mirror. *Glad to meet you, Prince Charming. My name is Ruby. I will marry you if you treat me nice, give me lots of babies, buy me diamond rings and nice cars, and build me a fine house.* Ruby paused, waiting for her imaginary prince to respond. *Oh, you will? Then you are my big man!*

A knock on the dressing room door pulled Ruby back from her fantasy. Cracking the door, she saw an elderly colored man holding a pair of overalls.

"Sorry, I'se just seein' if nobody's in there."

"You can use the room now, mister. I'm finished."

"I thank ya, miss."

Outside, she found the saleslady, holding the dress, now neatly bagged. "Thank you," she said.

"Oh, I'm glad to do it," said the saleslady, leading the way to the front of the store, where a big brass cash register sat on a wooden and glass display case filled with candy. "Will there be anything else, Ruby?"

"Do you have any ladies' hats on sale? I need to buy a gift for my mother."

"Look right in back of you."

Ruby turned around to see hats on a table marked "FINAL SALE—$1.75." Her mother would love the bright purple one with iridescent peacock feathers. She put the hat on the display case beside the register. "I'll take this one."

"Anything else?" asked the saleslady, pleased with the additional sale.

"No, ma'am. That's all for now."

"The dress is ten dollars...," announced the woman, punching in the numbers, "the crinoline is two dollars...and the hat is one dollar and seventy-five cents." With a punch of the Total button and a ding of the register's bell, she smiled. "That comes to a total of thirteen dollars and seventy-five cents."

Ruby dug deep into the pocket of her overalls to fish out a wad of dollar bills, happy that she had thought ahead to trade her coins in for paper money. "One, two, three...," she began, carefully counting and pressing each wrinkled bill to make a neat stack. When she had thirteen, she pulled a handful of pennies from her other pocket. "I found most of these on the sidewalk. Mamma calls them 'pennies from heaven.'"

Writing out the receipt, the saleslady smiled benignly, thinking how her own mother called them "nigger money." "Keep this to prove that you paid for it."

"Thank you, ma'am," she said, pleased that the woman was now treating her almost as well as one of her white customers.

Leaving the store with her new dress, Ruby felt a strange sense of inner worth and wellbeing, realizing for the first time that money had the power to blur the distinction between colored and white.

Chapter Twenty-Four

Ruby lay in bed reading the front page of the *Suwannee Democrat*, smiling to see that Dr. Adams, who had been designated the emergency room physician for the new hospital, would speak right after U.S. Senator Claude Pepper at the hospital's upcoming dedication ceremony. *Now, that's what I call a big man,* she reflected.

Turning to the society page — which, of course, was limited to white society — Ruby read, "Mrs. Lee Ledbetter entertained the Tuesday Bridge Club with a luncheon at the home of her mother, Mrs. Harold Wolfe, on Suwannee Street last Thursday afternoon. Seasonal flowers were placed at vantage points throughout the house." Ruby noted that Dr. C. Leroy Adams's daughter, Laverne, who had married Warren Jernigan, the head teller at Live Oak's Commercial Bank, was listed among the guests as "Mrs. Warren Jernigan."

Ruby threw the paper on the floor in disgust, thinking, *There'll never be a day when I'm 'Mrs. Sam McCollum' in this house! Those white women don't even have their own names.*

Feeling a deep emptiness inside, she looked at everything around her: the gift of handmade red crepe paper roses that Beulah had lovingly arranged in a vase on her dresser, her colorful collection of perfume bottles, and the bright floral-patterned wallpaper she had chosen to coordinate with her chenille bedspread. All of her rich surroundings seemed to have lost their joyful color, bleeding into lifeless shades of gray. It was obvious that the sparkle had gone out of her life.

Since she was a little girl, Ruby had known what she wanted: to get married and have a family. She would marry a big man, who would work by her side to fulfill her dreams. And now she had everything she wanted, but she had lost her big man, and the void he left was painful — almost unbearable.

Sinking deeper into despair, she closed her eyes. In her mind's eye she looked up to see a ray of light pierce through the gloom, revealing a hand reaching down to save her — and the hand was white.

Why hadn't she seen it all along? Hadn't that white man protected her from Sam when he hit her? Hadn't he been there to deliver her baby? Hadn't he been there to run the business when Sam was down in Ft. Myers? How blind she had been to all the little things he did to prove his love!

Ruby rolled over to reach for the telephone. "Operator, get me Dr. Adams's office, please."

"Dr. Adams," he answered.

"I really need to see you, Doctor," Ruby pleaded, her eyes brimming with tears.

"What seems to be the problem, Ruby?"

"I got an awful headache…and this terrible pain in my stomach, and—"

"I got one more patient, Ruby; then I'll drive on out there."

"Thank you, Doctor."

Ruby hung up the telephone to feel her sadness replaced by a sudden, inexplicable euphoria. Lying back in bed, she wondered what it would be like to sleep with a white man—not just any white man, but the most important white man in Suwannee County.

When she heard the doorbell ring, she ran to her dresser to splash on perfume, then pulled on her robe to hurry downstairs.

Adams stood at the door. "I just finished up down at the office. You ain't been sick in a coon's age."

Ruby lowered her eyes. "I know… It's been over a year now."

"You want to go on upstairs so I can examine you?"

"Yes, please," she said, stepping back for him to enter.

"Awful quiet around here," he said, glancing about. "Where are Sam and the kids?"

"Sam went down to Fort Myers, and the kids went with Matt and Bessie to church."

"I see," he replied, following her upstairs, thinking how odd it was that she was wearing perfume when she was at home by herself, sick in bed.

Ruby closed the bedroom door behind them. "Where do you want me, Doctor Adams?"

"Just slip off your clothes and lay down there on the bed."

Ruby removed her robe and slip to lie on the bed in her panties.

"Might as well take those panties off while you're at it."

Ruby slipped her panties down.

"That's good," Adams said, placing his satchel on the dresser. "Now, where did you say you hurt?"

"My head and my stomach," she moaned.

"Hmm," he murmured, pressing on her abdomen. "Does this hurt?"

Ruby grimaced. "A little."

"You've been cryin'."

Her lip trembled as tears welled up in her eyes.

"You might as well tell me what's wrong, Ruby; I know you're not sick—least it ain't nothin' physical."

"Seems like all I can do lately is mope around the house and sleep a lot. If it's not my rheumatism, it's my stomach or my back, or a terrible headache when I try to go outside...."

"Sam beat on you again?"

"No..." She hesitated a beat, then blurted, "I found out he's been sleeping with another woman."

"Well, hell, that explains it—you're depressed. And you don't get over that kind of depression until you get even."

A tear spilled from the corner of her eye. "But what can I do?"

"Now, now, don't get your panties in a wad," he said, sitting on the bed beside her. Reaching into his satchel, he pulled out a vial, filled a hypodermic, and gave her an injection in her arm. "There you go. That'll help get your mind off your problems."

"Thank you, Doctor," she said softly, beginning to feel her muscles relax. "You've always been there when I've needed you."

"That's right, Ruby. I can help you, and you can help me."

"Well, I guess the best I can do for my part is to pay—"

He stared at her, his eyes glowing with a lover's familiarity. "You ain't no green sprout, Ruby. You're a married woman and you have to know..."

"Yes...," Ruby agreed, aware of his intentions, yet hearing her voice trailing off as she turned to look out the window. "Oh, Doctor, I hear the most beautiful music outside—like angels playing on their harp strings. What was in that shot?"

"Just somethin' to help you relax," he chuckled, slipping down his trousers.

Ruby exhaled, running her hands down her nude body. "I feel...I feel just wonderful!"

Adams chuckled, stepping out of his boxer shorts.

Suddenly, Ruby realized that he was naked and obviously aroused. "Doctor!" she murmured. "I don't know... What if...?"

"Sure you do, Ruby," he reassured her calmly. "You've wanted me since the day we first met."

Looking at Adams standing nude beside her, she felt goose bumps. She had never seen a naked white man before. There was something exciting about his pink flesh and the graying hairs on his chest—something...exotic. At first she felt the impulse to resist, but it quickly melted as he kissed her nipples and ran his powerful hand all the way down her body to feel her yielding wetness. Then pleasure surged like a bolt of lightning through her body as she felt him plunge deep inside her, his powerful physique dominating her as she lay breathlessly beneath him, feeling like the very earth itself trembled.

"Damn! Damn!" he exploded.

"Oh, God!" she screamed, enjoying her powerful orgasm pulling him deep inside her, longing for everything he had to give.

Several thrusts later, Adams pulled out and rolled over, breathing heavily. "Damn, that was good!" he gasped. "What'd you think?"

Ruby lay catching her breath, enjoying the euphoric afterglow. "It was wonderful," she sighed, trying to remember the last time she had been so aroused.

Adams laughed. "Anything else?"

"Your...thing...it's so white."

"Yeah, they shipped it that way from the factory."

Ruby giggled, luxuriating in the giddy sense of well-being flowing through her body. Here was a "big man," the kind she had always dreamed about—a man who saw what he wanted and took it. There was something intriguing about that—a powerful, breathtaking, intoxicating aphrodisiac that made her body ache for more.

Then a scornful smile came to her face, thinking of Sam running around after his young mulatto schoolteacher while she was having an affair with the most powerful white man in Suwannee County. The doctor was right—getting even *was* the cure for her depression.

"How many kids do you have?" she asked him. "I know you've got a girl named Laverne—I saw her the other day down at your office when I paid my bill. She has your black hair."

"That's her," he said fondly. "She married Warren Jernigan down at the Commercial Bank. We call him Billy."

"Isn't he the one who works with Thelma on the books down at your office?"

"Yeah, that's him," he said, glancing at his Timex. "Then there's Sonny, my boy. He's joining the Air Force."

Ruby sighed. "Sam Junior is in high school this year.... They sure do grow up fast."

"Ain't that the truth?" Adams agreed, getting up to go to the bathroom.

When he returned, he said, "Why don't you come down to the hospital dedication next week? It'd do you good to get out and get your mind off Sam for a while."

"Well, thank you, Doctor. I just might do that."

"I'll look forward to seein' you," he said, sitting on the side of the bed. "Mind tellin' me what that is you're wearin' 'round your neck?"

"It's something my grandmother gave me a long time ago," Ruby explained, holding the amulet out for him to see. "She told me her mother brought it with her from Africa."

"Looks almost like a little bottle you could put somethin' inside of."

"Yes," she said, pulling out a tiny stopper on top of the amulet. "It's a bottle carved out of ivory and made flat on the back to wear on a necklace. Grandma believed it had some kind of magical power."

Adams grinned, going over to the dresser to pull a vial of white powder out of his satchel. "Here," he offered, handing her the vial. "Take this. You can put a little of it in that thing around your neck and carry it with you until you need it."

"What is it?"

"I call it Tinker Bell dust. But it ain't from no fairy—it's real magic."

Ruby opened the vial. "It looks like powdered sugar."

Adams chuckled. "It's sweet, all right. Here, let me show you." Touching his finger to the powder, he held it up to her nose. "Sniff it up like snuff."

Ruby sniffed the powder.

"Now, remember," he said gently, waiting for the cocaine to take effect, "we ain't just business partners anymore—we're friends. Anytime you want some company, you just give me a call."

Suwannee County Hospital

The spicy aroma of barbecued chicken and baked beans floated over the grounds of the newly constructed Suwannee County Hospital, where an eager crowd sat in a sea of folding chairs. Several rows in front were draped with red, white, and blue ribbons, reserved for visiting dignitaries.

At the head of the crowd, in the center of the hospital's circular drive, a dais was draped with an American flag. To one side of the dais was a folded Confederate flag, discreetly taken down at the request of Senator Claude Pepper, the keynote speaker.

Stationed at critical points around the gathering, whirring Movietone cameras captured the event for distribution to motion picture theaters nationwide.

Most of the hospital building was completed, and the landscaping was established, with bountiful azaleas nestled beneath the graceful moss-laden branches of the ancient live oaks. The hospital's interior was another matter — the new X-ray machine and the air-conditioning unit for the operating room would not arrive for another three months.

The Suwannee High School band joined the Branford and Jasper High bands in "Way Down upon the Suwannee River," backing up a tenor from the First Baptist Church choir. Aside from a few coloreds shifting nervously at "Oh, darkies, how my heart grows weary," the crowd was caught up in the theme song of its beloved county.

Friday's *Suwannee Democrat* had urged everyone to bring side dishes to complete the county-sponsored feast, and now dozens of folding tables stood under the shade trees, laden with squash casseroles, baked sweet potatoes, corn on the cob, and fried okra.

Just before noon, the all-male chorus from the Negro agricultural college in Tallahassee, ascended the dais to give a soulful rendition of "God Bless America" while the men in the crowd held their hats to their chests, recalling a war that had ended only three years ago. Many of the women wept silently, mourning lost sons, brothers, and husbands. As the women dried their eyes and the last choir member left the dais, the Reverend Bixler stepped to the microphone to deliver the invocation.

"Dear Lord Jesus," he intoned, "bring us your blessings by using the men and women who will staff this hospital as your instruments to heal the sick and the wounded who will soon come through these doors. Bless us, O Lord, and these thy gifts, which we are about to receive from thy bounty, through Christ our Lord. Amen."

Following the prayer, the Reverend Bixler introduced Senator Claude Pepper.

"Brothers and sisters," Pepper began, "I am delighted to be with you as we gather here on this historic site. This land upon which we stand was once the site of the Florida Memorial College for Coloreds, sponsored by the Florida Baptist Institute in 1879. The building served in that capacity until only about ten years ago, when the college moved to St. Augustine, leaving this site available for our new hospital."

"And so it is, my friends," Pepper continued, "that we are gathered here to share in the dedication of this monument to modern medicine. We will be privileged to have an X-ray machine, allowing our physicians to look into the innermost workings of God's crowning achievement, and to have the disease-destroying power of modern drugs to save our children from the ravages of a host of dreaded diseases heretofore considered incurable."

Some fifteen minutes later, Pepper came to the end of his speech. "In conclusion, I want to say that we assure you that medical care will be given without regard to the ability to pay, in keeping with the intent of the Hill-Burton legislation."

The crowd applauded as the senator introduced Dr. Steele, surgeon general of the U.S. Public Health Service.

"Thank you, Senator Pepper," Steele began. "I'm pleased to be invited here today to your beautiful Suwannee County. I had the chance to drive in early yesterday from the airport in Jacksonville and was treated by the good senator to a fishing trip just a short drive north of here. Can't say I caught much, but I can say I will always remember the great Suwannee River with its beautiful banks of moss-draped oak trees and its friendly people, who greeted me as I walked through downtown Live Oak after our trip."

The Movietone cameras panned across the throng of cheering spectators.

When the applause subsided, Dr. Steele continued, "I am proud to say that this hospital is the first in the nation to be funded by a partnership between the federal, state, and local governments under the

Hospital Survey and Construction Act, more popularly known as the Hill-Burton Act. Of the total cost of $295,000 to build and equip the hospital, the federal government is contributing $89,667.05."

"Finally, folks," Steele concluded, I want to assure your friend and mine, Senator Claude Pepper, that I will convey to my colleagues in Washington that the good folks down in Suwannee County still believe in 'hell, calomel, and the Democratic Party."

The crowd erupted in rebel yells when the doctor ended his speech and handed the federal check to J. E. Straughan, the governor's executive secretary, first in the line of state politicians to speak at the event.

After Straughan came speeches from representatives of both houses of the state legislature, Suwannee County officials, the mayor of Live Oak, and finally, Cary Hardee, a former governor and the president of Live Oak's Commercial Bank. Each speaker received the check from his predecessor and held it up for the crowd to see.

In the audience, an old man watching the seemingly endless procession of politicos relaying the check from the federal government turned to his friend and said, "After all them politicians get through pawin' that check, there ain't gonnah be 'nough left to buy a nickel Hershey bar."

"You got that right, Zeke!" his crony agreed, spitting a wad of tobacco onto the ground beside him.

When the politicians finished their speeches, Harold Gilmore, the state representative from Suwannee County, stood up. "Before I introduce our next speaker," he said, "I want to remind all of you to attend the free showing of Our Home Town, downtown at the Alimar Theatre. It's a movie about Live Oak, its history, its commerce, and its people. For those of you who saw the film being made in the last couple of months, look out—you just might find yourself in it. Anyway, why not go on down, get out of the heat, and watch this uplifting film, sponsored by the Live Oak Chamber of Commerce—I did mention it's free, didn't I?"

Laughter rippled through the crowd.

"Now, without further ado, I'd like to introduce our next speaker, Mr. Harold Schroeder, president of Blue Cross and Blue Shield of Florida."

"Thank you, Representative Gilmore," Schroeder said, taking the microphone. "What the gentleman didn't tell you is that I'm here to sell you health insurance."

The crowd laughed and applauded.

"At least, something like health insurance," Schroeder continued. "The big difference between us and them is that our sister companies, Blue Cross for hospitals and Blue Shield for physicians, are nonprofit service organizations. Since we don't make a profit, we pass more of the premium dollar back to you, the customer. To make a long story short, I've met with your new hospital board and signed up Suwannee County Hospital as the first hospital in Florida to participate in our plan."

"Thank you, Mr. Schroeder," Gilmore said, taking the microphone back during the applause. "I know all of you will want to pick up one of Mr. Schroeder's flyers here at the front table before you leave. Now, ladies and gentlemen, it is my pleasure to introduce you to one of our fine physicians, and current president of the Suwannee County Medical Society, Dr. Clifford Leroy Adams, Jr."

Florrie Lee, Adams's wife, along with daughter Laverne and her husband, rose with the crowd to give a thunderous ovation.

"Thank you," Adams called out to the crowd. "Thank you." After a few moments of applause, he raised his hands to calm his enthusiastic supporters. "Most of y'all know that I started out as a poor boy from Jasper, working hard to make his way through six long months of pharmacy school, and then all the way through medical school out in Arkansas with my wife and two kids to feed and nothin' but holes in my pockets. I stuffed cardboard in my shoes to walk to classes in the morning and to my job at the local drugstore every afternoon. Matter of fact," he said, lifting his foot to show his shoe sole to the audience, "you can see I've still got holes in my shoes from makin' house calls."

Tumultuous applause and wild cheering spread through the crowd as Ruby sat in the front of the colored section, daydreaming about her future with the biggest man in Suwannee County.

Chapter Twenty-Six

"Here we go, Miss Ruby," Beulah announced, struggling to bring a breakfast tray into her bedroom.

Ruby sat in bed, holding a mirror to freshen her lipstick. "How do I look, Beulah?" she asked.

"You looks just fine, Miss Ruby. You ain't gonna be in no beauty contest no how — Dr. Adams comin' out and you s'posed to be sick."

"Well, I'm feeling better now," she admitted, returning her mirror to the nightstand. "Especially with those shots he's been giving me. I'm beginning to feel a little down, though, like I'll need another one pretty soon."

"Hope you don't have to keep takin' them shots much longer — I don't know what they might be doin' to your system."

"Dr. Adams knows what's best for me," Ruby snapped.

"I guess you's right, honey...I guess you's right," Beulah agreed, recalling her sister's advice to mind her own business. "Better eat your breakfast 'fore it gets cold."

"I'm not hungry right now, Beulah."

Beulah's face fell. "Well, if you ain't gonna eat nothin', I'll take this on back downstairs and wait for the doctah. Be a sin to let good food go to waste."

Ruby carefully brushed her nails with her favorite Avon candy apple red nail polish. "You don't really need to bring me breakfast in bed anymore, you know."

"I know," Beulah admitted, picking up the tray on her way out of the bedroom. "I just wants to make sure you gets your nourishment, and you ain't been eatin' much lately."

"Was that the doorbell, Beulah?"

"I'll get it, Ms. Ruby," Beulah called back from the hallway.

"And one more thing, Beulah."

"Yes'm?"

"If it's Dr. Adams, be sure you don't disturb us."

"Yes'm," Beulah assured her, hurrying down the stairs to set the tray on the dining room table.

"He-e-e-y, kid," Adams said with a grin when she opened the door.

"Come on in, Doctah, Beulah giggled. How you doin' today?"

"Aw, I ain't so much," he beamed, stepping into the living room. "How's our patient this mornin'?"

"She's doin' a lot better today, Doctah."

Adams rolled his eyes toward the dining room table. "What's that over there smellin' so good?"

"That's Miss Ruby's breakfast. She say she ain't hungry."

"Well, maybe she ain't, but I'm starved."

"Let me grab this tray and take you on in the kitchen," Beulah suggested. "I gots you somethin' special."

Adams stepped ahead of Beulah to hold the kitchen door open. "That grits I smell?" he asked, taking a seat at the table.

Beulah ladled grits onto Adams's plate and returned to the stove to grab a frying pan. "That's not all I got."

"Good Gawd Almighty, Beulah! I can't remember the last time I had fish roe and grits."

"I caught me a mess of mullet down at the river last night," she announced proudly, placing two golden sacs of fish roe on his plate while she offered a silent prayer to ask forgiveness for the doctor's taking God's name in vain.

"You went out fishin' last night, Beulah?"

"Oh, yassuh. That be the best time to catch mullet—'specially with a full moon."

"You ain't afraid of the gators?"

"No, suh. Ain't no gator gonna tangle with my daddy's old shotgun."

"So what's the best way to catch mullet, Beulah?"

"You just leans out the boat and shines the lantern over the water and they jumps right in the net." Beulah gestured broadly to illustrate her technique.

Adams laughed. "Guess they ain't got much sense."

Beulah chuckled. "Good thing for us they ain't."

"You got that right," he agreed, cutting the fish roe to stir the tiny golden-yellow eggs into his grits. "By the way, where's Sam?"

"He be down in Fort Myers. If you ask me, I don't think Miss Ruby want him back yet no ways. She done pitched a hissy fit and had me throw all his things in that guest bedroom downstairs. She say he ain't sleepin' in her bed no mo'."

"You know how love goes," Adams replied between mouthfuls.

"Yassuh. I lived long enough to see all kinds o' things. One day two lovebirds be peckin' each others' eyes out, and the next they be puttin' sticks back in the nest and singin' like the Lawd give 'em good sense."

Adams laughed, standing up from the table. "Ruby better be careful—I just might decide to take you on over to my place."

"Oh, nossuh," Beulah returned with a dismissing wave of her hand, "I be here till they don't want me no mo'."

"Well, don't forget I asked," he said with a wink. "Anyways, you sure fry up the best fish roe I ever et."

"Glad you likes it," Beulah beamed.

"Well, guess I'd better go on up and see my patient," he said with a satisfied sigh.

"She's expectin' you," Beulah replied, clearing the table.

"Beulah, I won't be comin' by tomorrow," he said. "Seems like flu season hit early this year. Ruby don't need me to come by every day now, anyways—she's doin' just fine."

"Doctah," Beulah called, following Adams out of the kitchen, "I cain't tell you how much I 'preciates what you done for Miss Ruby. She ain't even complainin' 'bout her rheumatiz lately."

"Ain't nothin', Beulah," he called down from the staircase. "Just doin' my job."

She rolled her eyes toward heaven with a silent prayer. *Thank you, sweet Jesus, for that man. He sho' be a blessin' to this house.*

Chapter Twenty-Seven

On Thanksgiving Day, Adams drove into the courtyard of Blue's Lodge and parked beside Sim Howell's green Willys pickup. Getting out of his vehicle, he spotted a car with Columbia County tags, and another with Georgia plates.

Inside the lodge, he found LaVergne Blue and Sim Howell sitting around the fireplace with two other men he had never seen before.

"Happy Thanksgiving, Leroy," Blue called. "Come on over and join us. I want you to meet some fellas."

"Hey, LaVergne, hey, Sheriff," Adams greeted them, joining the men in front of the fireplace.

Howell blushed. "You know I ain't sheriff till next year, Doc."

"Hell, man, you won the election, didn't you?" He turned to the others. "You boys had your fill of turkey?"

"I took good care of 'em Leroy, right down to the pecan pie for dessert," Blue assured him. "Got you a plate covered back in the kitchen."

Blue turned to a tall, muscular man who, in spite of being in his early fifties, had a full head of black hair and boyish good looks. "Leroy," he said, "this is Jeff Elliott."

"Good to meet you, Jeff," Adams greeted, extending his hand.

Elliott stood up to deliver a beefy handshake. "Good to meet you, too, Doc," he boomed.

"Damn, son!" Adams exclaimed, nursing his hand. "Leave some of those fingers so I can do surgery."

"Sorry, Doc," Elliott apologized, looking like a little boy whose father had just scolded him.

Seeing the man's face, Adams laughed. "Hell, Jeff, I'm just jokin' with ya."

"Jeff here's a veteran law officer," Blue explained. "Spent his career up in Georgia, including serving as the commanding officer of the Georgia State Highway Patrol and as Governor Talmadge's personal bodyguard."

Adams fell into a chair. "That's quite a record, Jeff."

Elliott blushed. "After my doc told me I had to look after my blood pressure, I decided it was time to start lookin' for greener pastures.

Thought I might find somethin' down this way, where things are a little slower. You know, to keep me busy in my retirement. I told Governor Talmadge I wanted to move to Florida, then—bam!—just like that I get a call from Governor Warren's office, so here I am."

"So what are you doin' for Governor Warren?" Adams asked.

"Oh, he assigns me to odd jobs from time to time—gave me a badge and a gun and called me a 'special investigator.' First thing he done after I moved down here was tell me to drive over to Lake City and report to Mr. Black here."

"This is Keith Black," Blue said, turning to introduce a short, chubby, balding man with wire-rimmed glasses and a gray wool coat that looked overdue for a good pressing. "He's the state attorney."

"Good to meet you, Keith," Adams said, leaning over to shake his manicured hand and sizing him up as a stuffed shirt.

"Good to meet you, Doc. Governor Warren called over to my office and asked if we might find something in our neck of the woods to keep Jeff here busy. I called LaVergne and told him we might want to meet out here at the lodge tonight to put our heads together."

"Good idea," Adams agreed, pleased to be in the company of some of the major political players in the area. "Not much I can think of for Jeff to do, though."

"You got a radio in your car, Doc?" asked Elliott.

"A radio? Yeah, I got a radio, but it don't pick up much."

Elliott's face reddened. "What I meant to say was a two-way radio. Up in Atlanta we had a radio hookup with the gov's doc in case he needed him—he was prone to heart problems."

"Not a bad idea," Howell agreed. "It'd let us get in touch with you when we need you."

"Won't cost me nothin', will it?"

"Not a dime. Want me to help hook it up, Doc?" Elliott asked eagerly. "I'm pretty handy with that sort of thing."

"Why not? Seems like I ain't got nothin' to lose."

"Before you got here this mornin', Leroy," Blue said, "the boys and me were talkin' about your idea of runnin' for state senator in the next election."

Adams grinned. "You don't say!"

Black nodded, adjusting his necktie. "You come from a fine line of senators going all the way back to the Civil War. I think it'd be grand to continue that heritage."

Adams beamed. "Funny you should say that—I've been thinkin' the same thing."

Black continued, "I wish I'd thought to invite you to the Southern Governors' Conference down in Wakulla Springs this year. Had the most powerful names in the Southeast gathered down there to pass a resolution protesting Truman's civil rights initiative."

"Sorry I missed it," Adams replied, impressed with the man's political connections.

"The next big statewide event is scheduled right here on the Suwannee, over near Ellaville. Democratic senators are holding a convention to plan for the midterm election. I'll make sure you get an invite."

"I'd sure appreciate that, Keith—ain't gonna hurt to rub elbows."

"Won't be a problem introducing you, since Senator Pepper knew your grandfather."

Adams smiled at the mention of his grandfather, Frank Adams, who had retired after serving two terms as president of Florida's senate to become the president and third-largest stockholder, behind the Barnett brothers, in the Barnett Banks of Florida.

"In the meantime, I hear you and Sim here have pretty much taken over Sam McCollum's operation. I'd like to learn a little more about that."

Adams was stunned. Why did Blue invite this man out to meet him? Here was a state attorney asking about illegal gambling and liquor operations in an area where he was assigned to prosecute such activities.

"Relax, Doc," Black assured him, seeing the look on his face. "I've been trying to get a handle on bolita in Columbia County for a long time now. Liquor's still legal over there, so the only business is in moonshine where folks don't pay for the alcohol stamps."

Blue could see that his friend was still uncomfortable. "Like Keith explained to me before I asked him over here to meet you, he figures it's easier to control gambling if he's the one to call the shots—even if it's technically outside the law."

Adams could feel his heart slowing down, but made a mental note to ask Blue to warn him before he made any more surprise introductions.

"That's right," Black agreed. "If we had some sort of county or state lottery, then we wouldn't have to worry about folks breaking the law. But when folks vote gambling out, it tends to drive it underground where it's harder for us to keep an eye on."

Damn if he ain't a smart son of a bitch, Adams mused, stroking his chin. "Well, that's pretty much what the new sheriff and me decided — right, Sim?"

"Right, Doc," Howell replied, relieved to see that the state attorney was in camp.

"Then we're all agreed?" Black asked, monitoring the responses of the men around the room with an experience gained from selecting jurors.

"You can count on us, Keith," Adams assured him, thinking what a powerful ally this man could be. "Just let us know what we can do."

Black pulled out his pocket watch and squinted at it. "Glad to hear that, Doc. Now, I got to get on back to Lake City, but LaVergne or Jeff can get hold of me if you need me for anything. Sorry to have to run, LaVergne."

"Glad you could make it over here, Keith."

"I got to get on back, too," Elliott said, pushing back from the table.

When Black and Elliott had gone, Blue went to the kitchen to bring out the plate he had saved for Adams. "If this ain't enough, Leroy, there's more where that come from. I'll head on back to bring out a pitcher of tea."

"Thanks, LaVergne. Looks good. And don't forget some of that pecan pie."

"Saved a whole one just for you," Blue called back on his way to the kitchen.

Adams stuffed his mouth with turkey and dressing. "So, Sim, what do you know 'bout Black?"

"Smart man. Come up poor with a drunk for a father. Left home early and put hisself through college, then managed to marry well when he started out his law practice over in Lake City."

"Lucky bastard," Adams grumbled. "Ain't too many rich women out there."

Howell smiled. "Never did find me one."

"You talkin' about Keith? He earns pretty good money on his own," Blue shared on his way back from the kitchen. "Picks up property when folks get down on their luck and can't pay their taxes."

Adams stabbed a chunk of turkey. "Sounds like a good man to get to know."

Chapter Twenty-Eight

Thelma met Adams in the hallway coming out of the front white treatment room and said, "Dr. Adams, your uncle Claude is here."

Adams looked in the waiting room to see a thin elderly man stand up and shuffle toward him.

"Good to see you, Leroy," the oldster said with a smile.

Adams threw his arm around the old man's frail shoulders. "Uncle Claude! Good to see you! Thelma, why didn't you bring him on back to see me?"

"I'm sorry, Doctor. He didn't tell me he was your uncle until just a minute ago."

"He's shy that way, Thelma," Adams explained, patting his uncle on the back. "Come on back, Uncle Claude," he invited, ushering his uncle down the corridor into the first white treatment room. "What brings you to see me today?"

Claude put his hands in his pockets to conceal his trembling. "I'm sick, Leroy."

"Have a seat on the exam table so I can take a good look at you."

The pain on the old man's paper-white face was apparent as he managed to lift himself onto the exam table.

"What kind of medication you on?' Adams asked, noting the needle tracks on his arms while he tried to keep from trembling during the examination.

"I'm takin' laudanum for my back—sometimes a little morphine when the pain gets real bad."

Adams placed his stethoscope to the old man's chest to hear an irregular heartbeat and the telltale swishing sounds of heart valves worn out from old age. "It's been ages since I've seen you, Uncle Claude. Must've been at Granddaddy's funeral back when I was in medical school. Guess you didn't mention your back problem then."

"Got rear-ended by a drunk driver on the way home one weekend. My back ain't been the same since."

"Who's your doctor?"

"I ain't got one, Leroy—nobody'll see me."

Adams frowned. "Why the hell is that?"

They say I'm addicted to morphine so they won't give it to me anymore. The only way I can get it is on the black market over in Jacksonville."

"The hell with 'em!" Adams exploded, picking up a syringe and filling it with morphine. "We can't have you goin' 'round sufferin' like that."

The old man breathed a relieved sigh. "I'm mighty obliged, Leroy."

"What's family for, Uncle Claude?" Adams assured him, injecting the morphine in his upper arm.

"It costs a lot of money to keep up my medication," Claude continued. "And if I get caught buyin' the stuff on the street, I could get thrown in jail."

Adams stroked his chin, considering how he was going to handle the situation with his uncle. As a physician, he could obtain any quantity of narcotics, but he had to be careful to avoid gaining a reputation as the local supplier for addicts if he wanted to pursue his political ambitions.

Claude's eyes had the pitiful look of a hurt puppy. "I was hopin' you could help me out, Leroy."

Adams, hesitated, and then handed Claude a fistful of morphine vials. "You need to forget where you got these," he warned.

"Bless you, Leroy," he said gratefully, stuffing the little glass bottles in his pants pocket.

"Didn't Granddaddy leave you that stretch of farmland over near Lake City?" Adams ventured.

Claude looked up at his nephew. "Yes, he did. You remember, I was the only one of the nephews who didn't join in that competency hearing when the family tried to relieve him of his money and all those shares he held in Barnett Bank—nobody wanted it to go to that young nurse he married."

Adams chuckled. "I remember Granddaddy was hoppin' mad 'bout that."

He nodded. "Can't blame him. You remember how old Judge Adams cut right through all the fancy motions those Jacksonville attorneys filed for the rest of the family? Hell, they was as thick as a Sears Roebuck catalogue. Before the judge ruled anything, he called Uncle Frank back to his chambers for a few minutes and then come back out and declared him saner than any man he'd ever met."

Adams smiled and said, "Oh, I remember, all right."

"I stayed to congratulate Uncle Frank while the rest of the family flew out of the courtroom madder'n a nest of riled up hornets. They all hated Judge Adams's guts after that."

"I'll never forget. That was all Daddy could talk about back then when he found out most of the old man's money was goin' to that nurse of his — Granddaddy always was sweet on her."

Claude smiled. "Can't say I blamed him."

Adams sat on the stool beside the exam table. "Want me to get Thelma to bring you a Coke, Uncle Claude?"

"No thanks, Leroy. I ain't thirsty right now."

"So what are you doin' with that farm Granddaddy left you?"

"Guess it keeps me busier'n I need to be with this back of mine. Had to get the whole damn thing fenced in when the state passed that new law — too many motorists gettin' busted up runnin' into cows."

"Sounds like a burden, what with all the medical expenses you have right now," he ventured.

Claude nodded sadly. "Reckon it is…"

Adams looked thoughtfully down at the gray linoleum floor. "You know, Uncle Claude, what if you was to sign over the land to me and I made sure you had a lifetime supply of your medication — would that make life easier for you?"

Claude wrung his hands. "I don't know, Leroy. Your aunt Elizabeth'd be mighty sore at me — she wants that land to stay in the family."

Adams laughed. "It would still be in the family, Uncle Claude. And I don't plan to sell it if you sign it over to me. And you can stay out there all you want, same as if it was still in your name. And it'd be a hell of a lot less expensive — and dangerous — than gettin' your medicine on the streets. God knows what kind of shit they might be passin' off on you over there."

Claude's brow furrowed as he pondered the offer for a good half minute. "It's a deal, Leroy," he said. "Elizabeth and me don't have kids no how. And she's got plenty of cash tucked away from her side of the family, so she'll be fine if I kick the bucket before she does. I'll get my lawyer to draw up the papers."

"It's for the best, Uncle Claude," Adams assured him, accompanying him back to the waiting area. You think you can see your attorney first thing next week to get them papers signed?"

"Ain't no problem, Leroy."

"Thelma," Adams said loudly, "I want you to schedule an appointment with Uncle Claude at the end of next week so I can run a few tests and set him up on a medication schedule."

"Yes, Doctor," Thelma acknowledged, penning in the appointment.

"You take care of yourself, you hear?" Adams advised, patting his uncle on the shoulder.

"Thanks, Leroy."

At the back of the empty waiting room, Adams spotted a man in a three-piece charcoal gray suit and spit-polished brogue shoes. "Come on back, young man," he called, sizing him up as a salesman of some sort.

"Thanks, Dr. Adams," the man replied, picking up his trim black leather briefcase to follow the doctor down the hallway to his office.

"Pull up a chair," Adams offered.

"Thank you, Doctor. My name's Jason Simmons," the young man said, offering an eager hand.

Adams returned the firm handshake. "Glad to meet you, Jason."

Jason sat down and set his briefcase on his lap while Adams took a seat behind his desk.

"So, what can I do you for today, Jason?"

"Well, Dr. Adams, sir, I represent Blue Shield, the doctors' portion of Blue Cross and Blue Shield. I've been sent over by our Jacksonville office to ask you to join our network of participating physicians. We honor usual and customary fees as established by the Florida Medical Society, and we pay your billing within thirty days."

Adams leaned back and clasped his hands behind his head. "Sounds like a good idea. Problem is, son, I don't know anybody here in Live Oak who offers insurance to their employees. And I'm sure as hell none of the poor-assed dirt farmers can afford to pay for their own."

"We plan to change that," Jason explained with youthful enthusiasm.

"Who have you seen so far?" Adams asked, deciding to probe a little further into a possible source of extra income.

Jason smiled. "Dr. Black and Dr. Workman signed up this morning, and they both want to enroll their employees."

"'Zat so?"

"Yes, sir," he returned proudly. "After a small annual deductible, we offer our members eighty percent payment of claims for office visits and hospital admissions. And hospital emergencies are fully covered with no deductible."

"I see you been doin' your homework," Adams commented, considering that most of his hospital patients were emergency cases.

"I try, Dr. Adams," the young man said earnestly.

"Can a farmer buy insurance for his farm hands?"

"We insure any group of five or more workers who work fulltime for an employer, regardless of their occupation."

Adams rubbed his chin. "I just acquired a big farm north of Lake City, and I plan on hirin' on some help."

"Congratulations," Jason replied, eager to enroll his third physician of the day.

Adams stood up from his desk. "Why don't you leave the information up front with Thelma and let me look it over when I get a chance?"

Jason got up to shake hands. "Thanks, Doctor Adams," he said with a broad smile, pleased that he had enrolled another prospect.

Adams grinned and returned the handshake. "Be seein' you soon, Jason."

As soon as Jason left his office, Adams pressed the intercom button. "Thelma, give Keith Black a call. Ask him if he'll join me out at Blue's Lodge for supper next Friday night. Tell him I need him to look over some paperwork for me."

"Certainly, Doctor."

"Don't know what I'd do without you, sweetheart."

1949

Chapter Twenty-Nine

Seeing the Closed sign hanging out front well past the time Blue usually opened for business, Adams grabbed his satchel and stepped around to the front door of the adjacent cottage. "You in there, La-Vergne?" he called.

A feeble "Who's there?" barely penetrated the door.

"It's me—Leroy."

"Come on in, Leroy."

Adams opened the door to find the old man lying in bed. The entire cottage was one big room, with a small curtained-off bathroom beside the bed, and a combined kitchenette and dining area at the opposite end. A single table lamp illuminated walls of bookshelves filled with Civil War volumes and paraphernalia, and two gun racks with a half-dozen .22 rifles and several shotguns.

"Pull up a chair, Leroy," Blue invited.

Adams looked around the dimly lit cottage for an empty seat but found all of them littered with clothes and history books.

"Just throw everything on the floor, Leroy."

Adams took a stack of books from a ladder-back chair and set it on the floor. "You're gonna have to knock out a wall and add on a room if you collect any more Civil War stuff, LaVergne," he advised. He shivered and then looked at Blue's sunken face in the gloom, noting the old man's false teeth sitting in a glass container on a small table next to his bed. "It's cold in here," he said. "You ain't sick with the flu, are you?"

Tears rolled down Blue's cheeks. "No."

"Hell, LaVergne, I know somethin's the matter with you, so you might as well spit it out."

"I got a call from the highway patrol a little after midnight..." Blue's face froze, and his body heaved with the pitiful muffled sound that men make when trying to choke back their grief.

"Somebody die?" he asked, leaning forward in his chair.

Blue nodded, unable to answer.

"Somebody you knew?"

"My son. He was drivin' home from college..."

"Oh, my Lord! How'd it happen?"

"He was hit by a truck."

"Drunk driver?"

"Don't know yet. All I know is…" Blue went silent again, unable to utter the words that would make his son's death any more real to him than it already was.

Adams leaned over to hold his friend's hand while the old man closed his eyes, convulsing silently, his face contorted with grief.

When Blue finally opened his eyes, he looked up and said, "I'm an old man. When a man gets to be my age, he looks forward to having a son to carry on for him—to carry on whatever he started. For me, it's this lodge here, for whatever it's worth."

Adams nodded, giving Blue a chance to continue his grieving.

"Now all I got's a nephew—it ain't like he's my son." Blue started crying again.

Adams looked down toward the footboard of the bed to see the burled walnut butt of a shotgun sticking out from under the covers. "You want me to give you a shot to help you get to sleep?"

Blue nodded, feebly squeezing his friend's hand.

Adams rummaged in his bag, filled a hypodermic syringe with sodium pentothal, and then leaned over the bed to give the injection. "This should help you sleep through to the mornin'."

Blue looked up at his friend. "Thank you, Leroy. I can't take this anymore." Then the old man's eyes closed, and his sobs soon gave way to gentle snoring.

Pulling the covers up over Blue, Adams left his bed to search for matches in the kitchen. Lighting the kerosene stove, he rubbed his arms briskly. "Damn," he whispered, "guess I've got to stay here long enough to make sure the place heats up."

After warming his hands over the stove, he poked around the cluttered cottage until he found a file cabinet recessed into the bookcases near the kitchen. Opening one drawer and then another, he thumbed through the yellowed folders—which were in no apparent order—brushing off several silverfish from a file of crumbling newspaper clippings. At last, in the very back of the crowded third drawer, he found what he was looking for: a one-paged will, made out by Blue, leaving everything to his son. Looking over at the toothless old man with his mouth gaping open, he mused, *Guess he ain't got nobody to leave his place to now.* Carefully returning the file to its place, he quietly closed the file drawer.

Glancing at the angular lump beneath the quilt at the foot of the bed, Adams stepped over, lifted the covers, and slid out the shotgun, putting it back on its rack. Then, as he sat back down on the ladder back chair to settle in for the night, he looked at the pallor on the old man's sunken face. It was pretty clear that he had only a few years left to live.

Chapter Thirty

"Please come in, Sheriff," Ruby invited with a cordial smile, stepping aside for him to enter her home.

Sim Howell took off his hat and closed the door behind him. "Is Sam home, Ruby?"

"He's upstairs. Won't you please have a seat while I go up and get him?"

"Thanks, Ruby."

"May I get you something to drink," she offered.

"No, thanks," Howell returned, stepping to the fireplace to hold his hands out to the warmth of the glowing coals.

Upstairs, Ruby found Sam talking on the office telephone and scrawled a quick note to shove in front of him.

"Okay, Preacher," Sam said impatiently, "I'll get back with you tomorrow. Ain't nothin' we can do about it till then." Glancing down at Ruby's note, he hung up the phone to look questioningly at her.

She shrugged. "He didn't say."

Sam left the office with Ruby trailing behind him, wondering why the sheriff would come out to the house in the middle of the week.

"Good afternoon, Sheriff," Sam greeted Howell from the staircase.

"How's it goin', Sam?" he asked, turning around from the fireplace.

"I be just fine," Sam said, joining Howell at the fireplace to warm his hands.

"Why don't you and Ruby have a seat so I can talk with y'all for a few minutes?" Howell asked in a tone that sounded more like an order than a request.

Glancing nervously at Sam, Ruby took her place beside him on the sofa in front of the fireplace and looked up at Howell.

Howell folded his arms, adopting the intimidating stance and direct eye contact he had perfected as a prison guard. "Y'all know I got voted in 'cause I promised to run bolita and liquor outta the county. From what I hear, folks figured a prison guard was the kind of man they needed for the job."

Sam nodded nervously. It was obvious that the news was not going to be good.

"To cut to the chase, Sam," he blurted out, "the doc and me decided that you've got to leave town for a while."

"Yassuh. I understands that," Sam agreed, relieved to hear that the sheriff's demand was reasonable—nothing more than their usual charade to placate Wadsworth and defuse his editorial tirades against the evils of illegal liquor sales and gambling in an otherwise pristine county.

Realizing that he had not made his point, the sheriff said, "What I mean to say is that we want you to leave town for six to eight months or so, not just a week or two."

"Six months, you say?" he asked, hardly believing his ears.

"At least," Howard replied, holding his ground.

"That be a long time to be away from my kids, Sheriff."

Desperate thoughts raced through Sam's head. *Can't the sheriff and me come up with a plan to hide the liquor and gambling operations better? Or can't I leave for just a month or two like in the past?*

"I ain't got no choice, Sam," he explained before Sam could voice his thoughts. "We got to convince everybody that I've run Bolita Sam outta town for good."

Sam sat stunned, while Ruby braced herself, hoping that the sheriff's request was the only message he had to deliver. God forbid that he was working up to telling them they had to close their business down.

"Since Doc knows your men, and Ruby keeps the books, ain't nothin' gonna change. Besides, I'm sure your brother can use your help down in Fort Myers."

"That be a long time, Sheriff," Sam repeated, still unable to quite comprehend what he was being told to do—and why.

"You can still drive to Zuber and stay with your family, and Ruby can meet you down there with the kids. Hell, you can even drive out to your farm and stay with your family—just keep the heck out of Live Oak for a good while."

"You knows I'se gonna do what you say," Sam assured him.

"I don't like bringin' you the bad news any more than you want to hear it, Sam," Howell assured him, his voice softening. "I have a family of my own, so I know what this means."

"I sure 'preciates that, Sheriff."

"It ain't so bad, no how. Mr. Black asked the doc and me if we'd help him set up bolita over in Lake City like you did here in town. You can spend a month or two over there to help us get organized, and Ruby can drive the kids over to visit."

"That sound good, Sheriff," Sam said, encouraged by the possibility of expanding his business. "Do that mean I'll get a share?"

"If Ruby keeps the books and you set things up, Doc told me you could keep ten percent of the take."

Sam reflected that 10 percent, compared to the 20 he netted now, seemed paltry, but still, it was extra income. "That be fine with me, Sheriff."

Howell donned his hat. "Then I can count on you to leave town this weekend?"

"Ain't no problem, Sheriff—ain't no problem at all," Sam assured him, standing up to walk the sheriff to the door.

Ruby, still a bit stunned, remained seated, thinking how strange it was that she would not miss Sam during his exile.

Keith Black's Cabin
Private Island, Gulf of Mexico

The pilot moored the forty-foot cabin cruiser, and then jumped from the bow onto the dock to help the passengers ashore. "Watch your step, gentlemen," he cautioned. "The water's calm this afternoon, but you still need to be careful."

Keith Black stood on the wood stairs above the dock beside a flickering gas pole lamp, watching his guests make their way ashore, silhouetted against a horizon fired with sunset crimson and gold. "Good evening, gentlemen. Glad you could come. When everybody's dockside, we'll head on up to the cabin."

"Where exactly are we?" Adams asked, grabbing his satchel to join Black on the stairs.

"Welcome to my island."

Adams was incredulous. "You own the whole damn island?"

"'Fraid so," Black chuckled, taking Blue's arm to help him steady himself on the stairs.

"Good Gawd Almighty!" Adams blurted, looking down the long stretch of sandy beach. "That's one hell of a lot of waterfront. How much does a place like this cost?"

"Picked the land up for taxes, Doc—can't say the same for the house."

Sim Howell, Jeff Elliott, Louie Wadsworth, Adams, and Blue labored up the steep stairs to a sandy trail that led into dense palmettos and Mexican palms. When the men stepped off the wood and onto the sandy pathway, the ground seemed to come alive beneath their feet.

"What in hell are them things?" Adams asked, looking down to see thousands of sand-colored creatures scurrying sideways through the fallen fronds and into their burrows.

"Fiddler crabs," Black called back over his shoulder. "They won't eat ya, Doc—least ways not all at once."

"Funny little things," Adams commented, his shoe obliterating one of the little creatures beneath a sign that read, "Watch for Snakes."

Adams looked cautiously to either side of the trail. "You got snakes out here?" he asked nervously, suddenly aware that he had no antivenin in his medical kit.

"Not that I know of, Doc. I had my groundskeeper put rabbits out in a cage and then shoot the rattlers that ate 'em—snakes can't crawl back out of the cage with that kind of load in their belly. Since then he's shot a dozen rattlers, and we haven't seen any more in the last couple of months."

"Got to do that out at my place," Blue reflected. "One of my renters seen a diamondback the other day."

"When we get to the house, y'all go on in where it's air-conditioned," Black suggested. "It's still too hot this time of year out on the porch, and the no-see-ums are small enough to get through the screen and chew the daylights out of your legs."

"Thanks, Keith," Blue said with a relieved sigh. "My heart won't take much of this heat nowadays."

About fifty yards down the winding trail, a shiny tin roof appeared above the palmetto thickets. Around a shard turn a few steps ahead, the palmettos thinned to reveal a rustic log cabin with a wraparound screened porch, nestled between clusters of moss-draped scrub oak and slash pines.

Black held the door open for the men to enter. "Front door's un-locked," he said, "so y'all go on through to the living room and make yourselves at home."

On the porch, lined with a row of rocking chairs that ended with a swing, Blue noticed a strong lemony scent blending with the sultry evening breeze. "What's that smell, Keith?"

"Citronella candles—we keep 'em lit when we're here, to run off the mosquitoes. We don't get too many what with the salt water, but they still breed anywhere they can find an old tin can with rainwater in it."

The interior of Black's cottage was open with high vaulted ceilings finished in rough-hewn cypress, valued for its beauty and its resis-tance to termites. The walls were tongue-and-groove knotty pine, and the floors were golden oak planking covered with multicolored latch-hook rugs. Trophies of tarpon and swordfish hung on the walls alongside photographs of Black and his family enjoying their island retreat. Above a window on the far side of the room hung a Confeder-ate flag enshrined in a glass case.

In the middle of the room were two large folding tables draped with white linen and laden with pitchers of iced tea and a big tray of sweet rolls.

"Please have a seat, gentlemen," said Black, pulling out a chair for Blue. "Jeff told me y'all had your fill of fried oysters and shrimp back in Panacea, but if anybody gets hungry, I've got fresh sandwiches and beer in the fridge."

"Nice place you got here, Keith," said Blue, admiring the Confederate flag. "That come down in your family?"

"Came down through my wife's family," Black announced proudly.

"It's good you preserved it like that—gives your family something to remember their heritage," he said, taking a seat next to Adams.

While the men settled into their seats and helped themselves to the refreshments, Black opened his briefcase on the table and pulled out a stack of legal documents. "Gentlemen," he began, "as y'all know, we're here for a serious matter involving our friend Dr. Adams. I had a chance to speak with some of you about the problem, but I need to begin our meeting by asking if anyone has any questions."

"I did have one question before you begin, Keith," Wadsworth volunteered, pulling a pad and pen out of his shirt pocket and adjusting his bifocals. "Exactly why has the VA got its drawers in a bunch anyway?"

Black handed a subpoena across the table to Wadsworth. "A federal grand jury has indicted Dr. Adams on five counts of fraud against the Veteran's Administration, alleging filing false claims in anticipation of receiving financial remuneration. As you can see, he has been subpoenaed to appear in federal court in Tampa on the twenty-second of July."

Wadsworth studied the subpoena and jotted down notes.

"What does the VA have for evidence?" Howell asked, reaching for a sweet roll.

"They have the claim forms, signed by Dr. Adams, and the word of the patients whose names appear on those forms, claiming they've never seen the doc—not even once."

"Doc, what do you think happened here?" Wadsworth asked, returning the subpoena to Black.

"Some kind of mix-up is all I can figure," retorted Adams, visibly affronted by the whole affair. "There are days I see upwards of a hundred patients—I can't swear who I saw on any one day without looking at the records."

"I think people can understand that," Blue assured his friend. "For my part, I just wondered what in tarnation would motivate these men to swear they had never been treated by you. This whole thing's startin' to smell like a conspiracy of some kind."

"My concern is how it'll all look to the jury," Black explained, ignoring the old man's comment. "What we have here are veterans—simple country folks mostly—swearing they've never even seen the doc. Unless we can produce some hard evidence that Dr. Adams did see them—you know, prescriptions or whatever—then it's their word against his. And without any evidence on our part, it's just 'he said, they said' and everything will ride on how we pitch the whole thing to the jury."

"I don't write prescriptions for folks way out in the woods," Adams objected, looking both injured and annoyed. "Most of 'em call me out to their houses 'cause they got no car in the first place—they sure as hell can't get to no drugstore. I always carry a whole damn pharmacy with me and give 'em what they need right there on the spot."

Black stroked his chin. "That's good to know, Doc, but what I'm talking about is crafting an image of you as a physician that is unassailable, regardless of the testimony. In the courtroom there's only one truth: the truth the jury believes."

"Amen to that," Elliott concurred, chewing thoughtfully on a bear claw.

"That's why I want to stay on top of the jury," Black continued. "LaVergne, you're planning on getting down there ahead of us, right?"

Blue grimaced and stretched his frail legs out on the plank floor in front of him. "I sure am. I plan to settle into the Hillsboro Hotel and reserve a whole floor for whoever you get to come down and testify for Leroy."

"Mind if Jeff uses one of those rooms as a base to investigate the potential jurors? I think that'd give us a leg up."

"Use the rooms however you like—I'll pay for 'em as long as it takes."

"Thanks, LaVergne. I'll have Jeff communicate by radio with Sim here to fill us in on what he finds out."

"Who are you goin' to call for character witnesses?"

"I'll start with every man in this room. Louie, you know the doc volunteers his time to the Guards."

"He sure does," Wadsworth confirmed. "Every man who comes into my unit gets a physical from Dr. Adams."

"Just about all my patients would testify, too," Adams volunteered, relieved to see his friends rallying around him.

"How many patients did you say you see in any given day, Doc?" Black asked.

"Between fifty and a hundred, including hospital admissions, house calls, and office visits. Don't take more'n a couple of minutes to see most of 'em."

Black jotted the figure on his legal pad. "Make sure you have your office get me a list of all the patients you've seen over the past six months. I'll call some of them into my office and determine who'd be the best witnesses. By the way, are most of them colored or white?"

"Good Gawd Almighty, Keith, you know most of my patients are colored. How the hell do you expect those poor bastards to get down to Tampa?"

"I'm sure we can arrange transportation and find some place to house them down in Tampa for the trial," Black assured him. "Besides, knowing they must worship the ground you walk on, they'd sleep out on the sidewalks if they had to."

"Who's the judge in the case, Keith?" asked Wadsworth.

"Fellow by the name of William Barker."

"Know anything about him?"

A hint of irritation crossed Black's face. At heart, he despised the press, but it was apparent that he was exercising the same kind of control he had gained from years of courtroom appearances. Besides, Wadsworth could be a powerful ally. "Just that he can't afford bad publicity with the election coming up, so he's going to be pretty darn careful about public opinion—and coloreds are a good part of his voting base, from what I hear."

Wadsworth nodded reflectively. "I think I'll drive down there to talk with my fellow journalists at the *Tampa Tribune* before the trial, to fill them in on a few things."

"Excellent," Black replied, pleased to have the political support he needed to tip the scales of justice in his client's favor. "We could use a sympathetic press."

"What about the witnesses for the government?" Blue asked.

"I was just getting to that," Black explained, positioning his reading glasses. "Quinton E. Daughtry and Curtis A. Bass are the primary witnesses. Looks like they selected these men during their investigation because both of them claimed they hadn't been treated by a doctor at all during the time the claims were submitted—that way we can't suggest they might have been confused about which doctor treated them."

"How much money is involved here?" asked Wadsworth.

"It's hard to tell exactly, Louie. We're going to find out during discovery, but I spoke with Arthur Steed, the assistant U.S. attorney down in Orlando, and he says it's less than two hundred dollars."

"Good Gawd Almighty," Adams sputtered, jostling his iced tea and spilling it on his white shirtfront. "You mean the feds are gonna waste taxpayers' money holdin' a trial over less'n two hundred dollars?"

"It's not the money, Doc," Black explained. "The feds have to show that Uncle Sam's watching out for thieves with their hands in the federal till. Since the vets came home, the government's spent untold millions on VA claims, some of 'em bogus, and they have to answer to the inspector general for that sort of thing. Since the VA can't take on a New York doctor with those fancy Harvard Jew lawyers they got up there, they go peckin' around in deadwood to see if they can find a poor country doctor to hang out to dry. They're lookin' to parade your head on a stick, to put the fear of God in the heart of anybody who's even thinkin' about cheatin'."

"Well, I sure as heck ain't gonna sit around and watch 'em crucify Leroy," Blue retorted, raising his glass of iced tea to his friend.

Adams leaned back in his chair and clasped his hands behind his head. "Damn, boys, I don't know what I'd do without friends like y'all."

Chapter Thirty-Two

Mrs. Workman, a diminutive woman with a halo of tightly permed silver-gray hair framing a gracefully aging face, hovered over her husband seated at the kitchen table.

"Would you like some more gravy on your potatoes, dear?"

"I've got enough gravy in my arteries to kill off a platoon," the elderly physician snapped while he finished his black-eyes peas. "Can't believe that stuff's good for you."

"I'll take that as a no, then," she concluded with a smile, ladling red-eye gravy onto her mashed potatoes, unaware that some of it ran over the edge of her plate to drip onto the bright red-and-white checkered oilcloth. "Have you heard from Dr. Adams?"

The elderly physician sipped his iced tea. "I called down to Tampa last night and spoke to Leroy. He says they've got a whole floor of the Hillsborough Hotel filled with witnesses for him, and only four witnesses for the government. He told me Cary Hardee's reputation as a former governor impressed the judge, from what he could tell. He also said that even if he's convicted, Senator Pepper has talked with President Truman about a pardon."

"That's good," Mrs. Workman replied, spooning more black-eyed peas onto his plate. "I just can't understand what gets into the government to pick on a fine Christian like Dr. Adams. There's not a man in this country can lay claim to ministering to the needs of the poor more than he has."

"Don't I know it!" her husband grumped, raking the gravy off his potatoes. "I can't keep up with his patients in the office and down at the hospital—had to call Price in to help."

"Did Dr. Adams say when they expected the trial to end, dear?"

"Well, it started last Friday, and Leroy seems to think they might wrap things up by this afternoon."

"Thank goodness! It's been almost a full week. Lord knows we need Dr. Adams back so you can get some rest," she said, getting up from the table to take a pitcher of iced tea from the counter.

"Rest?" Workman snapped. "You were the one who wanted me to go back to work in the first place."

"That's true, dear," Mrs. Workman agreed, filling his glass with tea. "But not to kill yourself—whatever would I do without you?"

"Did you like that contraption I brought home?" Workman asked.

"Oh, this?" Mrs. Workman replied, picking up a miniature wooden house from the end of the yellow formica counter. "It's lovely, dear, but for the life of me, I can't figure out what it is."

"Here," Workman offered, "lemme show you." He set the little wooden house on the table, released a small pin, and one of the two miniature doors on the front swung open for a little boy in a yellow raincoat to pop out.

"Well isn't that wonderful!" Mrs. Workman exclaimed.

"That means it's gonna rain," Workman explained.

"Why, I Suwannee!" Mrs. Workman chuckled, standing up to rub her husband's shoulders and give him a peck on the cheek. "What a clever little gadget. I'll have to hang it up in the kitchen window by my African violets and show it to my bridge club."

"Darn!" Workman exclaimed, hearing the telephone ring. "Just when I was beginnin' to think about gettin' sweet on you."

"Hold that thought, dear," Mrs. Workman suggested with a coy smile, crossing to the telephone table. "Hello? ... Oh, my goodness, Dillard, it's Dr. Adams!"

Workman rushed to the phone. "Hello, Leroy?"

"Hey, Dillard. The bastards lost their case. We won!"

"Thank the good Lord!" Workman exclaimed, turning to his wife. "Honey, Leroy won!"

"Praise the Lord," Mrs. Workman rejoiced, clasping her hands.

"Is that music I hear in the background, Leroy?" Workman asked.

"Yeah. LaVergne took us all out to this fancy restaurant down here to celebrate."

"When are you drivin' back up here?" Workman asked, pressing the receiver to his ear to hear over the background music.

"Keith wants some of us guys to stop by his beach place to spend the weekend. Everybody else'll head straight back tomorrow mornin'."

"Well, I for one will be darn glad to see you. I ain't no spring chicken, you know."

"I really 'preciate what you've done, Dillard."

"Well, like they say, 'They also serve who stand around and wait.'"

"Please say hello to that pretty little lady of yours for me."

Workman turned to wink at his wife. "I'll give her that hug for you, Leroy. Ya'll enjoy your party, now...and have fun at the beach this weekend."

Adams hung up the telephone in the bright orange, yellow, and blue Spanish-tiled lobby of Ybor City's Columbia Restaurant to return to the darkly paneled private banquet room, where he was greeted by Sonny standing at the head of a table seating twenty supporters, proposing a toast. "Here's to Dad!"

"To the doc!" everyone cheered to a symphony of clinking glasses while Adams threw his arm around his strapping teenage son.

Taking a seat beside his wife, Florrie Lee, his daughter, Laverne, and her husband, Billy, Adams grinned, surveying the banquet table laden with steaming arroz con pollo, mounds of freshly baked Cuban bread, and pitchers of sangria with thin paper-thin slices of orange and lemon floating on top. "Looks like they brought mine out. Hope they have some more back in the kitchen for the rest of you."

"Y'all know he ain't foolin'," Blue cracked, starting a round of laughter.

Strolling musicians entered the room, dressed in colorfully embroidered black Spanish tuxedos and white shirts girded at the waist with scarlet red sashes to serenade the jovial diners with a slightly off-key "Vaya con Dios."

Blue laughed over the music. "I can still see their faces when Thelma got up there and testified that Leroy saw up to a hundred patients a day, most of 'em too poor to put food on their tables, much less pay their doctor bill."

"Those two little peckerwoods better go climb back in their holes," Howell crowed. "Ain't nobody gonna talk to 'em in Suwannee County."

Adams beamed, washing a mouthful of bread and butter down with sangria.

Former governor Hardee was next to share his favorite moment in the trial: "And what about when Louie Wadsworth got up there and told everybody that the doc was entitled to charge a dollar a head for almost five hundred National Guardsmen he sees every year, yet all he'll take is an invite to their annual banquet?"

"Yeah," Blue agreed. "If there was ever a better witness against the doc bilking the government, that put the lie to 'em—shoot, they should be givin' the doc a medal."

"Two hundred dollars!" Adams crowed, wiping his mouth with a napkin. "Two hundred dollars versus millions of dollars of big government waste by those crooks up in D.C."

"That's right," Blue chimed in, passing more arroz con pollo to his friend. "With all that paperwork they put on Doc, they oughta be ashamed to squabble over a little bookkeeping error like that. Hell, he'd of gladly paid it back out of his own pocket if they'd just asked him!"

While everyone celebrated the outcome of the trial, Blue passed out Romeo y Julieta oscuros. "I want everybody to know I got these from a friend who brought 'em back from his trip to Havana last week. And I'm here to tell you, they ain't your usual dime cigars."

Adams glowed. "Thanks, LaVergne. See you got my favorite: Romee owed and Julie et."

Amid the laughter, Adams stood to raise his glass. "I want to propose a toast!"

"Here, here!" Blue cried, tapping his wineglass with his spoon.

"To all the fine citizens of Suwannee County, my loyal friends and supporters, who I owe a deep debt of gratitude, I want to offer this toast—may you all live to be a hundred and enjoy the best of health, wealth, and happiness!"

1950

Looking past Thelma into the white waiting room for his next patient, Adams spotted a young blonde woman sitting near the entrance. *Damn!* he thought. *What a pair of tits.* "Thelma," he called distractedly, "would you come in here for a minute?"

Thelma left her desk to meet him in the hallway.

"Who the hell is that gal?"

Thelma rolled her eyes. "That's Evelyn. She's applying for the position you advertised on the radio. Of course, you'd be a fool to hire her."

Adams smirked. "What's the matter, brown sugar? You jealous?"

Thelma shot him a disapproving glance. "I'll tell her to come on back. You ain't gonna be worth a hill of beans till you got your eyes full." Tossing him her best you-know-I'm-right-but-you're-gonna-do-it-anyway look over her shoulder, she huffed back to the waiting room.

Adams stood in the hallway watching Thelma call Evelyn, mesmerized by the tight red knit sweater that clung revealingly to her full, gorgeous breasts. When she brushed a wavy lock of blonde hair to the side and flashed her sapphire blue eyes, she could have been one of the pinups he kept locked in his desk drawer along with a jar of petroleum jelly. *Good Gawd Almighty,* he thought, *please be eighteen.*

At the entrance to the hallway, Evelyn extended a demure hand and cooed, "Dr. Adams! I've so-o-o looked forward to meetin' you."

He took her soft, supple hand. *Strawberries and cream,* he mused, admiring her smooth young skin and inviting glossy red lips. *I'll bet she tastes like strawberries and cream.* "Thelma tells me you're lookin' for a job."

Evelyn smiled, her sensuous moist lips parting to reveal a perfect set of teeth. "Well, yes, Doctor, I am."

Adams felt a stirring in his groin. *Damn! Thelma's right. Have to be crazy as a bedbug to hire this gal.* "Why don't you come on back to my office so we can talk."

"Thank, you, Doctor," the young woman replied, following him down the short hallway into his office. "Oh, I just love your furniture. It's so...so masculine."

"Have a seat," Adams offered, anxious to retreat behind his desk to hide the growing bulge straining against his zipper.

Evelyn sat and crossed her silk-smooth legs, feeding his growing lust.

"So," Adams began, trying to maintain his composure in spite of his pinup girl sitting across from him. "What can you tell me about yourself?"

"Well, I'm seventeen, and I'm lookin' for work in a doctor's office after school until I graduate from Suwannee High.... I want to go to college to be a nurse."

"A nurse?" Adams reflected, wondering if she had the brains to match her perfect body.

"Yes, sir. I told myself that with summer comin' up and school bein' out, it'd be a good time to start workin' in a doctor's office to save up for college."

"Do you think you'd faint if you saw somebody bleed?" he challenged.

"No, sir, I wouldn't," she answered with the greatest of self-assurance. "I help my mama kill chickens every fall and I seen her cut off her finger with the axe. I stayed real calm while we carried her to the hospital."

Adams was captivated by the young woman's childlike innocence and the girlish lilt in her voice, attractively packaged in a decidedly grown-up body. "You mind watchin' somebody get sewed up?" he asked, deciding to raise the ante.

"That's what they done to mama. I didn't faint then, so I don't think I'd faint if I seen you sew somebody up—long as it ain't me, I mean."

Adams grinned, imagining suckling her luscious, taunting young breasts.

She grew uncomfortable with the pause that followed. "Please give me a chance, Dr. Adams," she pleaded, her lower lip trembling as tears welled up in her eyes. "I'll work really hard for you."

"You got yourself a job, Evelyn," Adams blurted out, intoxicated by the growing ache in his groin.

She jumped to her feet, squealing like a teenager at a pajama party. "Oh, thank you, Doctor," she gushed. "Thank you ever so much."

"Ain't nothin', Evelyn," he returned, captivated by her youthful enthusiasm. "Now, you just go on back out there to see Thelma. Tell her to give you the paperwork—and tell her I said you can start work first thing next Monday after you get out of school."

"Yes, sir," she gushed. "I can't tell you how happy I am."

"Would you be kind enough to flip that latch and close the door for me on your way out?" he asked. "I've got some business to take care of."

Evelyn gave a coy little wave underscored with a bat of her fake eyelashes, locking the door behind her.

When he heard the door click shut, Adams unlocked his pinup drawer, thinking, *What the hell have I gone and done now?*

Chapter Thirty-Four

Ruby sat in the colored waiting room, anxiously waiting for Adams to come out and call for his next patient.

It was mid-November, and almost two years had passed since they began their relationship. By now she knew that her marriage was purely one of convenience, not love. When Sam hit her, it had been one thing, but when he lied to her about his ongoing affair with Lucy — after swearing to give up womanizing — that had been the final straw. She had worked too hard to build their business and raise a family to be cast aside for a whore who kept one hand in Sam's pants and the other in the family till.

Ruby's affair with Adams had been exciting, as well as an instant cure for her depression brought on by Sam's betrayal. And having the biggest big man in Suwannee County, destined to be a state senator like the rest of the men in his family, had filled the void that Sam had left. But now, two years into her affair, she knew that something else was missing.

Separate bedrooms and separate lives did not make for a real family, the kind of family she had always dreamed about. A family was a husband, a wife, and children — not a man and a woman sleeping in separate bedrooms and leading separate lives, with their children bouncing between the two of them.

Now, aside from a broken marriage, the unthinkable had happened — she had missed her period last month and was past due this month, even though the last time she and Sam had slept together was on her birthday last August. The thought — the horror — of having a mulatto child was something she had not planned on and was not prepared to accept. Besides, he knew that Sam would kill her if she had a child by another man.

Oh God! she prayed silently, rolling her tear-filled eyes toward heaven. *Don't let this happen to me. Just give me another chance and I'll stop this craziness.*

Wiping the tears from her eyes, she rehearsed what she would say when she got in to see Adams. Suddenly, he appeared at the door. "Ruby," he called, "go on in the treatment room. I'll be in there in just a minute."

After Ruby entered the colored treatment room, Adams saw Evelyn coming out of a white treatment room and stepped behind her to give her a playful pat on the bottom.

"Why, Doctor!" Evelyn squealed, batting her eyelashes.

Opening the door to the colored exam room, Adams grinned, beside himself with desire.

Inside, he found Ruby standing by the exam table. "You here for a treatment?" he asked.

"Yes...but I came down to tell you..."

"Spit it out, woman, I don't have all day to fool with you."

She looked down at the cold gray linoleum floor and stroked her stomach. "I came down to tell you I might be pregnant."

"I knew it!" he exclaimed, sitting down on the stool beside the exam table with a proud grin on his face. "I can always tell."

Ruby played with her wedding band and then looked up with pleading eyes. "You don't understand. Sam and me...you know, we haven't had sex for some time now. If I'm pregnant, it has to be your baby."

Adams smirked. "So?"

Her face hardened. "I have to have an abortion."

Adams lunged up, grabbed her arm and backed her up to the exam table. "The hell you say! You kill that baby and I'll kill you."

Ruby fell onto the exam table, terrified. "But, Doctor! You don't understand!"

"You heard what I said, woman," he snarled. "I want all my babies—colored or white, it don't make no difference."

"But what about Sam?" Ruby pleaded. "He'll know it's not his when it comes out light."

"You don't worry yourself about Sam. I'll take care of him when the time comes."

Ruby sat up on the table, her eyes widening. "You're not going to..."

"Whatever put a crazy idea like that in your head, woman? I'm just talkin' about tellin' him the way things are. Hell, you already know he's got at least one woman on the side."

"I never meant to get pregnant," Ruby sobbed. "I thought that Sam and me might..."

"You need somethin' to help you calm down, Ruby," Adams interrupted, opening the pharmaceutical cabinet.

"I know," she agreed, rolling up her sleeve for her usual injection of heroin.

Instead, he handed her a bottle of sugar pills. "These'll keep you relaxed. Take one every time you start to worry—we don't want you gettin' upset now that you're pregnant."

"Thank you, Doctor," she said in a tone of resignation, taking the bottle. "What about my shot?"

Adams's face clouded. "I don't want you goin' crazy on me about this, so I'll tell you up front: I have to give you somethin' that won't hurt the baby—I ain't about to have that. You can come down and get more of them pills anytime you need 'em."

Her face fell. "But, Doctor…"

"There ain't no 'but' to it, Ruby. I'll ask Dr. Workman to follow up the pregnancy. I don't think it'd be a good idea for me to be your doctor right now."

Ruby looked terrified. "But what about my shots?"

"You deaf or somethin' woman? I already told you, I ain't givin' you no more till the baby comes. I'll give a call to my cousin; he's a doctor at Little-Griffin Hospital in Valdosta—it'd probably be better if you delivered the baby up there instead of down here."

"What about at my house like you did the last time?"

"I need better control over the situation, Ruby. When Sam's had a chance to see the baby, we'll know how he takes it…. I'll handle it from there."

"Whatever you say, Doctor," she replied meekly, hanging her head.

Pleased to see her spirit broken, he unbuckled his belt and peeled his boxer shorts down with his pants. "Glad to hear you say that, Ruby. Now, lay back and pull them panties down."

Chapter Thirty-Five

Adams sat at his desk, holding the telephone receiver to his ear with his left hand while signing a stack of insurance forms with his right. "That's what I got on my mind, Keith—I want to buy a place I can turn into a boarding house. Something I can pick up for back taxes—cheap."

"You might be in luck, Doc. There's an old two-story Victorian right downtown here in Lake City. Old lady without any relatives had a stroke and had to be put in the county nursing home. You can pick the house up for a song."

Adams poured himself a handful of roasted peanuts from a jar sitting on his desk. "How much is this song gonna cost me?"

"Oh, around five hundred...maybe less."

"What kind of shape's it in?" he mumbled through a mouthful of peanuts.

"It's real nice on the inside, but it needs a fresh coat of paint on the outside. It could use some yard work, too—place is overgrown."

Adams looked up at the fresh coat of green paint on his office walls. "Hell, I can hire a couple of niggers to clear out the yard. You got a good painter? The fellah I use don't have a car."

"I keep the one I have busy on my rentals, but I can spare him for your place. The old man's handy with carpentry, too, if you need to replace any rotten wood up around the eaves."

"I sure 'preciate that, Keith," Adams said, glancing down at his pinup drawer. "I've got to get this little gal I hired a job outside my office—her titties are drivin' me nuts."

Black chuckled. "Can't have that kind of distraction around the office. Ever consider hiring ugly ones?"

"All the time. Just never seems to work out."

"When do you want to drive over and take a look at the property?"

Adams looked at the stack of insurance forms he had left to sign. "What about this afternoon, say, around six o'clock?"

"See you then."

"Take care," Adams said, dropping the receiver onto its hook.

Hurriedly signing the forms and stacking them in his out-box for Thelma, he left his office to look for his next patient in the colored waiting room. His face fell when he saw Ruby sitting on the closest bench by an elderly woman who appeared to be dozing.

"I'm next," Ruby announced.

"Come on in, Ruby."

Ruby sat down on the bare exam table, seeing that the nurse had not had a chance to change the drape.

Adams straightened the counter and tossed a mass of bloody suture material into a waste basket by the door. "Ruby, I told you I can't see you now that you're pregnant."

"I'm not here to get a treatment," she explained. Her voice had a pleading tone. "I'm here because I'm still worried about having this baby."

Adams cocked a suspicious eyebrow. "You been takin' those pills I gave you?"

"I have."

"Then you ought to be fine," he shot back, recalling that he had given her a placebo.

She stared down at several fresh bloodstains on the exam table and climbed down in disgust. "But, Doctor, Sam will kill me when he finds out it's not his."

Adams held up an impatient hand. "You need to calm down, Ruby. I've already arranged for you to have the baby up at my cousin's hospital in Valdosta. I'll get Sheriff Howell to tell Sam to get out of town the whole month until you deliver. Then you can call him, and I'll run out to your house when he comes, so he thinks you delivered it at home."

"But he's got eyes, Doctor," she pleaded. "He can see it's a white baby."

He threw her a dismissing wave of his hand and wiped the counter down with alcohol. "I'll just tell him it's a throwback—everybody knows that once in a while a baby comes out light, even with two dark parents."

"Please get rid of this baby for me!" she moaned. "Please..."

"God-Almighty-damn, woman!" he exploded, turning his back to her to wash his hands. "How many times I gotta tell you? I don't want to hear nothin' more 'bout no abortion. After the baby comes, you can stay out at my farm if Sam goes crazy."

"But, Doctor..."

Ruby's protest was cut short by a swift wet slap across the face. Stunned, she gasped, tasting the warm saltiness of blood in her mouth.

"If you don't shut up, there's plenty more where that come from," Adams snarled, tossing a hand towel into the stainless steel laundry bin on his way out of the treatment room.

Thelma stood leaning against the wall in the hallway outside Adams's office, thumbing through the signed insurance forms. "Doctor, there are over forty hospital visits here for the same day. There ain't that many beds in the place."

"Damn, Thelma!" he snapped. "Do I have to tell you everything? Just change the goddamn dates to even 'em out and get 'em down to the post office on your way home."

"Yes, Doctor."

1951

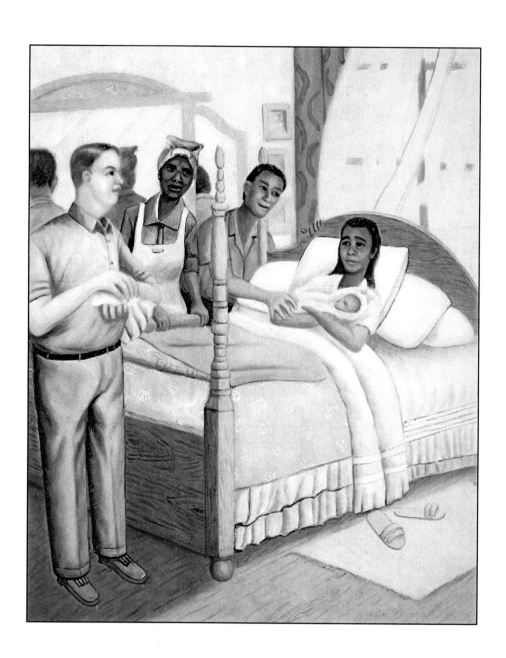

On July 18, three days after Ruby delivered her baby in Valdosta, Georgia, she lay in her bed with Sam and Beulah standing over her.

"What time did the baby come, Doctah?" Beulah asked, straightening the bedclothes.

"'Bout two this mornin'," Dr. Adams said, standing at the foot of the bed and drying his hands on a towel.

"Wish you hadn't made me take last week off," Beulah complained, kneading her apron. "I sho' woulda liked to been here when she come."

Ruby shot a glance at Adams, wondering how long she could keep up the charade of delivering the baby at home when he had actually spirited her away to his cousin's hospital to have it delivered by Caesarean section. "You needed some time off, Beulah. You're going to have plenty of work taking care of Loretta now that she's here."

"I still ain't had a chance to hold her," Sam complained. "Can't even see her face with that blanket you got her all wrapped up in."

Ruby held Loretta close to her side. "There'll be time later, Sam. I just want to hold her a little while longer."

"Sam, why don't you and Beulah go on downstairs," Adams suggested. "I need to check on Ruby's stitches."

"All right, Doc," Sam agreed, leaving the bedroom with Beulah in tow.

Adams closed the door and returned to sit on the bed beside Ruby. "So why the hell you lookin' so worried."

Ruby teared up. "Sam knows something is wrong."

"What makes you think that?"

She looked down at the baby. "Didn't you hear him? He wants to see her face."

"But that's natural, Ruby."

"I can't keep him from seeing her forever," she groaned.

"It ain't like it's his first, Ruby. Besides, he told me his brother's in the hospital, so he's got other things on his mind."

Ruby dried her eyes.

Adams stood up from the bed. "Tell you what, Ruby. I'll go downstairs and talk with Sam...see what he's thinkin'."

"Would you, Doctor?"

"Like I keep tellin' you—you don't have to worry 'bout nothin'."

Adams left the bedroom to find Sam having buttermilk and corn-bread in the kitchen while Beulah turned off the gas burner under a pot of coffee. "Can I get a cup of that coffee, Beulah?"

"Yassuh. Just made a fresh pot. Let me pour you and Mr. Sam up a cup. I sho' know you needs it after bein' up all night with the baby."

Adams pulled up a chair beside Sam, feigning exhaustion. "I'm used to it, Beulah."

"Yassuh, I guess you is," Beulah agreed, pouring coffee for the men.

Adams sipped his coffee while he studied Sam's face, trying to determine if he suspected anything. "Sam, you look a bit down this mornin'."

"I's worried 'bout Buck, Doc. Just heard he might lose his leg—it got mashed up pretty bad in that wreck the other night."

"I understand. Don't you think it might be a good idea for you to drive on down there and stay with him till he's better?"

"Well, I be worried 'bout Ruby…"

Adams held up his hand while he sipped his coffee. "You don't need to worry yourself about Ruby."

"She ain't herself, Doc. She ain't never held on to any of her babies like that befo'."

"It's just a mild case of postpartum blues, Sam," he said, eyeing Sam's cornbread and turning to see Beulah washing dishes in the sink. "Beulah, you got anything to eat over there on the stove?"

"Yassah. I got more of that cornbread in the oven. Made it fresh just a little while ago."

"Sounds fine to me," he said, turning back to face Sam. "Sometimes women are afraid of losin' their baby, Sam. Ain't nothin' real, you understand." Adams touched his head. "It's all up here."

"How long you think it'll take her to get over it?"

"I'd say in a few weeks she'll be fine. I know that if you go on down to stay with your brother, she'd feel like she had more time alone with the baby."

Adams watched Sam's face as a piece of cornbread appeared at his right hand. "Thanks, young lady."

Beulah giggled and returned to her dishwashing.

"I guess I can do that, Doc. The kids been askin' to see me, anyways, and I can stop by Mama Jackson's place on the way down there."

"That's a great idea, Sam," he said, biting into the cornbread.

"By the way, Doc, would you mind if I talked with you alone?"

Beulah dried her hands on a cross-stitched towel. "I'll go on back upstairs with Ruby while you menfolks talk."

Adams washed the cornbread down with a sip of coffee. "See you later, Beulah," he called after her through the swinging kitchen door. "So what's eatin' yah, Sam?"

"Well, Doc, I couldn't get a good look at the baby, but from what I could tell, she seem awful light."

"Hell, Sam. You've seen throwbacks; it happens all the time."

He nodded, apparently not satisfied with the answer. "Yassuh, but I was wonderin' 'bout somethin' else."

"What's that, Sam?"

"Well, I was wonderin' how long after a man has...you know..."

Adams laughed. "Sex?"

"Yassuh. How long after that can it take for a woman to get pregnant?"

"Well, Sam, I've heard of sperm stayin' up there alive and kickin' for up to a year."

Sam's eyes widened. "A whole year?"

Adams nodded, finishing the cornbread. "Strong little buggers."

"Well, I'll Suwannee. I sho' 'nuff never knowed that."

****

After Adams left, Sam decided to take a drive to sort things out. Caught up in his thoughts, he drove randomly through the neighborhood, and than turned onto Highway 90 to pass Blue's Lodge where he saw Adams's car parked at the main entrance.

Pulling between the twin brick lantern towers just past the railroad tracks, he stopped the car, opened his glove compartment and saw that his pistol was still there.

After taking several deep breaths, he slammed the glove compartment door shut and pulled back onto Highway 90 to head into town.

A few minutes later, he pulled in front of Lucy's house and parked, drying the tears from his eyes before he got out of the car to knock on her front door.

"Come on in," Lucy said, seeing the worried look on his face as he stood in the doorway with stooped shoulders.

Sam walked past Lucy like he had lead in his shoes and collapsed on the sofa before she could hug him.

"What's wrong, sugar?" she asked.

Sam covered his eyes. "The baby's not mine."

"What?"

"It belongs to Doc Adams."

"No!" Lucy gasped, sitting beside him on the sofa to put her arm around his shoulder while he buried his head in his hands. "Sam, honey, I know you said the baby was light when you called me, but sometimes there are throwbacks — the baby could be yours."

"That's what Dr. Adams told me," he said, uncovering his eyes.

"What's the problem, then?"

Sam looked into Lucy's eyes. "Did you forget that I'm a poker player, baby? I can see he's lyin'."

"But, Sam, how do you know for sure?" she challenged.

"Ruby and me hardly ever…"

Lucy laughed. "'Hardly ever' is all it takes, baby."

"It's not just that, Lucy. I found an electric razor in the hall bathroom. Sam Junior and me don't even own one."

"That's still not proof," she insisted.

"I feel like shootin' both of 'em!" he yelled, hitting the sofa with his fist. "All this time they been carryin' on right under my own roof and I didn't even know it."

"Now, honey, that's crazy talk. What if Dr. Adams brought that razor in the house while he stayed up to deliver the baby?"

"Matt says that man's been out to the house several times a week when I was at the juke or down in Tampa. Ain't nobody needs that much doctorin'."

"How long's this been going on, baby?" she asked, sensing that there might be some grounds for his suspicion.

"Best I can tell, since I stayed down with Buck after Ruby found out about you and me."

Lucy grabbed a tissue from a box at the end of the sofa to pat away his tears. "I hope you're wrong," she said, rubbing the back of his neck.

"I should shoot 'em both," he declared with quiet determination.

"Sam, you know you can't do that," she said, adopting the calm tone she used in her classroom. "If you shoot Dr. Adams, they'll string you up before you can make it to the jailhouse. Besides, you've got a family to take care of and a business to run."

Sam was quiet.

"And what about us?" Lucy pleaded.

He jumped up from the sofa. "If she thinks she can do this to me, she's got another think comin'."

Lucy stood up to hug him. "Now, baby, you need to calm yourself down."

"I'm gonna kill that fat-assed white bastard, too. I'm gonna kill both of 'em!"

"You've got to get a grip on yourself," Lucy insisted, pulling him back down on the sofa. "You know you can't do that—you'd end up in the chair."

"Just like Ruby to spite me by havin' his baby. I thought if we just spent some time apart...but now I don't see how things can be the same again."

Lucy stroked Sam's head. "If you're right about the baby, things stopped being the same when Ruby brought that man into your house. You never did anything like that to her—you always kept me on the side, and I was happy that way, just knowing I had a part of you that was all mine."

Sam laid his head on Lucy's shoulder, thinking how much he loved her.

Moving over, she took a pillow from the sofa and placed it on her lap, and then pulled him down so that his head was on the pillow. "The way I see it, you have only one solution," she said, gently stroking his forehead.

"What's that?" he asked, thinking how comforted he was by her touch, and how secure he felt in her lap.

"A marriage of convenience," she whispered. "You have me, and Ruby has Adams. That way you keep your business and manage a storefront marriage like a lot of people do for the sake of their kids."

"You mean just let those two keep carryin' on under my roof?"

Lucy felt the tension in his neck. "Do you have a choice? You aren't the first colored man to bear that cross, baby, and you won't be the last."

Chapter Thirty-Seven

Adams pulled into the McCollum's driveway to meet Ruby coming out of the house with Loretta. "How's our little girl?" he asked, rolling out of his car to smile at the baby.

Ruby leaned down to see Evelyn, dressed in a white nurse's uniform, sitting on the passenger side. "The baby's fine," she replied with a touch of irritation in her voice. "Can you bring in your doctor bag and give me a shot?"

After he had fetched his medical bag and rejoined her, she asked, "Who's that girl in your car?"

"That's one of my nurses. She goes out to house calls with me sometimes."

"I've never seen her before," she commented, entering the living room.

Adams closed the door behind him. "That's 'cause she works in the white side."

Ruby's face fell.

"How's my baby girl?" Adams said, grinning at Loretta and taking her from Ruby. "Itchy kitchy koo," he babbled, tickling her toes. "Where's Sam?" he asked, sitting on the sofa with the baby.

"How would I know?" she cried, pacing in front of the sofa. "He never tells me anything anymore. I know he's sleeping over at his whore's house most nights after the kids go to bed—stays out at the jooks all day during the week and takes the kids out to the farm after church on Sundays."

"Hell, woman, what you gripin' about? he asked, bouncing Loretta on his knee. "You two ain't been gettin' along for years now."

Ruby wiped her eyes and sat on the sofa beside him. "But I thought—it was just before I found out I was pregnant with Loretta— that there was a chance we might get back together again…that we might find a way to save our marriage."

Still dandling a cooing Loretta on his knee, he gave Ruby a cold stare. "You're dreamin', woman. After I win the election next year, you can move over to Tallahassee and get yourself a little place where I can visit if you want to."

"I don't want to leave my house," she replied, running her hand lovingly along the embroidered sofa cushion. "I have too many memories here."

"You ain't gonna be livin' high on the hog much longer anyways, with that new gamblin' law the feds passed."

"Sam said he's already registered," she protested. "Anyway, it's a cash business—the government's got no way of knowing how much money we're making."

Adams smirked. "You ain't gettin' it, Ruby. Guess you ain't seen this week's *Democrat*."

"No...not yet."

"Well, you just might want to take a look," he suggested, kissing the baby on the cheek.

Ruby walked over to the buffet and picked up the paper. "Oh, my God!" she gasped. "They're all here...including Sam...with all their addresses."

"Party's over, woman. Sam and his men might be legal by regis-terin' with the feds, but that county liquor law they passed back in 'forty-seven banned gamblin', too. Now that the whole passel of 'em are listed right there on the front page for buyin' a license from Uncle Sam to operate gamblin' in a county where it's illegal, Sim Howell's got to shut down his whole operation."

Ruby flopped down on the sofa and stared blankly into the fire-place. "So, what now?"

"You ain't gonna starve, Ruby," he said, handing the baby back to her. "Keith Black tells me they still need Sam's help over in Columbia County."

"Can I have that shot now, Doctor?"

"Why don't you take Loretta next door to your brother's house and come on back to meet me upstairs?"

"You'll give me the shot?"

"Don't I always?"

"All right, Doctor... I'll be right back."

When Ruby left with the baby, Adams went upstairs to her bed-room and pulled the door shut behind him. Holding the drapes aside to look out the window, he could see her with Loretta, crossing the street to Matt's house. *Time to stop this shit,* he told himself, going into the bathroom to undress and throw his clothes over the hamper. *Damn good thing Evelyn turns eighteen this year.*

A few minutes later, Ruby came in the bedroom and locked the door. Pulling her dress over her head, she said, "Matt said he could watch Loretta for about an hour before he had to go downtown to pick up Bessie."

"It won't take me that long, Ruby," he chuckled, lying naked on the bed with his hands behind his head and glancing over a mound of belly fat to admire his erection. My gun's about to go off and I've got house calls to make."

Ruby quickly finished undressing and lay passively on the bed next to him with her hands at her side.

"You know you got to throw your legs up, woman," Adams demanded impatiently, pulling her up beneath his belly to achieve the penetration he liked.

After a few thrusts, Adams groaned and rolled over onto the bed beside her. "Damn! I sure needed that," he said, still breathing heavily.

"Glad to accommodate," Ruby muttered resentfully, reaching over to pick up the "glad rag" she had placed on the nightstand.

After retreating to the bathroom to pull on his shirt and button his pants, he stepped in front of the mirrored closet doors in the bedroom to part his graying hair down the middle. "I need some extra cash this week, Ruby," he announced, looking at her in the mirror.

"How much do you need?"

"Oh, about five hundred—got a few extra bills to pay this month."

Stepping into her slippers on the bedside rug, she pulled on her plush pink robe and went to the office. Opening the safe, she removed five hundred-dollar bills and returned to the bedroom to find Adams sitting on the bed and looking over his list of house calls for the day.

Adams stood up to stuff the bills in his wallet. "Thanks, Ruby."

"Did you remember to get Loretta's birth certificate for me?" she ventured. "It's been a long time now."

"You don't have to worry yourself about it," he said with a dismissing wave of his hand.

"I need a copy to keep with my papers."

"I said, you don't need to worry yourself about it," Adams snapped. "I gave her my name, so I don't want you havin' a copy to go showin' around town."

Ruby sat on the bed and folded her arms, holding her position. "I need a diaphragm."

"I thought I told you I don't like those things."

"Sam's been really good about Loretta—he treats her just like she's his own." Tears welled up in her eyes. "But if I have another baby that comes out light, I know he'll kill me."

Adams returned his list of house calls to his black bag, ignoring her altogether.

Ruby jumped up from the bed and grabbed his arm. "Please, Doctor. Sam said he'd kill me if I got pregnant again."

Adams jerked his arm free. "Guess that puts you in a bad spot, Ruby, 'cause I'll kill you if you try to stop havin' my babies."

Ruby backed away, terrified. "I can't have more babies.... I just can't."

Adams shook his finger at her. "I'm tellin' you for the last time, Ruby, I don't want to hear about no diaphragm."

"Then I'll just have to get it from somebody else," she hissed.

Adams turned his back to her for a few moments, and then did an about-face, wielding a filled syringe like a weapon. Pushing her back onto the bed, he snarled, "God damn you, woman, you're gonna learn to do what I tell you if it kills you."

Ruby threw her arm up to block him. "No, Doctor! Please don't. Please!"

He sank the needle into her arm.

"You poisoned me!" she screamed.

Dropping the syringe into his satchel, he casually slipped on his worn leather loafers and engaged her with a cold stare. "You'll live—this time. Just don't make me have to teach you again."

Ruby grabbed her throbbing arm. "Oh, God...!"

Adams stood in the doorway, smiling. "Now you're gettin' it, Ruby. Enjoy your night in hell."

"Oh, sweet Jesus, please don't let me die!" she pleaded. Screaming, she felt the fire in her arm spread quickly through her chest and up her neck, then explode in her brain.

He stood a few moments watching Ruby convulsing uncontrollably on her bed, and smiled at how effective his extract of ground chinaberries and caladium roots was when given in just the right dose. It was always the discipline of choice out at the prison camp when the guards called him out to give "the shot" to a prisoner who had gotten out of control.

Casually closing the door, he left the house, wondering what Blue was serving for supper.

****

After making his house calls, Adams had a late meal of fried shrimp and hushpuppies with a group of friends at Blue's Lodge. Following the meal, Blue served the men hot chocolate around the fireplace.

Adams stood stirring the burning coals to kindle another log he had just placed on the fire. "Hear you're plannin' on runnin' for sheriff again next year, Sim," he said.

"That's right, Doc," Howell confirmed. "Speakin' of the election, before you got here this evenin', LaVergne was goin' over a few notes for your campaign speech with me and Mr. Black."

"Don't you think it's a little early, LaVergne?" Adams asked, continuing to poke the dying coals to kindle the log. "The election ain't till next year."

The old man glanced at the gently ticking mantel clock behind Adams. "At my age, Leroy, next year might not even get here."

Black blew on his hot chocolate, fogging up his glasses. "When it gets a little closer to campaign time, Doc, I thought we might meet back down at my beach place to introduce you to some folks."

"Good idea," Adams agreed, remembering how much he enjoyed Black's island retreat. "I'd like to be down there under better circumstances than last time."

"This time, I'll try to steal LaVergne's recipe for those fried shrimp of his you like so much and have my cook make up a batch."

Blue chuckled. "You know, Leroy," he said, growing suddenly serious, "the boys and me have been talkin' about Ruby."

Adams bit his lip, holding back the barrage of expletives that the mere mention of Ruby's name triggered.

"I know you and me have talked a lot—things I kept to myself—but now the boys here are tellin' me a lot of folks are talkin' 'bout you havin' a little nigger baby by that gal."

Impatient with his attempts to ignite the log, Adams threw kerosene from the tin onto the coals below the cast iron grate, sending a burst of flames up the chimney and a belch of smoke into the sitting area. "Good Gawd Almighty, LaVergne!" he exclaimed, jumping back from the fire. "Since when do nigger babies count? It sure didn't hurt my granddaddy none," he snarled, grinning in spite of himself.

Blue coughed, then pulled out his handkerchief and covered his nose against the smoke.

"LaVergne has a point, Doc," Black advised. "Times've changed since your granddaddy ran for the senate. If you want a girlfriend, you need to keep a white one—who knows how to keep her mouth shut."

"Damn, Keith!" Adams stormed. "It ain't just the pussy; it's the chance to take back a little piece of what the goddamn Yankees took away from us Southerners, and keep the niggers in their place at the same time."

"Better leave that to politics, Doc," Black cautioned, taken aback by the fervor in his friend's voice.

Wiping his eyes with his handkerchief, Blue fidgeted, wanting a way to ease the emotionally charged conversation. "What about that little Evelyn you're always talkin' about?"

The look on Adams's face changed. "I had to get that little gal out of the office—she flashed those big titties of hers around so much, my pecker was standin' at attention all the time."

The men sat grim-faced, unmoved by the attempt at levity.

"This is a serious matter, Doc," Black persisted, invoking his best prosecutorial tone. "I hear Ruby's been down at your office every day lately. Like I said, people talk."

"Yeah," Adams agreed, irritated at being called to account for his behavior yet aware that things had to change. "She's been goin' crazy on me lately. Ever since the baby came, she always wants me to see her in the white treatment room…Damn nigger bitch never did know her place."

"You can't keep playin' with fire like that, Doc," Black counseled. "You put ideas like that in that nigger woman's head and pretty soon she'll want all those 'rights' they been talkin' about up north. I don't care how much the Southern Governors caucus against Truman's plans to end segregation or how low he's ridin' in the Gallup Poll— you know as well as I do…"

"Yeah, yeah, I know," Adams interrupted, sitting down on the limestone hearth. "You might feel better knowin' that if things keep up the way they been goin', I'm plannin' on sendin' Ruby over to Brewster Hospital in Jacksonville."

"That the mental institution for coloreds?" Black asked.

"It's a nigger hospital with a mental ward."

"Why not Chattahoochee, Doc? They'll keep her over there as long as you want."

"I ain't through with her yet, Keith. I need her to keep the books just a little while longer so I can pay all the goddamn campaign bills."

Black nodded, apparently mollified by the response. "Fine...as long as you send her over to Chattahoochee right after the election— then we won't ever have to hear from her again."

1952

Chapter Thirty-Eight

Adams nodded off, then roused with a start to tug nervously at his necktie, struggling to stay awake while Judge Adams stood at the Lion's Club lectern, droning on about the dangers of Communism and how, even though every child in Florida was mandated to take the "Americanism versus Communism" course in high school, the evil menace could still take root right here in Suwannee County should its good citizens let their vigilance stray for even a moment. "Our boys in uniform won the fight for freedom," the judge concluded, "yet we best be on our guard against a new enemy—the enemy to democracy that arises from within."

When the judge paused to take a sip of water, the men stood from their banquet tables, cheering the elderly jurist for his patriotic message, based on the club's New Year's theme, "The Price of Freedom in 1952."

The judge smiled, motioning for the crowd to take their seats while several waitresses served coffee. "While y'all finish up your pecan pie and enjoy that fine coffee they serve here, it is now my considerable pleasure—and, indeed, a privilege and an honor—to introduce a man born and bred among us, the grandson and great-grandson of two of our finest Florida senators. All of you know him. Many of you have been visited in your homes by this tireless healer who leaves his home and family at all hours of the night to minister to your families in their time of greatest need. Others know him from visiting our new hospital, where he serves as the emergency room physician."

Adams quickly finished his dessert and wiped his hands on his napkin.

"Now, without further ado, it is, again, a privilege and an honor to yield the podium to your friend and mine, Dr. Leroy Adams."

While the audience applauded, the elderly jurist stepped aside to yield the podium and shake Adams's hand.

"Thank you, Judge," Dr. Adams said, fumbling with his notes. For a minute there I was lookin' around to see who you were talkin' about."

The crowd laughed.

"I think we all need to give Judge Adams another round of applause for his recent appointment as grand master of the Florida Masons, one of forty-eight men honored to travel to Washington, D.C., to represent that fine organization."

Again the audience applauded.

"You know," Adams began, waiting for the applause to end as the judge took his seat, "some of these folks might be tryin' to figure out how we're related, so I guess I should set the record straight right off the bat and tell 'em we ain't—not that I wouldn't be proud to have you as my uncle."

The room thundered with applause, drowning out the older man's "Thank you, Leroy."

"Hearin' the good judge warn us, I'm sure we'll all be on our guard against the advances of Communism in our community. And I want to add for my part that we'll also stand together to fight against all the other forces that threaten to destroy our way of life in the South."

"Go, Doc!" yelled a man in the audience. "The South will rise again!"

"Whoever said we fell?" Adams retorted, igniting a roar of laughter and applause. "Today," he continued, "we are surrounded by forces that would defeat us. We have the force of poverty. We have the force of limited funding for our schools. We have the growing force of outsiders moving into our fair state and seeking to change our way of life."

Monitoring his audience, Adams looked up from the notes that Blue had written for him to see sober nods of agreement throughout the room. "I have served this community going on seven years now. I've come out to your homes at all hours of the night, never worryin' about whether you had one thin dime to pay a doctor bill."

There were many nods, and several men looked at each other and applauded.

"So, after serving you as your physician for some time now, I would like to follow in the footsteps of my grandfather and my great-grandfather to serve you as your next state senator."

The room thundered with enthusiastic applause.

When the clapping subsided, Claude Pepper stood up at the head table and said, "Dr. Adams, I hope you don't mind if I take this opportunity to lend you my support. I can't think of a finer man for the job."

"Thank you, Senator Pepper," Adams replied as Pepper took his seat to another round of applause. "And I want to thank you for fighting those boys up in Washington to make sure we got the first hospital in the country under that Hill-Burton Act you sponsored."

The audience rose in a standing ovation.

Chapter Thirty-Nine

At four a.m. on February 1, 1952, Adams rolled over to answer the telephone on his nightstand. "Yeah," he mumbled, expecting a call from the hospital.

"Doc, Sim here," Howell said in a deadpan voice. "I'm real sorry to have to make this call."

Adams yawned. "What the hell's the matter, Sim?"

"Sonny's been in an accident near Amarillo Air Force Base—his car was hit by a milk truck just after midnight."

Adams sat bolt upright in bed. "Is he all right?"

Howell paused. "Doc...he didn't make it."

"Just a minute, Sim, I gotta change phones."

Adams placed the receiver on his nightstand and walked barefoot down the carpeted hallway and onto the cold linoleum floor of the kitchen to pick up the wall phone by the refrigerator. "I'm back. Now, look, Sim, Sonny just got off on furlough. He planned to be home today—hell, Laverne's already baked a cake and Florrie Lee's set the table up for supper tonight...." His voice trailed off.

"I'm sorry, Doc. They said they tried..." Howell halted, realizing that his friend had not yet accepted the dire news.

"Where'd they take Sonny?"

"The Air Force is puttin' him on a plane and flyin' him to the Moody base in Valdosta. He should be there around noon today. Then they're sendin' a special convoy down to Live Oak."

"Tell 'em to send Sonny on up to Jasper, to Reid's funeral home—don't send him down here. I need time to talk with Florrie Lee first."

"I'll get on the horn and tell 'em right now, Doc."

"Thanks, Sim."

Feeling numb, Adams hung up the phone. How could this happen? Maybe there was some mistake. Maybe it was somebody else. But no, the military would have made positive ID by now. It had to be Sonny. He walked back to the bedroom to hang up the phone.

Looking at Florrie Lee's face as she slept, he remembered a time when he had loved her. That time had long since passed, and the passion had faded over the years into a sense of familiarity, of being connected—something he would miss if he lost it, like a finger or a toe.

He knew he would eventually have to tell Florrie Lee about Sonny, but not now. First he had to adjust to the news in his own way, without the smothering closeness of a woman.

Stripping off his pajamas to pull on his clothes, Adams hurried to his car and turned the key to hear the slow, dull grind of the starter. "Goddamn piece of shit!" he yelled, pounding the steering wheel.

It wasn't supposed to be like this. Sonny was only twenty-two years old, a handsome young man in the prime of his life. He had been the star of his high school football and basketball teams before joining the Air Force. Everybody liked Sonny. Why him? Why not somebody else?

Turning the key in the ignition again, he was relieved to hear the engine crank. He pulled out of the driveway to head west along Highway 90 through the low-hanging early morning fog, feeling a raw fury raging through his body. If God wanted to punish him, why hurt Florrie Lee?"

The lanterns in the twin brick towers of Blue's lodge appeared dimly through the fog, like lighthouse beacons reaching out to guide a ship toward a safe harbor. Crossing the railroad tracks between the towers, he thought about how ironic it was that Blue had lost his only son a few years ago in an eerily similar automobile accident. If anyone could understand what he was going through, it would be Blue.

"Little early, ain't you, Leroy?" Blue asked, seeing Adams pull in front of the lodge as he was getting ready to open. "Good thing I got an early start this mornin'. You got a house call?"

"No, LaVergne, no house calls today."

Blue unlocked the door to the lodge. "Come on in, son. I'll start a fire and put on some breakfast."

Adams got out of his car. "I ain't hungry, LaVergne," he said in a detached voice.

Blue stopped and squinted to look closely at him. "What's the matter, Leroy?"

"My boy's been killed—run over by a truck out in Texas."

"Oh, my Lord!" Blue gasped. "Leroy, I'm so sorry."

Entering the lodge, Adams took a seat on the sofa while Blue put a few chunks of fat lighter and a couple of oak logs in the fireplace.

"After I lost my wife, and then my son, I still kept myself busy tendin' this place like I had some kind of tradition to pass on." Blue paused to throw kerosene on the logs and ignite them with a long match. "All that's gone now, blown away like dry leaves in the wind.

So I've changed my will to leave the place to my nephew." Satisfied at last with the fire, he sat on the sofa beside Adams and patted him on the shoulder. "But a nephew ain't like a son—a son's your own flesh and blood."

"I always hoped Sonny would want to be a senator someday," Adams lamented. "He was only twenty-two—had his whole life ahead of him."

Blue nodded sympathetically, staring into the fire. "He came from a great line of men, all great statesmen stretching all the way back to his great-great-grandfather."

"Damn!" Adams shouted, pounding his fist into the sofa. "Why did this have to happen to my Sonny? Why couldn't it be some poor goddamn son of a bitch who's not worth the dirt on the soles of my shoes?"

Blue sat quietly for a few moments to let his friend vent his grief and rage. "How are they bringing Sonny home?"

"They're flyin' him to Moody Air Base up in Valdosta," Adams said matter-of-factly. "They told me they'd call when the plane landed, so I'd have time to drive up to Jasper to meet 'em at Reid's place."

"I'd like to be an honorary pallbearer, Leroy, like you did for me at my son's funeral. It would mean a great deal to me."

"I'll call up to the funeral home and tell Reid."

A little over an hour later Blue, yawning, looked at the striking mantel clock. "Can't believe it's already six o'clock," he said.

Adams stood up and stretched, seeing the first glint of sunrise through the leaded-glass windows. "Guess I'd better run back home and tell Florrie Lee about Sonny. She should be wakin' up right about now. I always told her she's better'n any alarm clock."

Blue stood up and put his hand on his friend's shoulder. "Can I fix you a cup of coffee to take with you?"

"No, thanks, LaVergne. Right now I'd throw up anything that hit my belly."

"I can understand that," Blue empathized, following his friend out the door. "You sure don't want somebody else callin' Florrie Lee before you get a chance to tell her yourself."

When Adams got into his car, Blue leaned down to put his hand on his shoulder. "You know, Leroy, you're the only family I got left." Blue choked on his words, patting his shoulder. "The only real family, I mean."

Adams smiled and patted his friend's hand. "I'm glad to hear you say that, LaVergne."

****

"Thelma," Ruby cried over the telephone, "I simply must speak with the doctor."

"Ruby, Dr. Adams told me not to put your calls through. Don't you know he just lost his son in a car accident? Why don't you do the decent thing and just leave him alone?"

"Tell him it's an emergency."

"He'll just tell me to tell you to go down to the hospital and see somebody else."

Ruby paused, taking a deep breath. "You tell him if he doesn't come to the phone, I'll drive to his office."

"Ruby," Thelma whispered, "he told me that if you showed up, he'd have you committed. That man's tired of your craziness."

"Committed!" Ruby gasped. "He told you that?"

"I've already said too much. Good-bye."

"Thelma? Thelma, don't you dare hang up on me!" Realizing that she had done just that, Ruby slammed down the receiver so hard that Loretta was frightened and began crying loudly.

Hearing the baby's wails, Sam came downstairs to find both mother and child in tears. "What's wrong with you, Ruby?" he asked, bending down to pick the baby up and give her the bottle that was lying on the sofa beside her.

Ruby stared ahead blankly.

"Beulah!" Sam yelled. "Beulah!"

"Yessuh," Beulah answered, coming out of the kitchen.

"Take the baby and Ruby up to her bedroom."

"Yessuh," she replied, taking Loretta. "Come on, Ruby, honey," she urged, taking her arm. "Let's go on upstairs."

Sam paced the floor, not knowing what to do. Since the day Loretta was born, Ruby had steadily deteriorated. Not only had she asked Matt and Bessie to watch the children more often, she had also neglected her church and school functions—she had even neglected her appearance and put on weight.

Not knowing what else to do, Sam drove to Adams's office, thinking about all the things he wished he had done differently in his marriage. Hitting Ruby at the Christmas party five years ago had been his first mistake; getting careless about his affair with Lucy had been the second. If it took three strikes to be out in a marriage, he had made the first two, but Ruby had made the third—and far the biggest—by having Adams's child.

Parking in the alley beside the colored entrance to Adams's office, Sam sat for a moment to consider if there was any way to avoid involving the doctor. But since it was probably a medical matter, there was nothing he could do short of driving her out of town for treatment—and that, he knew, Ruby would never accept.

When he entered the office, Thelma Curry stepped out of a treatment room and gave him a flirtatious smile. "Well, Hello, Mr. McCollum. Ain't seen you in a long time."

"Hey, Thelma. How you doin'?" he asked, catching the scent of her rose cologne.

"I'm doin' fine, Sam. How 'bout yourself?"

Sam grinned, glancing down at her tight-fitting sweater. "Just fine. Mighty nice sweater you got on."

"Well, thank you, Sam," she replied sweetly, playing with her sweater buttons and batting her eyelashes. You know, I was just about to call you. Dr. Adams told me he wanted to speak with you."

"That so? I really need to talk with him myself."

Thelma sashayed ahead of Sam to Adams's office where he was busily rummaging through his desk.

"Dr. Adams, Sam McCollum's here," Thelma announced.

"Come on in, Sam," Adams said, barely looking up. "I've been tryin' to get hold of you."

"That's what I hear," Sam acknowledged.

"Close the door and pull up a chair."

"Thanks… Doctah. First of all, I wants to tell you how sorry I is to hear 'bout your son."

"Thank you, Sam," Adams returned in a detached voice.

"But the reason I come down here right now is, I thought I better talk with you about Ruby—she actin' mighty strange. She don't even pick up the baby when she cries."

"Like I told you, Sam, some women get that way after havin' a baby—only with her it seems to be gettin' worse."

"Is there anything you can give her?" he ventured.

"I sure as hell can't take care of her. I got Dr. Workman in here to help out 'til I can get back on my feet and I sure don't want to saddle the old man with Ruby. You've got to take her over to Jacksonville, to Brewster Hospital, and let them keep her on the mental ward for a few weeks."

"You mean where they keep crazy folks?" Sam asked incredulously.

"You can tell everybody she's sick with the flu if you want."

"I don't know, Doc," Sam replied in an anguished tone. "Can't you just give her somethin' to calm her down?"

"She's already got more drugs in her than the Live Oak Drugstore, Sam."

"I guess I ain't got no choice, then."

"And I guess I ain't got no choice but to follow you on out to the house and sedate her. You know how to find Brewster once you get over to Jacksonville?"

"Yes, suh. I knows my way 'round Jacksonville pretty good."

"I'll give her enough medication to keep her quiet for the drive over there."

"All right, Doc. Can I use your phone to call Matt?"

"Go right ahead, Sam," he said, shoving the telephone across the desk.

Sam picked up the receiver. "Operator, please get me five-six-OK... Hello, Matt? I'm down at the doc's office, and he say I got to take Ruby over to Jacksonville, to Brewster. If you can go on over to the house and watch out for the kids, I'd sure be obliged."

"Don't worry, Sam. Bessie and me'll keep the kids. I'll run on over to your house right now."

"Thank you, Matt," Sam said, hanging up the telephone.

Adams stood up to leave his office with Sam, locking his office door behind him. "You ain't got nothin' to worry about, Sam," he said reassuringly. "I'll call over to Brewster after you head out, and let 'em know you're comin'."

Five minutes after leaving the doctor's office, Sam pulled into his driveway with Adams right behind him.

Inside, Matt met them at the door, holding Loretta. "Ruby's a little better now, Sam," he said.

"Where's the rest of the kids?"

"I told Sam Junior he could spend the night at his friend's house, and Kay's taking a nap over there on the sofa. I was tryin' to let her sleep."

"Thanks, Matt. Ruby still in bed?"

"Yeah… I'll wait down here," he said, taking a seat on the sofa.

Sam and Adams found Ruby in bed, staring blankly at the ceiling.

"Ruby," Sam called, shaking her gently.

Her eyelids fluttered. Seeing Adams, she sat up with a start, pulling the covers up around her neck.

"I'm goin' to give you somethin' to help you sleep," Adams explained, filling a hypodermic.

"No! Don't!" Ruby screamed, scrambling out of bed. "Sam, help me!"

Enveloping her in his arms, Sam held her down on the bed.

"Hold still woman!" Adams demanded, at last managing to get the needle in her arm.

Ruby went limp, falling back onto the bed.

"Doc!" Sam exclaimed. "She look like she dead!"

"She ain't dead, Sam," Adams replied, monitoring her pulse.

"How we gonna get her out of bed?"

"We'll roll her out," Adams explained, turning her over. "You take one side and I'll take the other."

"All right," Sam agreed, lifting Ruby by one arm while Adams took the other to assist her downstairs to the living room.

Kay woke up to see her mother being carried down the stairs. "What's wrong with Mommy?" she whimpered.

"Mommy's asleep," Matt assured her. "Daddy and the doctah just drivin' her to the hospital. She's goin' to be fine."

"Can I kiss her good-bye?"

"No, baby," Matt answered gently, struggling to carry his share of Ruby's weight. "You might wake her up."

Kay jumped up and ran over to the dining room table to grab her mother's purse. "Here, Daddy," she said, handing him the purse. "Mama's gonna want this."

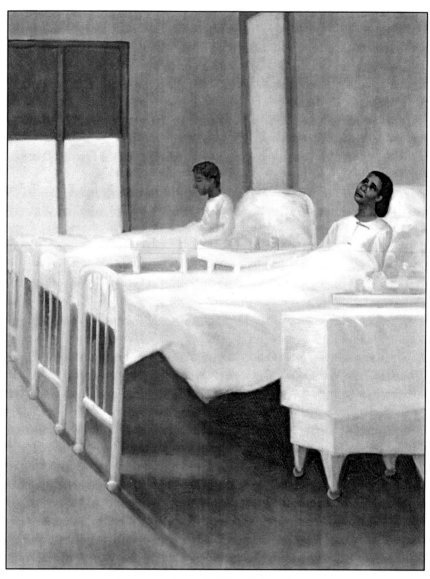

Brewster Hospital for Coloreds
Jacksonville, Florida

Chapter Forty

The morning after sending Ruby to Brewster Hospital, Adams sat in his office, hurriedly signing insurance forms when the telephone rang. "Hello, this is Dr. Adams."

"Dr. Adams, this is Dr. McCullagh. I'm the lead psychiatrist over at Brewster Hospital in Jacksonville."

"Good to speak with you, Dr. McCullagh," Adams said, laying his pen down on the stack of forms.

"Good to speak with you, too, Dr. Adams. I wanted to obtain some history on the Negro woman you sent over—I believe her name is Ruby McCollum."

"That's right, Doctor."

"Her husband was rather vague when I spoke with him. He said something to the effect that she was not acting like herself after having her last child—not taking care of the children or keeping the house, things of that nature. She's also complaining of some general aches and pains."

"She's a fairly long-term patient of mine. I should say a fairly difficult long-term patient of mine. I gave her a diagnosis of postpartum depression, but she's also hypochondriacal and tends to get hysterical from time to time."

"Yes," McCullagh agreed, "that makes sense. I'm deferring my diagnosis until I can run a series of X-rays and lab tests to see if there is any physical basis to her complaints. She's had some sort of situational crisis, but I can't seem to get to the root of that yet. She carries around this photo of a mulatto child and mumbles something about 'the doctor' being the child's father. When I asked her about it, she said, 'That's between me and the doctor.' Have any idea what that's all about?"

Adams fidgeted, considering how to answer McCullagh. "No doubt she's delusional. I had to sedate her for her husband to drive her over there. She's also addicted to heroin and cocaine."

"Certainly the suggestion of postpartum depression and the history of substance abuse make the prognosis guarded. Does her husband have the resources for her long-term care?"

Adams smiled. "Yes. You can keep her as long as you need to."

"Depending on the physical findings, I'm considering insulin shock therapy. She may suffer some transient memory loss as a result, but not as much as the blank slate we see following electroshock."

"Have you considered a prefrontal lobotomy?" Adams ventured, picking up his pen to twirl it between his fingers. "At times I've worried that she might be suicidal when she's having one of her episodes."

"That's a drastic and irreversible procedure, as you know, Doctor. We reserve lobotomies for the most violent of patients who fail to respond to more conservative therapy. Besides, we've had remarkable results with a new psychotropic, Thorazine. Some physicians consider it a reversible chemical lobotomy, since it has many of the same effects as the surgical procedure."

"So what should I expect as far as managing her?"

"As long as she's on the Thorazine, she'll be responsive but will not initiate any actions on her own. Her speech will be somewhat slurred, she'll walk with a shuffle, and her affect will be flat, with no emotional ups and downs. When you ask her a question, her answers will usually be limited to a word or short phrase. Obviously, you'll have to have someone look after her hygiene and nutrition."

"I can see why you chose Thorazine," Adams reflected, realizing that he now had the means to control Ruby's behavior. "I'll make sure she stays on it when she comes home. She has a maid in the house every day and a brother who lives next door, so she should be looked after just fine."

"Yes, I've met her brother, Matt, and spoke with him about wanting to keep her over here for at least four to six weeks to establish her diagnosis and manage her detoxification before releasing her."

"I understand."

"I appreciate your help, Dr. Adams. I'll stay in touch to let you know of her progress, and call you when she is scheduled to be discharged."

"Certainly, Dr. McCullagh. I'm here when you need me."

Dr. McCullagh hung up the telephone at the nurse's desk and entered the treatment room to find Ruby lying strapped to a gurney with an IV in her arm, an oxygen tube in her nose, and a rubber bite block in her mouth. A nurse stood monitoring her blood pressure with a cuff.

"Go ahead and prepare her arm for the injection," the doctor instructed.

The nurse swabbed the area over a vein in Ruby's left arm with mercurochrome while he stood ready with a hypodermic filled with insulin.

Ruby's eyes widened when she saw the needle. "Mm-mph!" she managed, struggling against her restraints.

"Now, Ruby," the nurse advised, putting a firm hand on her shoulder, "you need to get hold of yourself. Dr. McCullagh's going to give you something to make you feel better."

Seeing the approaching needle, she spit out the bite block and screamed, "Let me loose! Get me out of here!"

An orderly standing by the instrument cart stepped over to replace the bite block, and McCullagh injected her arm with insulin. He then held her eyelids back to watch her pupils as she lay convulsing on the table. "Nurse, insert the nasogastric tube for the glucose."

"Yes, sir," she said, turning to pick up a rubber tube from a tray on the nearby cart.

"Orderly, where's the blanket?" the doctor asked.

The orderly looked around nervously. "I'll get one, Doctor," he returned, stepping out of the room.

Obviously annoyed, McCullagh said, "From now on, make sure he keeps a clean blanket in this room."

"Yes, sir," the nurse replied, angry with the orderly for making her look bad in front of a physician—and one who had a reputation for strict adherence to protocols.

McCullagh felt Ruby's pulse. "Pulse is good. Take her temperature every half hour until she's stabilized."

"Yes, Doctor," she said.

McCullagh took the chart from the nurse to jot a quick note and then hand it back to her. "By the way, Nurse, I know you're new here, but Dr. Bedell tells me you've assisted with this procedure before."

She brightened and said, "I did some years ago up in New York, but I know there have been a few changes since I was trained."

McCullagh pulled up a stool to sit beside his patient. "I'd probably better review a few of the basics with you, then. First, I'm certain that you know the function of insulin in the body, and how an excess induces a coma."

"Yes, sir."

"As with any patient in a comatose state, we have to be extremely cautious in monitoring the vital signs. You'll take her temperature every fifteen minutes and use a blanket to keep her warm. Check her pulse every five minutes to make certain her rate and rhythm are regular. Do you know how to check her pupils?"

"Yes, sir."

He pointed to the bottle of glucose suspended above Ruby's head. "If you see she's under too deep, start that glucose running, stat. And be absolutely certain to have the orderlies remove those restraints and turn her over if she starts to strangle on her saliva."

"I will, Doctor."

"Here's, the blanket, Doctor," the orderly announced, closing the door behind him and weathering the nurse's disapproving look.

"Be sure to get a clean blanket and store it under the cabinet in the corner," McCullagh instructed.

"Yes, sir," the man said as the nurse took the blanket and covered Ruby, folding it back at her neck.

"When you have her cleaned up and stabilized in a couple of hours, take her down to X-ray to make sure she didn't fracture any bones during the seizure. With insulin, the convulsions aren't as bad as they are with Metrazole or electroshock, but we can't be too careful."

"Yes, Doctor."

"When you're done in X-ray, have the orderlies catheterize her and suit her up in a straitjacket before they send her down to the ward— she'll be a little disoriented when she regains consciousness, and we don't want her hurting herself."

"Yes, Doctor."

"After you get her glucose drip set up in the ward, let me know so I can check on her. I'll be right outside at the nurse's station."

"Thank you, Doctor. I'm sure I can manage her."

McCullagh found Matt sitting in the black-and-white-tiled waiting room near a bank of jalousie windows, looking through *Better Homes and Gardens.*

"How's Ruby, Doctah?" Matt asked anxiously, returning the magazine to the table in front of him.

"I believe you're her brother?" he asked.

"Yassah," he said, standing up. "My name's Matt."

"She's going to be fine, Matt," the doctor assured him, reaching to shake his hand. "She'll be a bit forgetful, but sometimes memories can contribute to depression."

"How long she got to stay in the hospital?"

"I'd like to keep her under observation for a few weeks to stabilize her on her medications. If she goes home too soon, chances are you'll just have to bring her back."

"I sure do 'preciate what you're doin', Doctah McCullagh."

McCullagh smiled. "I understand that you and Ruby's house-keeper will be taking care of her when she gets back home."

"Yes, suh, we sure will."

"That's good. She'll need lots of attention for several months after she's released. I'll have the nurse review her care and medications with you before she's discharged, and schedule her follow-up. Do you have any other questions?"

"No, suh, not right now."

"Well, I'm sure I'll see you around the hospital over the next week or so."

"Yes, suh, you sho' will. My wife's takin' care of the kids so's I can be here with Ruby."

After McCullagh left the waiting room, Matt looked over to the bank of telephone booths, trying to understand what had happened to his baby sister and wondering what he would tell Bessie when he called home.

Chapter Forty-One

A month after Sonny's funeral, Leroy Adams returned to his office, made house calls, performed surgeries, and visited his patients at the hospital. He also reserved time each week to meet with Blue to draft campaign ads for the *Suwannee Democrat*.

"I think you ought to say somethin' about old-age assistance," Blue suggested, enjoying the warmth from the roaring fire he had just kindled to take the early morning chill off the cavernous interior of his lodge. "I hear a lot of folks worryin' about havin' enough money to keep a roof over their heads and kerosene for their stoves when they retire."

Adams stood with his backside to the fire. "We got to watch our step there, LaVergne, or somebody might accuse me of bein' a Communist. I'm already the only doc in Florida who supports socialized medicine."

"You can strike a happy medium, Leroy. Grantham's goin' to push for the businessmen's interests, even though he's a fellow Democrat. He ain't got the least idea of what it's like to look forward to retirin' on nickels and dimes."

Adams laughed, hearing the blaring sound of the morning train approaching. "That's for sure." Looking across the room through the leaded glass windows, he watched an endless string of boxcars speeding by through the morning fog. "You know, LaVergne, I can't figure out why I've got so much energy lately."

"It's like that after you get past the first week or so, Leroy. I remember I started replacin' the rotten wood on the eaves around here a few weeks after my boy died."

"You might have a point there," Adams reflected, taking a seat beside the old man in front of the fireplace.

"Have you stopped takin' that little Evelyn out with you on house calls?"

"Yeah," Adams lamented. "Florrie Lee drives with me now. Keith said it'd look good for the campaign."

"That explains some of your energy right there, son—you ain't screwin' around so much."

Adams laughed. "Hell, LaVergne, a good hump gives me more energy, not less."

"Well, anyway, I'm glad to hear you're on the road to recovery.... It sure ain't easy."

"No," Adams agreed. "It ain't."

The two men fell silent for a moment, listening to the rhythmic "click-clack" of the train passing by.

"They let Ruby out of Brewster yet?" Blue asked.

"Not yet."

"You think she'll leave you alone when she gets back?"

"Hell, LaVergne, that nigger woman acts like she's my wife or somethin'."

"Wonder what put a fool idea like that in her head?"

Adams threw his hands in the air. "Beats me."

Blue lit his pipe. "Might give some thought to what you're goin' to do when she gets out. Be a shame to have her ruin your chances of winnin' the election."

"I'll send her over to Chattahoochee before I let that happen," Adams snapped.

"You might have to, Leroy." Blue paused, taking a puff on his pipe. "How's Florrie Lee?"

"She's still depressed—spends a lot of time on her church work."

"Everybody has their own way of gettin' on with life."

"Yeah, but I guess religion never did it for me."

"I'm not a churchgoer myself," Blue confessed. "After my boy died, I got out of the habit and never got back."

Adams stood and crossed the dining room to look out the window to see the train cut through the last wisps of ground fog still hugging the ground as the sun rose higher in the sky. Watching the caboose pass by, he drifted back in time, and recalled a moment from his childhood.

"Lotta people say they hate livin' close to a train track," Blue said, seeing the faraway look on his friend's face when he returned to join him in front of the fireplace. "I think you and me like it, though. Can't say I enjoy anything more than hearing a train go by during the night—'specially when it's raining and cold outside."

"You know, LaVergne," he said with a distance in his voice, "when I was a little kid—musta been around seven or so—I remember prayin' for a toy train one Christmas. I'd seen one in the Sears-Roebuck Christmas catalogue, and showed it to my mamma and daddy. My daddy told me he'd buy it for me, but I knew I could never depend on anything he told me. Hell, once he sobered up he always forgot what he promised — and on top of that I had just learned there was no Santa Claus — so I just kept asking Jesus for it to be on the safe side."

Blue smiled and gave a fatherly nod.

"When Christmas mornin' finally come, I jumped out of bed before the sun come up, and run like hell into the living room to play with my new toy train. But all I found was a goddamn box of little wood logs to build a toy log cabin. I knew right then and there that my old man had used the Christmas money to stagger around the corner and buy another bottle of his goddamn corn liquor. I also knew that Jesus don't answer prayers."

"That's sad, Leroy," LaVergne sympathized, seeing the look on his friend's face. "I'm sure you realized when you got older that it was your dad that let you down, not Jesus."

"Hell, LaVergne, after that, and now with Sonny, I'm not so sure there is a Jesus — or his daddy."

****

After leaving the lodge, Adams made a quick stop by the hospital, and then continued on to his office to park in the alley behind Thelma's car. Inside, he saw that there were no patients in the colored waiting room. Stepping into the corridor, he called, "Thelma, you got anybody up there?"

She stepped to the doorway at the end of the hallway. "No, Doctor. Guess you seen 'em all down at the hospital. Today is Sunday, you know."

In his office, Adams sorted through a stack of mail until he found a letter from Dr. McCullagh. Holding the envelope for a moment, he took a deep breath and stared down at McCullagh's name, knowing that Ruby would have had a chance to speak with him on numerous occasions by now. *What filth had she told him? Did he really believe anything she had to say?* "Good God Almighty," he muttered, ripping the envelope open. "What the hell am I worried about, anyways? I'm a damn doctor and she's just a nigger woman who's as crazy as a bed bug."

Reading the letter, he winced and then smiled. Placing it back on his desk, he leaned back in his chair and stared at it, considering his options. Then he picked it up again and read it once more to determine if McCullagh had picked up anything from Ruby that he might have to deal with later. *Hell,* he thought, dropping the letter into his center desk drawer, *he's turning her over to me with a diagnosis I can use to throw her in Chattahoochee if she gets out of line anymore.*

```
William McCullagh, M.D.
Brewster Hospital
7th and Jefferson Street
Jacksonville, Florida
February 14, 1952

C. Leroy Adams, M.D.
Parshley Building, Suite 2
201 South Ohio Avenue
Live Oak, Florida
```

Dear Dr. Adams:

I am releasing Mrs. Ruby McCollum, a 42 year old Negro female, to return to her home in Live Oak where I under-stand that she will continue receiving medical care under your supervision.

Mrs. McCollum is suffering from a severe case of de-pression and hypochondriasis with neurological overtones, exacerbated by her addiction to cocaine and heroine.

Mrs. McCollum has undergone several treatments of in-sulin shock therapy in conjunction with a course of Thorazine adjusted to maintain her in a calm and manage-able state during the acute stages of detoxification. Her prognosis remains guarded because of her history of substance abuse and her tendency to physicalize.

Should you need to refer her to my care in the future, please call in advance and forward any medical records that you feel would be relevant to her treatment.

Sincerely,

William McCullagh, M.D.

Adams leaned forward to press the intercom button. "Thelma?"

"Yes, Doctor?"

"Forgot to tell you that I 'preciate your comin' down on a Sunday."

"Only time I got to catch up with this paperwork," crackled her response.

Adams glanced at the unopened mail remaining on his desk. "Ain't that the damn truth. Anyways, I want you to order a supply of Thorazine—that's T-h-o-r-a-z-i-n-e. Check the dosage with Tom Kennon down at the drugstore, and next time the pharmacy rep comes in, get enough samples for a dozen patients."

"Yes, Doctor."

"I'm headin' out to make a house call, but I'll be back. You expectin' many patients today?"

"Just the ones that traipse in the back door."

Adams glanced at his wristwatch. "Looks like a good time for me to catch up on my paperwork when I get back."

Five minutes after leaving his office, Adams parked in the driveway of the McCollum house and used his key to open the front door. "Anybody home?" he called. Hearing no answer, he walked in, the smells of collard greens and frying pork chops beckoning from the kitchen.

He climbed the staircase to find Ruby in bed, staring at the ceiling. "Where's Sam?" he asked her.

"Sam...?" she repeated, her voice empty of emotion.

Adams noted her blank expression. "Yeah, Sam—your husband."

Ruby looked confused.

"Where are the kids?" he asked.

"Matt's place."

"Who's lookin' out for you?"

"Beulah."

"Where's she?"

"Kitchen."

Adams put his satchel down on the bed and sat beside Ruby. "How you feelin'?"

"All right," Ruby responded.

Seeing the bottle of Thorazine on the bedside table, he said, "Looks like the medicine's workin'. I'll be back later this evenin' to check on you."

Ruby's face remained masklike, her eyes glazed.

Leaving the bedroom, Adams went into the office, shut the door quietly behind him, and set his satchel on Ruby's desk. He then dialed the combination and opened the massive steel door to find a shelf of neatly stacked bundles of hundred-dollar bills. Grabbing a bundle, he stuffed it in his satchel and closed the safe.

Downstairs he found Beulah in the kitchen, stirring a pot of collard greens. "How you doin', Beulah?"

"Fine," she replied without looking up from her cooking.

Seeing that she was ignoring him, he said, "Mama, that sure smells good!"

"Thank you," Beulah replied noncommittally, taking the pork chops from the pan to stir in flour and water for gravy.

After waiting in vain for her usual offer to serve him, Adams finally said, "You feelin' all right today, Beulah?"

"I's just fine," came the indifferent response.

"What else you got there?" he asked, lifting the lid from a pot to find rutabagas simmering with strips of pork fat.

Beulah remained silent.

"I see Ruby's doin' all right," he ventured.

"She stays in bed all the time."

Adams opened the door to the living room. "That's a good thing, Beulah, 'cause she needs her rest. Make sure she gets her pill in the next hour, and I'll be back to check on her later this evenin'."

"You can count on me to take good care of Miss Ruby," Beulah replied coldly, stirring the gravy and adding water to make sure it thickened to perfection.

Looking out the kitchen window to see Adams pulling out of the driveway, Beulah picked up the telephone. "Operator, please get me 56OK.... Matt?"

"The doc's gone," Matt observed, looking out the window. "Is you ready for me to come on over?"

"Yes. I just fixed her dinner."

"I'll be right over," he said, hanging up the telephone and looking up at his wife, a woman who looked much like Ruby, with the exception of carrying a few more pounds and wearing simple house-dresses — except on Sundays.

Bessie looked out the window and said to her husband, "Don't worry 'bout me and the kids, honey. You just go on and do what you got to, to take care of Ruby."

Matt kissed his wife on the cheek and left the house.

Across the street, Beulah met him at the front door. "He say he be back tonight, Matt," she whispered.

"We need to get her up and out of here before that devil get back," Matt said, leading the way up the stairs.

"I's right behind you," she said, following him up to Ruby's bedroom.

Matt leaned over his sister and whispered, "Wake up, Ruby." Seeing how drugged she was, he snatched up the bottle of Thorazine from the nightstand. "This stuff turnin' her into a zombie."

"What you doin', Matt!" Beulah exclaimed, seeing him walk into the bathroom with the bottle of pills.

The toilet flushed in reply. "You don't think she need them pills?" Beulah asked, kneading her apron.

"That stuff's poison," Matt explained, coming out of the bathroom. "I drove downtown to the Home Pharmacy and talked to Doc Kennon. He say it's what they gives crazy people over in Chattahoochee to keep 'em quiet."

"Ruby may be sick, but she sho' ain't crazy," Beulah said, her voice rising in indignation.

"Ruby…?" Matt called again.

Ruby's eyes fluttered. "Yeah…Matt?"

"Come on, big sister, we got to get you up out of this bed."

"Where's Loretta?"

"Bessie just put her down for her nap over at our place. Your kids be fine. What I needs you to do is to get up and let Beulah and me help you get dressed."

"Here," Beulah said, picking up a robe from the chair. "This'll be easy to slip on her."

"You're gonna be just fine," Matt encouraged, helping her to sit up and slip her arms through the sleeves. "You hungry?" he asked, helping her stand and shuffle out of the bedroom.

"A little," Ruby mumbled, making her way slowly down the hallway with Matt holding her arm.

"Well, we're gonna fix you up a nice plate," Beulah said cheerfully, holding back her tears. "I got a big mess of collard greens, mash taters, and po'k chops and gravy cooked up for you in the kitchen."

Beulah and Matt struggled to help their semiconscious charge down the stairs and into the kitchen to settle her at the table with a plate of food.

She sat motionless, staring at her plate.

"You ain't hungry, baby?" Beulah asked.

"A little."

Beulah fed her several bites of mashed potatoes and sprinkled hot sauce over her collard greens. "Matt brung over these collards early this mornin'. They turned out real nice."

"Here, baby," Matt offered, "have some ice tea."

Ruby sipped the iced tea, dribbling it down her chin.

"I got it, Beulah," Matt said, wiping Ruby's chin with a napkin.

Beulah kept fighting back her tears, offering Ruby a forkful of collard greens. "I sho' done change my mind about Doctah Adams—he a devil in disguise."

"Yeah," Matt agreed, looking at the kitchen clock and seeing that it was almost half past noon. "When she supposed to take her next pill?"

Beulah glanced at the clock. "He say she s'posed to have it in just a little bit."

"Maybe we can get some of it outta her system before that man gets back."

Ruby managed to use her fork and eat several mouthfuls of collard greens.

"Good girl!" Beulah cheered. "Here, let me cut up those po'k chops for you."

Over the next half hour, Matt and Beulah helped Ruby to eat half a pork chop, several bites of collard greens and most of her mashed potatoes and gravy.

Matt wiped his forehead. "I think that's all we gonna get down her for a while."

"That was good, Beulah," Ruby said.

Beulah grinned. "You feelin' a little bit better now, Miss Ruby?"

Shaking her head slowly, she said, "That medicine must be real strong."

"I know," said Matt. "I flushed it down the toilet."

A trace of concern came across her face. "You don't think I might need it?"

"I think you needs to ride with me over to Jacksonville. Leona say she be glad for you to stay at her place for a few weeks."

"I don't want to leave my house," Ruby protested.

"It be good for you to get some rest," Beulah urged.

"And you need to get away from Doctah Adams," Matt added.

"He's the big man in Live Oak, now," Ruby announced proudly. "I have to do what he tells me."

"No, you don't, Ruby," Matt said sternly. "That man's a devil—a real, live devil. He just makin' you *think* he's helpin'."

"Sam and me depend on him for protection."

"Protection from what?" Matt scoffed.

"Everybody who wants our money," she replied.

Matt kissed his sister on the forehead. "We'll talk about all that later, Ruby. Right now we got to get you out of here."

"I'm not leavin' my house!"

"But, Ruby..."

"I said no," she said firmly.

Seeing that she was adamant, Beulah and Matt looked at each other and left the kitchen.

In the dining room, Matt teared up. "She don't remember nothin' 'bout that man. They done somethin' to her head over there in that crazy house."

Beulah cried on Matt's shoulder. "Lawd forgive me for leavin' this house and all the chillun, but I cain't see Ms. Ruby like this no mo'."

Chapter Forty-Two

Although she refused to travel to Jacksonville to stay with Leona, Ruby took Matt's advice about the Thorazine and kept her secret from Adams. Two weeks without the tranquilizer had left her with a clearer mind and a desire to get back to her housework, especially now with the chores piling up since Beulah's tearful departure. Still, even though she had come out of the Thorazine fog, the insulin shock treatments had left gaps in her memory, and she had trouble remembering things from the months before her hospital stay, including her interactions with Adams.

Bracing herself for the backlog of bookkeeping that awaited her in the safe, Ruby pulled open the steel door and was relieved to find Sam's bolita receipts stacked in neatly labeled brown paper bags on the lower shelves. With each week of receipts separately identified, it would be much easier to catch up with her accounting.

After four grueling hours of reconciling the bolita receipts against the cash — a job that would earlier have taken perhaps an hour — Ruby pulled the adding machine lever and read the grand total. No! That couldn't be right. Suspecting the drug's aftereffects, she made a second count, then a third, but the shortage was the same: two thousand dollars to the penny.

Picking up the telephone, she drummed her fingers nervously on the desk, waiting for the operator. "Operator, would you please get me the residence of Buck McCollum in Fort Myers? That's M-C-C-O-L-L-U-M." She waited for what seemed an eternity until the operator at last connected her.

"Sam?"

"Yeah, Ruby. You feelin' better?"

"I'm fine, Sam."

"Did Beulah come back?"

"No, Beulah told Matt she didn't want to work here anymore," she said with a touch of irritation in her voice. "Sam, I'm calling about something I just found when I reconciled January's work. From what I can see, we're exactly two thousand dollars short."

"What!"

"I said, we're two thousand dollars short."

"How'd that happen?"

"That's what I was about to ask you. Did you take that much money down there with you?"

"No, Ruby. I only took about five hundred. I'm staying here at Buck's, so I don't need much money."

"There's only one other person who knows the combination to the safe."

"You mean the doc?"

"Yeah."

"Ruby, you better be real careful 'bout accusin' him of takin' our money. There's no tellin' what he might do."

"I'm not going to accuse him of anything. I'll just bring it up the next time he's here and see what he has to say."

"You better watch yourself."

"I will, Sam. I will," she assured him, and hung up the telephone. Now she had to figure out how to approach Adams.

****

Late that evening, Adams found the front door of the McCollum house locked, so he used his key. Finding no one downstairs, he went in the kitchen to rummage through the refrigerator.

Upstairs, Ruby woke, hearing a noise downstairs. Sliding open the drawer to her nightstand, she took out Sam's Smith and Wesson .38 revolver and crept down the stairway.

Seeing no one in the living room, she tiptoed through the dining room toward the kitchen. "Jesus!" she screamed when the kitchen door slammed in her face.

Adams laughed. "I scare you?"

Ruby gasped. "I thought somebody had broken in."

"Well, it's just me," he said, glancing at the gun in her hand. "Might better put that thing away before you hurt yourself."

"I heard a noise downstairs that woke me up," Ruby explained, her heart still racing.

Adams yawned. "I got a big day ahead of me tomorrow, so I need to hit the sack. Kids asleep?"

"Yeah," she replied, following him up the stairs.

As they passed the office, Ruby asked, "Did you take any money out of the safe?"

"You accusin' me of stealin', woman?"

She stopped dead in her tracks, realizing that she should have been more careful with her words. "No, of course not. It's just that I came up short when I reconciled the books. I already checked with Sam, so I thought I'd ask if you took the money and planned to tell me later."

Adams stalked into the bedroom after her and threw his satchel on the dresser. "Good Gawd Almighty, woman! Who the hell do you think you're talkin' to?"

"It's my job to keep track of the money," Ruby protested, sitting on the side of the bed.

"It's your job to do what I tell you," he snapped back, taking a hypodermic and a vial from his satchel. "And I can see you ain't takin' your medicine like I told you to."

"But, I..."

"But nothin'," Adams interrupted, filling the syringe.

Ruby jumped up from the bed to try to escape, but he caught her easily and plunged the needle deep into her arm.

"No, please! Oh, God...oh...God..."

When she passed out onto the bed, Adams put the syringe away and picked up the telephone receiver. "Operator, this is Dr. Adams. Patch me through to Jeff Elliott, would you, please? It's an emergency."

He felt Ruby's pulse while he waited for his call to be patched through to Elliott's car radio. "Hello, Jeff?"

"Hey, Doc," he drawled. "What can I do for you?"

"I'm out here at the McCollum place. Ruby's done overdosed again. You think you can take her over to Brewster while I call and tell 'em she's comin'?"

"I'll fill 'er up and be burnin' the road in five, Doc."

Chapter Forty-Three

Adams walked into Blue's Lodge to find Blue, Howell, and Elliott laughing around a table with a six-layer cake topped with dozens of candles.

"Hey, boys," he called amid the convivial greetings, "looks like we got ourselves a party." He looked around. "Where's Keith?"

Blue glanced at the mantel clock. "He's late."

Adams leaned over the table, swiped up a finger-full of the icing, and sat down licking it. "He'd better get here soon or this cake ain't gonna make it."

"It's today, ain't it?" Howell asked.

"His secretary told me it was March twenty-eighth," Elliott confirmed. "We're a day late, but there's no way we coulda got him over here on a weekday."

"Hey fellas," chimed Black, coming in and hanging his hat on the hatrack at the front desk. "Jumpin' Jehoshaphat, LaVergne!" he exclaimed. "That cake's big enough to choke two mules."

Blue chuckled. "Had to be—how else could I fit forty-eight candles on it?"

"How've things been with your campaign, Doc?" Black asked.

"Pretty good," Adams reported through a mouthful of cake. "Got a passel of signs printed up, hired a bunch of teenagers to put 'em out after school every day, and Mrs. Workman's writin' up ads to plaster all over the *Democrat*, startin' in April."

"Sounds like you been busy, all right," Black acknowledged, pulling out a chair. "I haven't had much time to get out there stumpin' the trail, myself."

"Hell, Keith, you're a shoo-in," Adams assured him, chomping happily away.

Elliott glanced at Black. "I hear Ruby's back out of the hospital again, Doc. Why didn't they keep her longer?"

"They said she seemed to be doin' better."

"She givin' you any more trouble?"

"I ordered enough Thorazine to keep her quiet until after the election. This time I'm gonna make damn sure she takes it, even if I have to go over there and shove it down her goddamn throat."

Elliott laughed. "Let me know if you need any help."

"What's this Thorazine?" Blue inquired.

"New drug to keep the crazies quiet."

"Just what she needs, Doc," Black quipped, cutting a piece of cake. "Now that we got Sam workin' on settin' up bolita in Lake City, I wouldn't want him gettin' distracted by that crazy wife of his."

"How are Sam and his boys comin' along over there, Keith?" Adams inquired, helping himself to another piece of cake.

"They've already set up two jooks and thrown quite a few fish fries to introduce themselves to the colored community. Sam even set the payout high for his first week."

"He always was a smart nigger," Howell commented. "Evelyn give you any idea how much money he's takin' in, Doc?"

"She tells me he's runnin' about a thousand a week," he said, sucking the icing off his fingers.

"You got Evelyn keepin' the books for you now, Leroy?" Blue asked.

"Yeah. She's pretty damn good at it, too. I paid for her to take those bookkeeping courses out at the tech school—can't rely on Ruby no more. 'Sides, with us havin' to close bolita down over here, we won't need Ruby much longer no how."

"Saw two Live Oak cabs over at the county line yesterday," Elliott reported. "Looks like Sam's got the run goin' already."

"Yeah," said Black, patting his mouth with a napkin. "He told me his boys set up a few stills out at the river, but he's still havin' a hard time keepin' up with the demand for tax-free liquor over in Lake City."

"Might not be a bad idea for him to go slow till after the election," Howell suggested, leaning back in his chair. "We need to keep up the story that we've run Bolita Sam out of the county—don't need folks sayin' he just set up shop right next door."

"You got a point there," Black agreed. "On another note, I'm getting concerned that the IRS is going to start auditing the books, Doc. I showed Evelyn how to keep two sets so we have one to show 'em if they drop by...hope you don't mind."

Adams winked. "Now we know why you're our lawyer."

"You can't get any better, Doc. I'm afraid we're going to have to move on to other business, though. Bolita and shine are gonna be a thing of the past once the feds get to snooping around our neck of the woods."

"Guess you're right. We'll just have to come up with another cash cow."

A twinkle came into Black's eyes. "Don't think that'll be a problem with Governor Warren's new road project, Doc."

"How's that?"

"When we talked last week, he told me Highway Ninety's going to be straightened out to go right through downtown Live Oak. That means the price of property east of downtown towards Lake City is gonna go through the roof."

"God-Almighty-damn!" Adams blurted out, dropping cake crumbs on his belly. "Sounds like we need to buy ourselves some dirt, boys."

Chapter Forty-Four

Toward the end of Adams's campaign for the state senate, Mrs. Workman wrote a speech and asked his permission to present it to the Live Oak Garden Club. Adams readily agreed and went her one better, sponsoring a spot for her on the radio as well.

On April 21, Mrs. Workman sat proudly reading her speech to WNER's audience, reaching the citizens of the Seventeenth Senatorial District, while her husband stood alongside Adams, watching through the glass window of the sound booth.

"Friends and fellow citizens," she began, "I wish to speak to you on behalf of a man who bases his campaign for office on the amazing platform of the welfare of our children: Dr. C. Leroy Adams. In this web of politics and intrigue, this seems a clear call to parents to support a person whose primary interest is our greatest concern—our children."

With heartfelt conviction, Mrs. Workman pressed on through her three-page typewritten epistle, appealing to "the women, especially in this area, to join me in enthusiastic support of Dr. Adams. He is a man whose primary interest is our homes and our children. Surely we have here that which we seek in a man to represent our area."

Concluding her speech, she looked to the announcer, a tall, wiry man with red hair so frizzy he resembled a cartoon character who had just stuck his finger in an electric socket. "The foregoing was a paid political announcement," he said, "paid for by the friends to elect Dr. C. Leroy Adams state senator. This is Cousin Claire Parker comin' to you live from the studios of WNER, your radio station in Live Oak and the Greater Suwannee River Valley. Now, let's catch up with Hank Williams, who's mighty upset about 'Your Cheatin' Heart.'"

"How'd I do?" Mrs. Workman asked anxiously.

Parker winked, opening the door to the sound booth. "You were perfect, Mrs. Workman."

Adams gave her a bear hug. "Great job! How 'bout I get the whole thing printed up in the *Democrat*?"

"That'd be wonderful!" Mrs. Workman beamed. "I've never been published before."

Dr. Workman hugged his wife. "You did a superb job, dear....
Now it's your turn, Leroy."

"He'll do just fine when he gets up there to give his speech," Mrs.
Workman announced proudly, squeezing Adams's hand.

Driving the Workmans from the radio station along Highway 90
into Live Oak, Adams saw an old man hoeing in the rose garden of a
two-story colonial house. "Why, there's Doc Lee, out workin' in his
yard."

"I don't know where that man gets so much energy at his age,"
Mrs. Workman marveled, waving at the elderly dentist. "He certainly
devoted a lot of effort to our campaign for a dry county."

"Yes, he did," Adams agreed. "And it sure paid off," he said with a
smile as he turned right at the stop sign where Highway 90 became
Ohio Avenue. Driving slowly along the busy thoroughfare, he approached the courthouse, where Jeff Elliott radioed to his car. "Hey,
Doc, Gray'll show you where to park."

Picking up the microphone, Adams said, "Thanks, Jeff."

"Well, isn't that marvelous!" Mrs. Workman exclaimed.

"Comes in handy," Adams agreed, pulling into the space that
Deputy Gray pointed out to him.

Gray opened the passenger door and helped Dr. and Mrs. Workman out of the car.

"Thank you, sir," Mrs. Workman said, pulling her skirt into place.

Adams led the Workmans through the crowd on the courthouse
lawn to the campaign platform and helped Mrs. Workman up the
stairs, where she and her husband slipped past the other candidates
and their supporters to sit beside him.

Leon McDonald, the master of ceremonies, tapped on the microphone atop the flag-draped podium. "Ladies and gentlemen, may I
have your attention, please? It's a great honor for me to introduce to
you our fine candidates."

The crowd cheered enthusiastically.

"As y'all know, I'm a man of few words—but that's more than I
can say for the gentlemen sitting behind me today." Laughter rippled
through the crowd. "Having said that, let me first introduce Dr. C.
Leroy Adams, one of our two fine Democratic candidates for state
senator."

Adams stepped to the microphone before a cheering crowd.
"Thank you, Leon," he began, waiting for the applause to die down.
"Keep up the good work over there at the Suwannee Hotel. This fella

serves up a fine mess of black-eyed peas and cornbread if y'all want to stop by and belly up after we get done bendin' your ears." This elicited some merriment in the crowd. "Brothers and sisters," Adams continued, "I want to thank y'all for comin' out here today. I know y'all are goin' to do your jobs in a couple of weeks, when you drive downtown and pull that lever in the votin' booth."

He smiled at the cheering crowd. "And when you pull that lever, I want you to think about it like you're droppin' the trapdoor out from under those crooks over in Tallahassee so you can hang 'em high, like they deserve. And when you've done your job, I can go over there and tell 'em what we need right here in Suwannee County."

Watching the roaring crowd, he waited to deliver his next line. "It's about time we got our fair share of revenues from all those rich Yankees down in south Florida."

"You tell 'em, Doc!" a man yelled.

"That's just what I'm gonna do!" Adams yelled back. "Next month, when you send me over there to Tallahassee, I'm gonna tell 'em, and I'm gonna keep on tellin' 'em until we get what we deserve for the fine citizens of Suwannee County."

He paused for his cheering supporters, then said, "We need better schools for our children!"

"You tell 'em, Doc."

"We need free medical care for our poor and our elderly. We need lower taxes!"

"Yeah, you tell 'em, Doc!"

"We, the people of Suwannee County, will be heard!"

Adams raised his hand, giving the victory sign to chants of "You tell 'em, Doc."

Adams' Inn
Lake City, Florida

Chapter Forty-Five

Parking in front of his boarding house in Lake City, Adams grabbed a copy of the *Democrat* from the front seat and got out of his car.

Leaning against the fender, he admired the renovation of the old Victorian house with its gingerbread porch and fresh coat of blue paint with white trim. He smiled proudly at the sign announcing "Adams Inn" and the bright yellow clumps of narcissus that Evelyn had planted along the winding white brick walkway. Walking up to the gate in the whitewashed picket fence covered with climbing pink floribunda roses, he congratulated himself for managing to pick up the property for back taxes.

Reaching for the gate, his thoughts raced back in time to the day when his father and mother moved into their newly built Victorian home in his hometown of Jasper, just north of Live Oak. In many ways, it was a larger version of his current boarding house, with its blue paint and white gingerbread trim. Then he frowned, leaping forward in time to the day that his childhood homestead was thrown into his father's bankruptcy and he had to face the taunts of classmates in high school.

Ain't nobody gonna take this from me, he told himself, treasuring his most recent addition to the Adams Company, the land rich corporation he had acquired from his Uncle Claude in exchange for a lifetime supply of cocaine.

Crossing the front porch, he leaned over the railing to look at the spacious side yard. There he saw an overgrowth of scuppernong vines, just like he used to help his grandfather pick from his vineyard to make his special holiday wine. *Got to get that yard nigger to build me an arbor,* he told himself, wondering if his grandfather had passed along his winemaking secrets to his Uncle Claude.

Inside the unfurnished bed and breakfast, he admired the red brick fireplace and the newly refinished oak flooring and freshly painted crown molding. Going upstairs to one of the bedrooms along a hallway, he found a shapely pair of legs sticking out from under the lace bed skirt of the four-poster bed.

"Whatcha doin' sugah?" he asked, bending down to tickle Evelyn's bare feet.

"Ooh!" she exclaimed, wriggling out from under the bed with a fuzzy pink slipper in her hand. "You're such a bugger! What do you think about what I've done with the place?"

Adams looked around the room at the new white lace curtains and garish Victorian furniture that Evelyn had rescued from local thrift shops.

"Looks great," he said, giving her a peck on the cheek. "Got somethin' for you."

"Oh! Oh!" she said, taking the newspaper he handed her and eagerly leafing through it to find Adams's quarter-page campaign ad with a three-by-five-inch portrait shot. "I love it!" she squealed. "Who took the picture?"

"I had it made at Mims' studio down at the Suwannee Hotel."

"You look so handsome," she cooed, stroking his double chin. "I didn't even know you owned a suit."

"Had to get one made down at Sharple's."

"Let's see...," Evelyn began, reading the ad aloud...

To the Voters of the Seventeenth Senatorial District, composed of Hamilton, Suwannee and Lafayette Counties, Your Candidate For State Senator Will give you his QUALIFICATIONS, for the most IMPORTANT POSITION in your District:

- Born and lived all of my life in the 17th Senatorial District
- Graduate of Jasper High School
- Have First Grade Teacher's Certificate
- Am a Registered Pharmacist
- Have worked as a laborer during Hoover Days
- Rode turpentine woods and worked with timber for several years
- Am a Doctor of Medicine
- At present, I operate one of the largest farms in north Florida

I understand your needs, because:

- I was raised with many of you.
- I went to school with many of you.
- I dug ditches on the W.P.A. with many of you.
- I rode turpentine woods, and worked with timber, around many of your homes.

- I have served many of you, as a druggist in retail drug stores.
- I have visited in many of your homes.
- I have served you as your doctor in your time of sickness.
- I operate a large farm at this time; therefore, I understand the farmer's needs.

All this gives me a better understanding of your needs and wants. I shall do everything in my power to serve you to the best of my ability, with your wishes, happiness and prosperity always first in mind.

YOUR SERVANT,
LEROY ADAMS

"I love it! I love it!" Evelyn cried, jumping on the bed to the rhythm of squeaking bedsprings.

"Yeah," Adams grinned, falling onto the bed. "It's not bad."

"Let's see what the other guy has to say," Evelyn suggested, riffling impatiently through the pages. "Here it is: 'Even through the distressing days of the 30s when many of us were on WPA, or in dire financial stress, Wiley Grantham, through application of his intelligence and long hours of hard work, was promoting a growing and prosperous business.'"

"Get a load of this guy—thinks he's Mr. Big Shot!" Evelyn snipped. "Has to rub it in that he was gettin' rich while everybody else worked for the WPA." She turned back to Adams's ad and carefully tore it from the paper to place it lovingly on the dresser. Wrinkling her nose, she rolled up the remainder of the paper to toss it in the wastebasket. "The rest of this is trash."

Adams laughed. "Just don't forget to vote."

"You know I'd vote for you if I could, Big Daddy," Evelyn said sweetly, unbuttoning her blouse, but I ain't twenty-one yet. "Mama's gonna vote for you, though."

Adams pulled down his trousers. "I got a surprise for you, sugah!"

She giggled, tossing her blouse on the bed. "Oh, it ain't no surprise no more, Doctor."

"Not that, pussycat—I mean I got a place for your mama to stay."

"You mean a house of her own, with no rent to pay?" she asked, slipping off her skirt.

He grinned proudly, seeing the look of disbelief on her face, then held her by her silky smooth shoulders. "That's just what I mean."

"Oh, Doctor!" Evelyn squealed, pushing him down on the bed and covering his face with kisses.

Adams laughed. "Slow down, gal!"

"Do you think we can get married one day?" she asked, straddling him to stare directly into his eyes.

"Sure, sugah. Right after I win the election."

Evelyn rolled over to lie beside him and sighed, a tear running down her cheek. "I love you so much, Doc."

Adams put his arms behind his head to stare at the ceiling. "You know I love you, too," he whispered.

Her lip quivered. "That's the first time you've told me."

Adams grew almost teary-eyed. "If I weren't married to Florrie Lee, I'd marry you right now."

Evelyn laid her head on his belly to run her fingers playfully through his graying chest hairs. "Would that mean I'd get to call you Leroy?" she asked coyly.

He laughed, bouncing her head on his belly. "Sugah, you can call me Leroy right now—when we're alone, anyway. I don't give a damn."

"I'm gonna wait till I can say it in front of the whole world," she said wistfully, waving her hand in the air.

Adams took a deep breath, dreading what he had to tell her next and preparing for the inevitable tearful protest. "You know I'm gonna be hot and heavy on the campaign trail over the next few months."

"Yeah, I know. Is there anything I can do to help?"

"We need to take a little break, sugah—just until after the election. I need to be seen out with my wife more."

Evelyn gave a stoic sigh, apparently taking the news in stride. "You've got to do what you've got to."

Her matter-of-fact response caught him off guard. "I thought you'd be real upset," he said, feeling a bit disappointed that she was able to take the prospect of being separated from him so easily.

She gave him a peck on the cheek. "My mama told me all good things take time, and I should spend my time helpin' you any way I can. So I'll just get this place ready for somebody else to run, and dream about when you get to be a senator and maybe even governor and we can get married and have lots of babies and live in a great big white house over there in Tallahassee."

Chapter Forty-Six

Matt called from his garden, "Bessie, can you turn on that hose for me?"

Bessie stopped the porch squeaking swing's gentle sway and handed the baby to Sonja. "Can you be a big girl and hold your sister for a minute?"

"Yes'm," Sonja said proudly, taking her baby sister.

"Now, don't swing till I get back, you hear?"

"I won't, Aunt Bessie—promise."

Ruby sat nearby in a rocking chair, reading Adams's ad in the *Democrat* while Bessie walked down the stairs to turn on the faucet at the end of the porch.

"Thank you, Bessie," Matt called. "I's just tryin' to save some of the 'matoes from dyin'."

"Laws a mercy," Bessie sighed on her way back up the porch steps, "'fit don't rain none in the next few days, we ain't gonna get nothin' out of the garden this year.... What you lookin' at?" she asked, noticing Ruby's studious expression.

"Just reading the paper."

"Any good sales in there this week?"

"Sirloin's on sale down at the Blue Front."

"How much?"

"Eighteen cents a pound."

"That *is* good. I'll have to run down there later on this afternoon."

Ruby fell silent again, a smile spreading across her face.

"How's the 'matoes holdin' up?" Bessie called to Matt on his way back from the garden.

"Don't think they gonna make it. Looks like all we'll get this year is the melons and a little bit o' cane if we're lucky."

"I keep prayin' for rain—grass ain't even green enough for the yard hens to eat."

Matt brushed the dust off of his trousers and sat in the rocking chair beside Ruby's.

"Did you hear that speech Mrs. Workman gave on WNER last week?" Ruby asked.

"I heard it, all right," Matt huffed. "Read the whole thing in the paper, too. Guess he got her fooled like ever'body else in Suwannee County."

Ruby ignored Matt's comment.

"Mama," Sonja whined, "Loretta got my dress wet."

Bessie looked over at Ruby and saw that she was still reading. "I'll take her in the house and change her. Mama's busy readin' the paper."

"What about my dress?" Sonja whined, jumping down from the swing to follow her aunt through the screen door.

Ruby sat quietly, transported by the rhythm of her rocking chair to a vision of a platform festooned with flags and patriotic bunting, where she stood beside Dr. Leroy Adams, holding his hand as the crowds cheered his victory speech and tossed a snowstorm of confetti into the air.

"Thank you, my friends," Adams called out to the crowds, holding Ruby's hand up proudly. "I want y'all to know that I couldn't have been governor without this little woman. Without her behind me, I'd still be back down on the farm, cussin' at the buzzard who couldn't wait to get over to Tallahassee and strip the pickin's off our poor bones."

Matt turned to see a faraway look in Ruby's eyes. "If you knows what's good for you, you'll pack up the kids and stay down at Mama's place."

"I can't leave here, Matt," Ruby protested, rousing from her daydream. "It's my home. I worked too hard to get where I am, and I don't plan on leaving everything I've earned."

"That man gonna be the death of you, Ruby. Don't you remember? He's already th'owed you over there in Brewster two times now!"

"I know he can be mean sometimes, but he says he's going to take me over to Tallahassee with him when he wins the election. Just imagine! He's going to be a state senator—and one day he's going to be governor."

"Big sister, you been snortin' somethin' again and it sure ain't snuff."

Ruby turned her head away from her brother. "Not since I got out of Brewster the last time."

"You mean you had that stuff over at Brewster?"

"Yes," she confessed, holding the carved ivory amulet that hung around her neck. "They didn't know I had it."

"I thought they took everything away from you when you was over there."

"Not this," she said, holding on to the amulet.

"Ruby, I can't believe you'd disrespect Grandma like that. Our own great-grandmother brung it over with her from Africa."

"Sometimes I miss being able to get rid of my troubles," she confided, removing the top of the amulet to look inside at the little bit of powder that remained. "But the doc won't give me any more of it."

"Least that's one thing he done right. Does he know you're not takin' that medicine he told us to give you?"

Ruby smiled secretively. "He can't tell if I just act like I am. And he's real good in bed—all I have to do is just lay there."

"Ruby, you know I don't care to hear nothin' 'bout that mess," Matt protested. "You playin' with fire with that white man, and you gonna lose ever'thing you got. Why you think Beulah left you and won't even come by to see us no mo'?"

Bessie stood inside the screen door with Loretta, hesitant to interrupt the intimate conversation between Matt and his sister.

Tears welled up in Ruby's eyes. "Beulah's left me. Sam's all but left me. Now the doctor's all I've got, Matt—he's my big man now."

Bessie came out of the house with Loretta, unable to control herself. "What you talkin' about, Ruby? That man ain't all you got—you got this baby and all your other chillun, and you got Matt and me. Lord help you if you thinkin' he all you got."

Chapter Forty-Seven

On May 7, Adams drove into Blue's Lodge to find the parking lot full.

"Surprise!" Blue shouted when his friend went in to find the place strung with festive ribbons and decorated with balloons, celebrating Adams's triumph in the Democratic primary. In Suwannee County that was a good as winning the election, since no candidate ever ran on the Republican ballot.

While the men stood up from the confetti-sprinkled banquet table to greet their candidate with rousing applause, Black held up the front page of the *Democrat*. "Damn, Doc! Says here, you just flat wiped Grantham out: 5,936 to 2,837—that's over a two-to-one margin! Wish I'd done that well."

"I knew Leroy could do it," LaVergne Blue crowed, eagerly passing out his prized Romeo y Julieta oscuros.

After the congratulations died down, Adams took a seat, grinning broadly as he cut off the end of the black cigar with his penknife. "Didn't know you had more of these, Lavergne."

The old man gave a knowing wink. "Saved a few back for today, Leroy."

An uncharacteristically jovial Keith Black managed a broad grin. "That makes you the fourth generation of state senators in the Adams family," he noted, leaning forward to light the victor's cigar. "Nothin' like havin' a good bloodline."

"Sorry you didn't win this round, Keith," Adams consoled.

Black threw up his hands. "That damn Slaughter's been out on the campaign trail night and day—I just didn't have the time to put into it."

Adams blew a smoke ring. "Saw that wife of his out there right alongside him. Hell of a good looker, that one," he said with a twinkle in his eye.

"Darn good violinist, too," Blue commented. "Folks say she studied music in college."

Adams laughed. "She can damn sure play my fiddle anytime she wants to."

Blue saw that Keith Black found the remark distasteful. "Guess with the liquor still flowin', they figured Sim didn't run Sam McCollum out of Suwannee County after all," he interjected.

"Hugh's a good man," Black said. "If we can talk him into looking the other way when we need him to, he's the best bottleneck we've got. Slaughter sure as hell won't go out and play sheriff all by himself."

"I figure, what with Ruby under control and Sam workin' Columbia County, we're set to go," Adams concluded. "Sounds like all we need to do is have a little talk with the new sheriff."

"Anybody gettin' hungry?" Blue asked.

"Hell, yeah," Adams roared. "What you got back there for supper?"

"Got some chicken-fried steak, biscuits, mashed new potatoes and gravy..." Blue paused to watch his friend's face. "And some friend shrimp and French fries—your favorite."

Adams winked. "You sure as hell know how to feed a fella."

While Blue and his kitchen help, Jimmy, ferried platters of food to the table, Black asked, "Are you going to the Democratic National Convention in July, Leroy?"

"Damn straight," Adams announced proudly. "And since I started goin' to church to pump hands like you told me, I even got me a new suit to wear up there. Damn thing set me back fifty bucks. One of my nurses got so excited seen' me in church, she drove up to Georgia and bought me a Confederate tie to go with it."

"Dressed to kill, huh, Leroy? Guess there's hope for you yet," Blue teased as he set down a platter of fried shrimp. "Jimmy," he snapped on his way back to the kitchen, "fill up that tea like I told you."

Adams smiled, seeing the old man ride his helper. "That Jimmy's a piece of work. Asked me for a job the day I won—probably planned on doin' the same with Grantham if he'd come out on top. Problem is, I don't know as I'd have anything a fella like that could do."

Black looked up from his plate. "You thinkin' about runnin' for governor after you spend a term or two in the state senate?"

"That's the plan, my friend," Adams bragged, sucking the meat out of a shrimp tail and adding it to the growing pile on his plate.

"Kind of a shame, though, to waste all those years in medical school," Blue interjected, returning to the table to sit with the men.

"Hell, LaVergne, like I told you, medicine was always just a hobby with me. My granddaddy was right about that—politics runs in my blood."

Black grinned. "He sure was, Doc. You get to be governor and you can buy all the docs you need."

"That's what ol' Granddaddy used to tell me. 'It's all about power,' he'd say. 'Never forget that, son—leave heaven to the niggers and the poor white folks.'"

Black held up his champagne glass. "Well, boys," he toasted, "here's to our new state senator."

"Three cheers for Leroy," Blue said, clinking glasses with the men at the table.

Black sipped his champagne and looked over the top of his wire-rimmed eyeglasses at Adams. "When it all comes out in the wash, I guess I still have a job workin' with the doc—right, Doc?"

"Hell, yeah!" Adams said, and drained his glass. "Where else am I gonna get myself a lawyer like you?"

Chapter Forty-Eight

On Thursday, May 22, Adams found Ruby curled up in a fetal position on her bed. "You and Sam been fightin' again?"

"No," she moaned. "I think I'm pregnant."

Adams smiled proudly, throwing his physician's bag on the dresser. "I knew it—I always know. Guess you'll have to stop takin' that Thorazine—ain't no tellin' what it'll do to the baby."

"I already did."

His face darkened. "Next time you get it in that thick head of yours to make up your own mind, check with me first."

She looked up at him and whimpered, "If I'm pregnant, you've got to give me an abortion."

"What's the matter, brown sugah? You tired of havin' my babies?"

Ruby got out of bed and stood in front of her dresser with her back to the window. "You know Sam'll kill me this time," she cried, wringing her hands.

Adams smirked. "Sam'll do what I tell him, when I tell him."

"He swore he'd kill me if another baby came out light," Ruby sobbed, staring at her reflection in the mirrored closet doors across the bedroom, remembering that she and Beulah had cleaned out all of her maternity clothes after Sonja was born. It had been a day of celebration for her—the day she resolved that her childbearing years were over.

"Like I told you, Ruby, he ain't gonna do Jack shit unless I tell him to. I'm the one you should be afraid of. Do I have to throw you over there in Brewster again?"

"If you won't give me an abortion, I'll have to go out of town to get one."

"You ain't goin' nowhere," Adams snapped, grabbing her arm.

Recognizing the cruel look clouding his face Ruby backed against the window, feeling cornered and helpless. "Can't we just get rid of this one and go on with our lives?" she pleaded. "We can move over to Tallahassee like you said, and leave Sam here with his schoolteacher bitch."

"Since when do you think you're movin' over to Tallahassee?" Adams taunted.

"What do you mean?" Ruby asked incredulously.

"You heard me. You ain't goin' nowhere. You're gonna have this baby and you're gonna stay right here in Live Oak and do what I tell you, you understand?"

"You promised…"

"You've got two choices, Ruby," Adams interrupted, holding up a finger. "One, you can clean up your act and keep on runnin' what business there is left here." He held up a second finger. "Or, two, you can spend the rest of your life over there in Chattahoochee."

"I thought you wanted me with you," she said, a tear trickling down her cheek.

Adams grabbed her by the throat. "You dumb nigger bitch! How the hell did you get it in that crazy head of yours that you're somethin' special?"

Ruby gasped for air. "You're choking me!"

Adams loosened his grip. "You're livin' in this mansion, drivin' those new cars, and wearin' those fancy diamond rings because of me, you understand? So why don't you get over those crazy ideas of movin' to Tallahassee, consider yourself lucky to be a rich nigger, and make a life for yourself right here in Live Oak?"

"You hurt me," Ruby complained, rubbing her neck and taking a seat on the bed.

Adams laughed. "You always did look sexy when you were hurt. I'd fuck you now, but I don't have the time."

Looking at the nightstand next to her, the image of Sam's nickel-plated Smith & Wesson popped into Ruby's mind. She could see herself taking it from the drawer and emptying it into Adams's belly.

Adams grabbed his bag. "I'm leaving now," he announced indifferently from the doorway. "And I ain't comin' back unless I need some cash or a fuck."

Ruby sat on the bed, digging her fingernails into the bedspread to control the hand that so desperately wanted to pull out the drawer in the nightstand.

Downstairs, Adams passed Sam coming into the house.

"How you doin', Sam?"

"I be fine, Doctah," Sam replied, closing the door behind him. Looking around the living room, he saw that the children were not home, so he walked upstairs.

"Ruby?" Sam called, going to her bedroom. "Where the kids?"

Ruby wiped her face and looked up at him. "Sammy's at football practice, and Kay and Sonja went downtown with Matt and Bessie to see Snow White at the Alimar."

Sam smiled and turned to leave the room. "They'll like that."

"Sam," Ruby began nervously, "I don't know how to tell you this…"

"Tell me what, Ruby?" he asked, turning back to see the pained look on her face.

She could feel her body tighten up, preparing to defend herself. "I'm going to have a baby."

"What!" he cried in disbelief. "What are you gonna do about it?"

"I asked the doctor for an abortion, but he said he'd kill me if I had one."

"So go over to Jacksonville and have somebody do it over there," he said coldly.

"He'd know, Sam," Ruby pleaded, her face glistening with tears.

"So? It'd be too late for him to stop you."

Ruby jumped up from the bed to stand face to face with him. "He said he'd kill me, Sam. He said he wanted his baby."

Sam's face hardened. "You done got yourself caught between two guns, then, woman, 'cause if you have another baby by that bastard, I'll kill you. You done it to me once—you ain't gonna do it to me again."

"I don't want to have his baby any more than you want me to," she pleaded, reaching out to touch his shoulder.

"I don't want to hear nothin' more outta you, woman!" he snarled, pushing her hand away. "Seein' what I'm seein' out of that snake Keith Black, I drove over here today to ask you if you wanted to take the kids and leave town with me. But now you've gone and pushed me too far, and I don't give a damn what happens to you." He turned and stormed out of the bedroom.

Ruby fell back on the bed and lay there, her tears gradually drying as she escaped to a pleasant past, her ever more convenient refuge from an unbearable present.

****

Straightening the red rosebud in her hair and adjusting the strand of faux pearls around her neck, Ruby stood on her front porch, waiting for Sam to arrive for their prom date.

It was a special night, celebrating her graduation from Fessenden Academy, a private school to which her teachers had recommended her.

Though she wanted desperately to sit down, she had to stand for fear of wrinkling her treasured dress. Reminding herself that Sam was never late, she spotted a red Buick pulling onto the front yard. *Look at that shine!* she said to herself, thinking how it was polished like a shiny apple for a favorite teacher.

She didn't know a soul with a car that nice. But there was Sam, stepping out of it, wearing a white tuxedo with a red bow tie and cummerbund. How handsome he was with his hair slicked neatly back, stepping onto the front porch with a broad grin on his face.

Sam brushed her lips with a light kiss. "You're the prettiest girl I ever did see, Ruby," he said, admiring her dress.

"Thank you," she replied, looking into his sparkling steel-gray eyes. Straightening his bow tie and wondering why he held his hand behind his back, she said, "You're really handsome yourself. Whose car are you driving?"

"It's mine, Ruby. I won it in a poker game."

"Really?" Ruby exclaimed, thinking how nice she would look in a car that matched her dress. "You always were good at cards."

Sam grinned. "Sam's the name, and poker's my game."

Ruby laughed. "What's that behind your back?"

"Oh, nothing," he teased.

"Come on, give it to me!" Ruby insisted, reaching behind him to pull his hand forward.

With a sheepish grin, he held up a corsage of four red rosebuds with wisps of fresh green fern, nestled in red and white ribbons.

She felt a warm tingle up her spine, knowing that Sam must have driven up to Gainesville or down to Ocala to buy the corsage, since there were no florists in Zuber. "Oh, Sam, they're beautiful," she cooed, noticing that it matched her dress perfectly. "But, how did you know what color to buy?"

"A little bird told me," he confessed with a nervous laugh, unsure exactly how to go about pinning the corsage on her dress.

"Musta been a mama bird," Ruby shot back, knowing how much her mother liked her beau.

Sam fumbled with the corsage until Ruby broke the silence. "Well, are you going to pin it on my dress, or do you plan on just carrying it for me?"

Sam shuffled his feet, feeling the blood rush to his face. "Ruby, I don't know where this thing's supposed to go."

"Here, I'll show you," she offered maternally, taking the corsage from him and pinning it in place. "Next time you'll know how to do it," she said, surprised, yet pleased that he was inexperienced in this intimate ritual.

"I got somethin' else for you," Sam announced eagerly.

"You bought me a present?" Ruby asked with growing anticipation. "You know it's not my birthday until August."

"It ain't no birthday present," he assured her, enjoying the suspense. "Had to drive up to Lewis Jewelers in Gainesville to find it."

"Where is it?" she demanded eagerly.

He gave a boyish grin. "I got it in my pocket."

She thrust her hand into his pocket and grabbed what her hand hit first—soft, yielding flesh.

Sam jolted to attention. "Ruby! Not out here on the porch, baby!"

She felt the blood rush to her face. "I'm sorry, Sam!"

He fell back onto the porch swing, laughing. Unable to help herself, Ruby joined in, and the couple's harmonizing laughter ricocheted off the front porch, surrounding them with the music of young love.

After several rounds of alternately gazing at each other and breaking into laughter, Sam stood and reached in his pocket to fish out a small black velvet box.

She stood and opened it to find a yellow gold ring with a single small brilliant-cut ruby. "A ruby for my Ruby," he announced proudly. Knowing all he needed to know from the smile on her face, he slipped the ring onto her finger, then kissed her hand.

"Does this mean you're asking me to marry you?" she asked coyly, feeling like the leading lady in a romantic movie.

"Yes," Sam admitted shyly. "That's the only way you'll ever let me give you the other present you found in my pocket."

She slapped him on the shoulder. "You can give me that on our wedding night, lover boy!"

"And when do you want *that* to be?" he asked.

"Right after graduation."

Sam's jaw dropped. "You foolin' me?"

"We've got to start right away if we want everything we've been dreaming about," she said confidently, admiring her ring.

"Well, that settles it!" Sam declared with an emphatic slap to his knee. "I'll go down and see the preacher in the mornin', right before church."

"You know where we're going to spend our honeymoon?"

"Yeah," he said, grinning. "We're goin' up to New York like we talked about, so I can find a good-payin' job in construction."

"You're my big man, Sam," Ruby whispered, throwing her arms around him.

"You ready to go now, baby?"

Ruby grabbed his hand. "Let's make the good times roll, sugar!" she shouted, running with him to the car.

Chapter Forty-Nine

Ruby lay in foaming white bubbles up to her neck, finding little comfort in the hot bathwater that normally relaxed and soothed her. After yesterday's encounter with Adams, her night had been one of fitful sleep and vivid dreams—failed attempts to escape the living nightmare that her world had become.

Ruby reached up from the tub to grab her towel. "Damn!" she cried, seeing her dressing table mirror crash to the black and white floor tiles. "How did that get in here?"

Standing up to dry off, she looked down at the shards of mirror to see a shattered person, a broken soul scattered in a thousand pieces.

She stepped out of the tub to pick up the pieces, cutting her bath-softened fingertip on a sliver of glass. "Dear God!" she cried. The falling drips of crimson blood spattered against a background of black and white. Then she had the strangest feeling that all the torment that had filled her soul was draining out of her body, dripping out of her in the blood that fell to the floor.

After bandaging her finger and cleaning up the floor, Ruby glanced in the mirror over the sink and noticed a smear of blood on her amulet. Then the room faded to become her grandmother's clapboard cabin in Zuber, and she was a girl of eighteen again.

****

"You all right, Grandma?" Ruby asked the bent little woman with a face as wizened and wrinkled as if it had been fashioned from a shriveled apple.

"I be fine in a minute," the old woman moaned, pulling the crocheted lap warmer up over her legs. "I's just havin' one of my spells."

Her grandmother's "spells" were getting more frequent, and her leathery gnarled hands had grown colder to the touch as the days grew shorter heading into winter. Seeing that she had recovered, Ruby stood next to her and held out her hand. "Look what Sam gave me, Grandma."

"Laws a mercy, me!" Grandma Jackson exclaimed, holding Ruby's hand to admire the engagement ring in the dim light entering the only window in the room. "Sam's a good man, and I knows he loves you."

"Yes, he does," Ruby assured her, sitting beside her on the thread-bare crushed-velvet sofa to watch the dying embers in the fireplace. "Are you cold, Grandma?" Ruby asked, concerned that the chills might come back.

"Oh, honey chile, I's always havin' cold spells these days," she said, seeing the light fade from the sky as the sun sank below the horizon. "The blood's done drained outta these old bones." Grandma Jackson lifted a bony finger to point to the fireplace. "Would you put on another piece of fat lighter and that big oak log yonder? Fire startin' to die down again."

Ruby picked up a few pieces of resin-rich fat lighter wood from the small basket beside the fireplace and set them on the grate over the glowing embers. The fat lighter began hissing and sizzling like bacon, dripping down onto the coals to reanimate the dying flame. Then she heaved the heavy bolt of oak on top of the fat lighter and tossed kerosene from a tin can into the fireplace.

"Careful, child," her grandmother cautioned when the fire blazed up the chimney and flashed over the hearth.

"I'm fine," Ruby assured her, nestling into the sofa's dark wine-red nap, enjoying the velvety feel she remembered from earliest child-hood.

"You and Sam gettin' married soon?"

"Sam's going to talk to the preacher today."

Grandma Jackson chuckled. "Times sure be changin'. In my day, white folks didn't let coloreds get married. We just held hands and jumped the broom; then we tol' all the colored folks we was married."

Ruby laughed. "Is that how you and Grandpa were married?"

"Sho' 'nuff," the old woman said with a faraway look in her eyes. "Go on over there to the fireplace, chile, and pull hard on that brick jus' up over the kettle."

Puzzled by the odd request, Ruby went back to the fireplace, scooted the black cast-iron kettle aside, and wiggled the loose brick in the facing until it came free.

"Now, look inside the hole and bring me the box in there," the old woman instructed.

Unable to see inside the hole in the dim light from the window, Ruby lit the kerosene lantern on the fireplace mantel and held it up to the dark, square cavity. Still unable to see anything, she reached inside, and her fingers brushed against something hard and smooth. Closing her fingers around the object, she withdrew what she could now see was a small black box.

The old woman opened it by the light of the kerosene lamp, and Ruby could see a miniature bottle inside, round on the front side and flat on the back, carved out of ivory and strung by tiny handles on a thin leather necklace.

"Here," Grandma Jackson said, offering the necklace to her.

Ruby's hands trembled as she took it.

"This come all the way from Africa," the old woman told her as she held it in her hand. "My mama had it on when the slave traders th'owed her in a cage and brung her over here. How she hid it from them men, I cain't say. She tol' me it was magic, and nobody could see it but her 'less she want 'em to. I don't know if she was just tellin' me a story or if the magic be real, but I do know that she got it here, and that's enough to make me believe nobody could see it or they woulda took it. I want you to keep it safe like I always has."

"Oh, thank you, Grandma," Ruby said, carefully hugging the old woman's frail body to her.

Her grandmother held up her hand. "But before you puts it on, I want you to know some more 'bout it. You see that little stain on it?"

Ruby nodded, noticing a small spot of dried blood in a crevice by one of the handles.

"That blood belonged to my daddy. He died tryin' to fight his massa off my mama when he come in the cabin drunk that day and tol' her she was goin' to make a baby for him."

Ruby sat spellbound, unable to believe her ears. Could it be that her great-grandmother had been raped by her owner, and her great-grandfather had died trying to defend her?

"Daddy died right then and there, but the massa died, too. Took a whole week for him to die, though, 'cause he be rasslin' with the devil all that time not wantin' to go."

Ruby sat rapt.

"I wants you to keep that like I has," her grandmother said, coughing into her handkerchief. "Hol' on to it and keep it safe."

Ruby looked down at the amulet with its gruesome secret, wishing that her grandmother had not passed such a terrible responsibility on to her. "I will, Grandma," she promised. "But what happened to your mother...my great-grandmother?"

"Mama was sold to Massa Jackson down near here."

"You mean here in Zuber?" she asked, her eyes widening in disbelief.

"Right down near Ocala," her grandmother confirmed.

"Then what happened?"

"Well, Massa Jackson was a good Christian man. He treated all us real good. Then one day, Massa come and tol' us he had to go off and fight in the war or they'd shoot him. He say if he don't come home after the war was over, we was free, since he don't have no kinfolks left. He say we can take what we can from the house before the Yankees come and takes ever'thing."

Ruby listened intently, gazing at the flickering flames reflected in the clouded dark eyes, as the old woman recalled a day from her youth that she would always remember. "The day Massa Jackson rode off on his horse, some folks talked about runnin' away, while others was afeared o' what might happen if they just up and left the plantation, thinkin' they'd be shot for runaways."

"Well, suh," her grandmother continued, "the war ended, and our massa, he never come back home. Later on, we got word he died up north of Georgia somewhere. Then one of the house slaves tol' us he knowed where our massa kep' his gold, and then all the men pulls up the floorboard, opens this great big box full of gold, and passes it out to all of us."

"He must have had a lot of money," Ruby concluded, her eyes widening.

"Yes indeedy, honey — whole lot o' money. He was a big man." Grandma Jackson smiled at the recollection. "That why all us slaves took his name."

"Then what happened?" Ruby asked, intrigued by the story.

"Well, we all settled down near the plantation, got ourselves a little piece o' land, and started plantin' our own crops. It was real hard at first, but we had 'nuff money left to buy ourself some seed and a plow — tha's all we needed."

Ruby listened in rapt fascination to how her grandmother had gained her freedom and started her life as a free person. She could only imagine how hard it must have been to raise her own food with no help in the fields.

"After I plants the first crop and started hoin' the rows," her grandmother continued, "I looked up and seen one of Massa Jackson's field slaves come walkin' down the road in front of my place. Then he stops dead in his tracks just where I's hoin' and asks me right there on the spot to marry him. Well, suh, I took one look at that big young buck, and I took one look down the rows that needed hoin', and I says, 'Yassuh, that suits me just fine.' Then he puts this gold ring on my finger right then and there and tol' me he been watchin' me fo' some time now, and he made that ring hisself from one of the Massa's twenty-dollar gold pieces. Mind you, it was a mite big, so I wore it on my thumb and figgered I'd grow into it after I done had a few babies. Then I tol' him I has one gold piece left and I wants him to make a ring for hisself, just like the one he made for me. He say he would, but he wants me to watch him while he do it. Well, I follows him to the blacksmith shop where he gots a job shoin' horses, and I sits down on a bench and watches him while he takes the littlest hammer I ever done seen and taps on the edge of the gold, holdin' it just right on a big piece of iron. He keeps hammerin' and hammerin' and turnin' it real slow ever time he hammers. Then he tol' me, 'Ever' time I hammer, I's hammerin' your love for me deep inside this here gold. When it be the right size, I'll cut out the middle so's I can put it on my finger. Then I'll have enough of your love pounded inside that gold to last me the rest of my life, just like the one I made for you.'"

Smiling gently at the memory of her husband forging their wedding bands, Grandma Jackson closed the box with its previous contents and handed it to Ruby. "You's my oldest girl grandchile, Ruby, so I wants you and Sam to have these, baby. Always remember the story I tol' you, and pass it on down to your chillun."

"Grandma Jackson," Ruby said, hugging her, "this is the best gift I could ever get from anybody. I know Sam will be proud to wear the ring you gave him, and I will always wear mine."

****

When the cabin's dark interior faded in the mists of memory and the brightly lit bathroom returned in the mirror, Ruby took the amulet from around her neck and emptied the powdered cocaine into the sink, sending it swirling down the drain in a whirlpool of water. Then she held the amulet under the stream of cleansing water, feeling it wash away the chains she envisioned in her mind. After blotting the amulet dry on a bath towel, she put it around her neck again, then pulled on her bathrobe and walked back into the bedroom to sit on the edge of her bed.

Contemplating the nightstand drawer that held Sam's gun, Ruby thought about Adams. As long as he was alive, she was bound to do what he told her and to bear his children. There was no recourse in the court system, no law to stop him from doing what he was doing, no police she could call to keep him away from her.

And leaving town would be meaningless, since Adams would send his henchman, Jeff Elliott, out to find her, armed with the full force and authority of the law.

Then there was Sam. If she had another baby by Adams, he would kill her — he had already told her so. To stop having Adams's children and stay alive, she had only one choice.

Ruby took Sam's gun from the nightstand and put it in her purse, got dressed, and marched resolutely downstairs. Getting into her car and turning onto Highway 90 toward downtown, she experienced an inner strength that she had not felt in years. She now knew what she had to do, and summoned forces she could not see and did not fully understand to give her the courage to carry out her plan.

Passing Adams's house, she saw Florrie Lee in her yard, cutting roses, and considered how different she was from this woman — long-suffering, submissive, meek — and how perfect a wife this was for a man who abused his women and simply expected them to take it.

Several minutes later, Ruby pulled alongside Adams's car in the alley behind his office and put her purse under her arm. Storming through the screen door, she darted past the waiting patients to enter the white treatment room, where Adams was preparing to see his next patient. "I want an abortion," she demanded, slamming the door behind her.

"You ain't havin' no abortion," Adams replied nonchalantly.

"Sam said he'd kill me if I had another white baby."

"Like I told you, Ruby, you're caught between a rock and hard place, 'cause I'll kill you if you sneak off and get rid of my baby."

"I can't have this baby."

"How many times I gotta tell you, woman? When I say no, I mean no."

"You can't make me have this…" Ruby stopped, stunned by the words that were coming out of her mouth.

"Woman, I'm gettin' goddamn tired of you. You're talkin' like a crazy woman."

"You're callin' me crazy?"

"Well, Ruby, you go and try to get rid of this baby, and I'll throw you back over there in Brewster for sure. Maybe this time I can convince 'em to slice up your brain a little."

She gritted her teeth and opened her purse. "You're not going to put me away again."

"You tryin' to tell me what I can do, you nigger bitch?"

Ruby reached inside her purse for the gun. "You bastard!"

Adams held her hands, slamming her against the wall and sending her purse and the gun flying to the floor. When he let go, he slapped her across the face.

"Oh...!" she screamed, falling onto the exam table.

Looking down to see the gun that had clunked to the floor, Adams turned to fill a syringe.

"Help! Somebody help!" she screamed, fighting off the needle that hovered over her. "No!" she yelled, feeling it pierce her arm.

Moments later, as he positioned her limp body on the exam table, there was a knock at the door.

"You need help in there?" Thelma called through the door.

Adams yelled back, "Get Jeff Elliott on the phone for me — now!"

Chapter Fifty

Thursday evening, July 31, Adams sat around the table with his cronies at Blue's Lodge, recounting his trip to the Democratic National Convention in Chicago.

"There," Blue said proudly as he struck a match to set the sparklers ablaze on a sheet cake decorated with Old Glory.

"I feel like I should salute or somethin'," Elliott quipped.

"How was your plan ride, Leroy?" Blue asked, standing back from the table to admire his creation.

"Noisy damn thing," Adams complained with knife at the ready, waiting for the sparklers to die down so he could slice into the cake.

Making his rounds with the coffeepot, Blue quipped, "If God had meant man to fly, he would've given him wings."

"Good Gawd Almighty, LaVergne!" Adams chided, slicing into the cake and dragging extra icing onto his plate. "Does that mean if God had wanted man to have surgery, he would've given him a zipper?"'

Black shook his head, grinning. "You missed your calling, Doc— shoulda been a lawyer."

Adams laughed. "Wish y'all coulda seen the looks on those god-dam Yankees' faces on the flight comin' back down here when I took off my socks and shoes and walked barefoot down the aisle, tellin' 'em I was from the South and askin' 'em where the outhouse was."

Elliott grinned. "Guess you give 'em a run for their money, Doc."

"Hell, yeah! And that ain't all," he continued, enjoying the lime-light. "I asked for those little bags of peanuts three times, too, just to see the titties on that stewardess."

Elliott started to laugh, but Black shot him a sobering look.

"Did you get a chance to hear Stevenson's acceptance speech?" Blue asked, catching Black's disapproving look.

"Sat right up near the front so I could hear the whole damn thing. Florrie Lee's favorite was when he said, 'If this cup may not pass away from me, except I drink it, thy will be done.'"

Blue pulled out his pipe and tamped down the tobacco in the bowl. "Modest of him, I'd say."

Adams sucked the icing from his fingers. "Hell! Sounded to me like the man was plannin' to get crucified."

Blue chuckled. "Guess it does, if you think about it."

"Might have good reason to think so," Elliott commented. "Eisenhower's got a lot of support—even down here in the South, him bein' a general and a war hero and all."

"And everybody I've talked to thinks he'd do a better job fightin' Communism," Blue added.

"That's what I hear over my way, too," Black agreed, sipping his coffee.

Blue frowned, lighting his pipe. "Not like folks around here to vote Republican, but this time things might be different."

Adams scowled. "Let's hope that don't get to be a trend. Can you imagine Florida with a Republican governor?"

"Not to worry, Leroy," Blue assured him, "Florida will never go Republican, no matter who they vote in for president." Blue looked up to see a young, dark-haired man enter the lodge. "Can I help you?" he called, standing up from the table.

"Yes sir. I was wondering if you could tell me where the Gilmores live here in town."

Blue walked over to talk with the man.

"Looks like a goddamn Jew," Adams muttered. "Got a nose on him you could hook your hat on."

Black and Elliott finished their cake, waiting for the man to leave before continuing their conversation.

Blue closed the door behind the traveler and returned to the table to join his friends. "Fella's lookin' to stay with Harold Gilmore on his way down to Miami. Seems he's movin' his family down that way."

Adams pointed toward the front door with his fork, holding it like a weapon. "Get enough of his kind movin' down to Miami, they're gonna demand reapportionment one of these days—mark my words."

"Well, that day's a long ways off," said Black. "Right now we've got the legislature all sewed up—especially with seniority in the senate. We just have to keep sending you back over there until you can be president of the senate like your granddaddy."

"So, Leroy, how're your plans comin' along to move to Tallahassee?" Blue asked.

"Laverne's goin' to drive Florrie Lee over there this weekend to help her find a place."

"What about covering your practice?"

Adams pondered the question for a moment, as a locomotive whistle blew in the distance.

Blue glanced across the room at the mantel clock—the 4:45 to Tallahassee was running a few minutes ahead of schedule. "I don't think Workman's in any kinda shape to cover your practice by hisself," he ventured, more as an attempt to prime the conversation than to suggest a solution.

"Hell, no. The old man had to rest up for a month after coverin' for me when we were down in Tampa for that goddam VA trial." Adams stroked his jowl. "Maybe I can call my school in Little Rock and see who needs a residency."

"What about all your house calls?"

"'Fraid they'll have to make their way into town to the emergency room—ain't nobody gonna drive all those dirt roads like I did."

"That's for sure," Blue agreed, hearing a new and louder blast as the train approached the crossing outside the lodge. "Hardly a day you don't start out at sunrise and come out here for supper around ten in the evenin'." The old man's face saddened as he realized that his closest friend would soon be on his way to Tallahassee.

"You having any more problems with Ruby?" Black asked, studying the ripples that the train's passing produced in his coffee.

"Hell, Keith," Adams replied, raising his voice to be heard above the racketing train, "this time they let her out of Brewster after only a week. Right after that, she started back pesterin' me worse'n ever—sometimes she's waitin' out back in the alley when I leave the office at night."

"Just say the word, Doc, and I'll drive her on over there to Chattahoochee myself," Elliott suggested.

"I just wrote a note to Sam on his bill today, tellin' him to keep that goddamn crazy woman out of my office or I'll send her over to Chattahoochee." Adams looked at his wristwatch, hearing the final blast from the locomotive deepen a few notes as it receded into the distance. "LaVergne, you got any more of them fried shrimp back there in the kitchen I can take with me tonight on my house calls?"

"Sure do," Blue obliged, getting up from the table.

Black leaned back and inspected his manicure, frowning at a rough spot on his right thumbnail. "Far as I'm concerned, Sam's been slidin' lately, too, tryin' to handle that crazy wife of his. Don't think we can count on him to get much more done over my way."

"You really think Sam can manage her, Doc?" Elliott asked.

Adams looked miffed. "You got a better idea?"

"I guess I just get the heebie-jeebies when I hear a man sayin' a woman's chasin' after him like Ruby's doin' — usually spells trouble."

"Like I said, you got any better idea what to do about that woman?"

Elliott shot Adams a deadpan look. "You got a gun in your office?"

Adams reared back in his chair. "Good Gawd Almighty, Jeff! You tellin' me to shoot the woman?"

"No, Doc. I'm just thinkin' it'd be a good idea to keep a weapon in your office, in case she does somethin' stupid."

"You got any idea how that'd look in the *Democrat* if somethin' happened and I killed that nigger woman?"

"Actually, Doc, I had a four-ten pistol in mind. You ain't even got to aim it, and it's not likely to kill her unless you shot her right up close — sure as hell stop her, though."

Adams sneered, "My granddaddy called a four-ten a woman's shotgun. They make that in a pistol?"

"Yes, sir," Elliott assured him. "Have to special-order it, though."

"Here you go, Leroy," sang Blue, coming out of the kitchen with a paper bag. "Fried up a fresh batch of shrimp for you to take with you. Got 'em all boxed up where they'll stay nice and hot."

"Thanks, LaVergne," Adams said, still pondering Elliott's suggestion. "Now that I think about it, it might not be such a bad idea, Jeff. I'll give Tom Radford a call over at his store tomorrow mornin' and tell him to order one for me."

United States Post Office
Live Oak, Florida

Chapter Fifty-One

At the post office on Saturday morning, August 2, Ruby took her mail from her postal box. Sorting through the bills on the counter, she ripped open an envelope from Adams's office addressed to Sam. Inside was a bill for $116 for "two office visits" and "In-office D&C," with a handwritten note at the bottom: "Sam, I want you to keep that crazy wife of yours out of my office or I'll have to send her over to Chattahoochee."

"D and C...and who's crazy?" Ruby fumed.

Ruby stalked to her car to drive the one block north to Adams's office. On her way, the man's last words to her circled in her mind: *You're livin' in this mansion, drivin' those new cars, and wearin' those fancy diamond rings because of me, you understand?*

"Because of him?" Ruby mumbled to herself. "Where was he when Sam and me set up the business? Where was he when we built our house and raised our family?"

Circling around the Parshley building, she saw that Adams's car was not parked in the alley, though Thelma's was. Getting out of her car, she knocked loudly on the screen door, trying to be heard over the noise from the office window fan. "Thelma! Thelma, are you in there?"

Hearing no answer, Ruby walked out of the alley, around the Western Auto in the north corner of the Parshley building, to the white entrance to Adams's office. Knocking on the front door and ringing the doorbell yielded no answer.

Returning to her car in the alley, Ruby decided to drive by the hospital to see if Adams might be there. Again his words stuck in her brain: *So why don't you get over those crazy ideas of movin' to Tallahassee, consider yourself lucky to be a rich nigger, and make a life for yourself right here in Live Oak?*

"Stop it!" Ruby yelled, hitting her steering wheel as she turned onto Fifth Street behind the hospital. *I've got to get that man out of my life.*

Seeing that Adams was not parked in his space at the rear of the hospital, she continued home, passing behind Adams's house to see that his car was not parked under the covered driveway.

C. Arthur Ellis, Jr.

Several blocks later, she slammed on the brakes in her driveway and ran into the house to grab the telephone. "Operator, get me Dr. Adams's office, please."

Thelma answered.

"Hello, Thelma," Ruby said pleasantly. "This is Ruby. I saw you were down at the office, and tried to knock, but I guess you didn't hear me. I wonder if you would please tell me what a D and C is."

"It's when the doctor scrapes out the womb."

"Why?"

"Sometimes it's done when a woman bleeds too much during her periods."

"Any other reason?"

"Sometimes it's done to end a pregnancy."

"You mean an abortion?"

Thelma hesitated. "We don't use that word, Ruby."

"Can you tell me who had the D and C that Sam was billed for?"

"Ruby, you know I can't do that. That's confidential."

"I wonder if I might speak with Dr. Adams, please?"

"Do you know today's Saturday, Ruby? He's not here. You're lucky you even got me—I'm not usually down here on the weekend—just down here today to mail out the bills we couldn't get to yesterday."

"Well, you tell the doctor I got Sam's bill from the post office and I'm going to be there in five minutes."

"I already told you he's not here, Ruby. There's no way you can get in touch with him right now. He just got to the hospital from a house call to operate on a man with appendicitis. It'll be at least..."

"But I have to—"

The receiver clicked in Ruby's ear.

Ruby was furious. It was obvious that Adams had performed an abortion for Sam's girlfriend while refusing to give her one, even though she had told him Sam would kill her if she had another baby by him. She sat quietly, thinking of how she could reach Adams, then picked up her purse and stormed out the front door.

Turning onto Highway 90 toward the hospital, Ruby knew that if Adams did not relent on the abortion, she had to find some way to kill him. There was no way that she would let herself be thrown into Brewster again—or, even worse, Chattahoochee. The problem was how to do it without letting him overpower her again—and how to get away with it without anyone seeing her.

Parking at the rear hospital entrance, she entered the colored wing and walked to the operating room door to pick up the telephone labeled "For Emergency Use Only."

"Hello?" came a woman's voice over the telephone.

"Hello, I need to speak to Dr. Adams."

"He's in surgery. Who is this?"

"This is Ruby McCollum."

"You need to get off that phone—can't you see it's for emergency use only?"

"I need to speak to the doctor," Ruby demanded.

"Not now, you don't."

Adams clamped off the patient's appendix. "Who's out there?"

"It's that McCollum woman."

"Tell that goddamn crazy nigger woman to go to hell!"

"You tell the doctor I heard him," Ruby cried. "Tell him he needs to get out here right now."

"She is crazy!" the nurse exclaimed, slamming down the receiver. "I'm going out there and yank her tail straight."

"Thanks, Sarah," Adams called after the nurse, a former Army sergeant.

Sarah pushed open the first set of double stainless steel doors and then the second and marched into the hallway, where Ruby was still on the telephone. "Ruby!" Sarah barked. "Put down that phone right now or I'll have you thrown out."

"I have to speak to the doctor," Ruby insisted.

"Ruby," she said firmly, "there's a patient in there with his belly cut wide open, and the doctor needs me in there with the other nurse to assist. You want that man to die?"

"You have to let me talk with the doctor," Ruby demanded.

"You're crazy!"

"I'm not crazy!" Ruby shouted.

Two orderlies appeared. Each grabbed an arm, and down the corridor they went, dragging the screaming woman between them.

"Let me go!" Ruby shrieked, legs swinging helplessly.

Outside, one of the orderlies threw her to the pavement. "Now, don't you come back in here and bother the doc, you crazy nigger."

"Thanks, fellas," Sarah said. "Now I can go back in and scrub up."

In the operating room, Adams finished removing the appendix. "Nurse, keep up the peritoneal lavage until the saline runs clear; then go ahead and close up. I need to get some fresh air."

The nurse hesitated. "Dr. Adams...Dr. Sims told me I couldn't close unless you directly supervised me."

"To hell with Sims! I'm the doctor in charge here, and you'll do what I tell you."

"Yes, sir," the nurse replied, continuing the lavage.

In the locker room, Adams threw his scrubs in the laundry bin and changed into his street clothes.

Stopping by the nurse's station, he asked, "Any more emergencies?"

"No, Dr. Adams — guess you can call it a day."

"Thanks, sweetheart," he shot back, continuing down the corridor, where he met a man leaving the boardroom.

"Good morning, Leroy. Don't forget our peer review committee meeting Monday," the man called as he passed him in the hallway.

"Sorry, Sims, I don't have the time."

In marked contrast to Adams, the fiery young redhead, who had completed his residency at Emory University, had an air of refinement about him.

"You need to make the time," Sims insisted.

Adams turned to stand nose to nose with Sims. "Stick it up your ass, Sims!"

"Would you please step into the boardroom a minute so I can talk with you, Dr. Adams?" Sims asked in his best professional manner.

"You got exactly one minute," Adams barked, following him into the boardroom.

"Leroy, you already missed the training session on the defibrillator," Sims chided, taking a seat at the conference table. "That's a disservice to your patients. If you don't get trained on it by the end of the week and come to the peer review meeting, the medical staff has unanimously decided to ask J. C. to suspend your admitting privileges."

Adams crossed his arms and gave the man an icy stare. "Hell, without my patients, he'd have to turn this two-bit joint into a motel and rent it out by the hour!"

"Leroy, please," Sims pleaded. "J. C. is concerned that your claims to Blue Cross this past month were a hundred and twenty-five percent of our census — needless to say, that's a mathematical impossibility. Not only that, the dates have been altered. You know how the VA would look at this, Leroy. As it is, Blue Cross is a service organization of our fellow professionals, so they won't file fraud charges."

"What about all the patients I saw in the emergency room?"

"Did you get them to fill out their insurance papers?"

Adams pounded his fist on the conference table. "Good Gawd Almighty, Sims, I don't stop for paperwork when some poor bastard's lyin' on the table bleedin' to death! And what would you want me to do with that girl they brought in here last week with a coke bottle shoved up her vagina? Hell, it took me an hour to get the right tools to cut through the bottom, to break the vacuum and pull it out—suckers are damn near a half inch thick! If it was up to you, she'd still be walkin' around knock-kneed and cross-eyed with that goddamn thing rammed up her pussy."

"Blue Cross notified us that we have thirty days to correct the situation or the hospital will be dropped."

"Don't get your bowels in an uproar, Sims. I'm sure it's just a mistake."

"Leroy, if we lose Blue Cross, the hospital's ruined."

"Keep your britches on—we ain't gonna lose nothin'. I'll get through to the governor if I have to."

"J. C.'s going to be on you, Leroy," Sims warned. "If it turns out that you've been billing for patients you didn't see…"

"Good Gawd-Almighty-damn, Sims. You know I ain't good at fillin' out paperwork."

"It's not just the paperwork we're concerned about, Leroy. We also need to talk with you about that amputation you performed without having the patient's leg shaved. Not to mention your practice of having the OR nurse close up without supervision…"

"I've heard just about enough of this shit!" Adams yelled, storming out of the boardroom.

Sims left the boardroom to follow Adams down the corridor.

"Let it go, Sims," Adams warned. "Since when did you fellas become the goddamn Gestapo?"

"We can't just let it go, Leroy," Sims insisted. "As long as you practice here—"

"Fuck you!"

Sims stepped in front of Adams. "Leroy, if you don't straighten out this billing issue before you leave for Tallahassee—"

"Are you accusin' me of stealin'?" With one swift punch, Adams sent Sims crashing to the floor, his nose bleeding on the terrazzo.

A chubby nurse stuck her head out of a patient's room to see what was happening in the corridor.

"Looks like you've got another patient, sweetheart," Adams called over his shoulder on his way out the door.

Chapter Fifty-Two

On Sunday, August 3, 1952, a middle-aged colored woman with neatly braided hair, wearing a home-sewn short-sleeved smock, rocked nervously on the front porch of her tin-roofed bungalow.

Give me patience, sweet Jesus, she prayed, shielding her eyes from the sun to keep watch down the dirt road in front of her house. A few moments later, the distraught woman walked down the porch steps and into the neatly raked expanse of sand that established the boundaries of her front yard. Watching carefully for snake tracks in the sand, she went to the hand pump and prayed for a miracle.

The pump groaned and brayed like a jackass, but no water came.

Foolish old woman! If the chillun of Israel can wonder forty years in the desert, I reckon I can wait a little while longer.

Taking comfort in the thought of getting her promised water delivery, she returned to the shade of the porch, wiped the sweat from her forehead, and resumed her vigil.

Travelers along Highway 129, the two-lane blacktop south of Live Oak, would never have noticed the meandering dirt road that veered off toward the woman's house, through fields of withered corn stalks and flattened tobacco plants, now overgrown with the rich green dog fennel that was too stubborn to die even in the sweltering north Florida drought.

Again raising her hand against the sun's glare, the woman rejoiced to see a black Oldsmobile barreling toward her house through a cloud of dust. "Thank you, sweet Jesus!" she shouted. Her eyes brimmed with tears — not the kind born of sorrow, but the quiet, cleansing kind that sprang from the depths of desperate souls welcoming the coming of a savior.

Stopping in the front yard, Adams got out of his car with his medical bag.

"Oh, Doctah Adams! I's so glad you come out to see my boy on the Lawd's day. He done been moanin' all night with the fevah, and he don't sound so good in his breathin'...."

"Now, don't you worry yourself, Mama," Adams interrupted, slipping a reassuring arm around her shoulder. "The doc's here now — your boy's gonna be just fine." Following the woman up the steps onto the porch, he felt the soft, termite-riddled boards give under his weight.

Inside, standing in a tidy, simply furnished living and dining room, he savored the aroma of freshly fried bacon. Knowing that the family could ill afford his five-dollar fee, he made a mental note to employ the *Gee, Mama, what's that smells so good comin' from your kitchen?* technique to secure his breakfast.

He followed the woman through a door to the right to behold the familiar scene of a sick boy lying in bed. The boy's grandmother, a stout elderly woman, sat anxiously fanning him with a cardboard fan bearing a scene of Jesus surrounded by children on one side, and "HALL'S FUNERAL HOME—WE'RE THERE FOR YOU IN YOUR TIME OF GREATEST NEED" on the other.

The boy's mother rushed to her son's side. "You be fine now, baby. Doctah Adams is here to see you."

"You don't look like you're feelin' so good, son," Adams observed, sitting down on the edge of the bed.

"I got some chicken soup down him, Doctah," the grandmother volunteered.

"You ain't gonna give me no shot, is yah, Doctah?" whined the boy.

"What's your name, son?

"My name's Lavon."

"Well, Lavon, let's open those pj's so I can listen to your insides."

Looking fearfully at the biggest white man he had ever seen, the boy cautiously unbuttoned his shirt.

Adams took the stethoscope from his satchel, adjusted it to his ears, and placed the diaphragm on the boy's chest. "Now, I want you to take a deep breath, hold it as long as you can, then let it out, all right?"

The boy nodded.

"Good job, Lavon. Now, let me take a look at your ears."

Watching Adams return the stethoscope to his satchel and pull out the otoscope, the youngster said, "What you lookin' for in there with that flashlight?"

"Just lookin' to see if you've got any bugs in there."

The boy pulled away. "I ain't got no bugs!"

Adams chuckled. "I'm talkin' 'bout germs, son—they make your ears red inside," he explained as he peered into one ear and then the other. Putting the otoscope back in the satchel, he pulled out a wooden tongue depressor and a small flashlight. "Now, open your mouth and say, 'A-a-ah.'" Adams placed the tongue depressor onto the back of the boy's tongue and looked down his throat. "Mmm," he mumbled, handing the tongue depressor to the boy's grandmother. "I'm sorry to tell you this, son, but you need a shot of penicillin. You got yourself a bad case of pneumonia."

"Mama, I don't want no shot!"

"Now, son, you just lay still and do what the doctor say," his mother admonished.

"I don't want no shot!" the boy protested tearfully.

"Lavon," his mother said firmly, "you got to let the doctah give you a shot to help you get better."

"Now, roll over, and this won't hurt no more'n a pinch," Adams assured the boy as he pulled down the elastic waistband of his pajama pants to swab his hip and administer the injection in one synchronous movement.

"Mama, it hurt!"

"Now, there, baby, you gonna be all right now," the grandmother chimed in.

Adams threw the used hypodermic needle and the vial of penicillin into a separate container in his bag. "That'll fix you up, Lavon," he assured him, getting up.

The boy's mother followed nervously behind. "My man get paid this next week..."

Adams interrupted with a dismissing wave of his hand. "Families with sick folks don't need to worry themselves sicker 'bout no doctor bill. You pay me what you can when you can. After all, you did vote for me for senator, didn't you?"

"Me and all my kinfolks!" rejoiced the woman.

Adams grinned. "Well, consider us even." Sniffing the air, he asked, "What's that smellin' so good comin' out of your kitchen, Mama?"

The woman rushed to the dining room table. "Lawsamercy, Doctah Adams," she called, returning with a basket covered with a red and white checkered cloth, "I almost forgot. This be a little sump'm fo' yo' dinner, and a bit lef' over for supper."

Adams took the basket and pulled back the cloth to find a bonanza of fried chicken, biscuits, and a blackberry cobbler. "Mama, you sure know the way to this man's heart," he grinned, giving her a big hug.

"You's a blessin', Doctah Adams," the woman called to his back as he headed down the porch steps with the basket.

In his car, the mobile radio crackled. "Doc, Jeff here. You there, Doc? You got patients down at your office."

Adams reached for the microphone with one hand and cranked the car with the other. "I heard you, Jeff. Thanks for tellin' me. Elwood already called me at home about an hour ago. Tell all of 'em to go around back to the colored entrance and I'll meet 'em there in fifteen minutes."

"See ya later, Doc."

Adams replaced the mike to grab a drumstick and take a bite, sending a shower of crumbs to join the dried remains of doughnut and sweet roll wrappers on the floorboard.

Reaching the paved highway, he veered off the road to stop beside a stray dog rummaging through a mound of fly-infested garbage.

Taking his Colt .45 from the glove compartment, he opened his door, and with the chicken bone still in his hand, he walked around the vehicle, staying close to the passenger side. "Here, doggie, I got somethin' for ya."

The dog approached cautiously.

"Here you go," Adams called, tossing the drumstick toward the animal. After a cursory sniff, the dog grabbed it and started chewing off the remaining skin and gristle at the end.

Adams smiled as he slowly squeezed the trigger. The gun roared, and the dog fell to the ground, bleeding from its mouth and nostrils. "If there's anything I hate, its dogs, niggers, and Yankees," Adams sneered, getting back into his car. "But at least you can fuck niggers."

Whistling "Dixie," he put the pistol back in the glove compartment and pulled back onto the highway.

Driving along rows of two-story Victorian houses on Main Street, Adams found Live Oak quiet, with only the sounds of hymns coming from the opened stained-glass windows of the Methodist church, interrupted by ten laconic bongs from the courthouse clock. A broad banner stretching across the street announced, "1952 SUWANNEE COUNTY TOBACCO FESTIVAL — MUSIC — STREET DANCING — FOOD — PRIZES."

While the much awaited coronation of Suwannee County's 1952 tobacco queen was only a week away, the tobacco and corn crops had failed this year from what the *Suwannee Democrat* called the "drought of the century." Local merchants, foreseeing financial disaster, formed a committee to come up with a plan for attracting the few customers who still had cash in their pockets.

Following the committee's suggestion, business owners chipped in and bought a shiny new Ford farm truck at cost from the local dealer, to give away to some lucky family in a drawing during the Tobacco Festival. Having set the plan in motion, the businessmen's spirits were up, a night of celebration was declared at the Elks' Lodge, and Baptists became honorary Methodists for the evening to join in the libations.

Passing the courthouse square where the new Ford farm truck sat on display in front of the courthouse, Adams made a hard right turn into the alley behind his office to see Thomas Radford walking toward Dale and Radford's Hardware Store, where a sign on the door read "CLOSED SUNDAY." Adams stopped the car. "Mornin', Tom. You order that four-ten pistol for me yet?"

Radford hesitated, fumbling with the door lock. "Be a while, Doc. You just asked me for it on Friday, and there ain't no place around here I can get one. Why you want a four-ten, anyways? What's wrong with the Colt forty-five I got you last year?"

"Nothin'. I just want a four-ten."

"Might as well get yourself a sawed-off shotgun, Doc," said Radford, who had not placed the order, because Adams still owed him six hundred dollars for the materials he had bought on credit to fix up his house.

Adams cursed under his breath and pulled into the alley behind his office to find Chief Elwood Howard, in civilian clothes, leaning against his black and white Ford police cruiser. Standing alongside Howard was a colored teenage girl, her torn dress soaked in blood, with a blood-drenched cloth wrapped around her hand. With her was a colored teenage boy, his pant leg torn away to accommodate a blood-soaked bandage. The colored boy's sister was with him, helping him walk.

Beyond the police car was a '45 Ford pickup with a white teenager sitting behind the wheel, and his father, mother, and baby sister packed tightly into the front seat. The family was dressed in their Sunday best, their clothes drenched in sweat from the boiling heat, and the little girl was whimpering while her mother tried to comfort her. "There, there, honey," she consoled. "The doctor's here now. You're gonna be just fine."

In the alley outside the office were three colored women and an older colored man, holding a wet towel over his eyes while his wife held his arm.

Adams got out of his car and reached in his pocket. Finding the key, he opened the screen door to unlock the wooden door. "Y'all might as well come on in and sit down out of the sun," he called to the waiting patients.

Chief Howard led the two wounded youths in first. "Mornin', Doc. Thanks for comin' down on a Sunday."

"Glad to help out, Elwood. Hardly recognized you out of uniform."

The remaining patients bade their respective "'Mornin's" to the doctor as they filed into his office.

Following the last patient inside, Adams flicked the switches for the room lights and the big box fan in the office window, causing the lights to dim momentarily as the noisy fan motor drank enough current to build up speed.

Just as Adams entered the office, Ruby was pulling into the alley, but seeing the police car, she backed out and drove a block down Court Street to park facing the alley entrance. Several minutes later, she saw the police car pull out.

For the next twenty minutes, the alley was quiet until the police car pulled back into the alley, and Elwood Howard picked up the two colored youths, who now had cleanly bandaged wounds and were smiling and holding hands. Howard helped his charges into the back of the car, got into the driver's side, and pulled from the alley onto Court Street, heading toward the jail.

A single bong from the courthouse clock announced 10:30.

Ruby started her engine and pulled back into the alley, parking next to Adams's car. With tears streaming down her face, she looked at Loretta, asleep on the backseat, and then pulled a handkerchief from her handbag to wipe the tears and sweat from her face.

While Ruby watched the office screen door, a stout, elderly colored woman, her husband, and their daughter came out of the office, got in their car, and drove out of the alley. Ruby rested her head on the steering wheel, sobbing quietly.

"Mommy, why are you crying?" Sonja asked.

"Hush, baby. Mommy's thinking."

Ruby started the car again and backed up several feet; then, stopping suddenly, she pulled back to her original parking place and turned off the engine. Going back to the screen door, she saw the white man and woman coming out of the treatment room with their little girl. After the family drove their truck out of the alley beside the Suwannee Hotel, Ruby returned to her car and sat staring at the dashboard clock.

Within the next ten minutes, two more patients left the office.

Getting out of her car, Ruby approached the screen door and peeked in to see that the only patients in the waiting room were two colored women she did not recognize—one old, one young, conversing quietly—but she could not hear what they were saying over the noise of the window fan.

Ruby then returned to her car to check on her two children in the backseat. "I want you to keep an eye on your little sister while I'm in the doctor's office," she said. "Make sure she's all right."

"Yes, Mama," Sonja replied, yawning and stretching.

Ruby handed her one of the cardboard fans from Hall's Funeral Home. "Take this and fan your sister," she said.

"Yes, Mama," Sonja said dutifully.

Ruby grabbed her tan handbag from the front seat and, hooking the strap over her shoulder, went back into the doctor's office.

While her mother was inside, Sonja took turns fanning Loretta and herself. Quickly growing bored, she turned on the car radio to listen to WNER and sing along with the African Baptist Church morning service.

> Jesus loves me, this I know,
> For the *Bible* tells me so,
> Little ones to him belong,
> They are weak but He is strong.
> Yes, Jesus loves me,
> Yes, Jesus loves me,
> Yes, Jesus loves me,
> The *Bible* tells me so.

"Now, brother, and sisters," the minister began, "I want y'all to turn to our scripture for the day, Job 1:11. That's Job one eleven…"

Sonja heard an enormously loud bang come blasting through the screen door and echo into the alley, followed by a second, and then a third, completely drowning out the preacher's voice on the radio.

Suddenly, three colored women bolted out the screen door, yelling, "Help! Police! Somebody get some help! The doctah been shot!" Still yelling, the women ran out of the alley and across the street to the Cities Service Station.

Sonja clicked off the radio, grabbed Loretta, and pulled her down onto the floorboard to hear another gunshot ring out. Waiting a moment, she raised her head cautiously to see her mother coming out of the doctor's office. "Mama...Mama," she whimpered. "Are you all right?"

Ruby pulled the wooden door shut and let the screen door slam behind her. She could hear Loretta crying. Suddenly she was conscious of the revolver in her hand. Concentrating to regain her focus, she walked toward the car, holding the gun behind her. "Hush, child. Nothing's the matter. I just had to visit the doc to pay my bill. Everything's going to be fine now."

Crossing to the driver's side, Ruby dug in her purse to locate her car keys. She got in the car, put the pistol in the glove compartment, and started the engine.

When she pulled out of the alley to turn onto Court Street, the three colored patients who had run out of the office pointed her out to a cab driver, who jotted down her tag number when she turned south onto Ohio Avenue to avoid passing the police station.

On the drive home, Ruby realized that it was over. She had killed the man who threatened to have her sent away for good. Was it murder, or was it self-defense? In either case, what would happen to her now? What would happen to her children? What would happen to Adams's unborn child?

For now there were no answers, only questions. Wiping away her tears, she decided that she would have to sort all this out later—at least now Adams could no longer send her to Chattahoochee.

Pulling into her driveway, Ruby noted that Sam's car was gone. "Looks like your Daddy and Kay aren't back from church yet," she said to Sonja. "Why don't you run on over to Uncle Matt's place while I feed Loretta and get dinner on the table?"

Sonja got out of the car. "Okay, Mama."

Seeing that Sonja was out of sight, Ruby opened the passenger door to take the gun from the glove compartment and secure it in her purse. She then bent down to pick up Loretta, who had fallen asleep.

Inside, Ruby went into the kitchen to place a fretful Loretta in her high chair.

"Hey, Mama," Kay greeted, coming through the kitchen door.

"You back from church?"

"I didn't go, Mama. I told Daddy I didn't feel good, and he went by himself." When Ruby said nothing, she said, "Can I go over to play at Uncle Matt's house?"

"Sure, baby."

After Kay left, Ruby took a baby bottle from the refrigerator and put it in the electric bottle warmer on the kitchen counter, singing as she waited for it to warm.

"Hush, little baby, don't say a word,
Papa's gonna buy you a mockingbird.
If that mocking bird don't sing,
Pappa's gonna buy you a diamond ring..."

After puttering about the kitchen for a few minutes, Ruby squirted a few drops of milk onto her wrist to test its temperature, then picked up Loretta from her high chair, cradling her in her arms to feed her.

Upstairs in her bedroom, she laid the baby in her crib, taking off her shoes and clothes to pull the crib sheet over her bare legs. "Sleep, my love. Dream sweet dreams," she whispered, gently kissing the soft forehead.

Ruby undressed down to her slip. Bending down to turn on the water in the tub, she picked up a bottle of bubble bath and poured some into the running water. While the bubbles foamed up in the tub, Ruby stood in front of the mirror and held her amulet, feeling at peace.

Chapter Fifty-Three

Police Chief Worth Howard wiped the sweat from his forehead as he cruised along Ohio Avenue in his black-and-white. He reflected that downtown was quiet, even for a Sunday.

Turning onto Howard Street, the main east-west route through Live Oak, he parked across from the Wagon Wheel restaurant, set his parking brake, and got out of his cruiser. Taking a moment to tuck in his shirt and straighten his gun belt over his ample waistline, he strode past the Alimar Theatre's "Coming Soon" poster for High Noon.

In front of the Wagon Wheel, Howard stepped back to hold the door open for a gray-haired man in a white dress shirt, donning a broad-brimmed felt hat. The man greeted Howard with the kind of frugal smile that the affluent sometimes bestow on commoners. "Mornin', Worth. Looks like another hot 'un."

Howard tipped his hat to reveal his sweat-drenched chestnut brown hair. "Mornin', Mr. Crapps. Sure does."

Inside, a rush of cool air evaporated the sweat on his forehead. At a table toward the rear of the smoke-filled diner, closest to the main air-conditioning vent, he could see several men in short-sleeved white shirts, intently sorting stacks of papers.

Sliding onto a chrome-and-red-vinyl barstool at the counter, Chief Howard placed his hat on the neighboring stool and smiled at his favorite waitress, a haggard-looking middle-aged woman who had just glided through the swinging door and now turned smoothly in mid stride to lift a pot of coffee from the Bunn warmer with the grace of a ballerina.

"Mornin', Worth."

Howard winked. "Hey, good-lookin'. Whatcha got cookin'?"

The woman shot back a weary smile that barely flexed her crow's-feet. "Tell you the same thing I tell all the other fellas — you ain't no Hank Williams."

Howard grinned, having reached that stage of married life when a receding hairline and an advancing waistline concerned him less than earning a living for his family. "See you found your glasses, Suzie... Sure feels good in here with that new coolin' system."

"Yup, lot easier workin' here, too," Suzie agreed, leaning over the counter to pour his coffee.

Howard caught the familiar scent of rose cologne seasoned with fried bacon—a comforting reminder of his childhood. "Anything goin' on this mornin', Suzie?"

The furrows on her forehead deepened. "Heard those Yankee ni-grahs are plannin' on comin' down here to eat in our restaurants. You reckon they'll make it to Live Oak?"

Howard took a casual sip of coffee. "Doubt it, Suzie. They'll prob'ly end up in Jacksonville or Tallahassee."

"How's that?"

"More press."

She made her way around the counter to climb up on the stool be-side Howard. "You know I ain't against colored folk—I just don't want my baby girl havin' to go to school with 'em. They got lice in their hair, and..."

Chief Howard's eyes locked with Suzie's. "You need to leave that to us menfolk, sweetheart."

Suzie breathed a sigh—probably from concern rather than relief, since it wasn't followed by the usual twinkle in her eye that came when she felt comforted by what he had to say. "So how come you runnin' late this mornin'?"

"Had to pick up two cut colored kids out at the Three Spot. El-wood drove 'em down to Doc's office to get stitched up since I covered for him last night."

"Now I know why Elwood left a few minutes ago, sayin' he had to get back to Doc's office."

"Least these two settled their differences with knives instead of guns—lot easier for Doc."

Suzie frowned. "Ain't got no idea why a nice man like Doc Adams wastes so much time on the coloreds when decent white folks need him. 'Sides, now that he's won the election, he ain't got much time left 'fore he moves over to Tallahassee."

Howard nodded. "Had my way, I'd take 'em all down to old Doc Birch and let *him* sew 'em up."

Suzie laughed. "He sure does a bang-up job on our bird dogs."

"Good to see that smile come back, Suzie. Ain't seen one on your face for a month of Sundays."

"I can't help it, Worth. Seems like we just can't never get ahead— 'specially with the drought this year. Had enough rain to give a good crop of melons, but my old man had to pump water from the river to keep the 'bacca from fallin' flat dead in the dirt."

"Hear tell there ain't much to show out at the warehouses this year."

"Guess I should stop complainin'," Suzie confided. "After that hailstorm hit 'bout ever'body but us, our puny crop fetched a fair price—people gotta smoke, you know."

Seeing a man enter the restaurant, Suzie grabbed her coffeepot.

Howard nodded toward the dark-haired young man. "Hey, Mr. Jacobs."

"Mornin', Worth," Jacobs returned, intent on joining the men at the back of the restaurant.

"You got a copy of this week's *Democrat*, Suzie?" Howard asked. "I ain't had time to read it this week."

"Sure thing, honey. Soon as I pour some coffee for Mr. Jacobs."

After pouring the coffee, Suzie retreated to the kitchen with Jacobs's order, returning moments later with a copy of the *Suwannee Democrat* and a sticky cinnamon bun.

"Fresh out of the oven... Ain't much in the paper this week—'less you like readin' foreclosure notices. Mr. Crapps just dropped off another pile of papers from his bank."

Howard bit into the warm roll and sucked the sticky-sweet icing off his fingers. "Yeah. I seen him leave when I come in. Me and my boys been helpin' the sheriff's office serve all those poor cusses. Don't seem right them havin' to give up farms that's been in their families for God knows how long just 'cause of a drought."

Suzie placed a sympathetic hand on Howard's shoulder. "Sure you won't have some eggs and grits on me?"

"No, thanks, Suzie," he said, finishing the cinnamon bun.

"In that case, I better see what's up in the kitchen. Can't keep them buzzards waitin'," she said, rolling her eyes toward the men at the back table.

Howard grinned. "See you later." After skimming through the *Democrat*, he finished his coffee and threw a quarter on the counter.

Outside, somewhere between cursing the hot car seat and parking at the police station two blocks away, Howard ran through the to-do list he kept in his head. Opening his car door, he jerked it back to avoid a cab that came screeching to a halt beside him.

The cab driver leaned over to the passenger window. "Chief Howard! Come go with me to Doc Adams's office—quick!"

"What'd you say, Shorty?"

"Meet me at Doc Adams's office!" the cab driver yelled back, turning south onto Pine Street.

Scarcely a minute later, Howard swerved into the alley behind the doctor's office to find Shorty Raulerson standing beside his taxi in front of the screen door with its hand-lettered sign: C.L. ADAMS, M.D.—COLORED ENTRANCE.

"What's goin' on, Shorty?"

"Doc's been shot!" The cabbie pointed toward three women standing in the shade of a chinaberry tree across the alley. "Those colored women say they seen the whole thing."

"Tell 'em to stay put, Shorty," Howard barked, rushing to the office entrance. "Door's locked!" he yelled after Raulerson, who was approaching the women. "Run on around front and see if you can get in that way."

"Y'all stay right here," Raulerson called over his shoulder to the witnesses as he trotted off.

Another black-and-white pulled into the alley behind Howard's car, and a policeman jumped out. "Hey, Worth, what's goin' on here? Mr. Hill over at the gas station told me somebody shot Doc Adams and made a getaway out the Lake City road—turned out to be a wild-goose chase."

"Doc's been shot, all right, Elwood, and the damned door's locked."

"Jesus Christ! He still in there?"

Howard nodded toward the whirring window fan. "Never knowed Doc to leave that on when he's gone. I sent Shorty 'round front." He turned to look at the women standing under the shade tree. "Why don't you go over there and talk to those women? Shorty says they seen the whole thing."

"Sure thing, Worth."

Moments later, Shorty Raulerson ran back into the alley, out of breath. "The front door's locked, too. I called Brodie Harris's Funeral Home for an ambulance when I run past the hotel."

"Damn! Give me a hand, Shorty."

The two men rammed the door until it flew open. Inside, Doc Adams's corpulent six-foot-two body lay sprawled facedown on the waiting room floor, his hands crumpled beneath him. His white shirt was soaked in blood around what appeared to be two bullet holes in his back. Blood was also oozing from his nose and mouth. A penlight had fallen in front of him.

Bending down, Howard struggled to roll Adams over and was surprised to detect a weak pulse. "Hey, Doc, who the hell did this to you?"

Adams's lips quivered.

Howard's face hardened, recognizing the all-too-familiar rasping sound of the death rattle. Suddenly, Adams's massive chest sank, releasing a passive flow of air. Howard lowered the body to the floor, catching sight of a hundred-dollar bill clutched in the left hand. "He's dead, Shorty. Ain't gonna get nothin' more outta Doc."

"Guess not," Raulerson agreed, his voice trembling.

Howard pulled a handkerchief from his pocket to wipe the blood from his hands. "Why don't you step on outside, Shorty? Ain't nothin' else you can do in here."

Shorty nodded, happy to distance himself from the dead body.

A few minutes later, Howard came out of the office to find Elwood waiting for him in the alley. "I got their names down, Chief…" Elwood halted, seeing the bloodstains on Howard's hands.

"Go on."

"I'm afraid these witnesses don't know the suspect. They all agreed that she was a colored female, dark skin, medium build, a little over five feet tall, wearin' a tannish or brown suit and carryin' a handbag or purse… They ain't so sure 'bout that." Pointing to his temple, he whispered, "One of 'em seemed kinda slow."

"That don't give us much to go on, Elwood. You tellin' me none of 'em recognized the woman?"

"'Fraid not, Chief. Guess she was from outta town."

"Anything else?"

"They all say she was fightin' with Doc over her bill. They say they heard the woman demandin' a receipt and Doc tellin' her that weren't all she owed."

Howard studied the blood caked under his fingernails and glanced up at Elwood. "Doc had a hundred-dollar bill in his hand."

Elwood's eyes widened. "Only one nigger woman in Suwannee County carries around that kind of cash money."

Chapter Fifty-Four

Bessie settled Sonja at her kitchen table with a bowl of chocolate ice cream while Matt looked out the living room window to see if Sam's car was in the driveway. "Sam, that you?" Matt asked, catching the telephone before the first ring was complete.

"It's me. Everybody's at church talkin' about Ruby shootin' the doc. I drove near the house and saw all the police cars. Are they still there?"

Matt reached toward the window and pulled the curtain aside to look down the street. "No, Sam. They all gone now." He choked on his last words. "They done took Ruby."

The phone went silent except for heavy breathing at the other end of the line. "Get the children ready to leave town, Matt. I'll be there directly."

"Okay, Sam," Matt said, hanging up. "Bessie, can I see you a minute?"

Bessie hurried into the living room. "What's happenin', Matt?"

"Sam say to get the kids ready. He's takin' 'em down to Mama's house."

Wide-eyed, Bessie turned to go into the bedroom.

Matt continued looking out the window until he saw Sam pull into his driveway.

"You run on over to Uncle Matt's place," Sam said to Kay, satisfied that there were no more police cars. She hugged her father and scampered off, and Sam looked around cautiously before entering his home.

Matt met Kay on his front porch and took her to the kitchen where Bessie served her ice cream with Sonja. He then returned to his rocking chair on the front porch to watch the house while Sam went about his business inside.

Rocking nervously, Matt tried to consider the consequences of his sister's actions, but the possibilities were too terrible to imagine. White folks in Live Oak would never tolerate a colored woman shooting a white person—much less a man of the caliber of Dr. Adams.

Across the street, Sam ferried suitcases to the car, two at a time. When the last suitcase sprang open to reveal banded stacks of hundred and thousand-dollar bills, Sam quickly closed it and slammed the car trunk lid down. Turning to look at his house one last time, he got into the car and drove across the street to Matt's house, feeling a gripping pain in his chest.

Sam sat in his car for a moment in front of Matt's house, fighting panic. What was he to do? What would happen to Ruby? Without her, who would help him raise the kids? What would happen to his property and his business?

Sam knew that the moment Ruby murdered the most prominent white citizen of Suwannee County, there was no washing Adams's blood off his hands—he would be tried in the court of public opinion and found guilty, the same as if he had pulled the trigger himself.

Matt called through the screen door. "Bessie! Hurry up and bring the kids on out—Sam's ready to go."

Bessie, holding Loretta and a grocery bag full of coloring books and crayons, hurried out the screen door with Kay following. Sonja went back inside to grab her teddy bear, and then caught up with Kay to climb into the backseat of the car with her. Bessie handed the grocery bag to Kay and then went to the front passenger side to put Loretta on the seat beside Sam.

Sam shoved a small black leather satchel out the car window to Matt. "Matt, you're goin' to need some foldin' money until things settle down."

Matt took the bag to see banded bundles of hundred-dollar bills. "Lawsy, Sam, that's a lot of cash."

Sam shifted nervously in his seat. "The operator's gonna know who you're callin' if you call from your phone, so I need you to go over to the preacher's house and call Ruby's mama and tell her I'm coming down to her place. When you're done, call Sammy out at UCLA and tell him what happened."

"I'll do it, Sam. You drive safe, now."

Bessie rushed to Sam's side of the car and planted a kiss on his cheek. "You be safe."

Starting the car, Sam looked up and said, "Matt, be sure to call Buck and tell him to meet me in Zuber at Mama Jackson's house."

Matt put his hand on Sam's arm. "I will."

Sam looked into his eyes. "Pray for Ruby and me."

"That's all Bessie and me been doin' lately, my brother," Matt assured him.

Sam picked up Ruby's accounting book from the car seat and handed it to Matt. "Give this to Releford when he drives over here. He'll know what to do with it."

Matt stood weighted down with cash, and an accounting book that pointed an accusatory finger at practically every law enforcement official and many businessmen in the county. Numbed by the catastrophic outcome of Ruby's ill-fated love affair, he remained motionless as Sam pulled away, watching the children wave out the car windows until they disappeared down the dirt road in a cloud of dust.

Chapter Fifty-Five

Two hours after fleeing Live Oak, Sam drove onto his mother-in-law's front yard in Zuber, where Cecil and his wife, Bertha, ran out onto the porch to greet their brother-in-law.

Gertrude left her rocking chair on the front porch to greet her grandchildren with an exchange of tearful hugs and kisses until Bertha herded them into the house.

When she was alone with Sam, Gertrude said quickly, "Mr. Crews called and said he would be to the prison before Ruby and the sheriff, and Buck called, too, and said he would take a while gettin' up here from Tampa with that bad leg of his..." Gertrude broke down crying. "Sam, honey, please just tell me what happened."

Sam hugged his mother-in-law. "I'm tired and need some rest, Mama Jackson. I'll tell you everything in the mornin'. I would appreciate you callin' Buck again, though, and see when he's gonna make it up here."

"Sam, honey, you just rest up while I goes in and calls your brother. All this commotion ain't good on your heart."

On the front porch, Cecil greeted Sam with a concerned handshake. "How's my sister?"

Sam hung his head. "I reckon she's doin' as good as a body can do under the circumstances, Cecil."

"You think Matt can handle things up in Live Oak?"

"No," Sam answered without hesitation. "I've got to make some phone calls to arrange to pay Ruby's lawyer. And there ain't no doubt we got to get Mama Jackson and the kids up to Jersey."

Cecil's eyes widened. "You think you in for some harm from the white folks, Sam?"

Sam clutched his chest. "I know for sure I'm out of business and the white folks'll end up with all my property, but what they really want is Ruby's record book."

Cecil gave a sober nod.

"I've got to go inside and lay down, Cecil," Sam told his brother-in-law, feeling the pain run down his left arm. Going inside, he passed the dining room table, where Bertha was playing with the children, and went on into the kitchen to find Gertrude with a worried look, stirring a pot of collard greens and ham hock. "You go on into Ruby's old bedroom and get yo' rest, baby," she said. "I'll wake you up when its suppertime."

"Thank you, Mama," Sam replied, kissing her on the forehead.

In Ruby's old bedroom, he collapsed onto her flowered chenille bedspread and stared at the cracks in the ceiling. *Sweet Jesus*, he wondered, *why'd Ruby have to go and shoot the doc and bring down this misery on us all?*

Outside the open window, a crippled old man shaded his eyes to look through the screen into the bedroom.

Sam caught a glimpse of the figure standing outside the window and said, "Dooley? That you?"

"Yeah, Sam, dis yo' uncle Dooley."

"Come on 'round through the back door."

Dooley limped around to the back porch with his cane and came in the side entrance to the bedroom, where he pulled up a chair beside the bed. "I jes' come to visit with ya, Sam."

Sam reached out for his uncle's hand. "That's good. The good Lord done seen fit to chastise me, Dooley."

Dooley wagged his head. "That's for sure, Sam. That's for sure. And when de chastisement come, ain't nothin' better for a body to have than another body he's known for a coon's age jes' come and set a spell, like Mister Job's friends in the *Bible*."

"Dooley...you remember when you and me and Buck was young'uns 'round here?" Sam's smile spread to Dooley's face as the old man sat back in his chair with a faraway look in his eyes. "How we used to pick them oranges for a nickel a box? You remember them days, Dooley?"

"I sure do, Sam, jes' like it was yesterday. Me and ole Buck, we's allus gettin' in a heap of trouble. But not you, Sam—you never got liquored up and you never got in no fights."

The two men fell silent, retreating into their childhood memories.

"That's been a coon's age ago, ain't it, Dooley?"

"Reckon it be, Sam...reckon it be." The older man winced, rubbing his knees. "Lotta misery done crept into dese bones since den."

Sam smiled through his pain. "Dooley, you remember when Ruby was in school here...how smart she was? 'Specially in math?"

"I 'members, Sam. And I 'members how you won big in that poker game and bought that beat-up ol' Buick and painted it bright red to play it up big for her. And I 'members that fancy ruby ring you bought. Musta worked—I was dere at de weddin'."

Sam smiled at Dooley's words.

"I knows you figgered you had trouble gettin' Ruby...but she knowed who she got. She always used to tell ever'body, 'I picks my men off the top,' jus' like she figgered the best oranges was always at the top of the tree." Dooley paused, glancing proudly at his nephew. "Guess she figgered you right, Sam."

"I always done my best, Dooley," Sam said, feeling a sickness in his stomach. "But I let her down...messed around with the lady folks...left her for weeks all alone while I went down to Tampa on business."

Dooley leaned forward on his cane. "Sam, you a man, jus' like any other man. But you's always been good to Ruby, and dat's what counts."

Sam found comfort in his uncle's words, remembering that he had always been a friend.

Dooley shifted his weight in his chair to ease the numbness in his legs. "How long you figger bein' down here in Zuber, Sam?"

"I'm here, Dooley.... I guess I'm here as long as the good Lord sees fit to let me live...which I figure ain't gonna be much longer."

Dooley reached for his nephew's hand. "You ain't got no reason to die, Sam. You thinks de chastisement more'n a body can bear, but it ain't. De good Lawd'll let up on you in a day or two, you'll see."

Sam clutched his chest. The viselike pains were becoming more steady. "Dooley, there comes a time in this wicked world when a man dies just 'cause he can't do nothin' but."

Gertrude peeked into the room. "Sam, baby, supper's on the table."

"Thank you, Mama Jackson, but I can't eat nothin' right now. I got the heartburn pretty bad and I got to get some more rest. Dooley can come and join y'all."

"You done took yo' medicine, Sam?" asked Gertrude.

"Yeah, Mama Jackson, but the pain ain't passin' so easy."

"I'm gonna call the doctah, Sam," she declared. "You needs to be seen and get some medicine that'll work. I'll keep a plate covered in the ice box for when you can get up tomorrow."

Seeing the pained look on his nephew's face, Dooley grabbed his cane and got shakily to his feet, trying to retain his composure. "Sam,

I's gonna eat supper; then I's gonna mosey on down by the church house and get the Reveren' to pray for you."

"I thank you, Dooley."

After his uncle left, Sam could faintly hear Gertrude speaking with the doctor on the telephone. After she finished the call and returned to the table, he could hear the all—too—familiar low murmuring that he knew took place when there was a crisis in the family.

"You think they gonna send Ruby to the 'lectric chair, Mama?" That was Cecil's voice.

"Hush your mouth, Cecil!" Gertrude cried, devastated by her son's unfeeling words. "I don't want to hear no more talk like that in my house."

After Cecil's indiscretion, everyone sat silently for the rest of the meal. When the table was cleared, they retired to the front porch and mourned Ruby's plight where Sam could not hear them. They discussed what might happen to Sam and Ruby's business and property. They made plans to get the children up to New Jersey to stay with Ruby's sister. They talked about Ruby's chances of getting a fair trial in Live Oak. A host of other concerns were tossed around and opinions were shared, but the subject of Ruby's possible death sentence was taboo, forbidden even to be cast out into the world of possibilities.

By the time the talking was over and the children were tucked in bed, cool silvery moonlight filtered through the living room curtains, replacing the warm, golden rays of the setting sun. Except for the mournful cries of a whippoorwill outside, the house was quiet as the evening breeze flowing through the window screens carried away the heat of the day.

On a small table beside the living room sofa, the telephone rang. "Hello?" Gertrude managed with a start, her hands trembling.

"It me, Mama. Sheriff Howell's here, and he say Sam got to drive up to Lake City to see Mr. Black tomorrow mornin' first thing."

Gertrude glanced toward the door where Sam was sleeping. "Sam's feelin' sickly, Matt. You know how his heart's been givin' him trouble. Let me go peek in and see how he is." Gertrude cracked the bedroom door to see Sam resting quietly. "He sleepin', Matt. I'll let him know in the mornin'."

"All right, Mama."

"Good night, baby," Gertrude said lovingly, hanging up the phone. Looking up at a picture of a colored Jesus hanging above the telephone table, she folded her hands and prayed, "Sweet Jesus, please send your mercy down on all of us—our family need it now more than ever."

Chapter Fifty-Six

Late Monday afternoon, the day after the murder, Keith Black sat in his office, disturbed by a call from Jeff Elliott. "Dead? What the hell do you mean, dead?"

Black paused for an explanation, pressing the receiver close to his ear to hear Elliott's voice over the roar of the car engine on the other end of the line. "I don't care who told you Sam's dead. That smart nigger's switched out with some poor-ass bum and hightailed it up north with that book of Ruby's."

"What do you want me to do, boss?" Elliott asked, glancing down at his speedometer to see the needle hovering over the one hundred mark.

"Well, ain't no nigger's got Sam's gray eyes. You go in to that nigger undertaker down there in Ocala and you pull the cover back and you make damn sure you see Sam's eyes. You got that straight, Jeff?"

"I knew you'd tell me that, so while I was tryin' to get patched through to you I drove on down to Ocala."

"Good work, Jeff. Call me back when you know what's going on."

"Yes, sir." Elliott put the microphone back on its hook and slowed down on the outskirts of Ocala to pull off the road in front of a small whitewashed concrete block house bearing a lighted sign "Chestnut's Funeral Home."

Elliott knocked on the door of the combination funeral home and residence. Hearing no response, he pounded on the door with his fist until the porch light came on.

Charles Chestnut, a bewildered elderly colored man dressed in a night robe, opened his front door just enough to see his evening caller. "May I help you, sir?"

"Yeah," barked Elliott. "I want to see the dead nigger who's supposed to be Sam McCollum."

Knowing that there would be no refusing the white man, Chestnut opened the door. "Please come this way," he responded with a calm dignity. "The holding area is at the end of the hallway."

Chestnut shuffled ahead of Elliott down a hallway and past a chapel, where he opened a door to reveal two tables with covered corpses. He approached the first one and pulled the sheet back.

"Take the nickels off his eyes," Elliott demanded.

Chestnut hesitated but did as he was told.

"Now, open his eyes."

Chestnut was stunned, but Elliott persisted. "Open 'em up, god-damn it!"

Chestnut complied.

Elliott examined the corpse's eyes. "Well, that's Sam, all right. Ain't no other nigger got them gray eyes. When did he die?"

"The death certificate say he died at nine fifty in the mornin' on August the fourth," Chestnut replied.

"Who issued that certificate?"

"Dr. Jones, here in Ocala."

"What did he say was the cause of death?"

"He say it was a heart attack."

Elliott poked his finger into the old man's chest. "You're not to bury him until you get a call from Mr. Keith Black's office up in Lake City. Do you understand what I'm tellin' you?"

Chestnut winced. "Yes, sir."

Elliott did an about-face. "I can find my way out."

Once Elliott had gone, Chestnut bolted the front door and returned to the holding room. He then carefully placed the two coins back on Sam's eyes and, with a tender smile on his face, covered the body as gently as a father tucking his child into bed. "Well, Sam, guess now the white folks'll be convinced that even rich niggahs gotta die sometime."

Walking to the doorway, Chestnut turned back toward Sam's body. "While I's here, Sam, I needs to tell you Gertrude done took your chillun down to the railroad station to send 'em up to stay with Ruby's sister in Jersey." Looking at the clock on the wall, the old man added, "Matter of fact, they should be down at the train station right 'bout now."

Turning out the light, he said, "You can go back to sleep now, Sam. Your family's safe."

Florida State Prison
Raiford

While Elliott was in Ocala confirming that Sam was dead, a black Cadillac limousine pulled alongside a gray 1951 Oldsmobile in the visitors' parking lot of the state prison farm in Raiford.

The prison, reserved for society's worst offenders, was home to "Old Sparky," Florida's electric chair. Guard towers stood at all four corners, manned by armed sentries equipped with powerful arc spotlights to flood the prison yard with artificial daylight should any inmate attempt an escape over the fourteen-foot barbed-wire fence under the cloak of night.

When the limousine came to a stop, the door of the Oldsmobile swung open, and Pigeye Crews, after extricating his great belly from behind the steering wheel, lumbered to his feet. Leaning his bulk against the limousine, he stuck his head in the rear window. "Hey, Buck, Matt," he drawled, "how y'all doin'?"

"Well as we can be, I reckon," Buck replied.

"Y'all ready to go on in and visit Ruby?"

"Matt can go on in with you," said Buck, wincing. "My leg's givin' me trouble."

Pigeye opened the door for Matt. "Whatever you say, boss."

"Give Ruby my regards, Matt," Buck said.

Matt followed Pigeye to the guard station at the barbed-wire fence. The guard glanced up from his newspaper and waved the two men through. A few yards past the main entrance, Pigeye led Matt through the barred gates of the prison building, where another guard waved them through with a cheery "Howdy, Pigeye!"

Matt felt uneasy and closed in, and wished he could be as comfortable in this oppressive setting as the white lawyer beside him, who had visited dozens of clients here over the past three decades. As far as he was concerned, this was just a satellite office, complete with a cafeteria, where he could settle in with a plate full of food and make the necessary phone calls to free his clients: a campaign contribution here, a paid vacation there—whatever it took to free the fortunate few who could pony up the fee.

The guard got up, walked around his desk, and opened the barred gate sealing off the long corridor of prison cells. "Y'all stay as long as you like—we always got room for two more."

Pigeye stepped through the gate, grinning at the jailhouse humor. "Thanks, cuz."

The guard waited for Matt to enter and stepped inside to secure the gate behind him. "Now, Pigeye," he said, "you know what Judge Adams ordered, but cousin John tells me I can trust you to keep quiet."

"That's mighty kind of you, brother," Pigeye said, patting the man on the shoulder.

Matt felt a chill run down his spine as he followed Pigeye down the passageway lined with concrete and steel bars. The late afternoon sun angled through the small barred window of one of the cells, illuminating the face of an old man crouched in a corner.

Walking past the cell, Matt thought of the illustration in his family *Bible* showing Saul on the road to Damascus at the moment the sky opened and the voice of God questioned his life of persecuting others while offering a chance to atone. But, unlike Saul, who got a second chance, anyone in Raiford had likely reached the end of the line.

Approaching Ruby's cell, Matt saw his sister sleeping on her cot in a fetal position. She was dressed in loose-fitting drab prison garb, her legs covered with a khaki blanket.

Matt called softly, "Ruby…It me, baby."

Ruby roused and opened her eyes to see her brother. "Matt! I'm so glad to see you," she cried, jumping up to reach through the bars. "Good to see you, too, Mr. Crews. Thank you for bringing my brother to visit me."

"Glad to help out, Ruby."

Matt held on to her hand, fighting back the tears. "Mr. Pigeye said he already started workin' on your case, baby. And Buck's outside in his car—you know he has trouble walkin' with that stiff leg of his."

Tearing up at the sound of Matt's voice, Ruby squeezed his hand. "Buck's always been there when we needed him. Give him a hug for me."

"I will, baby," he said, feeling a tear roll down his cheek in spite of himself.

"Are the kids all right, Matt? Tell me they're okay."

"The chillun's fine, Ruby..." He paused, lowering his head to summon the strength he needed to deliver his terrible news. "It's Sam I come to tell you about."

Ruby grabbed the steel bars. "Did they hurt Sam?"

Matt reached for her. "No, Ruby—Sam done passed on of a heart 'tack early this mornin'."

Ruby gasped in disbelief.

"Sam dead, Ruby," Matt declared with a note of finality.

"Sam...," she murmured. Then, looking around her with wide eyes as if searching for something that might prove it all a lie, she wailed, "Sam... Oh, my God! I killed him... I killed my Sam...!" Falling onto the cot, Ruby rolled back into a fetal position, her high, keening cries echoing down the long corridor.

Across the corridor, an inmate stared through his cell bars with vacant eyes dulled by a lifetime of receiving and inflicting pain.

"Guess we oughta leave now," Pigeye suggested, uncomfortable with Ruby's grieving.

Matt loosened his grip on the bars, feeling a deep sickness in the pit of his stomach. He felt powerless to help the big sister who had protected him so long ago from the scary monsters that lurked in the dark of his bedroom.

In the dying light outside the prison, Matt's face glistened with tears shed in silence as the two men walked past the guard station and into the parking lot.

Matt opened the back door of the limousine to sit beside Buck.

"How'd she take the news?"

"She took it real hard," Matt replied, wiping his face with a handkerchief.

Pigeye opened the center passenger door and got in, huffing from the effort.

"Sam and Ruby had their troubles, but they still loved each other," Buck said.

Matt sighed. "Sam's troubles be over now, I reckon.... Ruby say hello."

As if on cue, Pigeye tried to console the two grief-stricken men. "I'll make sure they give her a shot to keep her rested till mornin'."

Matt said, "Wished somebody'd give me a shot."

Pigeye reached into his hip pocket and pulled out a stainless steel flask. "Here you go—this'll help you relax."

Gratefully, Matt took the bottle and downed a gulp.

Pigeye, pleased that he could render at least this small service, moved to a topic closer to his heart. "I know this is a bad time to ask, fellas, but I have a feelin' there ain't goin' to be a better one anytime soon…"

"Reach me that suitcase, Matt," Buck interrupted, pointing to the floorboard.

Matt hauled the heavy suitcase onto the seat, and Buck flipped the latches to reveal stacks of neatly banded hundred-dollar bills.

Pigeye's eyes bulged as Buck selected three banded stacks and tore out a slip from the receipt book. "I set this aside for your retainer, Mr. Crews. You'll find that there's four thousand and eight hunnerd—enough to buy yourself a new Cadillac if you want. Just sign the receipt, if you would, please."

Feigning nonchalance, Pigeye ventured, "Did I mention the money we need to pay Brother Cogdill for his assistance? You know he's the only reason we got in there to see Ruby without filin' a passel of legal papers with ol' Judge Adams."

Buck knew that the stacks of greenbacks were as addictive as Ruby's pills—a little always called for a lot more. "I like dealin' directly with people I pay cash money to, Mr. Crews—no offense."

"None taken," Pigeye assured him. "Miss Ruby's done bought herself one hell of a defense team."

Buck closed the suitcase. "That's what we're gonna need—one hell of a team for one hell of a mess."

"A big amen to that, Brother Buck."

"We need to let you get on home, Mr. Crews," Buck said, dismissing the man.

With a grunt, Pigeye heaved his considerable bulk out of the limousine, stuffing the money and the receipt in his pocket. "Well, it's good to be doin' business with you, Mr. Buck."

"I won't be seein' you again for a while, Mr. Crews."

"Well," he said expansively, "if you need me, you've got my number."

"I think we've all got your number, Mr. Crews," Buck replied with a touch of sarcasm. "You think you can give me that receipt now?"

"Oh, yeah…the receipt." Pigeye pulled a pen from his shirt pocket to scrawl out his signature. "I'll be sure to stay in touch," he assured him, handing the receipt through the open window.

"I'm sure you will…. Let's get on back home, Willie."

Watching the limousine roll out of the parking lot, Pigeye eased the hip flask out of his pocket, wiped it with his sleeve, and took a snort. *Sweet Jesus,* he prayed, gazing at the brilliant pink-and-gold-streaked clouds billowing above the setting sun, *thank you for lookin' out for us sinners.*

Suwannee Hotel
Live Oak, Florida

Chapter Fifty-Eight

Pigeye drove straight to Live Oak, paid a hundred dollars of his retainer to book a room at the Suwannee Hotel for the month, enjoyed a supper of fried catfish with hushpuppies at the Wagon Wheel restaurant, and turned in early to get a good night's rest for his meeting with Cogdill in the morning.

After a leisurely sunrise breakfast of fried ham, buttered grits and scrambled eggs in the hotel coffee shop where hushed talk centered around Adams's murder the previous day, he traveled north along Ohio Avenue to find the stores open early, with many of the shopkeepers standing at their front doors to greet the fortunate few whose crops had survived the drought and the hailstorm.

Turning left onto Howard Street at the light, he was surprised to find cars lining both sides of the street in front of Dees's barbershop. Rivaled only by Annie's Beauty Shop, its female counterpart, this was Live Oak's news center, broadcasting the local gossip more effectively than WNER ever could.

Seeing a car pull away from the curb in front, Pigeye pulled into the empty spot.

Inside the shop, he sauntered to the end of a long line of customers waiting in carved oak barrel chairs. Taking a seat, he looked across the room to see a wall of mirrors over marble-topped cabinets laden with Vitalis, Wildroot Cream Oil, Lilac Vegetal, and bay rum. A sign over a doorway in the rear of the shop advertised hot showers for fifty cents.

The customer sitting next to Pigeye glanced at him. "Awful crowded for a Tuesday mornin', don'tcha think? Guess everybody's gettin' gussied up for the doc's funeral this afternoon."

"Guess so," Pigeye agreed, showing a sudden interest in the *Suwannee Democrat* to avoid further conversation.

Bogue Dees, the owner of the shop, picked up on the customer's comment. "Just like a nigger to shoot the best doctor Suwannee County ever had."

Buford, Bogue's customer, called to the man sitting beside Pigeye. "Clyde, you worked with the doc down at the hospital, didn'tcha?"

"Yeah."

"What the hell you reckon was in that nigger woman's head?"

"All I know is, she was chasin' after him the day before she shot him. I was in the operatin' room with the doc when Ruby kept tryin' to use the phone outside to call in. Doc got madder'n a hornet. He yelled, 'You tell 'at goddamn nigger woman to go to hell!' But Ruby wouldn't' have none of it—kept on ringin' the phone till Sarah got two orderlies to th'ow her out the back door. Made the doc so mad, he left a nurse in the operatin' room to close up the patient by herself, then punched Dr. Sims out cold on his way out of the hospital."

"You mean he hit Dr. Sims?" one of the men exclaimed.

"I mean good night, Irene."

"Had to do with drugs, I hear," Bogue added, whipping up a mug of lather. "I cut old man Blue's hair just a little while ago, and he got real quiet when I asked him 'bout the doc givin' her those shots everybody's talkin' 'bout. People seen her down at his office every day when they let her out of that crazy house over in Jacksonville."

"The doc was pretty generous with the drugs, all right," agreed Buford. "My cousin musta had a dozen bottles of painkillers the doc give him. Seems like he took them pills most of the time he was awake. Then one mornin' he just didn't wake up."

Another customer volunteered, "I've heard a lot of talk around town about Ruby owin' the doc money."

Bogue laughed, brushing the warm, foaming lather onto Buford's neck. "That nigger's husband, Bolita Sam, made more money from runnin' the numbers and sellin' bootleg liquor than old man Crapps rakes in down at his bank!"

Another customer looked up from his *Argosy* magazine. "I heard her last baby belonged to the doc."

Bogue laughed, scraping a clean swath down Buford's neck with the straight razor. "Wouldn't be the first rich white man to pick a blackberry outta the back forty."

This brought scattered chuckles.

"Hey, Bogue," Buford protested, "you gottah warn me 'fore you come out with one o' those—You're like to cut a fellah's ear clean off."

Bogue grinned. "I never cut nobody's ear off—nicked a pecker, though, one time when the bum tried to skip out 'thout payin' me."

Amid the men's raucous laughter and knee slapping, one of the customers made a show of jumping up to hold his crotch while he checked his wallet.

When the laughter subsided, Buford said, "I hear tell Sam's done left the county with all his money—switched out with some dead nigger down near Ocala to throw the sheriff off the trail."

"Ain't no way they're gonna find that nigger and all that money," Buford scoffed.

A moment of silence followed as everyone contemplated the missing man and his fabled riches.

"I hear tell that state attorney feller, Keith Black, is gettin' ready to fry her black ass."

"Forget him," Bogue quipped. "Everybody in the county's out to lynch her ass—includin' the niggers."

"Ain't nobody lynchin' nobody long as Judge Adams has his say...and he does like to have his say, if you know what I mean," Buford said with a wink.

Bogue grinned. "Yeah, he carries a lot of weight with the marchin' boys. Otherwise they woulda tarred, feathered, and hung her black neck the same day she shot the doc."

Bogue stared at Pigeye. "You awful quiet over there, mister. You from outta town?"

"Yeah, Jacksonville—just passin' through. Ain't much been said over there yet, 'cept for what come out in the paper."

"Just give it time, brother," Bogue quipped. "Just give it time."

Methodist Church
Live Oak, Florida

Chapter Fifty-Nine

On Tuesday afternoon, the streets of downtown Live Oak were lined with people holding cardboard fans to stir air so hot it felt like a damp, stifling blanket thrown over their heads.

Mothers dressed in their Sunday best held their children by the hand, bending down occasionally to chide them for fidgeting. Whispering spread about how poor people had lost the best doctor in town at the hands of a mean colored woman—rich woman, too, so stingy she didn't want to pay her doctor bill.

Dozens of state and local police cars lined the block in front of the Methodist church, preparing to lead the funeral procession to the city cemetery just north of town. When the voices of the choir, overlaying the sonorous tones of the pipe organ, drifted through the open stained-glass windows, two ushers opened the front doors of the church for Judge Adams, the lead honorary pallbearer, and Harry T. Reid, the Jasper funeral director, to step outside.

Forty men dressed in dark suits and twelve uniformed state and local police officers waited solemnly at the foot of the stairs as the courthouse clock tolled four.

Reid whispered orders to his assistants, who disappeared into the church while he stood at the top of the stairs, ceremoniously stretching his arms out to the crowd like Moses raising his staff to part the Red Sea. "Gentlemen," he called out loudly, "may I have your attention, please."

The whispering crowd fell silent, and all eyes were riveted on Reid.

"We have eight limousines lined up to take y'all out to the cemetery. Governor Hardee and Judge Adams will ride in the limousine immediately following Mrs. Florrie Lee Adams and her family. The senators will follow in the third limousine, and the physicians will ride in the fourth. Limousines five through eight will carry the remainder of the honorary pallbearers as well as the active pallbearers. Members of the police force and highway patrol will travel in their official vehicles. When we arrive at the graveside, my assistants will escort the pallbearers to their stations. The honorary pallbearers will assemble with Judge Adams and will remain standing while Reverend Philpot, minister of the church, and Reverend Lloyd King, chaplain of the Florida Police Officers Association, give the closing prayers."

Reid paused to wipe the sweat from his face. "I want to thank the local police force and members of the Florida Highway Patrol for their assistance with the largest funeral in the history of Suwannee County."

Descending the stairs, Reid put his hand on Judge Adams's shoulder. "Now, if you gentlemen will get in your assigned limousines, my assistants and I will work with the active pallbearers to bring the casket out to the hearse."

Reid went back into the church with his retinue while Judge Adams and former governor Cary Hardee led the honorary pallbearers to the limousines, where liveried chauffeurs opened the passenger doors.

Inside the second limousine, Hardee turned to Judge Adams. "How in tarnation'd all this happen, Hal?"

"Can't say as I know for sure, Cary. From what I've been told so far, though, it seems that between Ruby and Leroy, the two succeeded in breaking all ten of the good Lord's Commandments."

"Thank God I'm not sittin' over there in the governor's chair right now. 'Specially with all the northern press settin' their sights on Live Oak, and those civil rights meddlers just dyin' for a cause."

"I want to keep it as local as we can," the judge stressed. "Florrie Lee's a God-fearing Christian lady who's lost a son and a husband all in the same year. Last thing she needs is that nigrah woman smearing the good name of her late husband in the newspapers."

Hardee noticed Sheriff Howell pacing nervously alongside the car. "Sim's about to pop a cork over Ruby's accounting ledger. Seems the McCollums have half the county law enforcement on their payroll and—"

Judge Adams held up his hand. "I've heard rumors here and there, Cary, but in my position I don't care to hear more than I have to. My main interest is to keep Ruby from talking with the press and proceed with the trial in a quiet and orderly manner."

Hardee fidgeted. "I hear Pigeye Crews is already on the case, and he's bound to claim that his client can't get a fair trial here. Once she's moved out of Live Oak, she can talk all she wants."

"That's a reasonable move on Mr. Crews's part, but I plan to ask Governor Warren to allow Ruby to be transferred back to Live Oak when things settle down. That way any motion for change of venue can't ride on the notion that the court's keepin' Ruby out of town to protect her."

Hardee chuckled. "Hal, you're one of the brightest legal minds I've ever known."

Outside the limousine, Sheriff Howell leaned down to the window to take advantage of the pause in the conversation. "I don't mean to be disrespectful, Judge, but can I see you after the funeral to get some search warrants?"

"Come on down to my office later this afternoon, Brother Howell. I'll see that you get what you need to perform your duties."

"Thanks, Judge," Howell replied with a crisp salute.

"Oh, Sheriff," the judge called after him.

"Yes, sir?" said Howell, bending back down.

"I don't want any late-night marches right now. Can you take care of that for me?"

"Yes, sir. Don't think we need to right now anyways—a lot of coloreds done cut the doc's picture out of the paper and hung it up right beside their pictures of Jesus."

When Howell turned to leave the judge's limousine, Reid and his two assistants came out of the church, followed by six pallbearers carrying Adams's mahogany coffin. Florrie Lee Adams walked arm in arm with Laverne and her husband behind the casket, with Adams's two sisters trailing behind.

While the casket was being loaded into the hearse, Reid escorted the family to the lead limousine. At his signal, the police and state patrol cars turned on their flashing lights to lead the procession north along Ohio Avenue.

At the corner of Ohio Avenue and Howard Street, the main intersection in town, a colored woman bent down to her son and pointed to the hearse. "That man there saved your life last Sunday, Lavon. I want you to always remember him."

Chapter Sixty

On the morning of August 12, the day after Sam McCollum's funeral at St. Peter's cemetery near Ocala, Buck, Matt, Charles Hall, and Pigeye Crews met around a folding table in the cramped back room of Chestnut's Funeral Home.

Charles Chestnut placed doughnuts and coffee on the table. "I gots plenty more hot coffee and fresh doughnuts if y'all wants 'em."

"Thank you, Brother Chestnut," Hall replied. "You done a fine job with Sam's funeral."

"We always tries our best, Brother Hall," Chestnut assured his fellow undertaker, closing the door behind him.

"Well, gentleman," Buck began, "Sam's gone and left us with Ruby's mess—I just wish he had lingered a little while longer to help us out."

"Amen to that," Matt agreed. "The sheriff keeps comin' by my place ever' day tryin' to find out if I knows where Ruby's book is."

"Yeah," Hall grunted. "I bet he does. Ain't much doubt lots of fine white folks been losin' sleep over that little book of Ruby's."

Buck winced, clutching his bad leg. "Y'all know the reason we're meetin' here is because I asked Mr. Crews to tell us about what's happenin' with the trial."

Pigeye grinned, standing to present his update. "First of all, I want to express my appreciation for trustin' me with Ruby's case. In matters of life and death like this, I'm always honored to be called upon for my services."

Buck squirmed, uneasy with Pigeye's unctuous manner.

"As I understand it, y'all asked me here to give you an update on the legal matters facin' Miss Ruby and to escort y'all up to Raiford to visit her so's you can take care of business matters. As I told y'all, I could get her to sign the power of attorney for you myself, but I understand how y'all might like to speak privately with her about other matters, seeing the nature and the gravity of circumstances—"

"Yes, sir, Mr. Crews," Buck interrupted, acutely aware of the attorney's skill at staying on the clock.

"Well, Mr. Keith Black, the state attorney, along with his assistant, Mr. Edwards, convened a grand jury, and on August ninth they indicted Miss Ruby with murder in the first degree, and Mr. Cogdill and me appeared in open court with Miss Ruby at the arraignment to enter a plea of not guilty. Mr. Cogdill and I have a court date of August twenty-first to present our motion for a change of venue — that's a motion to ask the court to move the case outside Suwannee County, where folks don't know Doc Adams. In Live Oak, the man's a saint."

"You think the judge will allow that?" asked Buck.

"We've drawn up a bunch of petitions maintaining that Ruby can't get a fail trial in Live Oak. If we can get enough people to sign 'em —"

"I wouldn't put my money on that," Buck interrupted.

"In case that fails," Pigeye continued, "Mr. Cogdill wants to file a motion suggesting that Ruby was insane when she shot the doc."

"Do anything you need to do," Buck concluded, anxious to draw the meeting to a close. "I'm countin' on you to keep my sister-in-law out of the chair, Mr. Crews."

"If certain events turn out the way I think they will, there ain't no problem," Crews assured him.

"What other business do we have, Mr. Crews?" Buck asked.

"Well, I guess there ain't nothin' else right now, 'cept to get that power of attorney so you can sell her shares of the Central Life Insurance Company. If you don't get 'em in your name soon, Black's goin' to seize 'em for the widow Adams, and then you'll find him down there in Tampa at your next board meetin', demandin' to look at your books."

"I can get Ruby to sign that the next time I see her," Matt volunteered.

Pigeye handed the power of attorney document to Matt. "Well, I guess that about does it. Brother Cogdill's got it all arranged with his cousin for y'all to visit Miss Ruby day after tomorrow."

Buck pulled himself up with his cane. "Thank you for all your help, Mr. Crews."

Pigeye picked up his briefcase and lifted his straw hat off the rack. "You're most certainly welcome, Mr. Buck."

After Pigeye left, Buck turned to Hall. "What's your take on this clown?"

"Man's full of hot air, but he's white, and he knows a hell of a lot of people over in Tallahassee — got voted in twice for representative from Jacksonville."

Buck nodded in agreement. "I can't tell what he's up to, but my poker guts tell me he's got somethin' up his sleeve."

Hall grinned. "Let's hope it's the ace of spades, brother."

Chapter Sixty-One

Briefcase in hand, John Cogdill followed the officer through the second gate of Raiford State Prison to the guard's station, where his cousin was enjoying a doughnut. "Cousin John!" the guard drawled, breaking into a broad grin to stand and pump his cousin's hand. "You come to see Ruby?"

"Shore would like too, cuz. She decent?"

The guard laughed, reaching for his keys. "She's been askin' for her lawyer all mornin'. Told her I'd have to tell the nurse to give her a shot with a dull needle if she didn't hush up—she ain't hushed up yet."

The men laughed, heading down the hallway to Ruby's cell.

Standing at the bars of her cell, Ruby smiled at the approaching men. "Mr. Cogdill, it's good to see you!"

"Good to see you, too, Ruby."

"Just give a holler when you're though, cousin," the guard said, letting Cogdill into the cell.

"Thanks, cuz," Cogdill replied. "Miss Ruby, have a seat. I've got some good news for you."

Ruby sat on her cot and folded her hands in the lap of her cotton prison dress.

"Judge Adams is moving you back to Live Oak."

"That's good," she said calmly. "It's been hard on Matt trying to get over here."

Cogdill fidgeted and licked his lips. "Ruby," he finally said, "from time to time I've heard you say some things about the doc that might not serve your case well.... As a matter of fact, they can only set the community—and the jury—against you."

"What things have you heard, Mr. Cogdill?"

"From what I hear, you've referred to some sort of relationship between you and the doctor that is...well, other than of a strictly professional nature."

"Yes, Mr. Cogdill, the doctor and I have had sexual relations for some time."

Cogdill scratched his head. "I've also heard rumors that you've claimed that your last child was his."

"Loretta is my child by the doctor," Ruby confirmed, pulling a wallet-size photo from under her mattress and handing it to him. "As you can see, she's the spitting image of the doctor."

Cogdill leaned down and positioned his bifocals. "She's a pretty little thing, but you can't talk like that if you want Pigeye and me to defend you. Why do you think they're keepin' you over here in the first place?"

She fixed him with a sphinx-like gaze. "What do you want me to do, Mr. Cogdill—lie?"

"Well, Ruby, if there's one thing I've learned in my long years at practicin' law, it's that there ain't no such thing as a lie—there's only different versions of the truth."

"Well, if that's so, I didn't shoot the doctor."

Cogdill laughed, appreciating her humor. "I forgot to mention one small detail. If somebody—in this case several somebodies—see you do somethin', then their version of the truth weighs heavier on the scales of justice than your version of the truth. That's what you might call the law of gravity in legal matters."

Ruby crossed her arms and held her ground. "I understand one thing, Mr. Cogdill: I'm paying you to be my lawyer because you know more about the law than I do. But I do know that Dr. Adams is Loretta's father."

"I don't think you're followin' me, Ruby. This case is a lot like ridin' a johnboat down a ragin' river while tryin' to steer clear of the rocks—we're in for one hell of a ride."

Looking at him with defiant eyes, she said, "Like I told you, Mr. Cogdill, I'm not a lawyer. That's what I'm paying you for."

Cogdill smiled at her spunk, knowing that she was accustomed to spending money to have her way. "That's what I like to hear, Miss Ruby. You keep your mouth shut like I told you, and I'll make sure you continue to get special treatment around here." Looking out the cell bars, he called down the hall, "Cuz, can you let me out now?"

"Thank you for coming, Mr. Cogdill."

"Certainly, Ruby. You get your rest and stop talkin' to all the prison employees. Just leave your case to me and Pigeye."

"I'll think on your advice, Mr. Cogdill."

"Good."

"Just one more thing, Mr. Cogdill. Would you get me a doctor...soon?"

"You sick, Ruby?"

"I just need to discuss...you know...something personal."

His cousin John opened the cell door, and Cogdill stepped into the corridor, leaving her standing at the bars of her cell. "I'll see to it, Ruby."

As soon as Cogdill was out of Ruby's earshot, he whispered, "Get somebody to give her that shot you mentioned."

The guard winked. "Sure, thing, cousin."

"Oh, and one more thing—see if you can't convince her to write that letter I called you about this mornin'. She ain't gonna last long over in Live Oak if she don't."

"I'll talk to Mr. Britt first thing in the mornin', cousin," the guard assured him. "He'll know what to do to get what you need outta her."

PART III

On Monday, November 24, the week following my visit with Lucy, I took my usual seat in the courtroom balcony to witness the aftermath of Pigeye Crews's clever attempt at forcing the judge to declare a mistrial. If he had pulled it off, Buck McCollum, being a gambling man with a reputation to uphold, would have paid off on the five-thousand-dollar bet, and Pigeye would have been that much closer to retirement.

But since his scheme had failed, we were now in the throes of what was, for all practical purposes, a second trial, and one that did not constitute double jeopardy.

Court was already in session, and the courtroom was packed with spectators anxious to witness the next episode in the town's favorite soap opera.

Ruby was seated with her new attorney, Odis Henderson, a slender, dark-haired young man from Adams's hometown of Jasper, just north of Live Oak.

During the silence, while everyone waited for Judge Adams to arrange his papers, my thoughts turned to my research. So far, I had spoken with Releford and Matt, heard a conspiracy theory from Blue regarding a forged will, and taken copious notes from my all-night visit with Lucy. I was beginning to feel that I had enough material to begin my "Life Story" series for the *Courier*, which would give me the leverage I needed to ask Nunn for a substantial payment on my contract.

After what seemed an eternity but was probably no more than a couple of minutes, the judge had his papers in order. Without preamble, he said, "This homicide is alleged to have occurred on August 3, 1952. The indictment was returned on August 9, 1952. On August 14, 1952, the defendant came before the court for arraignment, accompanied by her counsel, the Honorable John L. Cogdill of Jacksonville, Florida. Arraignment was duly had upon that date, and the defendant entered a plea of not guilty. At that time the court allowed a further time for filing of any motions or other procedural matters. That was fixed for August 21, 1952."

Judge Adams then outlined the defense's filing of motions for change of venue and suggestion of insanity, going into great detail regarding his reasons for denying both. "On November 18, 1952," he continued, "the venire was present and the trial proceeded after agreement by counsel for the state and the defendant that both were ready. The matter proceeded until noon, at which time one hundred twenty-five veniremen had been examined thoroughly, fully, and carefully, and forty-two qualified jurors at that time were left to be called into the box for trial service."

"During the noon hour, a representative of the Associated Press at Tallahassee discovered that on that morning of November eighteenth there had been filed in the clerk's office of the Supreme Court of the state of Florida an order suspending Mr. P. Guy Crews, the defendant's counsel, from practicing law for six months."

The judge thanked the members of the Associated Press who broke the news, as well as the entire chain of command of the Florida Highway Patrol, for dispatching the news of Crews's suspension in relay fashion between Tallahassee and Live Oak in time to prevent a mistrial.

Judge Adams paused to clear his throat and avail himself of his spittoon. "It developed that Mr. Crews, who had announced ready for trial on November 18, had summoned not one single, solitary witness to appear here, and I do not know what his line of procedure was. So there is very little to be done now except to submit the facts of the alleged homicide. Leaving out all other things, this is just another homicide case, that is, where one person is charged with shooting and killing another human being. That is all it is, and there is nothing extraordinary about it, because, in my time, I have tried over two hundred homicide cases."

"I think that the date of December sixteenth will grant a fair time to Colonel Henderson. I can draw the jury on the Saturday before that, and we will draw about one hundred twenty-five names. That way the sheriff won't have to go night and day to serve them."

"I will state frankly that if Mr. Crews has the right principles, he will go out of his way to advise Mr. Henderson of everything that he did and everybody that he contacted and all the information that he had obtained. If he doesn't, it would be a clear case of his lack of appreciation for the responsibilities which he should recognize under these circumstances."

Whereas carving out meaning and order from formless chaos is well beyond the ability of the average mind, it was the everyday business of this elderly jurist to simplify a complex set of circumstances and mount it all on the stage of human drama, where it would appear to the less informed to play itself out as naturally as the rising and setting of the sun.

After court was adjourned, I reflected on the judge's statement that Crews had not called any witnesses for the trial. Short of an outright condemnation of the man for attempting to create a mistrial, the judge had made his point.

Yet again I marveled at the awesome power of silence to communicate.

Suwannee Democrat Building
Live Oak, Florida

On the first Tuesday of Ruby's second trial, I decided that my frog had followed me around long enough. It was high time I fried him up for breakfast so I could wake up in the morning without seeing him staring me in the face.

The frog I had in mind was Louie Wadsworth, owner and editor of the *Suwannee Democrat*. I suspected that trying to speak with him would be the ultimate exercise in futility, but I might be able to sit in some back corner of his offices and read what he had published about the trial.

About twenty minutes after leaving Matt's house, I stood in front of the rather plain red-brick, two-story building housing the *Democrat* in downtown Live Oak, took a few deep breaths to steel myself, and opened the door.

Inside, I was greeted by a white receptionist who asked me if she could be of assistance.

"Yes, please. Would it be possible to see some of your back issues?"

"Of course," the young lady assured me. "You can step through that door to the left and ask one of the men to see anything you'd like."

"Thank you," I replied, pleased at having met no resistance. In fact, her reception was quite cordial.

When I entered the small room the receptionist had directed me to, a young colored man greeted me, and I asked to see copies of the *Democrat* from August fifteenth of this year up to the current issue.

"Yes'm," he said. "Just take a seat there while I go in back to pull 'em out of the stacks." He hesitated for a moment. "You sure you don't want the one about Dr. Adams, Miz Hurston?"

Once again I was embarrassed to be recognized. "No, thank you, I've already read that one."

While the young man went to get the back issues, I looked at the labels on the file cabinets lining the room and saw that they housed a photo archive containing a visual history of the county back to the 1930s, when I had last visited the area. I knew that the *Democrat* was older than that, so I assumed that the earlier issues must be stored elsewhere.

"Here's what you wanted," the young man announced, handing me the issues I had requested. "If you need anything else, just let me know."

"Do you think it would be possible to speak with Mr. Wadsworth when I'm finished?"

The young man stared at me. "I'll go tell Mr. Wadsworth you asked."

I thanked him and started in on the August 15 issue, which carried photos of the tobacco festival, with the Headline "UNIQUE '52 FESTIVAL ENJOYED SATURDAY." The festival, including a parade and a "crowd of thousands," attested to how quickly the residents of Suwannee County had buried their beloved physician and moved on with their lives.

The article also celebrated the award of a new Ford farm pickup truck to Mrs. Harlie Lee after her raffle ticket was drawn out of the concrete mixer used to shuffle the free tickets handed out at the tobacco festival. Then there was the announcement of the two candidates for the special election to replace Dr. Adams. Joseph Jacobs, a young lawyer who had already served as a state representative, was running against J. Graham Black, a former state senator from Adams's hometown of Jasper.

What caught my attention, though, was Louie Wadsworth's weekly editorial column, "Thinking Out Loud." It seems that Wadsworth had been out of town for "a pleasant two weeks encampment with the National Guard at Ft. McClellan" when Dr. Adams died. Scanning down the column, I read, "I have been impressed with a general feeling here that perhaps the slackness with which we here in Live Oak and Suwannee County approach this matter of cleaning out gambling and the evils that go with it might have played a part in the untimely and tragic passing of our beloved doctor."

This was the first time that I was aware of a public statement, however tenuous, between Dr. Adams's death and bolita activities in Suwannee County. Wadsworth went on to warn, "History records that when moral fiber begins to deteriorate in a people that nation falls." Then he mentioned that reporters from the *Atlanta Journal* had interviewed Sheriff Sim Howell.

What concerned Wadsworth about the interview was Howell's statement that he "closed the beer and whiskey establishments immediately after the tragedy." Wadsworth, noting that Suwannee was a dry county, wrote, "If the sheriff was rightly quoted, and I believe he was, then I think it would be well for him to continue to close beer establishments on Sunday as the law requires and to close permanently the whiskey places he closed some few weeks ago for a day."

In a town that spoke in ciphers and codes, this was the clearest indictment of any law enforcement officer that I had heard during my stay. Here was Louie Wadsworth—a decorated war veteran, a ranking officer in the National Guard, and the clarion of decency in the county's only newspaper—openly pointing a finger at Sheriff Sim Howell for his slackness in controlling illegal liquor sales in a dry county.

It was an unmistakable signal to the citizens of Suwannee County that they had chosen wisely when they voted Howell out in favor of their new sheriff, Hugh Lewis. Time alone would tell how the new sheriff would deal with Sam McCollum's legacy.

Moving on to the August 22 edition, I found the headline "ATTORNEY ASKS COURT TO NOT TRY RUBY MCCOLLUM IN COUNTY." This was Cogdill's motion for a change of venue. While the paper's take on the motion was simply expository, what I found interesting was the statement that Ruby was "brought to the court from Raiford where she is being held for safe keeping," and "was taken back to the State Prison at Raiford immediately after the hearing today. Nearly 20 patrolmen were in and about the court house during the hearing."

Turning to the August 29 issue, the only coverage of the trial related to the motion for a change of venue and the presentation of evidence from attorneys on both sides.

The September 5 headline read, "JUDGE ADAMS RULES NEGRESS CAN GET A FAIR TRIAL HERE," noting that the decision followed two weeks of legal arguments in a "packed courtroom." The article also reported, "The Negress was rushed to Raiford State Prison, where she was held for safe keeping." It also noted, "The Negress' husband, Sam McCollum, known in this section as 'Bolita Sam,' had died shortly after the shooting."

Again the code. A "Negress" could receive a fair trial in the county, yet she had to be held for safekeeping three counties away in a high-security state prison. All the dots, but no connections.

What I found particularly noteworthy was the closing statement: "The case is receiving nationwide publicity due to its racial implications." Judge Adams was quoted as saying, "The trial will be conducted so that fairness and justice will be had on both sides."

It was apparent that the national attention drawn by the trial was an unwelcome spotlight on folks who preferred to live in the shadows.

The September 12 and 19 issues extolled the virtues of Suwannee County in almost poetic language, reminiscent of Wordsworth. The area was presented as a hunter's and fisherman's paradise where colored and white communities lived in harmony. I had to chuckle at seeing Wadsworth-turned-Wordsworth try his best to take advantage of the sudden national attention brought by the trial to attract new residents to the land of Stephen Foster.

The September 26 issue ran the headline "MCCOLLUM TRIAL POSTPONED FOR INSANITY EXAMINATION." The first thing that struck me was the disappearance of the word "Negress" as the only reference to Ruby. I wondered if Wadsworth's fellow journalists had tipped him off about his unconscious bias in reducing Ruby to an unnamed "Negress" embroiled in a trial for her life.

In passing, I enjoyed a chuckle when I saw a reference to Ruby's age. The *Democrat* had consistently reported that she was thirty-four, but this issue put her at thirty-two. Although surely nothing would cheer her up at this stage, any other woman would have appreciated having two years shaved off her age—especially since she was actually forty-three to start with.

Having gone through all the editions of the *Democrat* since the murder, my mind turned to how best to approach Louie Wadsworth— that is, if he would see me.

When I stepped back into the tiny reception area about an hour later, the same young woman was still seated at her desk. "Did you get what you wanted?" she asked.

"Yes, I did, thank you," I said. "There was one more thing.... I sent word to Mr. Wadsworth that I'd like to see him if he has the time."

"Let me check to see if he's available," she offered, disappearing into the corridor behind her desk.

A few minutes later the woman returned. "Mr. Wadsworth said he can see you now."

I hadn't counted on this. Had the young man who helped me told Wadsworth who I was?

When I walked down the short corridor to an office with Wadsworth's name on the door, I found a dark-haired man in his mid-forties sitting at his desk behind a typewriter. From the ashtray full of cigarette butts on his desk, I assumed that he was a heavy consumer of Live Oak's primary cash crop. "Good morning, Miz Hurston," he greeted, adjusting his thick glasses and standing up with outstretched hand. "I'm Louie Wadsworth."

I returned a polite handshake to the only white man in Live Oak other than LaVergne Blue ever to offer one.

"I understand you're with the *Pittsburgh Courier*."

"Yes, I'm here on assignment until the trial is over."

Taking his seat, he said, "I was right in the middle of my weekly column when Thomas told me you wanted to see me. I have a few minutes, so please pull up a chair and tell me what you'd like to know."

I thanked him and settled into the oak chair in front of his desk. "Well, first of all, it's a pleasure to meet you, and I appreciate your taking the time to see me without an appointment."

"I can always spare a little time for a fellow journalist."

"I've read all your articles up until last Friday, and the only question I have relates to your statement that there might have been a connection between Dr. Adams's death and Sam McCollum's bolita activities."

He leaned back in his chair, apparently comfortable with my question. "It's no secret that I've been concerned about this bolita problem for a couple of years now. I consider bolita the root of most of the evil in this county. However, I see no connection between Sam McCollum and Dr. Adams just because Sam's wife shot the doctor."

"Are there any other reasons that might lead you to think that Dr. Adams worked with Sam?"

Wadsworth fidgeted. "I can't imagine a fine gentleman like Dr. Adams having anything to do with the likes of Sam McCollum other than in his role as a physician."

"What about Loretta?" I ventured, realizing full well that I was crawling out on a limb.

"I suppose we'll have to see what comes out in the trial," he responded circumspectly. "I make it a practice to deal in facts, not gossip."

"I understand," I replied, getting the definite impression that Wadsworth knew far more than he was admitting. "What about the connection between Sheriff Howell and bolita?"

"I've long said that bolita could not survive in Suwannee County unless it was protected by the law. Things are changing here, though."

"Yes," I agreed, seeing that he was growing defensive. "I read that Sheriff Howell lost the election a few months back."

Wadsworth nodded, glancing at his wristwatch. "I was glad to spend some time with you, Miz Hurston. Unfortunately, I have to get on with my column. You know how deadlines are."

"Yes, I do," I acknowledged, getting up. "Thank you for your time."

"Glad to oblige," Wadsworth replied, standing up to show me out.

As I left the *Democrat* offices, I concluded that Wadsworth's careful crafting of oblique references to illegal liquor sales and gambling activities had served to signal voters to kick the corrupt sheriff out, leaving the subterranean affairs of Sam McCollum and Dr. Adams to be washed away in the blood of the Lamb on Sundays.

Once again, I was witnessing how the South had a way of taking care of its problems without hanging out its dirty laundry in full view of the rest of the world.

Chapter Sixty-Four

Ruby's new attorney, Frank Cannon, stood pleading her case before Judge Adams. Odis Henderson, playing a secondary role as he had promised, sat beside Ruby at the table for the defense.

Cannon was a distinguished-looking gray-haired gentleman who resembled an older Cary Grant with his hair parted down the middle. His stage presence was apparent even before he uttered his first words. "I wish to state to the court, more or less in self-defense, that I got into this case last night. The court knows what has happened before when the previous trial was set. At that time, it is my information that seventy-two jurors were questioned by the court and excused for cause."

"Now, with that before the court, I feel bound to renew the motion for a change of venue on the ground that it is virtually impossible to get a jury from this county to give this defendant a fair and impartial trial."

Keith Black stood up to deliver his argument. "I would like to make inquiry of Mr. Cannon whether or not he is solicitor for the criminal court of record of Duval County."

"I think he is," volunteered Judge Adams.

"That is correct," Cannon acknowledged.

"The state would like a ruling on whether or not Mr. Cannon is qualified to represent the defendant, upon the grounds that he is solicitor of the criminal court of record of Duval County, Florida, and is therefore not qualified to be participating in this case by virtue of being an officer of the State of Florida." Concluding his argument, Black glanced at Cannon.

In that instant, I could see a hatred and resentment so deep that it was almost palpable. Black, already having lost the race for district attorney, now faced the unhappy possibility of having a worthy adversary steal the spotlight in the highest-profile case that Suwannee County had ever seen.

The judge stroked his chin. Even from the balcony I recognized the look on his face—I had seen it in his chambers when Diaz and I met with him to ask for a press table and to ask permission to speak with Ruby. Somewhere in that brilliant mind of his, he was consulting with his inner Solomon to render a decision that spared the baby from being cut in half.

"That is a brand new one," Judge Adams declared. "I have been in this business over forty-six years and this is my first time on that. This presents a question I can't rule on offhand."

A heavy silence filled the courtroom. Accustomed to being guided by its helmsman, the ship's crew was clearly adrift in uncharted waters.

Turning to the jury, Judge Adams broke the silence. "Gentlemen, we have something that will have to be settled before we can take up the matter of the venire. Court is recessed until further notice."

Watching the jurist disappear behind his hidden door, I had to decide whether to leave the courtroom or wait until he returned. My instincts told me that he would not take long to look into the matter, since his chambers had a law library, and I was certain that he would—perhaps with the assistance of the newly elected district attorney, Mr. Slaughter—comb through the relevant legal tomes and return in the jury's absence to announce his ruling.

Some of the observers in the balcony got up to leave, along with a few white people on the main floor of the courtroom below. But by and large, most people looked as though they were going to wait out the judge's decision.

"He ain't gonna let Ruby have no decent lawyer," an old man ahead of me told the woman sitting beside him.

"I ain't so sure myself," the woman disagreed. "I had me a dream last night that a tall white man rode in on this big red horse and he was a carryin' a flamin' sword and he grabbed Ruby up on that horse and rode off."

The man laughed. "Woman, you been eatin' too much 'fo' you go to bed."

A woman sitting a few seats down from me turned to her friend. "You think somethin' gonna happen today?"

"Can't say yet. But I's ready to run if somethin' do."

An old woman sitting to my left tapped me on the shoulder.

"I had a dream 'bout Ruby last night."

"You did?" I replied, a little surprised that anyone would speak to me.

"Yes'm. Ruby appeared to me at the foot of my bed like this cat person. She had these burnin' red eyes and these big white teeth, and she was howlin' like some kind of terrible beast."

"That must have been frightening," I said.

"Yes'm. She looked like she was sittin' in hellfire itself."

When the old woman fell silent, I knew that she would not speak to me anymore. Most of the people in the balcony knew I was a reporter for the *Courier* and were accustomed to my presence by now. None of them would speak to me directly about Ruby, so I wasn't surprised that anything they had to say would be safely locked away in the ciphers of dreams.

After all, we Negroes seldom talk about anything directly. We speak of dreams and visions and tell stories that have nothing to do with what is happening around us, yet everything to do with our thoughts. The woman who related her dream about the white man who rode in on a horse truly felt that Ruby would go free. Her companion made light of her words, fearing retribution. The woman sitting next to me conjured up a cat person to put a face on Ruby's suffering. Such is the way thoughts are shared among a people who have always lived in fear of speaking what they truly feel.

When Judge Adams returned to the courtroom an hour or so later, he again acknowledged Keith Black, who recited a precedent that, he maintained, barred Cannon from serving as Ruby's attorney.

Judge Adams listened patiently before rendering his decision. "The law books that we have been able to examine are about as devoid of any substantial discussion as was Mother Hubbard's cupboard when she went to get her poor dog a bone—they are practically empty. So the court is going to pass on it from a standpoint of what it deems to be ordinary, everyday reasoning, and as the old saying is, 'Let the hair go with the hide on that.' Mr. Cannon is solicitor of the criminal court of record of Duval County. His jurisdiction as such officer does not extend beyond that county unless it is enlarged by gubernatorial appointment. Otherwise, he is limited in his official actions to his own county."

Having set forth his reasoning, the judge continued for another five minutes or so before ruling: "As the court sees it, there is no legal barrier to his doing so, and the objection of counsel for the state will be overruled."

By overruling Black's objection, Judge Adams had allowed Ruby to retain competent counsel. I was beginning to think that the old man, as steeped in his history as he was, might conduct a fair trial after all.

Black then asked to respond to Cannon's renewal of Crews's earlier motion for a change of venue in the aborted trial.

After Black made his case, the judge ruled, "The motion for a change of venue is overruled, with the stipulation that a fair test will be made, and if we then feel any different, a further consideration will be given to the motion at a proper time."

Judge Adams then declared court recessed for dinner until one thirty, when the veniremen who had been called would be questioned to determine their fitness to serve as jurors.

Since I knew that the questioning of the prospective jurors would follow the same routine as it had with the previous attempt at a trial— with most of the men being questioned having either known Dr. Adams or used him as their family physician—I decided that the remainder of the afternoon would be better spent at Matt's house typing my notes to meet my publication deadline.

Chapter Sixty-Five

When I arrived at the courthouse around nine forty-five the next morning, I hoped that the jury box would be filled, so that the trial could begin. Fortunately, my evening had been productive in organizing my notes and further refining my work for Ruby's life story. The only interruption was my intrusive thought about how Ruby herself was faring, but this was something beyond my reach—and probably would be for the remainder of the trial.

Before court began, Matt sat down beside me. Knowing that he visited his sister every day, I asked him how she was doing this morning.

"She doin' good as she can. She say hello."

"I'm glad to hear she's well. Has she talked with you at all about the trial?"

"No'm. She keep on talkin' 'bout how much her lawyers cost her, but that's about all."

"I understand that they're going to continue with jury selection today," I said, marveling that a woman on trial for her very life could think only about how much her defense was costing her.

"Yes'm. I talked with Releford and he say Mr. Cannon gonna ask the judge to get the questions the lawyers ask the men put in the record."

"You mean they didn't do that yesterday?" I asked incredulously.

"No'm."

I had to wonder whether failing to record the jury selection process was a deliberate strategy. Without any record of what the prospective jurors were asked and how they answered, there would be no way to challenge their selection on appeal. Any of them could have admitted to using Dr. Adams as their regular family physician and no one would be the wiser.

Ruby followed Cannon and Henderson into the courtroom with a stoic expression and slumped shoulders. It was obvious that the trial was taking its toll. She was dressed casually, wearing her same green camel hair coat, so it was difficult to see whether she had lost weight. Sitting down at the table for the defense, she leaned forward, propping her elbow on the table and cradling her chin in her hand.

Judge Adams entered a few minutes later, calling court to order at precisely ten o'clock. The whispering in the courtroom subsided, and ten prospective jurors were led in by the bailiff to take their places in the jury box, leaving only two more, and the alternates, to be selected. At least I could see that progress had been made after I left yesterday.

The prospective jurors stood behind the railing in back of the tables provided for the attorneys, facing the front of the courtroom. Cannon asked each man whether Dr. Adams had seen him as his physician or whether he had treated any family members. Most responded that they had some sort of physician-patient relationship with Dr. Adams. All the stories I had heard about the doctor's tireless dedication in making house calls were certainly borne out, especially considering that these men represented a pretty fair cross section of Suwannee County's adult white male population.

In the middle of his questioning, Cannon addressed the bench. "Your Honor, if the court please, will you let the jury retire for the purpose of a motion?"

Judge Adams asked Cannon to approach the bench. After a brief consultation, he said to the prospective jurors, "Gentlemen, you can step out for a few minutes."

When the potential jurors left the room, Cannon renewed the motion for a change of venue. He explained that most of the men were excused because of their personal or professional relationship with Dr. Adams. That left six men in the jury pool, whom the defendant was compelled to accept because she had already exhausted six of her peremptory challenges. Thus, Cannon reasoned, his client was unlikely to get a fair trial.

Judge Adams differed. "The court cannot agree with that proposition," he said, "since whatever association they had with the doctor was casual and very infrequent, and of no serious moment, and transpired long ago."

What I found most interesting in the ensuing five minutes of the judge's monologue was his statement that it was practically impossible to select jury members who did not have at least a passing or casual knowledge of the parties involved in the case, yet he denied the motion, declaring, "A fair and impartial jury qualified according to law can be found in this county."

Cannon persisted. "The defendant would like to make this additional motion. Out of all sixty-two prospective jurors called in this case, only one out of the entire sixty-two that the court saw fit to retain is colored, and thereby the defendant has been deprived of the right to have called as jurors to try her case any member of the colored race other than this one prospective juror. We make a motion at this time to discharge the entire jury for that reason."

On the point of the racial composition of the jury, I knew that all but one of the colored men who had been called for questioning had eliminated themselves by answering either that they were against Florida's death penalty or that Dr. Adams was their personal family physician. Not that I blamed them—I could not imagine the pressure on those men and their families if they played a part in determining Ruby's fate.

Yet, Canon's argument that none of the colored men called felt that they could serve on the jury was a compelling argument for dismissing the jury already in the box, paving the way for a reconsideration of his motion for a change of venue.

"On this point," the judge began, "it is the long and well-established law in Florida that a defendant is not entitled to any certain juror to try him from any certain class or race of people."

The judge further pointed out that a number of colored men had been called to serve, some of them businessmen in their own communities, and that "white people looked upon them as being good, solid men."

I have always marveled at how our words betray our thoughts, even if we are unaware that our tongues are sweeping them right out of our heads for the world to hear. In the judge's case, it was apparent that for him, the ultimate determinant of a colored man's character is how he is judged by white people.

I sat feeling a bit depressed at the judge's ruling, having set higher standards for the man than he had shown himself capable of achieving. But then I suppose I've always been an optimist when it comes to our system of justice, differing from others of my race, like my sometimes friend, Langston Hughes, who wrote, "That Justice is a blind goddess/Is a thing to which we black are wise:/Her bandage hides two festering sores/That once perhaps were eyes."

As the judge called for the jury to return to the courtroom, I reflected that I had been appalled at Langston's poem—which he called "Justice"—not only because of the absolutely horrid metaphor, but because Justice, however she came to be blind, would still be unable to see the color of the accused to treat a colored man any differently than she would a white man. I remember telling my poet friend that he was at least merciful enough to give the coup de gras to logic in the space of four brief lines of iambic tetrameter.

After the jurors were seated in the jury box, Cannon, Henderson, and Black continued their questioning. Each excused potential jurors to the point that they had used up almost all their allotted challenges.

In all that questioning, what I found most intriguing was when a prospective juror named Carver tried to trivialize his association with Dr. Adams, and the judge stepped in.

"Brother Carver, you say you used Dr. Adams. Did you or some member of your family have any long illness, or was it just a casual visit?"

"Just little things; every time we used him along."

"About how many times?"

He fidgeted. "I don't know—several times, along at different times."

"Was it to bedridden members of your family that he was called?"

"How's that? I don't think I understand."

"Were they in bed when he was called?"

"Some of them was. I was myself—but just one time."

"Did he get pretty close to you?"

"He made a number of calls in the house."

"While you had serious sickness at your home?"

"Yes, sir."

"You can stand aside."

Black stood from his seat, quick to respond to the judge. "Is he being excused for cause?"

"I am excusing him for cause because of that association with the doctor."

I had to question not this particular action, but the lack of similar intervention by the judge when the defense had been obliged to use up its challenges on many previous occasions for the very same issue. In my mind, anyone who had an association with Dr. Adams should have been dismissed by Judge Adams.

The questioning continued until both Cannon and Black accepted the final jurors and they were sworn in. The prosecution's indictment was then read to the jury, charging Ruby with murder in the first degree.

Looking back, I felt comfortable that Cannon had made his case, concerning both the composition of the jury and the small likelihood that Ruby could get a fair trial in Suwannee County. There was no doubt that all this would be part of his appeal of the inevitable verdict of murder in the first degree.

Edwards's first witness was Dr. Workman, the same physician who was Dr. Adams's former associate. He was also the same Dr. Workman whose wife had supported Adams in his senate campaign, the same Dr. Workman who had followed Ruby's pregnancy with Adams's child, the same Dr. Workman whom Judge Adams had called to determine Ruby's sanity, and the same Dr. Workman who had performed Adams's autopsy. Dr. Workman had certainly been called on to wear many hats, so I wondered which one the prosecution was asking him to wear today.

After establishing Workman's identity and credentials as a physician and general surgeon, Edwards asked if he knew the woman "sitting over there in the green coat" as Ruby McCollum. After Workman acknowledged that he knew Ruby, Edwards moved on to question him about the day of the murder. Workman testified that he had responded to a call on that day, arriving at Dr. Adams's office somewhere between eleven thirty and noon. When he arrived, he met Dr. Black and Police Chief Worth Howard and saw Dr. Adams's body lying prone on the floor in the colored waiting room, with blood running from his nose and mouth. Workman stated that on examining the body, he found evidence of four bullets hitting the body, one grazing the right elbow, one entering and exiting the left arm at the shoulder, and two entering the back, with only one of the two penetrating the body to make an exit wound. The bullet that exited was found embedded in the floor directly beneath the body, so Workman concluded that it was fired from directly over the doctor after he had fallen to the floor. Most of the bullet wounds had powder burns around them, so he concluded that they had been fired at close range.

When asked about the victim, Workman testified that Dr. Adams was about six feet two inches tall, weighed about 265 pounds, and was 42 years of age when he died.

Edwards then asked, "In your opinion, which bullet or wound would have caused Dr. Adams to have fallen to the floor?"

"Any of the bullet wounds in the back," Workman responded.

"Were these wounds, or either of them that you found on Dr. Adams, sufficient to produce death?"

"They did."

"I believe you stated, Doctor, there was blood coming from Dr. Adams's nose and also from his mouth. What in your opinion was the cause of that?"

"That was caused by the bullet going through his lungs."

In cross-examination, Cannon asked if there was any disarrangement of Dr. Adams's clothing or of the furniture in the treatment room where he was shot. Workman testified that there was not. Evidently, Cannon was trying to establish whether there had been a fight between his client and Adams.

When Cannon asked if Workman was the one to remove the bullets from the doctor's body, he said that he was not. Cannon asked about the powder burns and reviewed each of the wounds, establishing that none of the bullets entered from the front side of Adams's body.

After Cannon finished his cross-examination, Edwards repeated his questions about the bullet wounds. Cannon objected that rehashing the testimony was neither right nor proper, serving only to prejudice the jury.

Judge Adams overruled Cannon's objection, allowing Edwards to lead Workman through his testimony a second time, asking several times about the last bullet fired into the doctor's back while he was lying facedown on the floor.

When Workman was dismissed from the witness stand, Judge Adams declared a dinner recess until two o'clock.

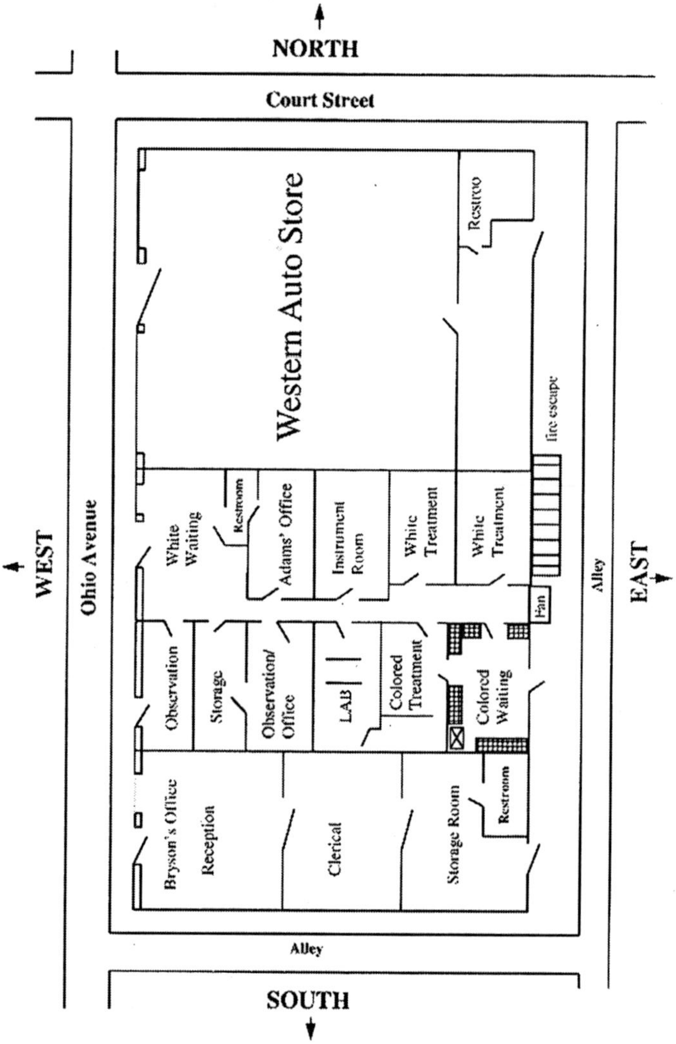

NORTH

Court Street

Western Auto Store

Restroo

fire escape

WEST

Ohio Avenue

EAST

Alley

White Waiting

Restroom

Adams' Office

Instrument Room

White Treatment

White Treatment

Fan

Observation

Storage

Observation/ Office

LAB

Colored Treatment

Colored Waiting

Bryson's Office

Reception

Clerical

Storage Room

Restroom

Alley

SOUTH

Floor Plan of Parshley Building
(Adams's Office Center)

Chapter Sixty-Six

After the dinner break, Edwards called Sheriff Sim P. Howell. After establishing his identity and that he knew Ruby, the sheriff was asked to describe the Parshley building and the location of Adams's office within that building.

Howell's description was exhaustive and delivered with mathematical precision—it was apparent that he had measured all the outside dimensions of the building as well as each room within Dr. Adams's office down to the inch. As I sat listening to his description, I could visualize the various rooms in the physician's office as clearly as if I had walked through each of them myself.

After Edwards finished questioning Sheriff Howell, he reserved the right to recall him for further testimony. Cannon had no questions for cross-examination, so Sheriff Howell was dismissed.

Edwards then called a parade of witnesses who testified that they had seen Ruby in the alley behind Dr. Adams's office, but because each of them had left before the murder, none of them could place her at the office when he was shot.

Carrie Dailey was Edwards's next witness. I recalled that she was one of the three colored women who had been sitting in the waiting room when Ruby shot Adams.

Dailey was a small colored woman, probably forty-five years old. I noticed that her hand trembled when she placed it on the *Bible* to be sworn in. I reflected that this was to be expected since, in the segregationist South, coloreds appeared in court for one of two reasons—to bear witness against other coloreds or to be tried for crimes themselves. In either case, they would not look at a courtroom as a place of justice.

Dailey testified that she and her daughter had walked from their home on the west end of town to the doctor's office that Sunday morning and arrived at about nine or nine thirty. Since the office was closed when she arrived, she and her daughter stood in the shade in the alley while other people arrived, including some "cut young people" with a policeman.

After Dr. Adams parked in the alley, he had unlocked the door, and all the patients waiting in the alley went inside. Adams first treated the two patients who were cut, then saw an elderly colored woman with heart dropsy. Next he treated some white patients, including a man with cement in his eyes, before continuing with the colored patients.

After all the patients had left except for Dailey and her daughter, Dailey said that Ruby walked into the waiting room and into the white treatment room, where Adams was alone, whistling. "She come in, and she come on in there where he was whistlin', and her back was to me then, and she says to him, 'I want that.' She said, 'I want that,' and he said, 'This?' and she said no, and he said, 'This?' and she said yes, and he said, 'Well, make up your mind.' She come on out and stood crossways of the door and opened her pocketbook and got somethin', got a bill out, and he went on around through in the colored treating room whistlin', and she stood against the door, and she got a bill out, and when she saw him she went to him with the bill this way, and said, 'Give me a receipt for this,' and he said, 'What?' and she said, 'Give me a receipt for this,' and he says, 'I don't keep no books.' He said, 'Come down here tomorrow and Thelma will run over the books and tell you what is owin', and she said, 'You can give me a receipt for this,' and he said, 'I don't write no receipts,' and she reached back and got a receipt book, and he was standin' in the middle of the floor, and she says, 'Here is the book,' and she walked over to the left around there where his bench was, where he examines colored people, and he said, 'I ain't got no books. I done told you. Furthermore, that ain't half of the money what you owe me,' and she said, 'How much do I owe?' and he said, 'You owe me more than a hundred dollars,' and she says, 'Well, I ain't goin' to pay no hundred dollars. I'm goin' to pay my part and the other fellow is goin' to pay his.' I could hear her, but I couldn't see her then. And he said, 'Well it matters a damn with me. I'm goin' to get mine if I have to carry it to the judge's office.' She said, 'I know you will. You can get yours.' He stood there a while and he throws the book there on the table and he said, 'Woman, I am tired of foolin' with you,' and he made one step and after he made one step toward the waitin' room, the gun fired and he hollered, 'Oh, oh, police, police!' And I looked down and said, 'Dr. Adams is shot; let's go,' and we ran out and as soon as we got out on the ground another pistol fired and we took off then. We run down to the fillin' station and told them."

Edwards led Dailey through each part of her testimony, verifying that she could see either Ruby or the doctor most of the time. He also established that Della Arnold entered the colored waiting room at the time Dr. Adams threw the receipt book down saying, "Woman, I am tired of foolin' with you."

"Now," Edwards paused, leafing through his notes, "immediately after the gun fired, Dr. Adams fell to the floor in the colored waiting room and Della left, and you and Avery left out the back door. What did you and Della and Avery do?"

"We took off to the fillin' station."

"Is that the filling station just across from the courthouse and which is located north of the Parshley building?"

"Yes, sir."

"Who did you see when you got to that filling station?"

During her testimony, I lost track of what she said and who was talking to whom, but apparently Dailey told someone at the filling station that Dr. Adams had been shot and someone else mentioned getting the police. She stated that the cab then left the alley with the two passengers still in the backseat and that she then saw Ruby come out of the doctor's office, get into her car, and drive away.

When Henderson cross-examined Dailey, I noted some discrepancies between her current statements and her earlier statements regarding the order in which Adams saw his patients, but there were no major differences in her retelling of the story until she reached the part about hearing the first gunshot. Henderson pointed out that she had testified earlier that she heard a slamming door, not a gunshot.

"Do you remember saying it sounded like a door slamming?"

"It went like a door slammin' when I first heard it."

"Did you hear it very good?"

"I can't hear real good."

"You can't hear real good?"

"Not with my left ear."

Henderson established that Dailey was sitting with her left ear, her bad ear, toward the door when she heard Ruby and the doctor arguing, as well as when she heard the gunshot. Referring to the first gunshot, he asked, "But you didn't know whether it was a gun or door slamming?"

"Not until I seen Dr. Adams fall."

When Dailey was dismissed and Della Arnold, the third eyewitness, was being called to the stand, I thought about Henderson's reference to Dailey's hearing problem and wondered if her testimony had been rehearsed before the trial.

C. Arthur Ellis, Jr.

Also, from what I could gather from Sheriff Howell's precise account of the relative positions of the colored waiting room and the colored and white treatment rooms that opened into it, if Dailey's left ear was positioned next to the colored treatment room, that meant that she was on the far side of the waiting room and could not possibly have seen what happened once Ruby had crossed from the white treatment room straight ahead of her into the colored treatment room—a good twelve feet to the left of where she was sitting.

Immediately after asking her name, Edwards asked Arnold if she knew Ruby McCollum. Arnold replied that she had known her for about nine years. When asked what time she had left home, she fixed the time fairly precisely at 11:00 because she had looked at her clock just before she closed her front door. She was uncertain of the time that she arrived at his office, but since I knew how long it took to walk from where she lived across the Seaboard Coastline Railroad tracks to the Parshley building, I estimated that it must have taken her less than fifteen minutes.

When she arrived at the doctor's office, she sat on a bench in the waiting room beside Avery Trawick and Carrie Dailey, whom she described as an "old lady" and a "young woman" since she did not know them by name at that time. The first thing she heard in the office was Dr. Adams saying, "Woman, I am tired of foolin' with you. You know you owe me more than that," to which she testified that Ruby replied, "No, I don't." Adams retorted, "It matters a damn with me."

I reflected how Arnold's testimony contradicted Dailey's account of Dr. Adams telling Ruby he was going to get what was coming to him, even if he had to take it to the judge's office. One version was of a doctor who never took steps to collect his bill, while the other was of a doctor who sued his patients for what they owed him. Clearly, I came down on the side of Della Arnold on this one, reflecting that the supposed motive for the murder being an argument over a doctor bill never made sense in the first place.

Asked what happened next, Arnold testified, "The next thing I heard was a shot." After that, Arnold ran outside, then looked back inside to see Adams sprawled prone on the floor. She then heard a second shot and saw both Dailey and Trawick jump up from the bench. Then she heard Dailey say, "Why, that man has been shot," on her way out the door.

When Henderson cross-examined Arnold, he asked if she had seen Ruby in the office, to which she responded, "I never saw her, period."

After Arnold stepped down from the witness stand, Judge Adams adjourned court near five o'clock.

While everyone else filed out of the balcony, I stayed seated, reflecting on the testimony of two of the three eyewitnesses to the shooting. Dailey did not testify that she actually *saw* the shooting—she only heard the shooting, or maybe a door slam, and saw Adams fall immediately thereafter. Arnold never actually saw Ruby *while* she was in the waiting room—she only saw her *leave* the office. From that standpoint, no one actually *saw* Ruby pull the trigger.

On my way out of the courthouse, the words of the witnesses kept circling in my mind like a dog chasing its tail. Heading toward the bench by the jail, I lit up a cigarette.

While I sat trying to relax, Matt came out of the jail and headed my way. "How is Ruby, Matt?" I asked.

"I don't know, Zora. She's done gone funny again. She thinkin' somebody's tryin' to pizin her food, and she's seein' the doc walk down the hall at night."

Although Matt must have forgotten that he had never mentioned this paranoia or these hallucinations to me, I had heard of this sort of thing before. Like any caged animal deprived of its natural environment, some prisoners crack up. The experts had a name for it: "prison psychosis."

"Ruby's had it hard, Matt. I've seen people get this way when they stay locked up so long. It's hard for a proud woman, especially a proud colored woman, to be at the mercy of the white man's court."

"That's for sure. But I like that new lawyer, that Mr. Cannon. He smart."

"I agree."

"He talked with me a spell—wanted to know about Ruby 'cause she won't say much to him. I told him what I could."

"Is Ruby prepared to testify, Matt?"

"She's ready...then she ain't ready. She keeps changin' from one minute to the nex'." Matt paused. "You mind tellin' me what happened there in the courtroom today? You know I ain't been able to sit through much of it. I musta gone in and out two-three times."

"Two of the three eyewitnesses testified, and I'm still going over their testimony in my mind. Aside from the fact that Carrie Dailey is hard of hearing and couldn't possibly have heard every word she testified to hearing between Ruby and Dr. Adams—in another room, with her back to them—something just doesn't add up about the doctor bill."

"No'm. Ruby always paid her bills on time."

I was dying to ask my next question but wondered whether I should. Then I decided that I had to sooner or later. "Has Ruby said anything to you about *why* she shot Dr. Adams?"

He hung his head. "She ain't talked much 'bout that man for a long time, but I know he had some kinda hold over her."

I nodded. "Try to keep her in good spirits, Matt."

"God and his angels are heppin' me, Miz Hurston. And it's takin' a lotta angel power."

I reached out to take Matt's hand.

"You want a ride back to the house?" he asked.

"No, thank you, Matt," I said, despite the temptation of an easy ride back to where I could take a nice warm bath. "I really need to have some time to myself. I'd rather walk back to your place, if you don't mind."

"Supper'll be on the table waitin' for you."

I smiled at him as he drove off—how simple a man, yet how kind-hearted. Then I looked across the street toward the Parshley building. I don't know what was bothering me, but I knew that I felt compelled to walk across the street and into the alley behind Adams's office.

There was little traffic as I crossed Ohio Avenue to reach the Western Auto on the north corner of the Parshley building. Walking along Court Street to the back of the Western Auto, I turned right to enter the alley, and a cold shiver ran down my spine.

Standing outside Adams's office, I tried to relive the testimony I had heard in court today. I saw the patients waiting for the doctor to arrive. I saw the police car pull up with the two cut teenagers. I saw Dr. Adams pull into the alley and open the waiting room door. I saw all the patients, colored and white, go into and out of the office. Finally, I saw Ruby pull into the alley with her children in the car and look through the screen door several times to see who was in the waiting room. Then I saw her go inside. Shortly afterward, I heard the gunshots and, in my mind's eye, watched three colored women running out of the office screaming, crossing the street to seek help from the cab driver. Then I saw Ruby come out the screen door with her handbag strap over her shoulder and a smoking gun in her hand. Were those tears in her eyes as she got in the car and drove away?

Popping out of my daydream—which many of my people would call a vision—I looked at the huge box fan that took up the entire bottom half of the window of Adams's office. It had to be running that hot August day, since his office had no air-conditioning. Then it hit me that my hunch about coached testimony was right: how could Dailey, who admitted to being deaf in one ear, hear every word in a conversation a room away with that huge fan blowing straight at her? Under those circumstances, how much had she actually heard, and how much had she agreed to say out of fear?

I walked out of the alley thinking how something as inconsequential as a window fan might discredit Dailey's entire testimony.

Chapter Sixty-Seven

When court began the next morning at ten, Edwards called Avery Trawick, Carrie Dailey's teenage daughter and the second of the three witnesses in the waiting room the day of the shooting.

After a few preliminary questions establishing her name, where she lived, and that Carrie Dailey was her mother, Trawick was asked about what she saw when she arrived at the doctor's office. Throughout her testimony, she was unclear about the type and number of vehicles in the alley and was unable to give a physical description of the patients in the waiting room.

Trawick did recall that Ruby, whom she had never seen before that day, had walked in when she and her mother were the only patients in the waiting room. Parroting her mother's testimony, she said that Ruby had argued with Dr. Adams about her bill, but she was unable to give a running account of the conversation.

When Cannon rose to cross-examine her, he asked, "How many people have you discussed your testimony with?"

"No one."

Cannon turned toward Edwards and Black. "Not even these two gentlemen sitting over here?"

"No, sir."

Now, I knew that Cannon was on to Black coaching his witnesses.

When Cannon cross-examined Trawick regarding the argument between Ruby and Dr. Adams and their positions in the office relative to where she was sitting, he grew frustrated with the youth's inability to distinguish left from right and east from west.

"Do you know east from west?"

"No, sir."

"Are you just as positive now that you haven't talked with these gentlemen here about your testimony?" Cannon asked, again turning to Edwards and Black.

"No, sir."

"How long would you estimate that Ruby was in the building over there?"

"I don't know."

"You were there and know all about what time you went there, but you don't have any idea how long she stayed there?"

"I just don't know."

From the look on Cannon's face, I could see the contempt he had for Black and Edwards for coaching a witness who was, as we say in the South, "slow."

After Avery Trawick was dismissed, Edwards called Thelma Curry to the stand. This woman, I knew, was privy to many of the doctor's secrets, and I sat on the edge of my seat to hear what she would say about the fateful doctor bill that Ruby opened at the post office downtown the day before the murder.

After asking her name and establishing her relationship with Dr. Adams, Curry testified that part of her job was to keep a daily accounting record of all the patients the doctor saw.

"Do you know whether or not Ruby McCollum had an account there with Dr. Adams for medical attention and treatment on August 1, 1952?" Edwards asked.

"She did."

"What, if anything, was done in connection with that account and debt that Ruby McCollum owed Dr. Adams on August 1, 1952?"

"We sent out statements."

"Were statements sent out for Ruby McCollum?"

"It was."

"What date was that?"

"On August first."

"That was on Friday before Dr. Adams was killed on Sunday, August third of this year?"

"Yes, sir."

When Edwards finished his questioning, I knew that this was the bill that Thelma had tried to tell me about that day at the Three Spot—the one that I later learned showed the charges for Lucy's abortion.

When Cannon questioned Curry about how often Ruby had visited Adams's office this year, she stated that it was "quite often."

"What do you mean by quite often?"

"Daily."

"Daily?"

"Daily."

"Now, during these daily visits you spoke of, did you ever see any altercation between Dr. Adams and this defendant—any trouble?"

"No, I did not see any trouble."

"Ever see him slap her?"

"I did not."

"Ever hear of them having any argument?"

"I have heard of an argument."

"How many times?"

Edwards jumped up like somebody had fired a shotgun. "We object to that on the grounds it is not proper cross. We only questioned her relative to her duties in connection with the books."

"The entire relationship between Dr. Adams and the defendant is certainly admissible," Cannon protested.

"Objection sustained," Judge Adams ruled.

Cannon then asked Curry why the bill for Ruby was sent out in Sam's name.

"We usually send out accounts in the name of the man of the house," Curry explained.

"How much was due on the bill of August first?"

"I don't know."

Cannon asked Curry why she would not know the amount of the bill if she prepared it.

"At the end of each month," Curry explained, "each person would take his books and fix out his records—the statements—and Dr. Adams would add up the amount and add on his house calls he had to the bill."

When Cannon asked if Adams had added any house calls to the bill, Curry responded that she would have no way of knowing. He then asked if she mailed the bills that month, and Curry replied that one of the other employees did.

What I knew that Curry was not admitting was that she had seen the bill after Adams had written the note to Sam. Now, I knew that either someone had gotten to her, or, to think the unthinkable, she was holding back evidence that could keep Ruby out of the electric chair.

After Curry was dismissed, Edwards called Bill Sanders to the stand. Sanders identified himself as a policeman and stated that he knew Ruby McCollum. Edwards established that Sanders lived on Highway 90, midway between the Suwannee County Hospital and the McCollum residence. He further testified that at about eleven o'clock on the day of the murder he saw Ruby's car turn left down Fifth Street so fast that it nearly collided with another car that honked loudly at her. He did not see who was driving Ruby's car.

Cannon had no questions of Sanders, so he was dismissed.

Edwards next called A. A. Raulerson, the cab driver known as "Shorty." Edwards established that Raulerson's cabstand was located at the Cities Service Station, just north across Court Street from the Parshley Building, where the three eyewitnesses had fled for help. Raulerson testified that after the three women told him about the shooting, he took off to the little police station next to Sam's Café and told Worth Howard to follow him back to Dr. Adams's office. On his way back to the doctor's office, Raulerson passed Ruby driving west along Court Street.

"What happened when Chief Howard arrived?" Edwards asked.

"He tried the door and said it was locked."

Edwards asked which door was locked, the screen door or the main door. Raulerson clarified that it was the main door that was locked. Raulerson then said that he ran to the hotel to call the Brodie Harris Funeral Home for an ambulance, after which he continued to the front of Adams's office to find that the front door was locked. He then returned to the alley.

"What happened then?" Edwards asked.

"Then we broke the door in."

I reflected that the three witnesses to the shooting had all testified that Thelma Curry had produced the key that opened the door. None of them testified that the door was broken in.

"What did you do then?" Edwards asked.

"I went in and looked at him and come back and told Worth Howard that he was dead."

I thought how strange it was that Worth Howard, the chief of police, would let a cab driver go in ahead of him to check on whether a gunshot victim was still alive.

I also noted that Raulerson's testimony differed substantially from Workman's in that he stated that Adams fell on his hands, whereas Workman testified that when he arrived, Adams's right hand was extended in front of him and he was still lying on his left hand. Furthermore, there was no mention in Workman's testimony of any pen in Adams's right hand or of a hundred-dollar bill in his left, even though he had to be able to see underneath the body to testify to an exit wound in Adams's chest.

I was betting that both the bill and the pen had been moved before Workman arrived and that neither would ever be entered into evidence. Certainly the argument that Ruby shot Dr. Adams over her doctor bill would be easier to support in court if there was no evidence that she actually paid most of the bill before she pulled the trigger.

When Henderson cross-examined, Raulerson was consistent in most of his testimony, but this time he forgot who first turned the body over so that he could see the bill.

Edwards's next witness was Police Chief Worth Howard. After identifying himself as the chief of police, Howard stated that he knew Ruby and Raulerson and that he saw Raulerson on Sunday, August 3, at around eleven thirty in the morning, when he drove up to the small police station and told Worth to follow him to Dr. Adams's office.

"Who was at the doctor's office when you arrived there at that time?" Edwards asked.

"Not anyone that I saw except Raulerson."

"What did you and Mr. Raulerson do immediately upon arriving there?"

Howard's testimony differed from Raulerson's only in stating that he, not Raulerson, had entered to find the body. Howard further testified that he left the body just as he had found it until Dr. Workman arrived a few minutes later, although he could not recall precisely when Dr. Workman, Sheriff Sim Howell, Brodie Harris, and others arrived, but he believed that it was Brodie Harris, the undertaker, who turned the body over.

At this point, I recalled that Raulerson had testified that Dr. Workman, not Brodie Harris, was the first to turn the body over. But since both Howard and Workman testified that Dr. Workman arrived before the funeral director, and Dr. Workman testified that Dr. Adams's right hand was extended when he arrived, both Howard and Raulerson had to be wrong. The body had to have been moved before either Workman or Harris arrived, and the only person who could have done that was Howard, possibly when Raulerson was not present.

"Immediately upon the body being picked up, did you examine that waiting room and treating room and white treating room?"

"Yes, sir."

"What did you find there in that waiting room where you saw the body of Dr. Adams?"

"Where the doctor was laying, I found a bullet embedded in the floor."

When questioned about the caliber of the bullet, Howard responded, "It looked to be a thirty-two caliber." When asked about the direction from which it appeared to have been fired, Howard said it was downward.

Howard also said he had found another bullet in the facing of the door leading from the colored treating room into the colored waiting room. Evidently the bullet had been fired in the colored treating room toward the colored waiting room and struck the door facing a little over four feet up. As with the bullet in the floor, it appeared to be a .32.

When Edwards showed Howard both the bullets he had found and asked him to identify them, Howard responded that they were the same ones.

Cannon asked Howard how he knew that the bullets entered into evidence were the same bullets, and Howard replied that he recognized the bullets from the identification marks on them. Cannon asked how the marks got there, and Howard explained that he turned the bullets over to Sheriff Howell, who gave them to the jewelry store for marking with a small drill.

Cannon objected to the two bullets being entered into evidence, because Howard could not possibly know that these were the same ones that he had found in Dr. Adams's office since they had been out of his continuous custody.

Judge Adams overruled Cannon's objection, and the bullets were entered into evidence as exhibits 1 and 2.

Since it was approaching noon, Judge Adams called a recess until two o'clock.

****

When the noon break was over, Judge Adams called court to order promptly at two o'clock.

The prosecution's next witness was Harry T. Reid, the Jasper funeral director who handled Dr. Adams's funeral. Reid stated that he received Dr. Adams's nude body from Brodie Harris at the Suwannee Funeral Home in Live Oak around three o'clock on the day of the murder. After transporting the body to Jasper, he and a Dr. Curry extracted a bullet from along the spine, about the middle of the back, and another from the left shoulder area, but he did not know the caliber of either bullet. He then delivered the two bullets to Sheriff Howell.

When asked if there were any other bullet holes, his testimony agreed with Dr. Workman's—the two bullets recovered from the body by Reid, combined with the two recovered by Howard, would account for a total of four bullets.

When Cannon cross-examined Reid, he wanted to know the depth of the bullet wounds, but Reid was uncertain. Reid was also uncertain about the angles of entry and exit. When asked about powder burns, he stated that he saw none because the clothes had been removed from the body by Brodie Harris, the undertaker in Live Oak, before Reid received the body.

After Reid was dismissed, Edwards called Brodie Harris. Harris testified that he was called to Dr. Adams's office and arrived at about eleven forty the day of the murder. Harris and several of the men present lifted the body onto a stretcher and transported it to the Suwannee Funeral Home, where Harris disrobed the body.

When Edwards turned Harris over to Cannon for cross-examination, he asked about powder burns. Harris responded, "I wasn't paying any attention to powder burns."

Cannon dismissed Harris, and Edwards called Elwood Howard to the stand. Howard stated that he was the constable in Live Oak and that he telephoned Dr. Adams's home on the Sunday morning of the murder to let him know that he had two colored youths, Marie Reese and Ned McQuay, who had been in a knife fight and needed medical attention. Adams agreed to see them at his office after he made a quick house call. Howard said that he drove the two, along with Ned McQuay's sister, to the doctor's office, where he arrived around nine fifteen.

Elwood Howard testified that he waited with the cut youths for about an hour before Adams arrived, during which time Coot Davenport and his wife drove into the alley. There was also an old colored woman with a man and a woman assisting her. Finally, there were two other colored women, who, he later learned, were Avery Trawick and Carrie Daily. Adams arrived between ten fifteen and ten thirty, and Howard estimated that the doctor spent about a half hour caring for the youths' wounds while Howard went out to the Wagon Wheel restaurant for a quick cup of coffee.

Howard testified that he then took the two youths to the jail, after which he got back into his car and turned past the Cities Service Station. The owner, a Mr. Hill, yelled at him that somebody had shot Dr. Adams and that the person was making a getaway out the Lake City Highway. After an unproductive high-speed run toward Lake City, Elwood Howard returned to the alley to find Worth Howard and

424   C. Arthur Ellis, Jr.

Raulerson inside Adams's office. He said that after conferring with his partner and questioning the witnesses, he drove immediately to the Three Spot, where he found a car matching the witnesses' description of the vehicle that fled the scene of the crime. He then came back to the filling station and used the phone to call Highway Patrolman Frank Millikin. Millikin told him to come to his house. When he got to Millikin's house, Millikin "done quite a bit of radio work, and then we come back to the office."

Edwards asked what Howard and Millikin did next. Howard stated that the three men then got into Sheriff Howell's car and drove out to Ruby McCollum's house, where they entered to find her coming down the stairs.

"What happened then?" Edwards asked.

"I believe the sheriff asked her if she was Ruby McCollum, I believe, or Sam's wife, maybe."

"What did she say?"

"She said no."

"What happened then?"

"Maybe he asked her again, and she said, 'Is something wrong? Has somebody done something?'"

"What happened then?"

"The sheriff and Ruby and me went upstairs and into a little hallway upstairs, and we talked to her some, and then we come back down the stairs. The sheriff went out to her car and I stayed in the house with her and the two kids, or three kids, I believe. The sheriff come back and about that time Mr. Gray, Mr. Sanders, and maybe Mr. Millikin, was there."

"After Mr. Gray got there, what happened?"

"We all went back upstairs, and she told Mr. Gray she wanted to talk to him privately. They went into the bathroom on the west side of the hall and closed the door."

I had to admit that I was now totally confused. First, since all the officers knew Ruby, why were they asking who she was or if she was Sam's wife? Could it be that Howard was attempting to distance both himself and the other officers from Ruby, knowing that the watchful eyes of the press were scattered throughout the courtroom?

Second, what on earth would motivate Deputy Gray to speak to Ruby alone in a bathroom?

"How long were they in here?" Edwards asked.

"Four or five minutes."

"What happened when they came out?"

"We all come back to the stairs and the sheriff arrested her."

"Then what happened?"

"The sheriff, Mr. Millikin, Ruby, and myself all come out the front door and got in the patrol car, and Ruby got in first and I got in the backseat with her, and Mr. Millikin drove and Sheriff Howell was in the front seat."

"You drove away?"

"Yes, sir."

When Cannon cross-examined Elwood Howard, he asked if he had seen any children in the house. Howard testified that he noticed three children in the house. "I would figure one of them was maybe seven or eight years old, or looked to be, and one was maybe ten or twelve years old. And the smaller one I would figure was two years old."

"Was it red, white, or colored?"

"I didn't pay a whole lot of attention to the kids. The baby was maybe a little shade lighter than the others, but I didn't pay much attention to it."

"Had you ever seen any of those children before?"

"If I had, I didn't know it."

"Now, when you say you got in the car with the defendant and you all left with her, where did you go?"

Edwards immediately objected, and Judge Adams sustained.

"Did you bring her to the Suwannee County jail?"

"No."

Edwards again objected and moved to strike the answer. Judge Adams sustained and ordered the answer stricken from the record.

Cannon asked if the officers searched the house, to which Howard answered no. He then asked if any of the officers other than Gray asked Ruby questions, and he answered no.

"When you say he arrested her, what did he do? Did he draw a pistol and tell her she was under arrest?"

"He told her she was under arrest for shooting Dr. Adams."

"Did he put handcuffs on her?"

"No, sir."

"How many of you got in the patrol car?"

"Sheriff Howell, Mr. Millikin, Ruby, and myself."

"Was there any other conversation that you know of between the defendant and you officers other than what you have related?"

Edwards objected, and the judge overruled.

"No, sir."

When Elwood Howard completed his testimony, I considered not what I had heard but what I had not heard. Howard had given no testimony about any of the officers recognizing Ruby, even through they all knew her and Sam. There was also no testimony about searching for anything in the house, even though I knew that the first thing they all would want was Ruby's accounting book. Not a word was mentioned about whisking her away to Raiford rather than taking her a mile away to the Suwannee County jail. Finally, there was no testimony about why it took a sheriff, a deputy sheriff, a constable, a policeman, and a highway patrolman to arrest an unarmed woman who stood just five feet two inches tall.

For his next witness, Edwards called Sheriff Howell to the witness stand. Edwards was brief, asking only about the two bullets that Harry T. Reid delivered to Howell. Howell testified that they were delivered to him on Monday, the day after the murder, at around four o'clock. Edwards showed Howell the bullets and asked if they were in the same condition as when they were delivered to him on that day. He responded that they were except for the jeweler's identification marks. Edwards then asked the court to enter the two bullets into evidence as exhibit 3.

Cannon objected on the grounds that they were not in the same condition as they were at the time they were extracted from the body, but Judge Adams overruled, allowing the bullets into evidence.

Edwards's next witness was Deputy Sheriff Gray. Gray testified that he first learned of Adams's death when he came home from Jasper and stopped by Elwood Howard's home. When Howard's wife told him that Dr. Adams had been shot, he immediately went to the doctor's office, arriving there at about eleven fifteen.

"What happened when you got to the doctor's office?"

"He was laying on a stretcher in the colored reception room with a sheet over his body and face, and I pulled the sheet back and looked at him."

"What did you do then?"

Gray testified that after staying at Adams's office for eight to ten minutes, he drove out to the McCollum house and entered to see Millikin, Elwood Howard, and a special deputy named Jack Andrews.

My list now included Sheriff Sim Howell, Deputy Gray, Special Deputy Andrews, Constable Howard, Police Chief Howard, Florida Highway Patrolman Millikin, and policeman Sanders—a total of seven law enforcement officers, representing every level of law enforcement in the state of Florida.

"After you got in the living room where Ruby McCollum was at that time, what happened next?"

"I walked up to where Ruby and Elwood Howard were standing, and I says to Ruby, 'Ruby, what in the world caused you to shoot Dr. Adams?' and she looked at me and says, 'Where is Sam?' and I says, 'I don't know where Sam is.' Then she says to me, 'I want to go upstairs,' and I said, 'All right, I will go upstairs with you.'"

Edwards stopped the questioning to tell the judge that he wanted to lay a predicate. The judge then asked the jury to retire into the jury room.

In the absence of the jury, Edwards asked Gray, "Then what happened?"

"We went upstairs, and it appeared to me that she wanted to speak to me alone, and I says to her, 'Ruby, do you want to talk to me alone?' and she said yes, and just beyond where she was standing there was a bathroom on the right, and so we stepped inside of the bathroom."

"In that bathroom, did you have a conversation with Ruby McCollum about her shooting Dr. C. Leroy Adams?"

"Yes, sir."

In rapid-fire succession, Edwards asked, "Did you force her to make those statements? Did anyone force her to make those statements? Did you threaten her in any manner? Did anyone threaten her? Did you give her a reward or offer her a reward to make such statements?"

To each question, Gray answered no.

"What were those statements?"

"When we got into the bathroom, I pulled the door to, and I says to her again, 'Ruby, what in the world caused you to kill Dr. Adams?' and she looked at me very calmly and coolly and says, 'Mr. Gray, I don't know why I shot him.' I said, 'Ruby, what did you do with the gun you shot Dr. Adams with?' Then she said she threw it in the hedge at the back of the house in the bamboos."

"Did she point out the place she threw the gun freely and voluntarily?"

"Yes, sir."

"She did that of her own free will?"

"Yes, sir. After she stated that, I says, 'Ruby, you realize you have shot one of the most important men that we have in this county? It is my duty as an officer to protect you, but you will have to do as I tell you to do.' She looked at me and says, 'I don't have anyone to leave with my children.' At that time we turned around and went back downstairs, and the sheriff took over, and I told the sheriff she was the one that shot Dr. Adams."

"That is all we have to submit," Edwards concluded.

"Let the jury come back," Judge Adams called to the bailiff.

After the jury returned to the jury box, Edwards asked Gray the same questions, and Gray responded with substantially the same answers. This time, Gray testified that Ruby looked out the bathroom window to point to an area in the bamboo where she had thrown the gun.

"Describe that gun," Edwards directed.

"It was a thirty-two Smith and Wesson. It had been nickeled, but it was worn pretty bad, and it was an old gun, and, of course, when I got it, I unbreeched it and there was four empty shells in the chamber, in the cylinder of the gun, and then I thought about fingerprints on the gun, and I snapped it back and put it in my pocket."

Edwards produced the gun that Gray had described for his inspection and offered it into evidence as state exhibit 5, without any objection by Cannon.

When Cannon cross-examined, he asked if Gray knew Ruby. I had the distinct feeling that Gray was more than a bit nervous under cross-examination.

"Well," he said, "I have seen her numbers of times over at Dr. Adams's office last year when I had a virus infection. I was over there for treatment and I seen her over there in the office with her little girl at different times."

Cannon then questioned Gray about his visit to the McCollum home at the time of the arrest, asking if he had searched the house for anything. Gray denied searching the house. When Cannon asked if Gray went back into the house after the arrest or if he talked with Ruby after the arrest, Edwards objected and Judge Adams sustained.

Edwards announced that the state rested its case, and Cannon immediately asked if the judge would allow a motion in the absence of the jury.

When Judge Adams asked the jury to retire, I reflected on Gray's testimony and how odd it seemed that Ruby felt comfortable taking him into her confidence, when he had claimed to have little or no relationship with her. Since I also knew that he was one of the people who had dealt with Sam and Ruby in their business, this was another example of how Black and Edwards conspired with the officers to silence any testimony that would link the McCollums' business with law enforcement in the community.

When the door to the jury room closed, Cannon made his motion: "The defendant, if the court pleases, at this time moves the court for a directed verdict of 'not guilty' as to the charge of murder in the first degree as alleged in the indictment, in that the evidence is not sufficient to go to the jury on the matter of premeditation. Therefore, the defendant respectfully moves the court at this time to instruct the jury that they are not to consider any degree of homicide above that of murder in the second degree. Particularly so because the last witness who just testified — and the state is bound by that testimony — said that the defendant told him, 'I don't know why I shot him.' I think that that would fail to come up to the rule and that nothing above second-degree murder could be submitted to the jury."

Judge Adams turned to Edwards. "Do you desire to be heard?"

Edwards emphasized the shots to the back and the final shot, fired at close range after Dr. Adams had fallen to the floor. He concluded, "There is ample premeditated design shown by the several witnesses and also by the physical facts."

Cannon replied that the evidence showed that Ruby went to the doctor's office, apparently for treatment, and apparently paid her bill. Cannon concluded, "Therefore, there is no premeditation that could possibly arise from the evidence other than that, and at the most it is a killing that happened between people who were on the best of terms before that."

I could hear murmuring in the courtroom on this last statement, since Cannon himself had tried to establish that the relationship between Dr. Adams and Ruby was an abusive one. Since the testimony to establish that abuse had not been allowed into evidence, though, I decided that this was a rather clever way to turn the prosecution's silencing of Ruby against them.

Judge Adams summarized Cannon's motion to strike the option of first-degree murder from consideration by the jury. He then added, "So far as the evidence shows, it appears that the defendant went to the doctor's office. The evidence also shows that the doctor was shot in the back and that one of the bullets went right through his body and stuck in the floor immediately under his body, which is a strong indication that he was shot at that time while he was prone upon the floor. All these things should go to the jury for their consideration in deciding as to the guilt or innocence of the defendant on any and all of the degrees contained within the indictment. Therefore, the motion is overruled."

After Judge Adams ruled, Cannon asked for a continuance to give him time to attend to other affairs before starting again in the morning. Judge Adams agreed, but only on the condition that the time be caught up by starting court early the next day.

Cannon then asked that the jury be taken across the street to view the scene of the murder, and Black joined in the motion.

At that point, the judge asked the bailiff to bring the jury back into the courtroom, where he instructed them that they were not to speak to one another during their inspection of the murder scene. He then asked Sheriff Howell and the two bailiffs to escort the jurors to Dr. Adams's office.

While I'm not schooled in law, I found it odd that Ruby and Cannon did not go with the jurors on their visit across the street. Instead, they sat quietly conversing at the defense table.

Unable to put my finger on what was bothering me, I seemed to recall that our legal system gives the defendant the right to be confronted by the accuser and presented with all of the evidence against him. Otherwise, the judge would just bring in the defendant to hear his sentence after being tried and convicted—without being given a chance to refute the testimony that had been presented to the jury.

I concluded that I would have to wait to find out what Cannon would make of this possible error on Judge Adams's part.

"Zora?"

I turned to see Matt standing beside me in the balcony. "I'm sorry, Matt, I didn't hear you come in. I guess I was too caught up in my notes."

He handed me a newspaper. "Releford wanted you to read this."

"Thanks," I said, noting that it was the Jacksonville *Florida Time-Union*. "Are you headed back home now?"

"No'm. I's gonna wait outside for them to take Ruby on back to the jailhouse. Thought I'd visit with her a spell 'fo' I walk on back home."

"Mind if I wait for you out on the bench? I'd like to walk home with you."

Matt smiled. "It be my pleasure."

When Matt left the balcony, I opened the newspaper to see Adams's campaign photo, accompanied by an article reporting the murder. The article appeared in the August 4 edition, a day after the murder, which was before the *Democrat* article came out the following Friday.

In striking contrast to Wadsworth's eulogy, the Jacksonville paper carried only an interview with Sheriff Sim Howell, stating, "Sheriff Howell averted possible trouble when he brought the woman from the courthouse and told a crowd of about 100 persons that he held another woman, one who was going to tell him who did the shooting. Howell and State Patrolman Frank Millikin put the woman in a car and 45 minutes later were in Raiford."

It was apparent that Releford wanted me to have the article to compare with the testimony of the officers during the trial. So far, Howard and Gray had said nothing about having taken Ruby downtown to the courthouse before rushing her off to Raiford. They also never mentioned that they had felt it necessary to deceive a growing crowd by telling them that the woman they were holding did not murder their beloved doctor.

I could only wonder if the Jacksonville reporters, onto the story so soon after the murder, had gotten to Howell before he had a chance to craft an account more in keeping with Judge Adams's depiction of this being just an ordinary murder in an otherwise peaceful community. It mattered because the judge's portrayal was the only one that could justify holding the trial in Live Oak.

When the jury came back a little less than a half hour later, the judge informed them that they were being dismissed a half hour early and that the time would be made up by starting at nine thirty tomorrow instead of ten. The court adjourned, and I sat with my notes while the remaining spectators filed out of the balcony.

Frank Cannon and Ruby McCollum

On Friday, December 19, every seat in the courtroom was filled with spectators eager to hear Ruby testify in her own defense.

On the main floor, white reporters from all over Florida had arrived early to stake their claims to the front-row seats and finally hear the woman who had been kept silent for almost five months now. I knew that most of them had not challenged Judge Adams's court order barring the press from speaking with her, choosing instead to honor a gentlemen's agreement of polite silence, sparing the community further embarrassment.

My boss, Sam Nunn, on the other hand, had kept the suspense going between the botched first attempt at a trial and the eagerly anticipated day when Ruby would take the witness stand. He was ready for it with the headline "WILL RUBY TALK? SENSATIONAL INTERRACIAL MURDER TRIAL STARTS SEPTEMBER 29 IN FLORIDA COURT."

Other than the members of the press who had traveled from various parts of Florida, I learned from overhearing conversations outside the courtroom that curiosity seekers had driven through the early morning fog from Jasper, Adams's hometown, and Lake City, where Keith Black practiced. Several lawyers had even driven from Jacksonville and Tallahassee—each separated from Live Oak by over eighty miles of two-lane blacktop—to watch Cannon in action.

Looking down at the table for the defense, I noted that Cannon had dressed Ruby down in a pale yellow wool dress and a green camel hair coat, with her hair kept in place by a loose-fitting hairnet. He was well aware that his client was appearing before a jury composed mostly of dirt farmers who would hate her for her obvious wealth if they saw her in her usual tailored suit and beauty shop hairdo. The misquoted Scripture "Money is the root of all evil" seemed as ground into them as the dirt in the furrows of their sunburned necks. Now they would finally get to hear the story of an adulterous, murdering Negress in her own words. Afterward, it would be their God-given responsibility to issue the sinner a ticket to "Old Sparky."

When I reached the chair that Matt had saved for me, Bessie was sitting at his other side, holding Loretta. When our eyes met, I smiled at her, wondering how she was holding up in her exile with the rest of the family.

"Why is Loretta here?" I whispered to Matt. "I thought she was in New Jersey."

"Mr. Cannon wanted her here," Matt explained.

"All rise," the bailiff called out, announcing Judge Adams's entrance into the courtroom at exactly 9:30.

When the judge was seated, the Reverend Philpot gave his usual prayer before court began. Sometime during the prayer, I saw the old lady with her knitting, occupying her usual front-row seat behind the attorneys. As I watched, I had the eerie feeling that the three Fates, the ancient Greek goddesses who controlled the metaphorical thread of life, were standing behind the silver haired lady, directing her every stitch. Time alone would tell the final story when Atropos, the Fate in charge of cutting the thread, performed her task.

When the minister finished, Judge Adams addressed the jury: "Gentlemen of the jury, I am advised that yesterday, on the occasion of the view, that the defendant was not over there with you. You are going to be sent back for a further view, and the defendant will go along with you."

The judge signaled Sheriff Howell to conduct the jurors out of the courtroom, and Cannon and Henderson followed with Ruby.

As the jurors filed out, I reflected that since Judge Adams had to be "advised" of Ruby's absence at the prior jury viewing of Adams's office, he had to have been absent as well. Whether or not this would have a bearing on the case was beyond my ability to determine.

When the procession had left, I turned to Matt. "So why does Cannon want Loretta here in court?"

"He say he wants to let Ruby tell everything 'bout her and Dr. Adams. He got a blood test done on Loretta and got the blood test from Adams's body, and he say they show the doctah could be her daddy."

From what I knew about establishing paternity, there were only two methods acknowledged by the courts: blood type compatibility and physical resemblance, neither of which is totally conclusive. Even though Cannon would have no actual proof, Ruby's testimony, along with blood type compatibility and the obvious physical similarity Loretta bore to her father, would be enough to lend credence to Ruby's claim of Dr. Adams's paternity.

While I was considering Matt's information, an old lady leaned over to whisper to him, "I dreamed Ruby come clean. She walked outta this courthouse a free woman."

"I thanks you, ma'am," Matt said, but I knew by the look on his face that he found little comfort in the woman's dream.

Another woman placed her hand on Matt's shoulder as she passed behind him on leaving the balcony. No words were spoken, but the communication was unmistakable, building a bridge of empathy across a chasm of silence.

At one point, Loretta became restless, shifting on her aunt's lap. "Now, baby, you needs to be quiet," Bessie urged. "Mommy's gonna be back in a few minutes, and she need you to be a big girl."

I was trying to note how long the jury was out visiting the scene of the murder, but I lost track. In any event, it was probably a half hour later that Judge Adams and Sheriff Howell led the procession back into the courtroom.

With the exception of occasional stifled coughs, the gallery fell silent after Judge Adams declared court in session. Cannon called Ruby to the witness stand, where she stood patiently with her green camel hair coat draped over her arm, waiting for the elderly bailiff to shuffle over with his *Bible*.

"Do you swear to tell the truth, the whole truth, and nothing but the truth, so help you God?" the bailiff asked, his intent stare portending eternal damnation to any sinner who dared violate the sanctity of the sacred book in his charge.

"I do," she said meekly, and took her hand from the *Bible*.

Noticing for the first time that the court used a copy of the Gideon *Bible*, I recalled the angel's words from the book of Judges, assuring the terrified Gideon, "Peace be unto thee; fear not: thou shalt not die."

In the short silence that followed, while Ruby draped her coat over the back of her chair to sit down, I considered her plight. Until her relationship with Adams took a turn for the worse, she had lived her life looking eagerly forward to the future, in the full flower of her prime. Now the rest of her life would be spent withering away in an emotional wasteland.

Waiting for Cannon to begin his questioning, she shifted her weight nervously from side to side like a caged animal. From her vantage point, she was barely tall enough to see her accusers in the courtroom.

The silence was broken by Cannon's opening question. "Would you please state your name for the record?"

"My name is Ruby McCollum."

"And what is your address?"

"My house is at 403 East Wood Street, here in Live Oak."

"How many children do you have?"

"I have four children."

"Could you please state their names and ages?"

"Sam Junior is nineteen, Kay is eleven, Sonja is three, and Loretta, the baby, is a little over a year old."

Cannon asked Ruby about the first time she had met Adams, and she testified that it was in 1945 when he delivered Sonja. "Beginning from there, tell the jury now, in your own words, all of the association and dealings that you had with Dr. Adams up until the time of this killing."

Edwards popped up like a jack-in-the-box. "We object, if Your Honor please. First, it is too broad, vague, remote, and indefinite as to time and place; second, it is shown to be undertaking to obtain testimony that is entirely irrelevant and immaterial; third, it is shown to be for the purpose of obtaining testimony that would constitute no defense to the charge that is included in this indictment; fourth, we think that she should be interrogated instead of asked to go ahead and cover a period of six years in the past."

Judge Adams sustained the objection.

Cannon again questioned Ruby about the period following Sonja's birth, and again Edwards objected.

Cannon was adamant. "By way of argument, if the court please, the state of Florida saw fit to charge her with premeditated murder. In every case, all of the relationships that existed prior to the alleged fatal occasion are admissible in evidence to show the state of mind of the accused. It is not remote and uncertain or vague and indefinite, but has a direct bearing."

With furrowed brow, Judge Adams rendered his decision: "On the question of premeditation, there might be some substance to that. The objection will be overruled."

Cannon repeated his question. "Now, how many times did Dr. Adams come out to your home for the purpose of treating you in the birth of the next to your last child, Sonja?"

Ruby was uncertain but said that it was a number of times.

"Beginning from there, did you have occasion to see him on numerous occasions? And if so, state what those occasions were."

Edwards rose to deliver his extended objection, centering primarily on obtaining testimony on "matters reaching back over a period of six or seven years, and which does not constitute any defense to the charge that the defendant is now being tried for."

Judge Adams sustained Edwards's objection and admonished Cannon to ask the question more directly.

Cannon continued questioning Ruby without objection until he asked, "Did he at any time have any other relations with you other than as a private physician and doctor?"

Edwards shot up like a bullet. "That is too broad, vague, and indefinite and remote as to time; it is undertaking to obtain testimony that is entirely irrelevant and immaterial; it is shown it is seeking to obtain testimony that could not apply to a defense under the charge which the defendant is on trial for; and it is too uncertain as to what relationship or association, and the question is too broad."

Cannon was quick to respond. "The relationship of doctor and patient was shown by the testimony of the state. The defendant is not confined in her testimony to the narrow bound established by the state."

Judge Adams again directed Cannon to ask the question more directly. Cannon objected vehemently. "I don't want to do it like the state did, and I couldn't write down every question and go over it with her on numerous occasions before I put her on the stand."

Judge Adams sustained Edwards's objection, ignoring Cannon's jab at Edwards for coaching his witnesses.

Cannon regrouped. "Beginning right after the birth of Sonja, did you ever have sexual relations with Dr. C. Leroy Adams?"

Edwards objected that Cannon was trying to obtain testimony about a "preposterous act, which can constitute no defense to this charge."

Turning toward Judge Adams, Cannon let loose with both barrels: "Since he objects to all testimony that the defendant might give, in fairness to the court, I propose to show by this witness that beginning several years ago that the doctor began having sexual relations with this woman and that continued right up to the time of the killing, and that was the very cause of the killing. I know you can't foresee it, but I can state the purpose of those questions and I certainly know that this is the most material and most relevant testimony that ever could be offered here, and nobody knows it any better than the state of Florida in this case."

Suddenly, there was one audible communal gasp, as though all the air had suddenly been sucked out of the room. As for Edwards, he looked like Cannon had slapped him upside the head with a turnip and called his pappy a carpetbagger. Nevertheless, the man had a job to do, so he was the first to see if enough air yet remained for him to object. "I think that is also a very improper statement to be made in the presence of the jury."

"I rather think so myself," the judge managed, in the briefest statement to come out of his mouth in all the time I had known him. Maybe he was testing the air as well.

"May I ask that the court charge the jury to disregard that statement of counsel?" Edwards asked.

"I think I better," the judge agreed. "Gentlemen of the jury, in the trial of many cases, counsel for either one or the other side may get a little overenthused sometimes and make statements that are not just right in line with the situation. So you will go by the testimony without regard to the observations of counsel. The objection will be overruled."

From the moment Cannon let the cat out of the bag, I knew that this was no ordinary house cat—no, this was Alice's Cheshire cat, and no matter how hard everyone tried to ignore it, for the remainder of the trial there would still be that persistent, enigmatic grin beaming down from the balcony.

After the judge's admonition to the jury, Cannon asked that his question be read back.

"Beginning right after the birth of Sonja, did you ever have sexual intercourse or sexual relations with Dr. C. Leroy Adams?" the court reporter read.

"No, I didn't right then," Ruby answered.

"Will you tell the jury where and when it first began and the circumstances under which it first began?"

Edwards again objected, referring to the question as "seeking to obtain testimony pertaining to some preposterous and purported act and matter which could constitute no defense to the charge that the defendant is being tried on."

"The first objection," Cannon began, "is that it is no defense. It goes to the jury as a matter of mitigation as well as defense. It may be in mitigation of the alleged crime that it is most material."

"The objection will be overruled," the judge ordered.

Cannon nodded at Ruby.

"It was in my home in 1948, the first time I had ever had any sexual relations with Dr. Adams."

"Tell us now how it came about, and the conditions under which it came about, and everything that he said to you and you said to him in reference to it."

Could it be that Judge Adams had opened the door for Ruby to tell the whole lurid story of her affair with Adams? Was that possible in this courtroom, in this town, in this day and time? If so, it would be the most significant trial in the history of Jim Crow, sending shock waves throughout the segregationist South. Never before, to my knowledge, had a colored woman been allowed to take the witness stand and testify about the paternity of her child by a white man.

"We object on the same grounds as to the previous question," Edwards protested.

I had the feeling that he had grown tired of his prepared chant, so he decided to reduce it to a convenient size, ready to pull out of his pocket every time Ruby tried to tell her story.

This time Judge Adams responded, "The objection is sustained to the question as asked."

"How did you come to have sexual relations with him?"

Another objection, also sustained, but the judge added, "The question is, 'Did she have sexual relationships with the deceased?'"

"She testified positively that she did," Cannon protested.

"I understand that, but all of this other is not admissible."

Cannon paused, no doubt to bite his tongue, because I could see the blood rush to his face even from where I was sitting. "Maybe in your mind it might be," Cannon replied. "And maybe in my mind it might be. But for the state to get up here and show that she shot Dr. Adams was and would not be sufficient to go to the jury on, and the details of this intimate relationship are entitled to be shown and not merely the uncorroborated answer that he did have relations with her."

Judge Adams leaned forward. "If you want that, then ask the direct questions and not ask general questions that cover a wide spread of time and events."

Cannon reframed his question: "Did Dr. Adams solicit you to have sexual relations, or did you solicit him?"

"We object to that—"

"Or did he take it away from you? I will take it all three ways."

The courtroom exploded in laughter. Some of the colored men in the balcony slapped their knees.

Needless to say, the judge was furious, pounding his gavel until I thought it would break. "We are not going to have any of that giggling all along through this case," he chided. "If you can't stay here without that, you ought to save yourselves trouble, because I don't like to be exercising power unless I have to, but I am going to maintain the best of decorum while this is going on and I hope you will help me."

Edwards objected that Ruby had not yet testified that she shot the doctor, so there was no proper predicate for her to testify about a motive.

"That is foolishness," Cannon retorted.

Judge Adams overruled Edwards's objection, clearing the way for Ruby to answer Cannon's question.

"Dr. Adams came out to my house that afternoon before the morning of the beginning of this sexual relationship and he told me that afternoon, 'I will be back in the morning as soon as I finish all of my work, I will be back, and I will show you what I was talking about.' He came back out there next morning about nine thirty and took me upstairs and laid me down on the bed and began the intercourse. When it was finished he left, and he said, 'I will be back some other time.' 'You'll call me?' I said, 'Yes, I will.' I didn't call him directly or in three or four days, and so when he came out to the house and I wasn't there, when I got back he was out there, I said, 'I didn't know you were coming to my house today.' He said, 'You didn't call me, but I came back out here for the same thing I had before.' I said, 'Yes, okay,' and he said, 'I am not up for any foolishness and you are not green, and if I ever have to tell you about it again you will be sorry of it. I am not afraid, and I don't want you to be afraid of it. No one is going to bother me. That is definite.' Then I told him, 'Okay,' and that made me begin to be afraid of him. I had to either yield or maybe die, so I couldn't tell him no. Anytime he came out to my house it was all right, and he continued this for quite a while. In 'fifty, I said, 'I am almost afraid.' And he said, 'Afraid of what?' And I said, 'Well, you know what I will be afraid of.' He said, 'That doesn't make any difference.' And I say, 'Why not use a diaphragm?' and he told me, 'To hell with a diaphragm. I don't use such things as that.' Then, later on, along about November it was, I spoke to him and told him what had happened. He said, 'I know it. I knew it to start with. You don't have anything to worry about.'"

I sat listening to Ruby recount her sexual encounters with Adams, marveling at how totally detached she was from any emotion. Certainly she expressed having felt fear when she testified, "I had to either yield or maybe die." Yet this expression of fear differed from what she had told McGriff about being able to pick any man she wanted, colored or white.

About the time I was beginning to wonder if Edwards was still breathing, he sprang to life and raised an objection, which the judge overruled.

"Did you continue then," Cannon asked, "after this time, to have sexual relations with Dr. Adams up until the time of his death?"

"Yes, sir."

The question of the wheres, whys, and hows of Ruby's encounters with Adams continued without objection, including the code between the two to let Adams know if Sam was home when he called the house.

"Now, after you began having sexual relations with Dr. Adams, did you ever become pregnant?"

"Yes, sir."

"When was that?"

Again Edwards jumped up, objecting with his usual statement of the testimony being irrelevant. This time, the judge sustained the objection, asking Cannon to rephrase the question.

"Did you become pregnant by Dr. Adams after you began to have sexual relations with him?"

"Yes, I did," Ruby replied.

"We object to that upon the same grounds," Edwards said.

"I think that is a direct question," Judge Adams responded.

The audience, already warned about giggling, was relatively quiet with the exception of a few smirks here and there around the room. I could see by the way people leaned forward in their seats that this was the high point in the trial for every whispering gossipmonger in town.

"Yes, I did. I became pregnant in 1951 in October."

"When was the child born?"

"She was born July 15, 1950. No, this was in 1950, and the baby was born in 1951. Now she is a year old."

When Cannon paused for a few seconds between questions, Ruby looked up to the balcony to see Loretta sitting in Bessie's lap. What I saw on her face was piteous, especially since I knew that this may be the last time she would see her baby.

Cannon confirmed Loretta's age and then asked, "Did Dr. Adams have anything to do with taking care of you during that childbirth or making any arrangements for your care during that childbirth?"

"He told me to go to Valdosta, to Dr. Saunders at Little-Griffin Hospital."

A line of questioning continued in which Ruby detailed Loretta's delivery at Little-Griffin by Dr. Saunders, Adams's first cousin, and Adams's care of her after she returned home. The testimony went uninterrupted except for Edwards's objections to the question of why Adams wanted Ruby to go to that particular hospital and the question of why Adams refused to give Ruby a copy of Loretta's birth certificate. In each case, Judge Adams sustained Edwards's objections.

"Will the court let the jury retire," Cannon asked, "and let me state what purpose I propose to offer on that question? I will be happy to do it in the presence of the jury, but it may be improper."

After his previous "improper" statement, I had the impression that Cannon was not going to push his luck with the judge.

When Judge Adams recessed the jury, Cannon asked Ruby to recount her conversation with Dr. Adams regarding the birth certificate.

"I told him that I had not received a birth certificate for my baby yet, and I was supposed to receive a certificate around a month after the baby was born. I asked if he would get it for me, and he told me, 'Why, I have it, and I am going to keep it until you tell me, until you do as I say do.'"

"Did he tell you how he had it made out?"

"Yes. He told me that the baby's name was made in his last name."

Cannon walked Ruby through her statement, confirming that she had never gotten a birth certificate for Loretta. Afterward, he addressed the court.

"Now, we submit that that goes to the jury for whatever credence it may have, and every word of it."

After that, the interchange between Cannon and Edwards was like two roosters going at it in a cockfight. Cannon jumped up at Edwards; Edwards jumped at Cannon; feathers flew—the only thing missing was the cheering and the betting. The audience sat mesmerized.

Finally, when the dust settled, Judge Adams sustained Edwards's objection, and Cannon asked the judge if his ruling was set.

"The court has ruled, the objection is sustained. Just proceed."

Cannon was livid. "With that statement, I am going to ask her all about it for the record. This is a trial for murder."

"If objections are made, they will be subject to being ruled upon," Judge Adams retorted.

"I feel that it is right and proper and necessary to protect the rights of the defendant and not in any disrespect of the court's ruling," Cannon added.

While Judge Adams summoned the jury, I had to wonder how many lawyers in his district had ever challenged him to the extent that Cannon had. I was willing to wager that few, if any, had done so and still remained in the circuit.

When Cannon resumed his questioning, he made good on his promise to pursue the issue of the birth certificate. This elicited the predictable objections and the equally predictable rulings sustaining them.

Then Cannon referred to the presence of Loretta in the balcony, suggesting that Ruby identify her and that she be presented to the jury. Again, the predictable objection and the ruling sustaining it. It was apparent that at least in Judge Adams's courtroom, Loretta's paternity would be as elusive and hard to pin down as the Cheshire cat.

Cannon moved on to ask Ruby about her pregnancy at the time of the murder. "Now, I will ask you if, sometime prior to August third of this year, and on August third of this year, if you were pregnant at the time you were in Dr. Adams's office over here across the street?"

"Yes, sir."

"By whom?"

"By Dr. Adams."

Edwards objected, but Judge Adams overruled.

"Did you have any conversation immediately prior to August third with Dr. Adams in reference to your being pregnant at that time?"

Edwards objected again, and this time Judge Adams sustained.

"How many months or how far had your state of pregnancy developed on August third?"

"Two months."

"Now, had you continuously had sexual relations with Dr. Adams up until August third of this year?"

Edwards again objected, but Judge Adams overruled.

"Yes, sir," Ruby replied.

"About how often, say, during the last six months prior and during the entire year prior to August third of this year, or of this year during his lifetime?"

"I couldn't answer that right off. I don't know. Many times."

"On August third, were you indebted to Dr. Adams in any sum of money? Owe him anything?"

"Yes, sir."

"How much?"

"I knew that I owed him six dollars. I didn't know anything about the other money."

I knew from my conversations with Lucy that the "other money" that Ruby was referring to was the charge for Lucy's abortion. Even now it appeared that the memory of this was too painful—or too embarrassing—for her to talk about.

"Prior to August third," Cannon continued, "had you ever had any altercation or any trouble with Adams?"

Following Edwards's objection, Cannon posed the question in six different ways, each raising an objection that was sustained.

Cannon halted his line of questioning to return to the topic of whether Ruby had had sexual relations with Dr. Adams in his office. Edwards objected to the questioning as repetitious, and Judge Adams sustained.

"Do you remember what day of the week August third was on of this year?"

"Yes, sir."

Battling through several objections, Cannon delved into the circumstances of Ruby's trip to Dr. Adams's office that Sunday. When asked why her children, Loretta and Sonja, were with her, she replied that there was no one to take care of them at home.

"Tell us what you did when you left home," Cannon asked, obviously wanting an uninterrupted account of Ruby's trip to Adams's office.

"I went to the doctor's office, and when I first got there it was full of people. I left my two children in the car."

"Go ahead."

"Since it was so full of people, I stayed out to the car with the children for a while. Later on, I went back to the office and sat down and talked with some more of the people that were waiting there until the doctor came out, and when he came to the door he told me to 'Come on in, Ruby,' and I said, 'Okay.' I said, 'Are you folks ahead of me?'

and he said, 'That is all right; you can come on in.' I walked in and I told the doctor that I had a pain in my right shoulder or arm and that I could hardly get in and out of my clothes when I first get up in the morning. He gave me a shot of penicillin."

Clearly, Ruby's testimony differed from the earlier testimony of the witnesses who were in the colored waiting room when she entered. I had to reflect that it sounded a bit self-serving, presenting this picture of her concern for those who had been waiting longer than she, as opposed to the earlier witnesses' version of her barging in ahead of them.

"What part of the building were you in when he gave you the penicillin?"

"On the right side — in the white side."

After a few questions about the shot, Ruby continued her account of what had happened that day: "Then I asked him, 'Doctor, I owe you for two calls, don't I?' He said, 'Yes, and this one will make three.' I gave him ten dollars and he gave me back one dollar, and I put the money in my bag. Then I thought about the bill. When he came back, I said, 'Dr. Adams, a bill came out to the house for Sam for a hundred and sixteen dollars. He said, 'Yes, I am going to get my money, too, if I have to turn him over to the county judge.' So I said, 'I have a hundred dollars I want to pay on it. May I peep and see who made that bill?' and he said to see Thelma about that. I said, 'That is all right; just give me a receipt for it, please.' I said, 'Then I will owe you how much?' And he said, 'Ten dollars,' and I said, 'Okay.' I said, 'I will bring it back sometime when I come in next week.' And he said that would be all right. Where we were at that time, I was leaning on that table in the back."

Listening to Ruby recount her conversation with Adams that day and the details of her payment, I reflected how it differed substantially from the previous witnesses' testimony. According to Ruby, the conversation was entirely civil.

What failed to ring true in my mind, even if I discounted the testimony of the witnesses, was Ruby's implication that Adams kept track of patient billing, down to the point of knowing that the hundred-sixteen-dollar medical bill consisted of a hundred ten for Sam's portion and six for Ruby's portion, and that she owed three dollars more for the current visit. The arithmetic was meticulous, tracking her paying a total of nine dollars for her portion and receiving change for a ten-dollar bill, then their both agreeing that her payment of a hundred dollars on Sam's bill would leave a balance of ten dollars.

In fact, the calculations were so meticulous that they seemed to be consistent with Ruby's thinking, not Adams's. From everything I had been told, he was a "Pay me what you can when you can" kind of country doctor—his real interest in his patients was in their value as political capital.

"Go ahead," Cannon instructed her. "After he signed the receipt, then what happened?"

"He told me to get on the table. I told him, 'Well, can I wait until another time?' and he said, 'No.' He said, 'I want you to get up there now.' I said, 'Well, maybe I can't get up there today.' He said, 'Yes, you can get up there today.' Then I told him why, and he grabbed me and started beating on me with his fist, and he turned around and grabbed the gun and stuck it in my stomach and I pulled it away from him and he snatched it back, and I grabbed it again and the gun went off, and it went off again, when he fell, and it went off again, and he makes out of the room and went and stood up in the door that entered into this room where the chairs are."

While Ruby was recalling the gun going off, she looked down at her right hand, the one that had held the gun, as if it were something separate and apart from her body—as if it had a will of its own.

"He stood there awhile, and gradually he went down to the floor, and he laid there flat out." She looked down and stretched out her arms. "He laid something like that. Anyway, when I started out by him, he grabbed the gun out of my hand. Then I asked him to give me that gun, please, and he wouldn't give it back to me. I asked him for it again and I caught his arm that way, and I don't know anything else that happened."

Cannon tried to question Ruby about other details of the shooting, but her recollection was vague at best. Again I marveled at how different Ruby's testimony was from the witnesses'.

Witnesses aside, after the first gunshot Ruby had blown holes in any possible claim that it was an accidental shooting. Any other shots would have to be portrayed as being fired in self-defense, out of fear for her life—a difficult trick since they were fired into Adams's back.

"Do you actually have any remembrance of it going off in that waiting room?" Cannon persisted.

Ruby looked up at the ceiling, and there was an abrupt halt in her testimony. In that instant, it was as though the film had broken in the middle of the movie, and in the moment before the celluloid melted, Ruby's world stood still.

In her silence, something from the depths of her tortured soul inhabited her face, reflecting the anguish of the months before the killing, the indescribable emotions of her resolve to slay the evil that possessed her, to blot it out from the world — to tighten her finger on the trigger. And then there were the memories of it all, the monsters imprisoned deep in the dungeons of her soul, instilled with a life that she could bestow but could not take away.

In a flash, I comprehended the infinitude of the human mind, mother of monsters and angels, and the ineffable glory and unspeakable horror of its creations. What I beheld in Ruby's eyes during her silence, when the agony of her memories robbed her of speech, may God have the mercy never to let me see again.

When Ruby was finally able to speak, all that she could say was, "I was just frightened, and I don't remember all that stuff."

Cannon led Ruby through her movements that day, starting with her reason for going to the doctor's office. She recalled little, but she knew that she had eighteen or nineteen hundred-dollar bills in her handbag. That was enough to send whispers throughout a courtroom filled with people who earned less than that in an entire year.

"Did you close the door as you went out, or do you remember?" Cannon asked.

"I don't remember."

Cannon asked what happened after she left the office, but again Ruby could not remember. She did recall taking a bath and changing her dress when she got home, as well as warming Loretta's bottle before the authorities arrived.

I had to reflect on the power of forgetfulness to shield a troubled mind from events too painful to revisit. As the slighted Montresor had done in Poe's "The Cask of Amontillado," forgetfulness had walled up the monsters in the dungeons of Ruby's mind, one brick at a time.

Turning to the arrival of the authorities at her home, Cannon asked Ruby about her conversation with Deputy Gray, since he had earlier testified that he spoke with her privately in an upstairs bathroom.

"Tell how you got in there," Cannon said, referring to how Ruby and Deputy Gray ended up in the bathroom together.

"I walked upstairs and he came up behind me, and he told me, 'Ruby, I know your husband. I know Sam and I have been doing quite a few things for him. I want to know who Sam's wife is.' I didn't say anything for a while, and then he said, 'I am here to protect you. Tell me where the gun is and where is Sam's wife.' I said, 'The gun is out there on the back.' Then someone opened the bathroom door and told me to go ahead on with them, and I told him I wanted somebody with my children, and he said, 'The children will be all right,' and I went with the officers."

"Where did they take you?" Cannon asked.

"We object to that," Edwards interjected. "It is irrelevant and immaterial."

After the judge sustained Edwards's objection, Cannon turned Ruby over to Edwards for cross-examination.

"Would the court give us a few minutes?" Edwards asked. "We have got to lay some predicates and we haven't had an opportunity to talk to the witnesses."

After a short recess, the judge announced that it was already past the noon hour, so he extended the recess until two.

Looking at the court clock, I saw that it was about twelve thirty.

Bessie stood with Loretta. "Look like we might as well take Loretta back home, Matt," she said. "Mr. Cannon ain't gonna be able show her nohow."

Matt nodded.

"Can I do anything to help, Matt?" I asked.

"Yes'm. You can look after the house whiles I drives over to Lake City to put Bessie and Loretta back on the bus."

"I'll do that," I said. "Good to meet you, Bessie."

"Good to meet you, too, Zora. You take good care of Matt for me until I can come back home."

While Matt and Bessie left the balcony with Loretta, I pieced my disintegrating notepad back together.

"Care to get a bite to eat?"

Recognizing the resonant baritone voice, I looked up to see Releford McGriff. "I'd love to," I replied. "I didn't know you were here."

"I was sitting in the back taking notes. Cannon and I have already been planning for the appeal, so I had to be here for Ruby's testimony."

"I'd love to have lunch. I have so many questions."

****

Releford and I comforted ourselves at Sam's café with warm chicken soup and hot tea, the latter being a rarity in a land where the drink of choice was iced tea syrupy enough to ladle over pancakes.

Annie Mae, who had adopted me by now, winked and served my soup chock-full of chicken.

"I was stunned at how many times Judge Adams sustained Edwards's objections," I lamented. "If only Ruby could have told her whole story, Cannon might have been able to make a case for second-degree murder."

"Even though I know you're coming from a journalist's point of view, Zora, it's not what Ruby could have testified that will save her from the chair—there's no doubt that she will be found guilty. What's going to save Ruby from the chair is Judge Adams's reversible errors when the case is appealed."

"Care to share some of your points?"

"Since I'll be on the defense team for the appeal, I can't talk about strategy, but I can tell you that I believe we have a strong case."

"Can I ask you about some other parts of the testimony?"

"Fire away. I'll answer if I can."

"I considered Ruby's upstairs bathroom conversation with Deputy Gray the most confusing testimony in the trial. According to Ruby, Gray tells her that he knows Sam, her husband, and that he has worked with him, and then immediately asks where Sam's wife is. What did you make of that?"

Releford took a moment to light his pipe. "Having Ruby on the stand was undoubtedly the most difficult ordeal any of the officers have had to deal with in their lives. As you know, this trial opened up a can of worms for the entire community, and especially the officials who were paid protection money by the McCollums."

"Yes," I agreed, "I've come to learn that the disappearance of Ruby's accounting book has been a problem for a good part of the town."

"Ironically, that book is a problem for Ruby as well."

"Oh?" I asked, surprised to hear that Ruby would try to protect the very men whose duty it was to bring her to justice.

"Ruby and Sam were involved in illegal gambling and liquor running. More than anything, Ruby wanted to avoid talking about their business because she feared attention from the IRS. She told me she had worked too hard to lose everything for taxes."

"Yes, I can understand that. But why would she be concerned about money when she is on trial for her very life?"

Releford indulged in a sardonic laugh. "Ruby is a woman who has lived her whole life acquiring wealth and the things that money can buy. As far as she's concerned, she's paying her attorneys to win her case, and she plans to spend as little as possible to accomplish that goal."

"So am I to understand that both Ruby and the officers played this little game of cat and mouse, each withholding their association with each other from the court in hopes of holding on to what they could?"

"Exactly. Ruby could at least hold on to the hope of keeping her money and her property, and the officers could hold on to their jobs and their reputations."

"Sounds like a fair trade," I agreed, reflecting on a twist in an already complex story that I had not yet considered. "Does that mean they were trying to secretly rush Ruby out of town to freedom when they told the crowd she was not the one who shot Dr. Adams?"

Releford relit his pipe. "I suppose we'll never know the answer to that question. There is the possibility that they were just trying to get Ruby over to Raiford to avoid any problems from a growing mob. But there is also the possibility that they were striking a deal with Ruby to get her out of town in exchange for her accounting book. In any event, Ruby isn't talking about that part of the story."

Suddenly, I realized that I had not asked Releford about how the McCollum estate was faring. "When I first met you," I said, "you told me you were handling the probate portion of the case. Would you mind sharing where all that stands?"

"Sam died intestate—without a will. In Florida that means that Ruby, as Sam's wife, receives a child's share of her husband's estate. In this case, Ruby receives an equal share with Kay, Sonja, Loretta, and Sam Junior. Bottom line: she's entitled to twenty percent of everything."

"Not much for a wife," I commented, thinking how a woman who worked alongside her husband to build his career and raise his children was reduced in the eyes of the law to having the rights of a single child.

"In this case, that might be a good thing," McGriff explained. "You see, her share of the estate is the only portion subject to any claim the state might file against her for court costs, not to mention the claim the doctor's widow has filed for the wrongful death of her husband. The rest of the estate, under Florida statute, isn't subject to claims resulting from her actions."

"How much do you think the estate is worth?"

"Aside from the cash that was recovered from the family safety deposit box down in Tampa, I've been able to document title to a couple of farms, numerous rental properties and jooks, and the McCollum home with its contents. If I had to guess, I'd say it'd all add up to about five hundred thousand—unless more cash is found. When everything is liquidated, Ruby's share would be a hundred thousand or less, a good bit of which will no doubt be spent on her appeal."

I tried to imagine what that much money would buy. For one, it would buy five hundred houses like the one I was trying so desperately to buy. To me, that was true wealth.

"How often do you talk with Ruby?" I asked, enjoying the apple scent of Releford's pipe and lighting my cigarette.

"Off and on. She prefers to talk with me more than she does Cannon—she's made it quite difficult for him to defend her."

"How is that?"

"First of all, he's white, and from what I can tell, Adams is the only white man she ever felt comfortable around."

"Can you share some of the things she told you—especially about why she shot Adams? I know I'll never have a chance to speak with her myself."

"In Ruby's own words, she was 'caught between two guns'—Sam threatened to kill her if she had another white baby, and Adams threatened to kill her if she aborted his child."

"Do you buy into her story that Dr. Adams hit her the day of the murder?"

"I have no doubt that he hit her, but not that day. In a real way, it's a lot like the cotton-patch Negro boy accused of raping the white woman he has had many times with her consent. When she screams and he protests his innocence, the white community can't admit the truth, the prosecution has to find a lie and stick to it, and the jury dishes out a verdict that far outweighs the severity of the crime. Ruby gets the chair, but if Evelyn, the doc's white gal, had gone crazy and shot him, she would have been sentenced to ten years for manslaughter—and out on parole in five."

As we waited for the end of the dinner hour, the conversation shifted from Ruby's trial to Releford's other cases around Florida, one of which was his fight to have coloreds on juries. I knew that one day he would bring a case before the Florida Supreme Court to overcome the Judge Adamses in the state.

Hearing Releford's passion underscored my belief that there are enough laws on the books to guarantee fair treatment for individuals without Congress having to pass federal civil rights legislation. What our society lacks is enough world-changing colored attorneys like Releford McGriff to argue for the equal enforcement of existing laws.

I had to reflect that until the day comes when our people look to themselves and not to others to solve issues of racial inequality, they will always be "slave ships in shoes."

****

Cannon was the first to speak when Judge Adams called the court to order after the dinner break. He said, "May I ask an additional question of the defendant, if it pleases the court?"

"Yes, sir."

"Ruby, you testified this morning that you were pregnant on August third. I ask you if you are pregnant now."

"That is irrelevant and immaterial as to the condition of the defendant at this time," Edwards objected.

Judge Adams quickly sustained.

"I will ask you if, sometime after August third of this year, if you had what is known as a miscarriage."

Edwards again objected and the judge sustained.

When Cannon turned Ruby over to Edwards for questioning, he asked her about the kind of handbag she was carrying, the details of her position in Adams's office at various points of her visit, how she carried and disposed of the murder weapon, which route she took home, and what she did when she got home. For most of the questions, Ruby responded, "I don't remember."

Edwards moved on to the letter that Ruby wrote from Raiford Prison after she was arrested. "On or about August 23, 1952, did you write a letter at Raiford, Florida, to a Mr. Crews, which letter went into the possession of Mr. R. H. Cox, Director of the Women's Division of the State Prison, in which letter you state and wrote that you had no relations with the doctor, referring to Dr. C. Leroy Adams, or with any other man other than your husband, or words to that effect?"

Ruby asked, "Was that all of the letter? May I ask that, please?"

Edwards persisted in demanding that Ruby answer his question, though he failed to produce the letter. Finally, Ruby said she had written a letter with "words to that effect," denying having relations with Dr. Adams.

When Edwards turned Ruby back over to Cannon, Cannon's first question was, "Will you tell the jury now why you wrote that letter?"

"That would be self-serving," Edwards objected.

The judge sustained.

"Did anyone do anything to you to force you to write such a letter?"

"That would be self-serving," Edwards reiterated.

"If somebody drew a gun on her, I wouldn't say that," Cannon objected.

The judge overruled Edwards's objection.

Cannon asked, "What did the nurse do to you?"

"She gave me a shot. Seemed to be about two cc's of whatever it was—of phenocin, I think—and this shot started me to sneezing, and I got to where I couldn't sleep, and I was supposed to get another one if I didn't stop crying. Then I got afraid and didn't know what was going to happen to me or what else would take place—"

Edwards objected that Ruby's statements were self-serving, and Judge Adams again asked Ruby to restrict her testimony to what the nurse did to force her to write the letter.

"The shot made me nervous. I got where I couldn't sleep, and I got real sick from it, and I asked for a piece of paper, an envelope, and a three-cent stamp, and it was given to me. I sat down and wrote that to Mr. Crews because I was afraid."

Edwards again objected that the testimony was self-serving and not responsive to the question. After Cannon protested, Ruby's answer was read back, and the judge determined that it was responsive, and allowed it in the record.

Cannon continued to question Ruby about whether officers in the jail pressured her to write the letter.

"I don't know whether he was an officer or not," Ruby responded. "But there was one that came in there with the nurse, and he spoke about it and held my arm while she gave me the shot."

"Had they asked you many times concerning your pregnant condition prior to that time?" Cannon asked.

Edwards objected that the question pertained to sometime other than when the letter was written, and Judge Adams sustained.

"When you say that you were afraid when you wrote that letter, what were you afraid of?" Cannon asked.

"I was just afraid of being in such a place, and I didn't know exactly what they were going to do to me. I was also afraid that I would get another one of those same shots after it was stated that I would get a bigger one next time."

"Who told you that you would get a bigger one next time?"

"The same nurse."

Edwards objected, and Judge Adams sustained.

In cross-examination, Edwards questioned Ruby about the names of the nurse and the officer. She recalled the officer's name as "Mr. Britt," but all she could recall about the woman was that she was a "young, very fat lady."

After Edwards ended his cross-examination, Cannon said that he had no further questions, and Ruby stepped down from the witness stand.

When Ruby took her seat at the defense table, Edwards called Carrie Dailey back to the stand for a rebuttal of Ruby's testimony. I knew this would be interesting since there were so many discrepancies between their testimonies.

When Edwards asked Dailey to recount her testimony, Cannon objected that this was simply repetition.

Edwards then became more direct in his questioning. "Did he put his hands on Ruby McCollum?" "Did he grab her?" "Jerk her?" "Beat her?" "Put a gun in her stomach?" "Did he grab her just before the pistol was fired?"

To each question, Dailey answered either "No, sir" or "I couldn't see her."

After Edwards finished questioning her, Cannon said he had no questions.

Edwards then called Avery Trawick and asked questions similar to those he had asked Dailey. To each, Trawick answered with an unequivocal no.

I reflected that in her previous testimony, Trawick had said she could not see Ruby at all. From that standpoint, since Trawick did not qualify her statements this time, she was testifying to what she could not have seen—certainly, without seeing Ruby or Adams, she could not deny the possibility of his grabbing her or putting a gun to her stomach.

When asked if he wanted to cross-examine Trawick, Cannon said he had no questions.

After Trawick was dismissed, Edwards stood to address Judge Adams. "We have one witness who is on the way here. We don't know whether we will use the witness or not, but we do not have any other testimony."

"Is that the witness you haven't had a chance to confer with?" asked Judge Adams.

"Yes, sir," Black replied. "One who we had no knowledge of until this morning — and that rather later in the morning."

Cannon stood. "I don't want any witness or evidence withheld from this jury, but with counsel telling you that he doesn't know whether he is going to use him or not, I don't know whether that can legally justify delaying the case."

Judge Adams replied that he didn't want to rush the case, so court would stand at ease until Black's witness arrived.

I used the break to review and organize my notes, which had, despite my best efforts, deteriorated into hen scratch.

About a half hour later, Edwards called a Mr. A. D. Rozier, a rather stodgy-looking middle-aged man, to the stand to be sworn in.

Edwards asked Rozier if he knew Ruby. It turned out that the man was known as "Mr. Britt" to the inmates at Raiford. Apparently, Edwards had gotten on the phone during the dinner break to ask Rozier to testify.

Edwards then asked, "Did you or a white nurse in your presence give to Ruby McCollum a hypodermic and cause her to write a letter to a Mr. Crews?"

"No, sir."

Cannon stood up. "I ordinarily don't make any objections to anything that has got anything to do with a case, but that is not rebuttal of anything that the defendant has testified about. She hasn't testified that this man did anything to her. She hasn't testified that she knows the man, but to bring that in here is just prejudicial."

"That is the rebuttal about him being present and holding her arm and giving her a hypodermic," Edwards explained.

Judge Adams ended the interchange, saying, "He said he is the man. The objection is overruled. Answer the question."

Edwards led Rozier through a statement that he had never forced Ruby to write any letter.

When it was Cannon's turn to cross-examine Rozier, he asked in rapid-fire succession, "Who put her over there? Was she serving any sentence over there? Was she charged with any crime in the county in which Raiford is situated? How long did you have her in the state prison at Raiford?"

Each of Cannon's questions was followed by an objection, and each objection was sustained.

Cannon relinquished the witness, but he had clearly gotten into the record that it was unusual to haul a person all the way to Raiford after arresting her unless the crime had occurred in the county where the prison was located. The fact that Ruby was spirited to a lockup three counties away would, I was certain, reflect badly on Judge Adams's decision to deny a change of venue when the case was appealed.

At this point, Edwards stated that the prosecution had concluded its case, and Cannon did the same.

"Will two hours for each side be enough time for argument?" the judge asked.

Cannon and Black agreed that it was.

"Does the court have in mind adjourning at five o'clock or running right on through?" Cannon asked.

"No, I am not going to run right on through," Judge Adams answered. "The defense has the closing."

When Henderson began his closing argument, there was no doubt that the man was a skilled communicator and every word flowed from his heart.

His hour-long presentation to the jury could be reduced basically to this:

"Ladies and gentlemen of the jury, I wish to thank you for your time, your patience, and your personal sacrifice in serving on this jury. I know that all of you have families and loved ones who are anxious for you to come home. But you still have a job to do. And that job is the most important one that our society ever places in the hands of anyone: the decision of life or death. In this courtroom, you have seen a defendant who has been denied the most fundamental of rights guaranteed under our Constitution. She was denied the right to fully testify, and therefore to fully defend herself. When you were listening to the objections of the state, did you take in how many times the defendant was silenced from telling how she was treated at the hands of Dr. Adams? Did you notice how the state would not allow her to tell what contributed to her state of mind that led her to commit the alleged act? Did you hear her testify that Dr. Adams forced her to have his baby, yet she was not allowed to present proof of a birth certificate? Did you hear the witnesses testify that they could not fully see what happened between Ruby McCollum and Dr. Adams before he was shot? Did you hear the noise from the window fan when you visited the scene of the shooting, and wonder how a witness who admitted she was practically deaf in one ear could hear a conversation word for word in the next room? As reasonable men, listening with your own ears, you certainly must have your doubts. As reasonable men, you also know that people, even the most outwardly kindly people, are not always as they seem. 'Oh,' you may say, 'Dr. Adams was a saint. He never would do anything to hurt anybody.' Can you really, truly know that? Can you really, truly know what a person is like in their personal lives, when the doors are closed and the lights are turned out at night? I ask you to question. I ask you to doubt not what you've heard in this courtroom, but what you were not permitted to hear. Why has the state silenced this woman—a woman who is on trial for her very life—when they could have allowed her to tell her story and let you as a jury determine whether she was telling the truth or not? Why has the press been barred from speaking with her? Finally, gentlemen, I ask that you turn to the still, quiet voice deep inside your hearts and consider that this woman is on trial for her life. She deserves to have a determination beyond all reasonable doubt that she planned and executed a cold-blooded murder for you to bring back the verdict the state is seeking. Otherwise, I ask that you consider one of the lesser charges, including the choice of setting her free."

While I listened to Henderson, I tried to get a sense of how the jury was thinking by looking at their faces. Unfortunately, it may as well have been a group of professional poker players—none of them gave the faintest hint of a reaction to Henderson's words. Instead, they all sat there with masklike expressions mirroring a hollowness of spirit that I have witnessed before when uneducated men are exalted to positions above their intellectual capacity. Like Pontius Pilate, they seemed quite capable of washing their hands of the matter and yielding to the will of the mob.

After Henderson took his seat, it was Edwards's turn to present the closing argument for the prosecution.

"Gentlemen of the jury, you have been most patient with us during this trial. You have taken time from your homes and families to render your civic duty, and for that we are most thankful. Now it is time for you to take upon your shoulders the heaviest of responsibilities that can be asked of you in a court of law, the responsibility of determining the guilt or innocence of the defendant, and the possibility that she may be sentenced to death for her crime. To make its case, the state has presented not one, not two, but three eyewitnesses. Three women who saw with their own eyes this woman, Ruby McCollum, take a gun and shoot the most generous and kind man in this county in the back—not one time but multiple times. And all over her doctor bill, and all, as the witnesses testified, without provocation. Could the gun have gone off accidentally? you might ask. In the most generous of considerations you might allow for a single accidental discharge of a weapon. But three more times? Gentlemen, I would submit that this woman, not the gun, determined the fate of Dr. C. Leroy Adams, and now it is up to you, as you have sworn to do, to decide hers."

Edwards, although brief and to the point, was much less skilled in his delivery than Henderson. Seeing the forbidding scowl that had become chiseled into his face over time, I had the impression that he did not feel the need to convince the jury of what they had already decided.

And indeed, listening to the closing arguments, it was clear to me that they fell upon deaf ears—the trial was over.

Chapter Sixty-Nine

With only five days left until Christmas, Judge Adams called court to order at nine thirty. After the invocation, he asked Frank Cannon to give his closing argument.

Evidently, the procedure was to allow each attorney, Edwards and Black for the state, and Henderson and Cannon for Ruby, to make his closing arguments separately. After the closing arguments by Henderson and Edwards yesterday, I had to wonder what else remained to be said.

When Cannon began his argument, it was clear that he was a gifted communicator with a compelling stage presence. He recounted Henderson's general line of argument, adding points of doubt for the jury to consider. He emphasized that the verdict of first-degree murder asked for by the state was not supported by the testimony, since no premeditation had been established. He also repeated that the witnesses, one of whom had a hearing problem, had been rehearsed by the state prosecutors to the point that they repeated many of the same lines verbatim.

Cannon concluded by appealing to the jurors to forgo the verdict of murder in the first degree and consider a verdict of manslaughter since Dr. Adams had abused Ruby and forced her into what amounted to slavery.

When Black rose to make his argument, he emphasized the irrefutable testimony of three witnesses. He acted out Ruby's shooting Adams in the back and ridiculed her testimony about describing the killing as an accident. He portrayed the doctor as a compassionate servant of the people, whereas Ruby was a rich, money-grubbing woman who begrudged him his rightful fees.

By the time both attorneys had finished, there wasn't a pair of eyes in the jury box that didn't look glazed over. Clearly they had had their fill of the whole matter and were ready to deliver their verdict with little or no deliberation.

At the conclusion of the arguments, Judge Adams read his written charge to the jury. He then asked if the possible verdicts had been agreed on by the defense and the prosecution.

Having assured himself that the attorneys were in agreement, Judge Adams addressed the jury: "Gentlemen, for your convenience, counsel for the state and the defendant have agreed on forms of verdicts, which you may use if you care to. However, you can write your own verdict if you so desire. If you find the defendant guilty of murder in the first degree, you may, if you so desire, use verdict form number one. If of murder in the first degree with a recommendation to mercy, you may, if you so desire, use verdict form number two. If of murder in the second degree, you may, if you so desire, use verdict form number three. If of manslaughter, you may, if you so desire, use verdict form number four. If you find the defendant not guilty, you may, if you so desire, use verdict form number five. You may retire and consider of your verdict."

After Judge Adams advised the jury of their possible verdicts, they retired to the jury room at eleven thirty a.m., and I decided to retire to Sam's Café to have a bite to eat.

****

About three hours after the jury had retired to deliberate their verdict, I decided to return to the courthouse to see if there was any indication of how long they might be out, when a young Negro man whom I had never seen before burst into the café. "Miz Hurston! Come quick! Mr. McGriff say the jury's comin' back in!"

When I made the two-block walk to the courthouse and took my seat, I was just in time to hear Judge Adams address the jury.

"Have you agreed on your verdict, gentlemen?"

Harry Howes, the jury foreman, stood and said, "Your Honor, we have."

"Pass it up. You will harken to our verdict as you have found it and as it will be read by the clerk."

The clerk secured the note from the foreman and adjusted his glasses. "We the jury find the defendant, Ruby McCollum, guilty of murder in the first degree. So say we all. Signed, Harry L. Howes, foreman."

Judge Adams addressed Cannon. "Any motions or notice?"

"No, sir."

"No motions or notices?"

"Naturally, we will make a motion for a new trial."

"I would want to know that because I would not want to proceed further with that pending now. Do you want the usual fifteen days?"

"The court knows that position that I came into this case, and I am like everybody else—I have got to get my business at home straightened out. If the court will give us thirty days within which to file the motion, we would appreciate it. If you can do that, we will have time in which to study the matter. If we could get the testimony written up, I would like to have it written up before I file the motion."

"I don't think I have any authority to accommodate you that long."

"It is done in our courts; you can give an extension of time for filing motions for a new trial."

"The usual statutory time is four days, with an extension of time for fifteen days if request is made therefor."

"I suppose you would then give us the additional fifteen days within which to file motion for new trial?"

"Yes, sir. Mr. McChesney, you will make note that counsel has requested in addition to the usual four days allowed by rules and statutes a further period of fifteen days for the filing of motion for a new trial. In the meantime, further proceedings in the case will be held in abeyance. Is there anything further to be brought before the court, Mr. State Attorney?"

"Not at this time," Black answered.

The judge pounded his gavel. "Court will take a recess subject to being reconvened on order."

Leaving the courthouse, I again considered how neat and tidy justice was in Live Oak, with the jailhouse conveniently located just a stone's throw from the courthouse. In Judge Adams's court, justice seemed to be a matter of getting down to the barest evidence to support the sentence, while summarily dismissing any inconvenient facts.

As a matter of fact, throughout the entire trial I had the distinct feeling that the argument of Ruby having a fight with Dr. Adams over her bill held center stage, while the real story was silently playing itself out backstage, behind a curtain of secrecy.

Chapter Seventy

After hearing the verdict, Cannon sat opposite me in Sam's Café, smoking a cigarette. When I took one out of my purse, he reached across the table to give me a light. "Thank you," I said, taking a deep draw. "You know, my step-mom used to tell me that ladies don't smoke."

"Oh?"

"According to her, ladies dip snuff."

Cannon laughed. "In that case, I know a lot of ladies who must have gone wrong somewhere along the line."

I smiled. What a stellar man this was, sitting in front of me! He had represented Ruby, had fought for her rights, and had shown no sign of giving up, even though Releford had informed me that the estate was dwindling and had no money for an appeal. "You are a very brave man to meet me in a public place," I said.

"Why is that, Ms. Hurston? It's obvious to everyone that I'm Ruby's attorney."

"There's obvious, Mr. Cannon, and then there's admitting the obvious."

He smiled.

"Do you mind if I ask you a question?" I ventured.

"I suppose it depends upon the question."

"Spoken like a true lawyer. Actually, I wanted to ask your opinion of the trial."

A pensive look came over Cannon's face. "Things went downhill when I tried to get Ruby to testify about Adams abusing her. I can't believe that Judge Adams is sending that woman to her death without letting her give testimony as to motive. Not a single word has left her mouth to explain the events leading up to the murder."

"I counted forty-eight objections by the prosecution, with thirty-seven of them sustained by Judge Adams — seems like pretty high odds in their favor."

Cannon nodded.

"I have always had an incredible faith in our system of justice, but now I have to consider that it is I who am blind, not Lady Justice."

By the look on Cannon's face, I could see that he was taking pity on my naïveté. He said, "According to Releford, this is the first trial where a colored woman has had the opportunity to testify to the paternity of her child by a white man. Regardless of how frustrated I am about Black and Edwards suppressing the rest of the testimony, that gives me some small consolation."

"I was thinking about that aspect of the trial as well," I shared, realizing that he was a political realist who measured social progress by the inch, not by the yard. "Without boring you with a long story, I first came to know this area back in the thirties, when I collected folk tales among colored lumberjacks working in the turpentine camps. It was there that I discovered something referred to as 'paramour rights.'"

Cannon nodded. "Yes, I'm aware of the common-law concept of paramour rights in the South."

"Then you know that countless women of color have been forced into sexual servitude since slavery ended."

He leaned his head back and sighed, exhaling a long plume of cigarette smoke. "Jim Crow is still alive and well in the South, and colored people still have little or no access to the courts. It often concerns me, as a student of history, when any group of people is not allowed to redress their grievances—it generally means a revolution will not be long in the making."

I reflected that our country's own Bill of Rights came out of the same situation—when a people loses its voice, there can be no lasting peace. Then I said, "It's a good thing the Releford McGriffs of this world are out there fighting for racial equality in the legal system."

"I've known his firm for some time," Cannon said. "They've already made a difference in our state courts. If you really want something to chew on, how about this? Releford told me that Loretta, as Adams's child, is entitled to a child's portion of his estate."

I sat dumbfounded. "That thought had never even remotely occurred to me."

"I have to admit that it had not to me, either. There has never been a case in this country, let alone in the South, where a colored woman or her bastard child has sued a white man for a share of his estate."

I sat listening to Cannon, feeling that I was in the presence of a truly great man. "So how would you set the odds for Ruby?"

Cannon looked me straight in the eye. "Ruby's accounting ledger may be the only thing standing between her and the electric chair. At some point, she's going to have to decide which she wants the most—her life, or her money."

I recalled how Releford, sitting at this same table with me, had mentioned the danger for Ruby in giving the go ahead to release her accounting book. But he, in contrast to Cannon, had placed his faith in Judge Adams's reversible errors to overturn the murder verdict and free Ruby—at least for a new trial.

How ironic, I thought, that a colored attorney would place his faith in the power of the courts while his fellow white attorney had more faith in the power of fear.

Lynching Postcard

Chapter Seventy-One

There was a thunderstorm on New Year's Day, and I sat on Matt's front porch to enjoy the patter of the rain on the tin roof. Settling into my rocking chair, I could feel the cool morning breeze caress my face, carrying the fresh scent of a winter rain.

There is something about rain that invites melancholy, the sober thoughtfulness of things that might have been, and people whose faces have gently receded into the past.

Recalling a line from Keats's "Ode on Melancholy," I mused that the mood does indeed visit those who enjoy bursting joy's grape against their palates—perhaps it is simply joy's aftertaste.

Looking forward to the New Year, I had no prospects of a job. In fact, I had no prospect of any income at all since Nunn had evidently reneged on our agreement and sent me only a paltry sum to travel back home. But I have never been one to give up hope, yea though I walk through the valley of the shadow of unemployment.

I had stayed through New Year's Day at Matt's house so he could spend the holidays with his family in Zuber. I was glad to hear that Ruby's sister was taking the train down from New Jersey with Loretta. It had to be tough on the family, being split up for over five months now.

A thunderclap echoing in the distance brought me back to my thoughts of Ruby sitting there alone in the Suwannee County jail, just outside the courthouse where she had been sentenced to death. Here was a woman mourning the loss of her husband, her family, her beautiful home, her wealth, and, perhaps, her life.

To me, that kind of loss was unimaginable. Although I have been married more than once, I have never had any children. For that matter, I have never owned a home of my own, and I have certainly never acquired any wealth. Perhaps I had trouble relating to Ruby's loss because I had no context for it, never having had what she had to lose in the first place. And I would never hear from her own lips what she was feeling, which might have helped me to understand.

What I *could* relate to was her loss of voice. For me, there is no agony like bearing an untold story inside—to be isolated from the rest of the world, unable to tell your story, is the greatest loss I can possibly imagine.

Matt had left a postcard with me that Ruby received in jail. Along with the jailhouse abortion that she still would not talk about and the Klan march on the same evening, the postcard, which bore a photograph of a lynching, undoubtedly contributed to her paranoia. Although such cards had been banned by postal regulations in 1911, this one had been mailed in a plain brown envelope, addressed to "Ruby McCollum, Suwannee County Jail," with no return address.

I had seen such cards before, but this one was different in two ways: for one, the victim was a woman; and for another, the card seemed to have been used several times, being readdressed using a different label, along with a new stamp. Each recipient would add a line about how they had enjoyed the picnic at the lynching — it was truly a community celebration. Looking through the various comments, I found one in heavy lettering, stating, "You're next, nigger" — evidently intended for Ruby.

Knowing that her appeal would take a year or more to play itself out, I had to wonder how Ruby would fare in the Suwannee County jail. She had already lost weight and was showing signs of a mental breakdown, fearing poison in her food and seeing Adams walk the hallways at night. Certainly there was enough hostility in the community about losing Adams at the hands of a "Negress" that Ruby's fears of being harmed were credible, even if her delusions were not.

With Ruby's death sentence slated to be announced in court in January, Releford had told me that he and Cannon had already begun crafting her appeal, counting at least fifty points that they considered reversible errors. Since appeals are notoriously slow, I knew that they had plenty of time to refine their pleading.

Looking back, the question I had posed early in the trial — whether the judge would support the local myth about the shooting being over a doctor bill, and if he did, whether this was because such thinking was native to his spirit or because he was rooted in the Southern traditions and sentiments of his ancestors — proved to be irrelevant, since either answer resulted in the same outcome for Ruby.

I suppose I should not have expected Judge Adams to act otherwise, but something in me stubbornly persists in believing that a person's better nature will prevail. It is the same kind of faith that leads me to plant a seed in the earth and believe that a beautiful plant will spring up to reward me with bouquets of flowers, even though sometimes it develops a canker and never blossoms.

It was that thought that led me to stop at Mizelle's Feed Store on my last walk downtown. I bought seeds—collard greens, string beans, sweet corn, and mustard seed—and opening the mustard packet, I took out a single seed to tape inside my thank-you note.

"Dear Matt," I wrote, "I have never known a kinder, gentler man than you. You have been generous to a fault, taking me in and treating me with dignity and respect. I can only hope and pray for the best for you and your family, and enclose this mustard seed to remind you that your faith, however small, will carry you through your troubled time. With faithful feelings, Zora, your kindred soul in loving the things that spring from the soil."

PART IV

1953

Zora Hurston in her Garden
Eau Gallie, Florida

When I returned home to start the New Year right by rocking on my front porch and watching the world go by, I decided that it would be best for me, like Voltaire's Candide, to tend my own garden. Life in the outside world had been challenging, but there were journeys that even my seven-league boots had trouble making.

My trip to Live Oak had been a fascinating study in the drama of human nature. There I had discovered, in the person of Dr. Adams, a man with tremendous drive to be a state senator like his grandfather and his great-grandfather before him. Enter a colored woman named Ruby McCollum, who rose above her race and her class to acquire more wealth than Adams could from practicing medicine. Could it be that Dr. Leroy Adams had met his equal and yet, strangely, his opposite, in the person of Ruby McCollum?

Was this how the ancient conundrum of what happens when an irresistible force meets an immovable object played out in real life? Obviously, when the two meet, one or the other has to give—in this case, it was Dr. Adams.

From Eve to Pandora, there have been many women, in history and in myth, who were cast as overreaching and bringing traumatic change to a world heretofore considered idyllic. And reading some of the letters to the editor printed in the *Courier*, I wondered if the same would be true of Ruby McCollum when the history of the segregationist South could finally be written.

While readers admitted that Ruby was wrong to resort to murder, they also suggested that her crime questioned Jim Crow and all it stood for in the South. Many argued that since Ruby had no access to the white man's legal system to protect her from Adams's cruelty and abuse, she had simply resorted to the only justice available to her.

Focusing on more mundane matters, I considered that my final article on the trial would run this month, with my piece on Ruby's life story scheduled to be serialized beginning in March, even though Sam Nunn and I had parted company after he reneged on his agreement by sending a miserable sum that barely covered my expenses.

I have never thought of myself as a quitter, but somehow the thought of leaving Live Oak without being able to tell Ruby's whole story gave me a deep sense of failure—and the drive to find someone who could take up the job where I had to leave off.

After giving it some thought, William Huie came to mind. Huie was a freelance writer who had published articles in American Mercury magazine, the same periodical that had carried my work. Making a trip to the library, I had found that Huie's latest endeavor was a book about Private Slovik, a naturalized U.S. citizen who was executed for desertion toward the end of the Second World War. Huie took up the story after learning that over twenty thousand U.S. soldiers were convicted of desertion during the war and that forty-nine were sentenced to death, but only Private Slovik paid the ultimate price. In fact, he was the only U.S. soldier to be executed for desertion since the Civil War.

Since Mr. Huie had established himself as a champion of other lost causes and was a known crusader for civil rights, I decided that he was the man for the job. But what would I say to interest him in Ruby's case?

After much pondering, I saw two primary issues: paramour rights and First Amendment rights. Having already written a piece about paramour rights based on my research in the North Florida timber camps in the 1930s, I searched through my papers until I found the piece I had intended to publish. Along with it, I also found a postcard from the same period, promoting Florida's turpentine industry.

My, oh my, how long it had been since I drafted these pages! As I sat leafing through the article, it seemed written by a pen not my own. My writing style had changed over the years, but the message was as meaningful today as when I wrote it.

Regardless of my interests, though, the real question was whether Huie would take up the issue of paramour rights, or whether even he would consider it tilting at windmills.

Turpentine Camp
1930s Florida Department of Commerce Postcard

Chapter Seventy-Three

I wanted dreadfully to tell Huie about the paramour rights issue, which I felt was crucially important in this trial. After several days of picking it up and putting it back down, I finally returned the postcard and my article to where I had found them, concluding that the issue would be repugnant to his white readers.

So instead, I appealed to his journalistic instincts by fashioning a letter describing how Judge Adams had denied Ruby her First Amendment rights. My mother always told me that if I wanted to catch a fish, I had to use the right bait, and for this particular fish, I felt intuitively that I had chosen wisely.

Dropping the letter at the post office with my last three-cent stamp, I resigned myself to wait until Huie decided whether he was interested in taking up the story where I had left off. From what I knew of him, he was a real scrapper who reveled in sensationalist reporting. Knowing that it would take the stoutest of hearts to deal with Judge Adams, I chuckled, imagining how the judge, who wanted to "avoid sensationalizing the trial," would rassle with the likes of Mr. William Bradford Huie.

On my walk back home, I felt a gentle ocean breeze coming from the Atlantic and looked up to see midafternoon thunderclouds rolling in. I looked forward to sitting on my front porch and enjoying the rain.

Just as I reached the welcomed comfort of my rocking chair, a flash of distant lightning transported me back to my childhood home and the warm, strong safety of my father's arms. There I sat entranced by countless raindrops splashing into the mud puddles in our front yard, magically transforming themselves into thousands of tiny ballerinas performing grand allegros to a symphony of clashing cymbals in the sky.

Angel tears — like a whisper through time, I looked up as I heard my mother's name for raindrops. "Look, Zora," she used to say, "See the raindrops out there? You know they be tears fallin' from the angels' eyes 'cause they weepin' fo' the woes of folks all over the world."

In that moment, I had a feeling deep in my soul that surely some of those tears fell for Ruby McCollum.

Epilogue

While Ruby sat waiting in the Suwannee County jail for her appeal to be heard by the Florida Supreme Court, the *Courier* ran Zora Hurston's "Life Story" series, exposing Adams's treatment of Ruby. Meanwhile, the widow Adams won a wrongful-death case against Ruby's portion of the estate; Ruby, believing that her lawyers were too expensive, fired them all (only to be countermanded by Judge Adams); and a second Sam McCollum Jr. surfaced in Ocala, claiming to be Sam McCollum's son and maintaining that he was entitled to a child's portion of the McCollum estate.

In 1954, the Florida Supreme Court declared a mistrial in Ruby's case, based on Judge Adams's failure to attend a jury viewing of the scene of the crime. The Supreme Court opinion stated in part that, "This is a right that cannot be frittered away by the act of a trial judge in voluntarily absenting himself from the proceeding."

When Judge Adams scheduled a new trial and Ruby was examined by physicians, she was declared insane and committed to the Florida State Mental Hospital at Chattahoochee.

In 1959, Zora Hurston suffered a stroke and died in the St. Lucie County Welfare Home.

In 1973, Frank Cannon—who had stayed on for Ruby's two-year appeal to Florida's Supreme Court without being fully paid—took it on himself to have her mental status reviewed under Florida's newly-enacted Baker Act and filed the necessary legal papers for her release.

In 1974, Ruby was discharged from Chattahoochee and given to the foster care of Ella Caskin in Ocala, Florida, near Silver Springs, where she lived for almost twenty more years. Ms. Caskin described Ruby as a "stubborn old lady," yet "sweet, easy, and quiet."

Ruby's retirement was paid for by a forty-thousand-dollar trust account funded by William Huie in exchange for the movie rights to her story, and she was given an allowance of a dollar and fifteen cents a day.

In 1975, Sam Jr. was sentenced in Pensacola to a three-year federal prison term for ten counts of illegal gambling. Kay, Ruby's oldest daughter, was killed in an auto accident in 1978, while traveling to meet Sam Jr. upon his release from prison. Ironically, the IRS returned a substantial sum of money to Sam Jr. following his release, after collecting penalties and interest for unpaid taxes from the money they had seized during his arrest.

In January 1980, Al Lee from the *Ocala Star Banner* interviewed Ruby and wrote, "There is a touch of aristocracy, self-ordained in her bearing." The reporter also said that Ruby had read Huie's book, *Ruby McCollum: Woman in the Suwannee Jail*, published by E. P. Dutton and Company in 1956. When asked about her impression of Huie's account of the murder, Ruby responded, "I just don't remember about it. But I do remember we had plenty of money and always paid the doctor bills." Asked about what she planned to do with the rest of her life, Ruby answered with a faraway look in her eyes, "I'd like to go home sometime, clean up my house."

In a side bar article, Lee also reported that "Keith Black of Lake City, the former state attorney who prosecuted Ruby McCollum on a first degree murder charge in 1952, was indicted in 1977 by a federal grand jury on charges of conspiracy to obstruct justice in connection with alleged racketeering in the Live Oak-Lake City area."

Cocaine addiction, the trauma of almost two years in the Suwannee County jail while facing the prospect of the electric chair, insulin and electroshock "therapy," and years of Thorazine and other sedatives had left Ruby, in her eighth decade of life, with little more than faded memories echoing through a distant past. In that respect, she joins the many victims of the living hell known as Chattahoochee, and an indictment of how our society drugged and warehoused the mentally ill in the 1950s.

On May 23, 1992, at 4:45 a.m., Ruby died of a stroke at the New Horizon Rehabilitation Center, at the age of eighty-two, following the death of her beloved brother, Matt, by less than a year. She now lies buried beside him, surrounded by a grove of moss-draped live oak trees, in the cemetery behind the Hopewell Baptist Church, north of Live Oak.

Ruby was embalmed in Live Oak by Charles Hall, who also cast the concrete headstone that marks her grave. Her name was entered on her death certificate as "Ruby McCollumn," and her burial place as a "rural cemetery" near Ocala. The misspelling of the McCollum name may or may not have been intentional, since the name was often misspelled, as seen in Hurston's rendering of the name as "McCollom." The misrepresentation of Ruby's place of burial was, according to reliable sources, designed to deter desecrators.

The "rural cemetery" referred to on the official, however misleading, birth certificate issued by the State of Florida Office of Vital Statistics is actually in Zuber, Ruby's birthplace. Today, Zuber is nothing but a crossroads with a convenience store, and the cemetery referenced is Union Cemetery, located off a road paved with crushed pink granite, down a winding stretch of overgrown, barely passable farm trail. The family graveyard contains the remains of Ruby's relatives, including Sonja, her second-born, who died of a heart attack.

All who remain of Ruby's family are Sam Jr., who lives in Live Oak, and Loretta, who was last reported living in New Jersey with her husband and children.

As for the town of Live Oak, the Parshley building, where Adams had his office, the Suwannee County Hospital, the jail where Ruby was incarcerated for over two years, the offices of the *Suwannee Democrat*, and the Suwannee Hotel no longer stand. The McCollum residence is in disrepair, its grounds overgrown with weeds and strewn with the remains of rusted vehicles. The Adams residence remains almost exactly as it appeared in the 1950s, with the exception of a new metal roof to replace the asphalt shingle original.

Live Oak is now bypassed by Interstate 10, and the usual chain outlets and fast-food franchises greet travelers who take the Highway 129 exit into town, hoping to find the "real story" of Ruby McCollum.

Suwannee Democrat

111th Year, Number 96   **MIDWEEK WEDNESDAY, OCTOBER 25, 1995**   Live Oak, FL   3 Sections 40 Pages   35¢

DOWN - BUT NOT OUT!

History burns with half a block of Live Oak

BY VIOLET MCDONALD
Staff Writer

History was made and destroyed all at once Friday night when over a century's worth of historical documents burned along with half a block of businesses located around the *Suwannee Democrat.*

As of Monday night, fire marshals still had not determined the origin of the fire. As of noon Saturday, three fire marshals were about to enter what was left of the three businesses. Live Oak Fire Chief Russell Avery did indicate that the fire was believed to have begun in Holiday Treasures and Gifts.

Although Avery estimated another five hours from noon Saturday for cleanup, smoke could still be seen rising from the rubble throughout the weekend and well into Monday.

Spokesperson Johnny Wooley said he did not see an early conclusion to the origin or cause of the fire. When questioned about the validity of arson rumors, Wooley responded with, "That's, I think, very premature. The investigation is just beginning."

Two firefighters suffered injuries fighting Friday night's blazes. "The wall fell on Greg Stevens and Mike Blackmon," Avery began. "Mike went to the hospital, but he's back out here. He was back out here within two hours. Greg's got a bad sprained ankle. He'll be back to work tomorrow, but he's home now resting."

Monroe Williams of Holiday Treasures and Gifts had this to say to the community, "Thanks to our customers. Thanks to the community and we need their prayers."

When asked if they had any plans to rebuild, Monroe replied, "At this point, we don't have any plans. We're just taking it one day at a time."

Mack Skipper and his wife, Susie, are scouting for a new location for

> "This community
> is kind of like a
> family ... They've
> got a common
> bond, and it really
> showed up here."
> – John Hale

Afterword

After the *Suwannee Democrat's* building and archives were burned to the ground by an arsonist on October 19, 1995, the October 25 edition, published from a remote facility, proudly proclaimed, "DOWN — BUT NOT OUT!" with the slug line, "History burns with half a block of Live Oak."

History Burns. Those words reverberated in my brain until I realized why they bothered me: history cannot burn. Over the millennia, many people have believed that history can be destroyed in one way or another. In China, the "First Emperor" eradicated all references to his predecessors. In the Nile Valley, pharaohs had the names of earlier rulers chiseled away from their statues and tombs. Often entire groups of people, finding it too painful to face past injustices, find it easier to sweep them under the rug. Thus, we hear Turks denying the Armenian genocide, Japanese minimizing and euphemizing the Nanjing massacre, and people in America today denying the Nazi Holocaust — as if negating those gruesome chapters of history might make them disappear.

In Suwannee County, people take a different tack: they hope to destroy history not by doing or saying anything, but by starving it with silence. Some things, you understand, are simply not the subject of polite conversation. Some things could hurt people's feelings, embarrass the community. Silence, it seems, will make things better, and eventually the unpleasant parts will go away.

I am reminded of my grandmother, who used to give us kids a nickel to sit quietly during the lightning storms that moved across north Florida each summer. Talking, she maintained, attracted the lightning, which could burn down the house.

While most folks in Suwannee County no longer believe that silence makes the lightning go away, they still cling to the notion that it can make history disappear — or at least make it more palatable.

But history is resilient. Embedded in myth and legend, folklore and song, it has survived ethnic purges and holocausts, wars, epidemics, and famine, passing down through the generations what is too important to be forgotten.

And a small part of that history, which we forget only at our peril, is the strange case of Ruby McCollum.

Acknowledgments

My heartfelt thanks to Leslie, my wife and constant companion through almost 40 years of joyful sharing of ideas, for lending her insights into the psychological makeup and motivations of the central characters, as well as their interaction with their social environment, so that I could bring the story to life for my readers.

My thanks also go out to all the research librarians and custodians of records at the University of Florida (Zora Neale Hurston collection and historical periodical collection), the University of South Florida, and the University of Ohio (William B. Huie collection) for their kind assistance. Deepest thanks also to the historical societies of Suwannee and Duval Counties for sharing their records. Finally, the Florida Supreme Court Library and the Florida State Archive and Photo Archive personnel were most kind in helping me with research in their extensive collections.

I also wish to thank Mr. Min Zhang, who served as my interpreter and agent in having the oil paintings for this volume completed by members of a wonderfully talented artist community in China.

And special thanks to the readers of my first book on this story, *The Trial of Ruby McCollum*, who shared their personal insights and memories.

Finally, my editor, Michael Carr, was an inspiration, lending his exceptional talents with patience, sensitivity, and understanding, giving me the second wind I needed to finish the manuscript. Thanks, Michael.

Printed in the United States
142335LV00002B/34/P

9 780982 094006